P9-DMH-929

The Wild Duck

AND OTHER PLAYS BY

HENRIK IBSEN

The Wild Duck

AND OTHER PLAYS BY

HENRIK IBSEN

Pillars of Society

The Wild Duck

The Lady from the Sea

Little Eyolf

John Gabriel Borkman

When We Dead Awaken

Newly translated, and with an introduction, by
EVA LE GALLIENNE

THE MODERN LIBRARY · NEW YORK

THE MODERN LIBRARY

is published by RANDOM HOUSE, INC.

BENNETT CERF · DONALD S. KLOPFER

839.822
Ibs

Contents

Introduction

BY EVA LE GALLIENNE

IN A LETTER to Frederik Gjertsen, written in 1872, Ibsen has this to say about translating: "To translate well is a difficult matter. It is not simply a question of rendering the meaning, but also, to a certain extent, of remodeling the expression and the metaphors, of accommodating the outward form to the structure and requirements of the language into which one is translating. . . . The foreign effect which it [the foreign metre] produces on the language acts like a disturbing melody coming between the reader and the sense of what he is reading."

In most of the existing English translations of Ibsen's plays, notably those in the standard edition edited by William Archer and largely translated by him, this "foreign effect" continuously gets in the way. Archer's devotion to Ibsen as an artist made him overconscientious: he clung assiduously to the letter, translating many of the Norwegian idioms so literally that they frequently entirely fail to convey Ibsen's thought; they present a series of stumbling blocks to the reader's mind and of tongue-twisters to the actor. Instead of translating the meaning they confuse and occasionally actually falsify it. This "disturbing melody" has undoubtedly had much to do with the prevalent notion that Ibsen's plays are "difficult" and "obscure." Archer himself seems to have been aware of this, for he wrote in *The Critic* of July 1906:

"What would we think of a man who, knowing no French, should sit down to write a critical study of Victor Hugo? Or who, knowing no German, should take upon himself to weigh Goethe in the balance and find him wanting? Yet this is inevitably the position of nineteen out of twenty critics who deal with the works of Ibsen."

The style of Archer's translations gives very little hint of the clarity, the powerful economy—what Huneker calls the "dramatic stenography"—of the original. Archer's dialogue is reminiscent of Pinero or Jones, of the conventional stage clichés of the nineties. Archer was after all a Victorian litterateur, whereas Ibsen was an innovator and a genius.

Ibsen's ideas—in themselves so startling that they struck the smug, complacent society of the time with the force of a tidal wave, and revolutionized not only plays and players but the pattern of thought of men and women everywhere—emerge, of course, to a very great extent, in spite of the tempering gentility of Archer's prose; but they seem less savagely alive and at the same time less austere. The great Viking ship, with its clean, eliminated, uncompromising lines, has been muffled under Victorian drapery.

It would be wrong to minimize the immense service Archer performed in introducing Ibsen to the English-speaking world, nor should one minimize the tremendous difficulty of the task he undertook so gallantly.

To translate Ibsen's poetic dramas—particularly *Brand* and *Peer Gynt*—is quite impossible; the rhythm, the very *sound* of the language, is inextricably bound up with the thought, the passion, the satire, the mysticism; it is like the blood pulsing through a body; there is no life without it. The prose plays, on the other hand, particularly the so-called "social plays" that started with *Pillars of Society*, should on the face of it seem easier. And yet one despairs of ever being able to convey that deceptively simple, lucid style—a style from which everything extraneous has been whittled away with a craftsmanship so superb as to be unnoticeable—a style that seems to spring inevitably from the thoughts and emotions of each character, revealing the essence with a minimum of words. And to make things more difficult, this style, so spare, so frugal, is alive with poetry; and so one begins to feel that to translate Ibsen's prose is impossible too!

It was sheer necessity that made me attempt to translate a few of Ibsen's plays; I wanted to produce them and act in them, and I realized that the existing versions were clumsy, old-fashioned and quite frequently misleading. Also they resisted all efforts on the part of the actor to make them come to life on the stage. They loomed like formidable barriers between the actor and the play. I wanted to try to avoid what Shaw described, in speaking of an English performance of *John Gabriel Borkman,* as ". . . a funereally unreal tradition which is likely to end in making Ibsen the most portentous of stage bores." I felt pretty sure that the Archer translation had contributed a great deal to this impression. So I went back to Ibsen himself and tried to evolve a text that would enable us to bring some truth and life into the plays. At that time there was no question of my translations ever being published; if anyone had raised this point I should probably never have had the temerity to undertake them.

Even though it has been fashionable in recent times in certain critical circles to minimize the importance and originality of Ibsen's ideas—a position that may very easily be challenged—there can surely be no question that his influence on dramatic structure, on the whole concept of playwriting— as well as on methods of acting—was revolutionary.

Ibsen's earlier plays were said to be reminiscent of Oehlenschläger, Schiller, and Wergeland and, though Ibsen was always unwilling to acknowledge the influence of others, it is probable that he—in common with most young poets—reflected in his writing much that he had read and admired. His development was slow, and it took him many years to arrive at a style and a way of thinking that were peculiarly and passionately his own.

He was forty by the time he wrote *Peer Gynt;* and he was

in his fiftieth year when he wrote *Pillars of Society*, the first of
the "social plays" which were to make him world famous and
which, to the English-speaking world, constitute his most
important and familiar work. It is on these plays that the great
bulk of English criticism and commentary has been focused.
Ibsen was hailed as the chief exponent of the "well-built"
play—a term flattering at first but, in recent years, tinged
with a somewhat patronizing disdain. Much has been written
of Ibsen's great debt to Scribe, and the influence of Hebbel,
and even of Dumas *fils*, has been interminably discussed.

Ibsen himself has given no definite clue, not even the
smallest hint, that might pin down any of these conjectures. A
young woman said of him during his early Grimstad days
when he was a boy in his teens, "He went about Grimstad like
an enigma secured with seven seals," and the stage manager
of the Royal Theatre in Copenhagen described him in 1852 as
"a small, close-mouthed Norwegian with wide-awake eyes."
"A small, shy woodchuck" was another description of him
during his Bergen years. Later on, in the nineties, when he
had become "the Great Silent One," such flippancies had
grown dignified and he was usually referred to as "the
Sphinx of the North." But, flippant or dignified, from first
to last in his long life the sense of reserve—of almost pathological secrecy—seems to have been a trait in his nature
universally recognized.

There is one influence, however, that—particularly to a
worker in the theatre—demands no proof, no corroboration
from Ibsen or from anyone else, for it is self-evident. For five
years, from 1851 until 1856, he was stage manager and official dramatic poet to the theatre in Bergen; and from 1857
to 1862, for another five years, he was director of the Norwegian Theatre in Christiania (Oslo): ten consecutive years
of practical theatre work. What better way for a young playwright to learn his craft! With the exception of Shakespeare
and Molière, no other playwright of modern times has had a
comparable opportunity.

His duties at Bergen—apart from being the theatre poet

and being obligated to write at least one play a year—seem to have been those of stage manager and assistant director. He was given no real authority and was often contemptuous of the plays presented there. He attended all the rehearsals, marking down positions and stage business; he followed the script, and we are told of his insistence on the actors' keeping strictly to the written text—a fact which no doubt added little to his popularity!

I have examined some of his prompt-copies, preserved at the old Bergen theatre, now a museum, and have often held them up as an example to stage managers of my own, who felt it beneath their dignity to keep their scripts in proper order; but it was not beneath the dignity of a genius to do so.

As official poet Ibsen had the opportunity to see five of his early plays produced in Bergen; of these five only *The Feast at Solhaug* was successful; it was Ibsen's first theatrical triumph, and in answer to the applause, he made a speech in which he said: "Your appreciation shall strengthen me in my work toward the aim for which I am striving, and which *I shall attain.*" And we are told he laid peculiar stress upon the final words.

In Christiania, Ibsen was given full authority as director, but only two of his own plays were presented there—*Lady Inger of Östraat* and *The Vikings at Helgeland.* These five years were full of struggle and discouragement. He tried in vain to raise the level of the plays, as well as of the acting and productions; but his attempts ended in failure and in 1862 the theatre was forced to close. Yet in spite of the defeat of Ibsen's program, which filled him with a bitter sense of humiliation, an invaluable groundwork had been laid in these ten years for the work that lay ahead. One can be sure that nothing escaped those "wide-awake" eyes of his.

The art of the theatre must be practiced; no amount of theory or speculation can take the place of actually being a part of the work itself. The constant daily closeness to the actors; the opportunity to watch night after night the re-action of the audiences; the incessant planning of stage busi-

ness and scenic effects—no wonder that Ibsen's craftsmanship became superlative. Even if other influences existed, they
could only be incidental compared to this.

The word "realism" is closely connected with Henrik Ibsen. But he was realistic in the sense that a great painter
might be called realistic: he did not agree with what he
called "photographic art." He resented being classed with
such a realist as Zola, for instance, of whom he said: "Zola
goes down into the sewer to take a bath; I, in order to cleanse
it." Halvdan Koht in his excellent *Life of Ibsen* very rightly
says: "He resembled Flaubert more than he did Zola. He
was a romanticist who had become realist—a man who
thought romantically, but wrote realistically. He did not
wish—did not even wish to seem—merely to study society in all the forms and consequences of vice and lust. The
thing which filled his mind was the individual man, and he
measured the worth of a community according as it helped
or hindered a man in being himself. He had an ideal standard
which he placed upon the community, and it was from this
measuring that his social criticism proceeded."

The most important difference between Ibsen's plays and
the theatre-pieces that preceded them was the light they
cast on the inner, secret lives of the characters presented in
them. The effects he created were not dependent—or very
little—on ordinary dramatic action. They were dramas of
the mind, of the spirit. Most of the action had already taken
place before the rise of the curtain, and the drama lay in
the effect of this action, the results of it, the response to it.
Ibsen's plays remind one of an iceberg: the greater part of it
lies hidden beneath the surface. This is the quality above all
others that presents such a challenge to the actor; external
virtuosity is not enough; his plays demand a subtler, far
more delicate technique. One might almost say that the most
important part of the actor's performance lies in what is
not said; it can never be a question of mere words and ges-
tures—the inner content is what counts. From start to finish
of the play the actor must sustain a consistent, unbroken line

of thought. Ibsen demands of his interpreters the most absolute concentration, and he demands it of his audiences too.
He must have agreed with the words embossed in gold letters
above the proscenium arch of the Royal Theatre in Copenhagen: *"Ej blot til Lyst"*—"Not only for amusement." To
him the theatre was a place of truth, of ruthless analysis: a
place where the minds and souls of human beings were revealed with an honesty that sometimes seems unbearably
harsh, and with a perception that is uncannily clairvoyant. If
people find his plays "difficult" and "obscure," the fault lies
with them, not with Ibsen. His meaning, even in his later
plays with their slant toward mysticism, is never blurred or
devious—only one must listen and observe. Then the reward
is very great. But one must not expect compromise from
Ibsen, and he makes no concessions. As Huneker says: "It is
his aloofness that his audiences resent most of all." Ibsen did
not write to please.

It is not surprising that most of the Ibsen pioneers have
been women; in nearly every country they were the first to
introduce his plays. In England it was Janet Achurch and
Elizabeth Robins; in America, Modjeska and Mrs. Fiske; in
France, Réjane; in Italy, Duse. A great actress once thanked
Ibsen for creating such wonderful roles for women, to which
he angrily replied: "I have never created roles. I have written
of human beings and human destinies." But the fact remains,
whether he liked it or not, that to a great actress the Ibsen
repertoire is as stimulating and rewarding as the Shake-
spearian repertoire is to a great actor. The range and variety
of his portraits of women are incomparable. His grasp of the
intricacies of female psychology is miraculous. Especially in
his later plays, when more and more he dealt with the hidden
subconscious forces of human beings, he became increasingly
absorbed in his studies of the feminine mind. It was perhaps
the poet in him that gave him such a sensitive understanding
of the mysterious invisible life of these women he portrayed
—so mercilessly and yet so delicately. Björnstjerne Björnsen

once used the expression "we women and poets," and Ibsen might well have used it too. It was indeed as if he had the power to transmute himself, and in his imagination actually to become these women of whom he wrote, so intimate and so accurate in every smallest detail is his knowledge of them.

The women of the Sagas, with their wild, deep natures, had always held a great fascination for him; and something of their sharply individual, fearless spirit—warm and strong at the same time—undoubtedly crept into many of the women in Ibsen's plays; they are a combination of ice and flame. And the woman he married, Susannah Thoresen, was, according to Halvdan Koht, "the embodiment of Saga womanhood."

It is probably this quality of fearless individualism that makes the Ibsen women seem so strange, even distasteful, to many people. Such a monument of hypocrisy, such comfortable fallacies have been built up about women, particularly in plays and novels. In most fiction—especially when Ibsen's plays first made their appearance—women were either blondly good or darkly bad. But to treat a woman as a rounded human being capable at once of courage and cowardice, tenderness and cruelty, honesty and deceit, self-sacrifice and merciless rapacity—in short as a creature whose being was torn by the torments of spiritual as well as of emotional conflict—was startling in the extreme. No wonder these plays have such appeal to women on both sides of the footlights. Here is a man who sees them as they really are; he never spares them, yet he understands them; and by focusing on them the light of uncompromising honesty, he accepts them as man's equal.

Not that Ibsen's plays are exclusively—or even preponderantly—concerned with women; his gallery of men is equally impressive. But, with Ibsen, woman was for the first time allowed to dominate the stage as a full-fledged individual—interesting and complete in herself, quite apart from the men with whom she shared the action; and to the Victorian mind, this must have seemed shocking and unseemly.

One critic described Ibsen's women as ". . . without affection, an unlovable, unlovely and detestable crew"; and another one dismissed them pompously as a lot of "crazed, hysterical geese."

Pillars of Society was published in 1877 and met with great popular success. As William Archer says, "The theatrical success of *Pillars of Society* was immediate and striking."

It was the first of the so-called "social" plays. Several years had elapsed between *Emperor and Galilean* (frequently referred to by Ibsen as his most important work) and this first attempt at a "well-made" theatre-piece.

Of all Ibsen's plays *Pillars of Society* seems to us the most old-fashioned. While the plot is ingenious and cleverly worked out, the mechanics are all too obvious. The "happy ending" (rare in Ibsen's plays) is flat and conventional. The sense of "truth will out, right must prevail" is also rare in Ibsen's work. Did he, for once, deliberately try to write a popular hit? If so, he succeeded. Perhaps the play's near-banality contributed to its popular appeal. There was nothing to shock and infuriate; it blazed no new trails; it traveled a familiar road; nothing in it soared above the commonplace. As Ibsen himself expressed it, "The ghost of the excellent Scribe still walked in him."

And yet, in spite of its shortcomings, as Professor Weigand says, *"Pillars of Society* has nevertheless stampeded countless intelligent audiences to wild applause, and even today it can count, whenever well staged, upon an enthusiastic reception."

Of course, when one considers the majority of plays written in the '70's, *Pillars of Society* presents many innovations: there are no "asides," no stilted soliloquies; and the characters, who seem shallow and conventional when compared with those in Ibsen's subsequent plays, are infinitely more alive and human than the lay figures to which the public was then accustomed. And what a boon they must have been to the actors of the period!

Its success is not surprising, for there is something highly engaging about the play. In spite of the virulence of its attack on the shams and hypocrisy of society, it manages to create a good-natured atmosphere. The structure of the play is so blatantly artificial and contrived that one cannot take the violence of this attack too seriously. It is fun to watch the "good" characters triumph in the end. It is fun to laugh at the "virtuous ladies," and to see the ridiculous schoolmaster robbed of his prey. Of all Ibsen's plays this is surely the least "Ibsenesque"!

And yet we see numerous indications of future plays in *Pillars of Society;* and in it we find preliminary sketches of characters to be met with in later works, developed and transformed into fully-rounded complex human beings.

Ibsen's loathing of the smugness and self-righteousness that marked the provincial society of his time—particularly of the greed of officials, and the hypocrisy of "leading citizens"—is expressed in several of his plays. In *An Enemy of the People* he uses it as his main theme, but in almost all his works he contrives to satirize and ridicule these evils, even by means of minor characters, as in the "chamberlains" in the first act of *The Wild Duck.* In *Pillars of Society,* too, this is the main theme of his argument (in fact this play and *An Enemy of the People* have much in common, though the later work is infinitely superior) but he touches on many other themes as well. Ibsen felt that this provincial society was completely dominated by the male ego—was a "society of bachelors," a man-made world in which woman was relegated to a subservient position, robbed of her freedom, and of all opportunity to develop a personality of her own. This thought led directly to *A Doll's House* and *Ghosts*—the plays immediately following *Pillars of Society*—in which Nora and Mrs. Alving both rebel against man-made laws and conventions. Ibsen was not a "feminist" in the ordinary sense of the word, and almost certainly did not believe in "votes for women"; but he did believe that women were equal to men in the sense of being human beings, and that they should be free to develop their own individuality, and become people in their own right.

In *Pillars of Society* Lona Hessel strongly represents this point of view, and Dina Dorf has in her elements of Nora and —though faintly—of Hilde Wangel too. Hilde might well exclaim as Dina does: "How I hate all this respectability! . . . I don't understand all this business about duty—I never could." While Dina's lines to Johan after consenting to become his wife: "But first I must work; make something of myself; become a real person, just as you are," are repeated almost word for word by Nora in her famous last-act scene, when she tells Helmer: "I believe that before all else I am a human being, just as you are—or at least that I should try and become one."

Bernick's insufferable contempt for his wife: "My dear Betty, the situation was far too complex for you to grasp." . . . "It can't possibly interest you, my dear Betty." . . . "And as for our good women—come closer, ladies, this is for your ears . . ." etc., reminds one of Helmer, Hjalmar Ekdal, Kroll, and innumerable other Ibsen men of this same type. The attitude reaches a peak in Borkman's remark in that incomparable later play *John Gabriel Borkman:* "My dear Ella, if the worst comes to the worst, one woman can always take the place of another." In fact there is much in Bernick that anticipates—though in a tentative way—the great "sick wolf" of this play written nearly twenty years later. But where we believe Borkman to be indeed a fallen Titan, a man whose vision and ambitions truly transcended all thought of personal gain ("I dreamed of exploiting all the sources of power throughout the country. I wanted to become master of all the wealth that lay hidden in the earth, in the mountains, the forests and the sea; so that, through me, it might benefit the lives of countless thousands." And again: ". . . spreading friendship and understanding—bringing light and warmth to thousands of homes. That's what I dreamed of doing!"), we see in Bernick only a selfish, grasping opportunist, in spite of the fact that he never stops reiterating that his scheme will result in "a permanent asset to the whole community and to the many thousands of workers whose well-being will depend on it." In *Pillars of Society* Ibsen also introduces the theme, developed so poignantly in *John Gabriel Borkman*, of the woman deserted by the man she loves and who supposedly loves her, for the sake of worldly gain. It is interesting to compare the scene between Lona and Bernick in Act II of *Pillars of Society* with the marvelous second-act scene in *John Gabriel Borkman* between Ella and Borkman. In both these scenes the woman accuses the man of having sold her love for money and for power. But what a difference twenty years have made in Ibsen's handling of the situation! The germ of the scene is clearly detected in the earlier play, but, compared with Borkman, Bernick seems hollow and unreal. One cannot conceive of Borkman, for instance, making the incredible *volte-face* that Bernick makes in the last ten minutes of the play. Borkman is too powerfully consistent; he is "John Gabriel Borkman—myself, and not another." Bernick's sudden reformation means nothing to us; we simply do not believe in it. It is just a means to a cozy, happy ending, and we can only hope that all those nice women are not totally taken in by it.

In Lona Hessel—a fine part for an actress (one can see why Mrs. Fiske made such a success in it)—Ibsen gives us the female and beneficent side of the medal of which, in *The Wild Duck*, Gregers Werle is the male and evil side: a fanatic zealot for the truth, a person who has no fear of disrupting someone else's life in order to, as Lona says, "put firm ground under your feet." The victim—in both plays—struggles frantically, but there is no escape. Both Lona and Gregers are inexorably bent on doing good to the soul of the person they profess to and, in fact, do love. Since *Pillars of Society* is a contrived theatre-piece, the well-meaning meddler is successful and Bernick and the other characters intimately involved in his confession are filled with happy gratitude. In *The Wild Duck*, however, Ibsen takes a directly opposite point of view, and shows the meddler Gregers Werle—also well meaning in his misguided way—as a miserable failure who sows the seeds of destruction in his own and other people's lives, and is the direct cause of little Hedvig's suicide.

Pillars of Society is very long, and at times redundant. Karsten's speech to Lona in Act II, for instance, telling her of the critical situation in which he found his mother's business affairs, is almost exactly repeated in Act III—though he is speaking to the same person. In Ibsen's later plays it is almost impossible to make the slightest cut, they are so closely packed, so telling in their strict economy, but many places in *Pillars of Society* can benefit by pruning in performance.

Like many other great artists, Ibsen learned to whittle away everything unnecessary, to strip down to the essential, to the clean, firm line, without ever sacrificing richness of content, or creating a sense of sparseness. The last four plays he wrote, *The Master Builder, Little Eyolf, John Gabriel Borkman,* and *When We Dead Awaken,* are all extremely short. Yet the characters are so superbly drawn—so vividly alive—that we know the life history of every one of them, and understand them fully in all their complexity, whereas the people in *Pillars of Society* are more "parts" than human beings; they are puppets used by Ibsen to advance the action, or to provide the "comic relief" in which the play abounds. The "virtuous ladies," the businessmen, the priggish schoolmaster are all "stock" types. We have met them—and will probably continue to meet them—in many a theatre-piece. As Archer rightly says: ". . . even Lona Hessel is an intellectual construction—formed of a blend of new theory with old sentiment—rather than an absolute creation, a living and breathing woman."

Yet how rapidly Ibsen learned to conceal his craftsmanship. We have only to compare the crudeness of exposition in *Pillars of Society*—the old-fashioned device by which the gossiping ladies reveal to the audience the background of the play's principal characters just prior to their appearance —with the subtle way in which in *Ghosts,* written only four years later, Ibsen reveals the events of the past twenty years that have led so inevitably to the situation with which the play specifically deals.

In spite of its many faults, there is no doubt that *Pillars of Society*, if well acted and produced, could still provide an entertaining evening in the theatre. The ingredients that contributed to its popularity have lost none of their power to please. Had it not been written by Henrik Ibsen we might judge it less harshly.

Between *Pillars of Society* and *The Wild Duck* Ibsen wrote two of his most controversial plays, *A Doll's House* (1879) and *Ghosts* (1881). They aroused, in public and critics alike, a veritable storm of indignation. Ibsen was accused of trying to undermine "the sacred ties of marriage." As Huneker wrote of Nora, "That slammed door reverberated across the roof of the world." As for *Ghosts*, William Archer tells us it inspired a "frenzy of execration." Clement Scott, one of the leading English critics, described it as "an open drain, a loathsome sore unbandaged, a dirty act done publicly, a lazar-house with all its doors and windows open." These two plays established Ibsen in the Victorian Age as a dangerously immoral writer. The reputation still, surprisingly enough, clings to him in certain circles.

In retaliation against the mass of hypocritical nonsense and abuse that had been showered upon *Ghosts*—even by the so-called "Liberals" from whom Ibsen had expected support—Ibsen wrote his "merry comedy" *An Enemy of the People* (1882), in which he heaped contempt and ridicule on the liberal newspapers through his hilarious caricatures of the editor, reporter, and printer of *The People's Monitor*. In June 1884 Ibsen wrote to his friend Theodor Caspari: "All this winter I've been revolving some new crazy fancies [*Galskaber* in the original, an almost untranslatable expression] in my brain; I went on doing it until they assumed dramatic form; and now I have just completed a play in five acts—that is to say, the rough draft of it; now comes the elaboration, the more energetic individualization of the persons and their mode of expression."

By the end of the year the play was finished. Ibsen called it *The Wild Duck*. Many critics have considered it Ibsen's finest work. It is true that the exposition is handled somewhat clumsily, and one could wish—especially if one happens to be the producer—that the entire action could have taken place in Hjalmar Ekdal's studio, for the first-act dinner party scene at old Werle's house, introducing many minor characters who never appear again, presents a painful problem in performance. Then, too, the subject of Hedvig's hereditary weakness of the eyes seems unnecessarily overstressed, and Mrs. Sörby's remark about old Werle's imminent blindness strikes one as a trifle pat—a most convenient coincidence. But these are minor faults in a wonderful play. It is a marvelous comedy! Yes, *comedy*—in spite of little Hedvig's pathetic death. Such a mixture of moods was an extremely daring innovation in the '80's, when plays were firmly labeled "tragic" or "comic," and it was not considered proper to blend the two.

Professor Weigand very perceptively writes: *"The Wild Duck* does not begin as a comedy and end as a tragedy. It is a comedy from start to finish. Ibsen injects tragedy into comedy, to make comedy but the more poignant. With Ibsen we must look down from the heights upon the human menagerie assembled in the studio, and we must keep a close tether on our emotions."

And how vivid and human are the members of that "human menagerie"! For once even Ibsen himself had to admit that he had written a play full of rare acting opportunities, for in a letter to his publisher Hegel he refers to the manuscript of *The Wild Duck* in these words: "For the last four months I have worked at it every day; and it is not without a certain feeling of regret that I part from it. Long, daily association with the persons in this play has endeared them to me, in spite of their manifold failings; and I am not without hope that they may find good and kind friends among the great reading public, and more particularly among the actor tribe—to whom they offer roles which will well repay the trouble spent on them." This is a most unusual concession on Ibsen's part; he did not usually think in terms of the "actor tribe."

But the "actor tribe" certainly responded with enthusiasm, and *The Wild Duck* has always been a favorite among theatre people. It is not surprising, for even the minor characters are drawn with uncanny perception. As for Hjalmar Ekdal—he is surely one of the greatest comedy parts ever written. But how difficult to play! It takes a great actor to avoid the pitfall of being consciously funny in the role, for Hjalmar, of course, takes himself most seriously; it is this that makes him so deliciously human. He is totally unaware of the comic aspect of punctuating his most grandiloquent statements by large mouthfuls of bread and butter. Ibsen's stage directions are most specific on this score. In the second act, for instance, Hjalmar is holding forth on the subject of Old Ekdal: "You don't seem to understand how humiliating it is for a man like me to see his old father treated like a servant. But someday the pendulum will swing the other way; it won't be long now—I feel it! (*Takes another sandwich*) I have a sacred duty in life, and I intend to perform it to the full!" And, in the last act, when Hjalmar sees himself at his most desperate and tragic, the pattern is repeated: "Poor lonely old man. (*He takes some bread and butter and smoked tongue, and finishes his cup of coffee*) . . . Those two scoundrels! Vicious, infamous brutes! I'll have to pick up a hat somewhere on the way. (*Takes some more bread and tongue*) Something'll have to be done about it. I've no desire to risk my life. (*Looks for something on the tray*)." Gina asks: "What are you looking for?" and he answers: "Butter." In the hands of a bad actor such things can easily become mere buffoonery.

Hjalmar's return from the dinner party (and here we see one of the chief values of that awkward first act) is hilariously funny; from that point on we can never take him seriously again, no matter how seriously he takes himself, no matter how often he carries on about his "integrity as a human being" or refers complacently to his "ardent, sensitive temperament." When, in the last act, Gregers urges him to uphold the standard of the Ideal against which his comfort-loving, shallow nature rebels so furiously, one can't help feeling sorry for him as he exclaims: "I wasn't made to bear unhappiness, Gregers. I need security; I must be surrounded by peace and comfort." And when Gregers reminds him of his mythical invention, his childlike answer, "That's a doubtful proposition, I'm afraid. . . . What on earth do you expect me to invent? Other people have invented practically everything already," is touchingly human. This is comedy based on timeless human foibles. This is why "in spite of manifold failings," as Ibsen said, there is something so endearing about the man. This is the quality that inspires the kind of devotion Gina and Hedvig feel for him, and Gregers Werle, too—that Gregers Werle who is Lona Hessel's counterpart, the dark, obverse side of the same medal. For in this play Ibsen chooses to present the seeker after truth as a meddlesome neurotic. Lona is an eminently sane and healthy person, whereas Gregers Werle is warped and sickly—a pathological case; as Relling says: "Can't you see the fellow's mad? He's a crackpot—a lunatic!" It's true that in this play "the lie" does not affect society as a whole, but only the immediate family life of Hjalmar, Gina, and little Hedvig. Here it is a personal matter, involving only the domestic happiness of the Ekdal household. And it is the personal happiness of individuals that Relling, with his mixture of kindness and cynicism, wishes to preserve: "Rob the average man of his basic lie and you rob him of his happiness as well." An unadmirable point of view, perhaps, and one with which, as a rule, Ibsen would have disagreed; but in this play he chooses to build up a strong defense in favor of it. He uses the character of Gina as witness to the fact that evasion of the truth does not always prevent a human being from being basically good and honest. Gina is the salt of the earth; a peasant woman born to serve; touching

in her devotion, but by no means blind to Hjalmar's faults
—far from it. She understands him thoroughly—sees through
him—yet accepts and loves him. This is a woman's job according to her lights. There is nothing of the rebellious "Ibsen woman" in Gina Ekdal. She knows precisely how to
handle Hjalmar. Her shrewd common sense never fails her,
even when she is most exasperated and unhappy.

Hedvig is in many ways very like her mother. She has a
precocious understanding of her father's weaknesses, yet she
adores him. Her one desire is to please him and, like her
mother, she studies his every mood. His absurd flamboyance
appeals to her; life is never dull to Hedvig when Hjalmar is
around. His cruel behavior to her in the last act of the play is
almost unbearable to watch; yet one feels that had it not
been for Gregers Werle's meddling, the child would have
managed to weather the storm; her natural sanity would
have enabled her to survive. But Werle's unhealthy sugges-
tions, against which she instinctively rebels—"but I didn't
think so much of it—after I'd slept on it"—come at a moment
in her life when, as the pragmatic Relling says, "Young girls
are apt to behave strangely." She kills herself out of bewildered misery and despair, thinking her beloved father
hates her; she perhaps found it impossible to sacrifice her
precious wild duck on the altar of her love for him—as
Gregers had suggested—and decides to sacrifice herself instead.

The Wild Duck is so filled with fascinating people that one
is tempted to touch on all of them: the eccentric, tragicomic
figure of Old Ekdal; even poor "daemonic" Molvik, who
spouts his drunken nonsense at the very moment of Hedvig's
poignant death. It is best to meet them in the play itself; for
Ibsen has brought them to life so completely that to attempt
to comment on them is really an unnecessary impertinence.

Much has been written about the "symbolism" of *The Wild
Duck*, that symbolism so often associated with Ibsen's work,
and which he always indignantly denied. Critics have
asked: "What is the hidden meaning of the wild duck, the

attic-forest, and Old Ekdal's ancient gun that can no longer shoot?" I may be very naïve but, for the life of me, I can't see why they shouldn't be just what they seem to be. Old Ekdal, broken by disgrace and ruin, uses the attic-forest as an escape from the reality he cannot bear to face. It is the "basic lie" that permits him to go on living. As Relling says, "He discovered the cure for himself, you see."

To Hjalmar the attic-forest is a means of avoiding the routine work of earning the family living. He leaves such boring things to the faithful Gina and spends blissful hours, puttering away, perfecting his "improvements." Most men have a touch of Peter Pan about them, and resent the tiresome business of "growing up." When Gregers asks him about the old gun, he answers, "It won't fire any more. It's fun to have it, though; we take it apart, grease it, give it a good cleaning—and then put it together again." And he adds, rather sheepishly, "That is—*Father* does; he likes puttering about with things like that." But it is obvious that he delights in these things too. When Old Ekdal comes out of the attic carrying the dead rabbit, his remark to him, "And you skinned it without waiting for me!" is surely proof enough.

To the child Hedvig it is only natural that the attic, with its old desk complete with pigeonholes, its "great big clock," its paintbox and the books filled with marvelous pictures, as well as the doves, hens, rabbits, and her pet wild duck—her pride and joy—should be a magical world. She is an only child and spends much time alone; and there, in the "boundless deep" of the old attic, she can enter the secret realm of her own imagination. Yet she is perfectly sane and realistic about it all: "After all, it's only an old attic," she says to Gregers. And when he replies, "How can you be so certain?" she "is silent and looks at him open-mouthed." It is only Gregers, "the crackpot," who tends to attach a symbolic meaning to the "wild duck's world."

It's easy to see that to Gina the attic-forest is only another cross to bear. One can imagine her efforts to combat the dirt and smells. Hjalmar solemnly tells Gregers: "These contraptions are all my own invention. . . . Gina doesn't like the hens and rabbits to get into the studio, so it's important to keep all this in running order." Poor Gina!

We have proof that Ibsen took pleasure in deliberately mystifying his readers and his critics—particularly the latter. He was well aware of his growing reputation as a "juggler of symbols." In the letter to his publisher that accompanied the manuscript of *The Wild Duck* he wrote: "My critics will, at any rate, find several things to squabble about and several things to interpret." We can almost see the malicious grin that lurked behind those formidable whiskers.

The two plays that followed *The Wild Duck, Rosmersholm* (1886) and *The Lady from the Sea* (1888), are both studies of women—this time real "Ibsen women." Our critic quoted earlier in this introduction would no doubt have labeled the one "unlovely and detestable," and the other "a crazed, hysterical goose."

Huneker, who wrote most perceptively of Ibsen's works, described Rebekka West in *Rosmersholm* in these words: "As cunning as Becky Sharp, as amorous as Emma Bovary, as ambitious as Lady Macbeth, Rebekka West is the most complete portrait of a designing woman that we know of; she is more trouble-breeding than Hedda Gabler."

The Lady from the Sea is very different. Where Rebekka West was clever, scheming, ruthless, and predatory—until she succumbed to the "Rosmer way of life"—Ellida Wangel is a woman of shifting moods, withdrawn in spirit, romantic, and superstitious—unpredictable and elusive as the sea itself.

Before starting on this play Ibsen had spent the summer on the northern coast of Denmark, and the influence of the sea permeates the entire work. The atmosphere is subtly charged with the acrid smell of seaweed, the harsh cries of sea birds, the plaintive mewing of the gulls, and the sting of salt spray from the great breakers. The personality of Ellida herself is as though enveloped in the mysterious gray mists that swirl in from the oceans of the North.

One wonders what a modern psychiatrist would have made of this woman. Ibsen, of course, created her—and offered the solution of her problem—long before the advent of Freud and of the psychiatric era. This solution is based on his knowledge and understanding of the human heart—the sixth sense of his genius. And it is simple and logical enough. A wild creature (and there is something shy and untamed in Ellida Wangel) imprisoned in a cage—even under the care of such a kind keeper as Dr. Wangel—will dream of freedom and the "mysterious world of the unknown" with its combination of fascination and terror, and beat against the bars. But once the door of the cage is opened by love and faith, and it is "free to choose," to "act on its own responsibility," the lure of the unknown loses much of its power, and the creature may, as long as it knows the door is open, decide to remain and accept the tenderness and care.

The Lady from the Sea is not an ensemble play, like *The Wild Duck* or *An Enemy of the People;* the focus is always on Ellida and her problem; the other characters are not as fully drawn, but they are lively and original. There are some delightful comedy scenes—relaxed and pastoral—almost in the manner of Turgenev: the passage between Bolette and Arnholm in the last act, for instance.

Turgenev, however, would never have thought of creating that frightening young woman Hilde Wangel. She is little more than a child in *The Lady from the Sea,* but we meet her again, in grown-up form, in *The Master Builder.* I think this is the only instance in which Ibsen deliberately picked a minor character from an earlier play for fuller development in a later work. He must have been impressed himself with Hilde's potentialities! There can be no question that these two Hildes are one and the same person. Apart from inherent traits of temperament—the brashness, the ruthlessness, the "bird-of-prey" characteristics, the strong need of hero worship, and the trollish charm—the actual mode of expression is identical.

The theme of the dead child's eyes is used again, though

in a different context, in *Little Eyolf*, in which the sea also
plays a dominant part. And the Rat-woman in this later play
—with her power to hypnotize and lure creatures into the
unknown—is, in a curious way, akin to the stranger in *The
Lady from the Sea*. Both these characters—though they appear only briefly—are the motivating force behind the action.

The Lady from the Sea is the first of the "domestic plays"
in which the strong mystic element in Ibsen's nature begins to
emerge. It deals with things that, in Wangel's words, "defy
all explanation." And when Arnholm asks him, "Do you believe there *are* such things?" we feel Ibsen himself joining in
the answer: "I neither believe nor disbelieve. I just don't
know."

In his later years Ibsen was to become increasingly engrossed in these imponderables. In such plays as *Little Eyolf*,
The Master Builder, and *When We Dead Awaken*, the focus
of his interest shifted from the solution of purely social and
psychological problems to subjects that "defy all explanation," subjects that even his powerful intellect could never
fully penetrate.

Ibsen followed *The Lady from the Sea* with another portrait of a woman, probably his most famous, *Hedda Gabler*
(1890). In spite of the fact that the subject matter is essen-
tially undramatic, it has always been one of Ibsen's most popular works. Henry James described it as "the picture not of an
action but of a condition"; yet there are few plays that have
such power to grip and hold an audience.

Then, in 1892, came *The Master Builder*, the first of the
last four plays of which Shaw wrote: "His [Ibsen's] magic is
extraordinarily potent in these four plays, and his purpose
more powerful." The second of them was *Little Eyolf* (1894).
This play is relatively unknown in this country, and is very
seldom acted. As far as I can discover, it has been presented
only once, in a professional performance, in the United States,
in the past fifty years—and then only for a very limited run.
Perhaps this is because it was so ahead of its time; even today

it strikes a distinctly *avant-garde* note. Perhaps another reason is that William Archer—despite his devotion to Ibsen's work—never really liked or understood these last four plays, particularly *Little Eyolf* and *When We Dead Awaken,* and this fact is strongly apparent in the weakness of his translations.

Little Eyolf is one of the shortest of Ibsen's plays, startling in its strict economy. There are no long speeches; the dialogue is crisp, and terse, and rapid. It exemplifies to the full that "dramatic stenography" of which Huneker wrote. It would require the most perceptive acting, the kind of acting for which Ibsen was so largely responsible, acting *in depth*— "rich, not gaudy."

Here again we have the death of a child. In *The Wild Duck* it ends the action, in *Little Eyolf* it begins it. As Shaw says: "He[Ibsen] is ruthless enough with Hedvig and Eyolf because he wants to use their deaths to expose their parents."

Two themes, introduced in *The Master Builder,* are carried over into *Little Eyolf:* that of the "helpers and servers," and that of the high peaks, or towers.

Surely the Rat-woman is a "helper and server" summoned subconsciously by Rita Allmers—for "the helpers and servers never come of their own accord," as Solness says; and, once they make their appearance, they are not easily exorcised.

The peaks and towers, which reappear in the "Dramatic Epilogue" *When We Dead Awaken,* stand for freedom of spirit. ("Then let me see you again free and high up!" Hilde says to Solness when she urges him to climb the tower, to "do the impossible again.") It is on these heights that a man loses his everyday self, sheds the paralyzing fears that prevent him from achieving his highest purpose, finds the strength to transcend himself.

Little Eyolf begins normally enough, even brightly, on an "early summer morning with warm sunshine." But, with the coming of the Rat-woman, ominous clouds gather, and the atmosphere rapidly becomes bleak and sinister.

The scenes between Rita Allmers and her husband are

surely, in their stark and savage honesty, as uncompromising
as anything written today by our most "modern" playwrights
—our angriest of angry young men. No wonder the more
reticent generation of the '90's shied away from them.
Shaw wrote: "If ever two cultivated souls of the propertied
middle class were stripped naked and left bankrupt, these two
are. They cannot bear to live; and yet they are forced to confess that they dare not kill themselves."

Huneker finds Allmers slightly reminiscent "of Hedda Gabler's husband." But to me he seems more akin to Rosmer.
There is nothing in him of the jovial, bustling Tesman; and
there is certainly nothing comical or endearing about him.
Like Rosmer he is a curiously bloodless creature—"infirm
of purpose." We never believe in his power to write his book
on *Human Responsibility*, any more than we believe in Rosmer's power to save society; and both men are deeply in-
secure at heart. Allmers is totally self-centered. He never
really lives life; he stands away and watches himself taking
part in it. He is that maddening combination: a vain man in-
clined to arrogance who, at the same time, doubts himself and
is incapable of firm conviction. Rita, with her frank and
healthy sensuality, has, by the power of sheer animal mag-
netism, forced him into some semblance of passion, but because true passion was not inherent in his nature, he could
feel no joy in it—only a sense of guilt. It is a case of the frigid
male seduced by the predatory, greedy female. Allmer's first
feeling for Rita was, he admits, one of fear; and, though he
succumbed to her—or perhaps more accurately to the combination of her "devastating beauty," which appealed to his
esthetic sense, and her "gold" and her "green forests," which
provided for his material comforts—his love for her was
strongly tinged with hate.

Of the two, our sympathy goes out to Rita Allmers. She is
at least honest in her all-consuming love, or lust, for him. In
spite of her violence, and her insanely possessive jealousy, she
is a human being. As she herself says, "I have blood in my
veins, not water." Allmers was indeed an unsatisfactory man

for such a woman! Asta, with her deep, pure, almost nunlike nature, would have been a better mate for him; though one can't keep being glad, for her sake, that she escapes him and goes off with Borghejm, who seems like a thoroughly nice person, a simple, forthright man, blessed with the power to enjoy life and generous enough to wish to share the joy—a man capable of true devotion, a "faithful soul," as Allmers says.

The final scene is very moving and leaves one with a sense of hope. Perhaps, after all, it will be possible for these two so different people—Rita and Allmers—to find a new life based on mutual understanding. The anguish and despair they have gone through—the bitter recriminations they have mercilessly heaped on one another—have changed them both. He has been touched by the warmth of her humanity, and she has come to realize that passion is not all of love. Allmers is perhaps right in saying, "The law of change may keep us together after all." Apart from being fascinating and provocative, *Little Eyolf* deals with problems that seem very close to us. As Huneker wrote: "It is a profound character study. Ibsen was writing for another theatre—the theatre of the twentieth century."

In 1896 Ibsen was ready with another play, *John Gabriel Borkman*. Every two years, with clocklike regularity, he produced a new work. During the period covering his twelve "domestic plays" (from 1877 to 1899) he made only two exceptions to this rule: he retaliated for the abuse heaped upon *Ghosts* by writing *An Enemy of the People* in one year. And he spent three years on his last play, *When We Dead Awaken*.

Huneker says of *John Gabriel Borkman:* "It is a play of great power, of a frugal, constructive beauty, and in it from first to last there sounds faintly but distinctly, an antique note." And indeed—in spite of its "airless rooms," its atmosphere of "lavender and dried rose leaves," its stuffy Victorian furnishings—it reminds one of a Greek play in the inexorable drive of its action, and in its unity of time and place.

The acts are very short, and the play suffers from inter-
missions. It should ideally be played without interruption. In
the theatres of Europe, which are usually equipped with
built-in revolving stages, this is a simple matter. Here it involves many technical problems, but the solution of them is
not impossible, and the result is rewarding.

While this play seems, at first glance, to be a realistic
study of a man consumed by a passion for power and money,
it is in fact a study of the mystique of power. As Shaw says:
"Ibsen does not make him [Borkman] superficially: he goes to
the poetic basis of the type: the love of gold—actual metallic
gold—and the idealization of gold through that love." But I
think it is power, rather than actual gold, that Borkman
loves. He refers to himself as a "Napoleon"—a "wounded
eagle." He is a romantic, glamorous figure. And, of course, it
is he who is the poet—not poor little Foldal with his poetic
"tragedy." It is all this that makes him so different from
Karsten Bernick in *Pillars of Society*, who seems a pigmy by
comparison.

In *John Gabriel Borkman* Ibsen reaches the peak of technical perfection. Two-thirds of the first act consists of a scene
between two elderly women—the twin sisters Ella and Gunhild—and for sheer clarity of dialogue and exposition, it
is unsurpassed. Though it involves no action, it is charged
with electricity, and holds the audience enthralled.

Every character in the play, even the tiny part of the maid
Malene, is drawn with consummate art. And in Ibsen's
gallery of superb "secondary roles," which includes such
figures as Old Edkal in *The Wild Duck*, Dr. Rank in *A Doll's
House*, Ulrik Brendal in *Rosmersholm*, and others too numerous to mention, the touching—truly adorable—Vilhelm
Foldal surely holds a place of honor.

Into the composition of *John Gabriel Borkman* Ibsen, with
an unerring sense of the dramatic, wove the music of Saint-
Saëns' *Danse Macabre*. Music and play are so closely inter-
twined it is impossible to think of one without the other. It's
as though the action were framed in the music—starting with

the tolling of the midnight bell, and ending with the cock-crow that sends the ghosts hurrying back to their respective graves.

We now come to Ibsen's last play, which he himself called "a dramatic epilogue," and which Shaw described as the "The Quintessence of Ibsenism": *When We Dead Awaken.*

We are told by Dr. Elias that Ibsen wrote this play "with such labor and such passionate agitation, so spasmodically and so feverishly, that those around him were almost alarmed." Many critics felt this to be an indication of the failing powers of a man of seventy, and most of them dismissed the play as the work of a faltering mind on the verge of senility. Even the faithful Archer condemned it. He writes: ". . . to his sane admirers the interest of the play must always be melancholy, because it is purely pathological. To deny this is, in my opinion, to cast a slur over all the poet's previous work, and in great measure to justify the criticisms of his most violent detractors. . . . One could almost suppose his mental breakdown to have preceded instead of following the writing of this play. . . . To pretend to rank it with his masterpieces is to show a very imperfect sense of the nature of their mastery."

The majority of critics have agreed with Archer; they did not understand the play, and therefore condemned it.

Shaw, however, who, being a bit of a genius himself, did understand it, slyly remarks: "The simplicity and the brevity of the story is so obvious, and the enormous scope of the conception so difficult to comprehend, that many of Ibsen's most devoted admirers failed to do it justice. They knew that he was a man of seventy, and were prepossessed with the belief that at such an age his powers must be falling off. It certainly was easier at that time to give the play up as a bad job than to explain it."

"At that time"—yes, indeed! It is no wonder that in 1899 people thought the play "pathological"—or just plain crazy.

There had never been anything like it. In the same way the Archers of the art world condemned the Impressionist school of painting and found the works of Cézanne, Gauguin, Monet, and Van Gogh crazy too.

Archer's chief quarrel with the play is what he considers to be a lack of consistency. He writes: "He [Ibsen] sacrificed the surface reality to the underlying meaning"; and he continues complainingly, ". . . we are confronted with the wholly impossible."

Huneker, who agrees with Shaw in his evaluation of the play, writes: "Wm. Archer sees in this closing drama of the social series little else than a resuscitation of the characters and motives that have done duty in his [Ibsen's] earlier plays. It is true that there is much familiar music, that the themes have been treated in previous works; nevertheless the variation is of enthralling interest."

There is, indeed, a certain kinship between Halvard Solness in *The Master Builder* and Professor Rubek in *When We Dead Awaken*—yet the two men are really very different. Solness is more robust, more obviously ruthless; he is more the craftsman than the artist. It seems unlikely that a woman would call him "poet." And while Maja has certain tricks of speech and behavior that remind one of Hilde Wangel, she has none of Hilde's fierce idealism, none of her all-consuming hero worship. She is more of a woman and less of a troll. As for Irene, who hovers between sanity and madness, she is like no other Ibsen woman one can think of. Perhaps Beata (whom we never meet) in *Rosmersholm* comes closest to her; yet one feels that Beata was more commonplace; and, while she had the negative courage to destroy herself by plunging into the mill race, she would never have dared to climb upward to the peaks.

Neither can the character of Ulfhejm be said to be "resuscitated" from other plays. He, too, stands alone. It is a masterly portrait. This "satyr," this coarse, foul-mouthed hunter of bears and women, somehow succeeds in winning our sympathy; we realize that he has resorted to this hideous

suit of armor to hide a deep hurt, an emotional and spiritual
wound. We can't help feeling that Maja will be happier with
him than she could ever be with Rubek.

It is not surprising that Ibsen should have written this play
with so much difficulty and anguish. It is, after all, clearly a
confession of his own views on art in relation to life. Speaking
of Solness in *The Master Builder,* he once said: "He is a man
who is somewhat related to me." What would he have said
of Rubek? Would he have agreed with Shaw who uses as a
subtitle in his remarks on *When We Dead Awaken* the
phrase "Rubek as Ibsen"? And he goes on to say, "He [Ibsen]
knew quite well that he was one of the greatest men living; so
he simply said: 'Suppose ME to be a sculptor instead of a
playwright,' and the thing was done. Thus he came forward
himself to plead to his own worst indictment of modern cul-
ture."

Rubek certainly expresses Ibsen's own feelings as an artist:
his contempt for "the masses," for "all the world," his growing doubt as to the value of the work itself; in Rubek's words:
"It suddenly struck me that this whole business about art—
this cant about an artist's vocation, an artist's sacred mission
—was a lot of hollow nonsense; basically unsound and meaningless." And when Maja asks him, "What would you have instead?" he answers, "Life, Maja . . . beauty, sunshine, life
itself. Isn't that the all-important thing? Far more important
certainly than burying oneself in a dark dismal hole, exhausting one's strength in a constant battle with lumps of clay and
blocks of marble."

Had not Ibsen spent his whole life in a battle with pen and
ink and paper, capturing those figures he saw and heard so
clearly in his imagination, and forcing them to remain alive
on the written page, so that others might see and hear them
too?

As the years went by Ibsen must have realized, no doubt
with the surprise common to us all, that he was getting old—
and that, as a human being, he had scarcely lived at all. Even
when he was not actually writing he seemed lost in another

world, meeting new creations of his mind, listening to their
points of view, noting their arguments. Then, as the theme
became clearer and the characters more and more insistent,
he would be chained to his desk for weeks, months—oblivi-
ous to everything but the work before him. He was helpless;
he had to submit to the ruthless discipline of art. As Rubek-
Ibsen says: "I'm an artist . . . I was *born* to be an artist."

There must have been times when Ibsen realized how hard
it was on those around him—his wife, his son, all those who
loved him. "Poet!" Irene says to Rubek "harshly and coldly,"
"I should never have served you—poet." Yet if she had not
served him she would never have "seen the sunrise," as she
says. She would never have climbed "high, high up on a
mountaintop." As usual Ibsen sees both sides of the question.

Of course the play is not consistent: it is a great poem—
and one does not demand consistency from great poetry. It
is a work of art that springs from the unconscious, as most
great poetry must, not from the calculated logic of the con-
scious mind. It undoubtedly makes strong demands on the
imagination and sensitive understanding of the reader or
spectator. He must not analyze it and dissect it—he must
yield to it, allow himself to come under the spell of its
strange magic.

It is not surprising that the play has so seldom been performed (at least in English-speaking countries) in the sixty
years since Ibsen wrote it. It was quite incredibly ahead of its
time; even now it strikes one as definitely *avant-garde*. I believe that in performance it would prove fascinating and provocative; one should remember that Ibsen called it a *dramatic
epilogue*. It would demand the most exquisite skill on the
part of all concerned—particularly the actors. Its production
could certainly not be lightly undertaken. But, while it would
in all probability never become popular in the sense of *Hedda
Gabler* or *The Wild Duck*, I believe it would prove rewarding
to the kind of audience capable of appreciating adventures
of the spirit. And, perhaps, were it not signed *Henrik Ibsen*,

it might even be accorded the kind of critical reception so generously extended to many of the young contemporary *avant-garde* playwrights. However, with Ibsen's name attached, the usual epithets, "dusty relic," "museum piece," "outmoded" (that ghastly word!) would probably be trotted out.

Now that Archer's monopoly of Ibsen in the English-speaking world has at last come to an end, and that his plays are available in several new translations both in this country and in England, might it not be a good idea for some of our critics to read the plays again—with an open mind? They might find their past opinions—almost inevitably based on the Archer versions—slightly "outmoded" too.

"Punctually on the stroke of one, there, entering the doorway, was the dour and bristling presence known to all the world in caricature . . . the great ruff of white whisker, ferociously standing out all round his sallow, bilious face, as if dangerously charged with electricity . . . the immaculate silk hat, the white tie, the frock-coated martinet's figure dressed from top to toe in old-fashioned black broadcloth, at once funereal and professional, the trousers concertinaed, apparently with dandiacal design, at the ankles, over his highly polished boots, the carefully folded umbrella—all was there apparitionally before me; a forbidding, disgruntled, tight-lipped presence, starchily dignified, straight as a ramrod; there he was, as I hinted, with a touch of grim dandyism about him, but with no touch of human kindness about his parchment skin or fierce badger eyes. He might have been a Scotch elder entering the kirk."

My father, Richard Le Gallienne, described Henrik Ibsen in these words when he went to interview the great man in Oslo in the late nineties; and this is the picture that comes to mind when the name of Henrik Ibsen is mentioned today. One immediately wonders—how could such a man have been a poet—an artist? How was it possible for this starched, stuffy, respectable "Scotch elder" to penetrate, as few other writers have ever done, the most complex, secret motives of the human mind and spirit?

We must not forget the "enigma sealed with seven seals" of his Grimstad days. This forbidding exterior was the armor Ibsen chose to wear both as a very young man to hide his basic insecurity and shyness, and as an old man to hide the vulnerability of his sensitive poetic nature.

Like all very great artists Ibsen was a creature of a thousand facets. To say one "knows" such a man is always incorrect; one may know a certain aspect of him—that is all. It is doubtful if anyone knew *all* of Henrik Ibsen—except, possibly, his wife. The chief clue to his complete personality lies in the characters he portrayed in his works, for there was a part of himself in literally all of them.

In a speech to the Oslo students in 1874 Ibsen made a very important and revealing statement: "All I have written . . . I have mentally lived through. . . . Partly I have written on that which only by glimpses, and at my best moments, I have felt stirring vividly within me as something great and beautiful. I have written on that which, so to speak, has stood higher than my daily self. . . . But I have also written on the opposite, on that which to introspective contemplation appears as the dregs and sediments of one's own nature. . . . Yes, gentlemen, nobody can poetically present that to which he has not to a certain degree and at least at times the model within himself."

In reading some of the biographies that have been written about Ibsen (of which I think Halvdan Koht's is probably the best), one finds passages on his high ideals, his aspiration, his moral indignation, his indomitable will, his relentless search after truth in his own soul—and one thinks: "Ah, yes! Brand; of course!" Then one comes across descriptions of violent, savage behavior; of cowardice in the face of danger; of colossal boastings, and of a black-bearded man lying drunk in the gutter—and who could this be but Peer Gynt?

Ibsen's delight in titles and decorations is worthy of Mayor

Stockmann, or George Tesman; yet he can write to Björnsen, referring to a request for sorely needed financial aid made to the Norwegian parliament: "You say that the Storthing *must* grant my petition. Do you really believe it will? I have an impression that my new work will not dispose the members more charitably towards me; but hang me if I can or will, on that account, suppress a single line, no matter what these 'pocket-edition' souls think of it. Let me rather be a beggar all my life!"

This sounds more like Dr. Stockmann than his brother Peter!

In another letter we catch a glimpse of Master Builder Solness: "There is, of course, a certain satisfaction in becoming so well known in these different countries. But it gives me no sense of happiness. And what is it really worth—the whole thing?"

There are traces of Ibsen himself in Lövborg as well as Tesman, in Gregers as well as Relling. And Halvdan Koht even goes so far as to say of Hedda Gabler: ". . . the mysterious one, who carries the contrasts and the strife within her. In this feminine soul Ibsen has laid down much of that which strove within himself."

It is easy to see why a man of this complex, paradoxical nature should have chosen the dramatic form as his medium. Since in his own being he experienced and understood so many widely divergent impulses, was constantly—all his life through—torn by violent conflicts of mind and spirit, he could quite honestly and positively agree with the many different points of view, the completely opposite patterns of behavior, of the characters he created in his plays. This is what makes Ibsen's men and women so alive and so convincing, and is also perhaps the reason why his work—in reality so personal—nevertheless seems so objective. He shows us the situations, reveals the human beings, but he never imposes judgment. He was himself too well aware of the infinite convolutions of the human soul. He knew that there were always at least two sides to any problem—and the last words he was heard to speak were the words, "On the contrary."

Alfred Kerr, a well-known German critic who was present at the imposing funeral with which the Norwegian state honored its great poet, wrote: "The ruling men in Norway had a daemon among them, and they buried a grandee." But it was both Peer Gynt and Mayor Stockmann that lay in that coffin.

Ibsen once wrote to a Norwegian student association: "Support from the young is dearer to me than support from anyone else. Moreover I hope confidently that the years shall never bring me to the point where I should feel a stranger among the intellectual younger generation."

It is now over fifty years since Henrik Ibsen's death, yet I know that at this present time it is still the "intellectual younger generation" that appreciate Ibsen best. Even here and now he would not feel a stranger among them; for he, perhaps more than any other writer of the nineteenth century, "allied himself most closely with the future."

Chronology

1828   Born in Skien, Norway—March 20.

1836   His father's business failed.

1843   Becomes apprentice to apothecary in Grimstad.

1849   Completed his first play, *Catiline,* under the pen name of Brynjolf Bjarme. His first poem appeared in *Christiania-Posten.*

1850   Ole Schulerud published *Catiline.* Ibsen moves to Christiania to enter the university. *The Warrior's Barrow* staged at the Christiania Theatre.

1851   With Botten-Hansen and Vinje edits a literary and political free-lance paper, *Andhrimner.* Abandons pen name and from now on writes under his own name. November 6. Signs contract with the Bergen Theatre as dramatic author and stage manager.

1852   First trip abroad to Copenhagen and Dresden.

1853   *St. John's Night* produced at the Bergen Theatre.

1855   *Lady Inger of Östraat.*

1856   *The Feast at Solhaug.* First success. Meets Susannah Thoresen. *Olaf Liljekrans.*

1857   Becomes artistic director of The Christiania Norwegian Theatre.

1858   Marriage to Susannah Thoresen. *The Vikings at Helgeland* produced in Christiania.

1859   Birth of his son Sigurd.

1862   Failure of the Christiania Theatre. *Love's Comedy*.

1863   *The Pretenders*.

1864   Leaves Norway for Italy. Settles in Rome.

1865   *Brand*.

1867   *Peer Gynt*.

1868   Moves to Dresden.

1869   *The League of Youth*. Visit to Stockholm. Sent as Norwegian delegate to Egypt for the opening of the Suez Canal.

1873   *Emperor and Galilean*.

1874   Visit to Norway.

1875   Settles in Munich.

1876   *Emperor and Galilean*, first of his plays to be translated into English by Miss Catherine Ray.

1877   *Pillars of Society*.

1878   Visit to Rome.

1879   *A Doll's House*.

1880   Settles in Rome.

1881   *Ghosts*.

1882   *An Enemy of the People*.

1884   *The Wild Duck*.

1885   Visit to Norway. Settles once again in Munich.

1886   *Rosmersholm*.

1887   Visit to Denmark and Sweden. Returns to Munich.

1888   *The Lady from the Sea.*

1890   *Hedda Gabler.*

1891   Moves to Norway. Settles in Christiania.

1892   *The Master Builder.*

1894   *Little Eyolf.*

1896   *John Gabriel Borkman.*

1898   Celebration of his seventieth birthday. Visits Stockholm.

1899   *When We Dead Awaken.* Opening of the new National Theatre in Christiania.

1900   Suffers first paralytic stroke.

1906   May 23. Ibsen's death.

Pillars of Society

A PLAY IN FOUR ACTS

1877

CHARACTERS

CONSUL BERNICK

MRS. BERNICK, *his wife*

OLAF, *their son, a boy of thirteen*

MISS BERNICK (MARTA), *the Consul's sister*

JOHAN TÖNNESEN, *Mrs. Bernick's younger brother*

MISS HESSEL (LONA), *her elder stepsister*

HILMAR TÖNNESEN, *Mrs. Bernick's cousin*

MR. RÖRLUND, *a schoolmaster*

RUMMEL
VIGELAND } *merchants*
SANDSTAD

DINA DORF, *a young girl living in the Consul's house*

KRAP, *the Consul's chief clerk*

AUNE, *foreman at the shipyard*

MRS. RUMMEL

MRS. HOLT, *the postmaster's wife*

MRS. LYNGE, *the doctor's wife*

MISS RUMMEL

MISS HOLT

Townspeople and others, foreign sailors, steamboat passengers, etc.

The action takes place in Consul Bernick's house, in a small Norwegian seaport.

ACT
ONE

SCENE: *A spacious garden room in* CONSUL BERNICK'S *house. Downstage left, a door leading to Bernick's office; further back in the same wall a similar door. In the center of the opposite wall a large entrance door. The back wall is almost entirely composed of glass; an open doorway leads to a broad flight of steps shaded by an awning. Beyond the steps part of the garden can be seen, enclosed by a railing in which there is a little gate. Beyond the railing and running parallel with it, is a street of small, brightly painted wooden houses. It is summer, and the sun shines brightly. Now and then people are seen passing along the street; they stop and speak to each other; customers come and go at the little corner shop, and so forth.*

In the garden room a number of ladies are gathered round a table. At the head of the table sits MRS. BERNICK. *On her left sit* MRS. HOLT *and* HER DAUGHTER; *next to them,* MRS. *and* MISS RUMMEL. *On* MRS. BERNICK'S *right sit* MRS. LYNGE, MISS BERNICK, *and* DINA DORF. *All the ladies are busy sewing. On the table are large piles of linen, cut into patterns, and various half-finished garments. Further upstage, at a little table on which are two pots of flowers, and a glass of barley water, sits* MR. RÖRLUND *reading aloud from a book with gilt edges; now and then a few words can be heard by the audience. In the garden* OLAF BERNICK *can be seen running about and shooting at a target with a popgun.*

Presently AUNE, *the foreman of the shipyard, enters quietly by the door on the right. The reading breaks off for a moment;* MRS. BERNICK *nods to him and points to the door on*

3

the left. AUNE *goes quietly ot the door of* BERNICK'S *office, knocks softly, pauses a moment, then knocks again.* KRAP, BERNICK'S *clerk, opens the door and comes out with his hat in his hand and some papers under his arm.*

KRAP: Was that you knocking?

AUNE: Yes. Mr. Bernick sent for me.

KRAP: I know; but he can't see you now. He's asked me to—

AUNE: You? I'd really much rather—

KRAP: He told me to tell you this: Those Saturday talks of yours to the workmen have got to stop.

AUNE: Indeed? I should have thought my free time was my own.

KRAP: You've no business using your free time to make the men useless during working hours. Last Saturday you went on again about the new machinery·—the new working methods we're inaugurating. You told the men they were unfair to labor. Why do you persist in doing this?

AUNE: To protect the interests of Society.

KRAP: That's odd! The master says you're undermining Society by that kind of talk.

AUNE: Mr. Bernick's idea of Society is not mine, Mr. Krap. As head of the Workers' Union it's my duty to—

KRAP: Your first duty is to Mr. Bernick's shipyard. As foreman your first duty is to that part of Society known as Bernick and Co. We all depend on that company for our livelihood—remember that! Well—now you know what Mr. Bernick wished to say.

AUNE: But that's not the way he would have said it, Mr. Krap. I think I can guess who I have to thank for this. It's those damned Americans and that wreck of theirs. Those people expect us to do the work as they do it over there; that's why—

KRAP: I can't waste my time on details. You know what the master wants, and that should be enough for you. Now get back to the shipyard; I expect you're needed there. I'll be down myself directly—Excuse me, ladies!

(*He bows and goes out through the garden and down the street.* AUNE *goes quietly out to the right. After a moment* MR. RÖRLUND, *who has continued reading during this conversation, closes the book with a bang.*)

RÖRLUND: There, my dear friends! That is the end.

MRS. RUMMEL: Such an instructive story!

MRS. HOLT: A truly moral tale!

MRS. BERNICK: A book like that certainly gives one something to think about!

RÖRLUND: Yes, indeed. It's a salutary contrast to the things we read daily in our newspapers and magazines. The great nations of the world display a gaudy flashy exterior, it's true; but what does that exterior conceal? Hollow, empty corruption—if I may so express myself. These great communities have no moral or ethical foundation; in short, ladies, I think we may say that they are nothing but whited sepulchers.

MRS. HOLT: True—all too true!

MRS. RUMMEL: Take, for example, the crew of that American ship that's in port at the moment—

RÖRLUND: Scum of the earth! Such people are beneath discussion. But, even in higher circles, what do we find? Doubt and unrest seething everywhere; no peace of soul, no standards of behavior. In such countries we find family life completely undermined; the most sacred truths ignored and scoffed at.

DINA (*Without looking up*): Still—they accomplish lots of great things, don't they?

RÖRLUND: Great things? I don't quite understand—

MRS. HOLT (*In astonishment*): Good heavens, Dina!

MRS. RUMMEL (*Simultaneously*): Dina! How *can* you—?

RÖRLUND: Let us hope and pray that "great things" of that sort never gain a footing here. Let us thank God that conditions here at home are as they are. There are tares among the wheat here too, unfortunately; but we strive to weed them out as best we can. We must try and keep our community pure, ladies; we must resist all these newfangled experiments that an impatient age seeks to force upon us.

MRS. HOLT: Unfortunately there are all too many of these newfangled notions.

MRS. RUMMEL: Last year it was only by a miracle that we escaped having a railroad thrust upon us.

MRS. BERNICK: Luckily Karsten put a stop to that.

RÖRLUND: Providence, Mrs. Bernick. Depend upon it—when your husband refused to support that project, he was an instrument in a Higher Hand.

MRS. BERNICK: That didn't prevent his being horribly abused in all the newspapers. But we're quite forgetting to thank you, Mr. Rörlund. It's really more than kind of you to give us so much of your time.

RÖRLUND: Well—school's out, you know; and during the holidays—

MRS. BERNICK: Still—it's a sacrifice all the same, dear Mr. Rörlund—

RÖRLUND: Don't mention it, dear lady. Are you not, all of you, making a sacrifice in a good cause? And I'm certain you do it gladly and willingly. I think of these fallen sisters whom you strive to help as soldiers wounded on the battle-field; you, ladies, are the Red Cross workers—the Sisters of Mercy—who prepare the bandages with which to bind up the wounds of these unhappy victims. You nurse them —you heal them—

MRS. BERNICK: It must be a great blessing to be able to see things in such a happy light!

RÖRLUND: It's largely a natural gift; but it can be acquired to some extent. The main thing is to see life in a serious light, and for this one must have a serious vocation. What do you think, Miss Bernick? Don't you find that your life has more stability, more purpose, now that you've taken up your school work?

MISS BERNICK: I'm not quite sure. Every now and then, as I sit there in the classroom, I can't help wishing I were somewhere far away—perhaps sailing on some stormy ocean—

RÖRLUND: We are all subject to temptation, my dear Miss Bernick; but we must bar the door against this disturbing guest. You say "some stormy ocean"—you don't mean that literally of course. You have in mind the great surging ocean of humanity in which so many souls are wrecked. Does this violent tempestuous life out in the great world appeal to you so strongly? Take a look at the people in the street outside. Watch them milling about, sweating in the glare of the hot sunshine—tormented by a thousand petty cares. Think how fortunate *we* are to be sitting here in the pleasant shade, turning our backs on all that distracting turmoil.

MISS BERNICK: Yes; I suppose you're right—

RÖRLUND: And, above all, how fortunate we are to be sitting in a house like this; a good, pure home—where family life is to be seen at its very best; where the utmost harmony prevails—(*To* MRS. BERNICK) What are you listening to, dear Mrs. Bernick?

MRS. BERNICK (*Who has turned towards the door of* BERNICK'S *study*): They seem to be talking very loudly.

RÖRLUND: Is anything special going on?

MRS. BERNICK: I don't know. There are evidently several people in there with my husband.

(HILMAR TÖNNESEN, *with a cigar in his mouth, comes in by the door on the right, but stops on seeing so many ladies.*)

HILMAR: Oh, I beg your pardon—(*He turns to go.*)

MRS. BERNICK: Don't go, Hilmar; do come in. You're not disturbing us. Was there anything you wanted?

HILMAR: No, I just thought I'd look in. —Good morning, ladies. (*To* MRS. BERNICK) Have they come to a decision yet?

MRS. BERNICK: A decision? What about?

HILMAR: You know Bernick called a meeting, don't you?

MRS. BERNICK: Indeed? What for?

HILMAR: That nonsense about the railroad has come up again.

MRS. BERNICK: Surely not that!

MISS BERNICK: Poor Karsten! I thought his worries on that score were over!

RÖRLUND: How very extraordinary, Mr. Tönnesen. I thought Mr. Bernick had made it quite clear that he would never consent to having a railroad here.

HILMAR: Yes, I thought so too. But I ran into Mr. Krap just now and he says the question has come up again. Bernick's having a conference with three of our local capitalists.

MRS. RUMMEL: I was certain I heard my husband's voice!

HILMAR: Yes—Mr. Rummel is one of them of course. Then there's Sandstad and Michael Vigeland—"Holy Michael" as they call him—

RÖRLUND: Hm—

HILMAR: I beg your pardon.

MRS. BERNICK: Oh dear! Just when things were so nice and peaceful too!

HILMAR: Let them start their squabbling again, as far as I'm concerned! It livens things up a bit!

RÖRLUND: We can dispense with that kind of liveliness, it seems to me.

HILMAR: That depends on one's temperament, you know. To some people a thoroughly good row now and then is highly stimulating. Unfortunately small-town life doesn't provide many distractions of that sort; we're not all able to— (*Turning over the leaves of* RÖRLUND'S *book*) *Woman as the Servant of Society*—what's this rubbish doing here?

MRS. BERNICK: You mustn't say that, Hilmar! I'm sure you've never read it.

HILMAR: No—and I don't intend to.

MRS. BERNICK: I'm afraid you're not feeling very well today.

HILMAR: I'm not.

MRS. BERNICK: Didn't you sleep well last night?

HILMAR: No, I slept very badly. I went for a walk yesterday —my doctor recommended it. Then I dropped in at the club and read a book about a voyage to the North Pole.

It's very bracing to read about men battling with the elements—

MRS. RUMMEL: It doesn't seem to have done you much good, Mr. Tönnesen.

HILMAR: No; quite the contrary. I lay awake, tossing about all night; and when I finally did doze off I dreamt I was being chased by a huge walrus.

OLAF (*Who has come up the steps from the garden*): Were you chased by a walrus, Uncle?

HILMAR: I dreamt it, you little idiot! Are you still fooling about with that ridiculous popgun? Why don't you get yourself a real one?

OLAF: I only wish I could, but—

HILMAR: There's some point in having a real gun; it makes your nerves tingle just to pull the trigger.

OLAF: Yes; and then I could shoot bears too. But Father won't allow it.

MRS. BERNICK: Hilmar—you mustn't put these ideas into his head.

HILMAR: A fine new generation we're bringing up! There's plenty of talk of action, and achievement; but what does it amount to? It's all a kind of game. It's quite a different thing when it comes to looking danger squarely in the face! There's no discipline—no daring! Don't point that thing at me, you little fool!

OLAF: It isn't loaded, Uncle.

HILMAR: You never know; it could be dangerous all the same. Take it away, I say!—Why the devil don't you go to America on one of your father's ships? You might see a buffalo hunt—or a fight with the Red Indians.

MRS. BERNICK: Really, Hilmar—!

OLAF: I wish I could go, Uncle; I might even see Uncle Johan and Aunt Lona too.

HILMAR: Hm—don't talk nonsense.

MRS. BERNICK: You may go down into the garden again, Olaf.

OLAF: May I go out into the street too, Mother?

MRS. BERNICK: Yes; but mind you don't go far.

(OLAF *runs out through the garden gate.*)

RÖRLUND: You shouldn't put these notions into the child's head, Mr. Tönnesen.

HILMAR: I dare say not! I suppose he's to stay at home and vegetate like everybody else!

RÖRLUND: Why haven't you ever been to America yourself?

HILMAR: I? With my precarious health? But, of course, no one here ever takes that into account. However—quite apart from that—one has certain duties towards the community in which one lives. *Someone* must keep the flag of the Ideal flying around here. Ugh! There he goes—shouting again!

LADIES: Who is shouting?

HILMAR: Don't ask me! All that loud talk makes me nervous!

MRS. RUMMEL: It's probably my husband, Mr. Tönnesen; he's so accustomed to addressing public meetings—

RÖRLUND: The others aren't exactly whispering either.

HILMAR: No. God help us, when it comes to squabbling about money—! That's all anybody ever thinks of here. They concentrate on nothing but petty material things; it's positively disgusting! Ugh!

MRS. BERNICK: At least that's better than concentrating on nothing but idle dissipation, as they did in the old days.

MRS. LYNGE: Were things in the old days really as bad as that?

MRS. RUMMEL: Indeed they were, Mrs. Lynge. You can count yourself fortunate that you didn't live here then.

MRS. HOLT: There have certainly been great changes here. When I think back to the time when I was a young girl—

MRS. RUMMEL: No need to go back as far as that! Even fourteen or fifteen years ago—the things that went on here! There was a dance club, and a musical association—

MISS BERNICK: And a dramatic club too; don't you remember?

MRS. RUMMEL: They presented a play of yours, didn't they, Mr. Tönnesen?

HILMAR (*In the background*): Oh, for heaven's sake—!

RÖRLUND: A play by Mr. Tönnesen?

MRS. RUMMEL: It was long before *you* came here. And it was only for one night, you know.

MRS. LYNGE: Didn't you tell me you played the heroine in it, Mrs. Rummel?

MRS. RUMMEL (*With a glance at* RÖRLUND): I? I really don't remember, Mrs. Lynge. But I remember all those noisy parties people used to give.

MRS. HOLT: Yes; I actually know of one family that gave two large dinner parties within a week.

MRS. LYNGE: And didn't I hear something about a touring company of actors?

MRS. RUMMEL: That was the worst of all—!

MRS. HOLT (*Uneasily*): Hm, hm—

MRS. RUMMEL: Actors did you say? No—I don't remember that.

MRS. LYYNGE: I was told they caused no end of trouble. What really happened?

MRS. RUMMEL: Nothing, Mrs. Lynge. Nothing at all.

MRS. HOLT: Dina dear, would you hand me that piece of linen?

MRS. BERNICK (*Simultaneously*): Dina dear, would you just go and ask Katrine to bring the coffee?

MISS BERNICK: I'll go with you, Dina.

(DINA *and* MISS BERNICK *go out by the upstage door on the left.*)

MRS. BERNICK (*Rising*): Excuse me a moment, ladies. I thought we'd have our coffee out on the veranda.

(*She goes out on the veranda and begins arranging a table;* RÖRLUND *stands in the doorway talking to her.* HILMAR TÖNNESEN *sits outside smoking.*)

MRS. RUMMEL (*In a low voice*): Oh, Mrs. Lynge! You gave me such a fright!

MRS. LYNGE: *I* did?

MRS. HOLT: It was actually you who began it, Mrs. Rummel.

MRS. RUMMEL: I? I don't see how you can say that, Mrs. Holt. I never said a word!

MRS. LYNGE: What *is* all this about?

MRS. RUMMEL: How could you bring up the subject of—! And with Dina in the room too!

MRS. LYNGE: Dina? Good gracious! What's *she* got to do with—?

MRS. HOLT: And here of all places! Here in this house! Don't you know that it was Mrs. Bernick's brother—?

MRS. LYNGE: What about him? Remember, I know absolutely nothing. After all, I'm a comparative stranger here—

MRS. RUMMEL: Haven't you heard that—? Hm—(*To her daughter*) Hilda, why don't you go out into the garden for a little while?

MRS. HOLT: And you too, Netta. And be very kind to poor Dina when she comes back; do you hear?

(MISS RUMMEL *and* MISS HOLT *go out into the garden.*)

MRS. LYNGE: What's all this about Mrs. Bernick's brother?

MRS. RUMMEL: Didn't you know he was the cause of all that dreadful scandal?

MRS. LYNGE: Hilmar Tönnesen a cause of scandal?

MRS. RUMMEL: Good heavens, no! Hilmar's her cousin, Mrs. Lynge. I'm speaking of her brother—

MRS. HOLT: —the one who's so disreputable—

MRS. RUMMEL: His name is Johan. He ran away to America—

MRS. HOLT: *Had* to run away, you understand.

MRS. LYNGE: So the scandal was about him, was it?

MRS. RUMMEL: Yes; it was a sort of—; I really don't know how to put it. It had to do with Dina's mother. I remember it all as if it had happened yesterday! At that time Johan Tönnesen was employed in old Mrs. Bernick's office; Karsten Bernick had only just returned from Paris— it was before he became engaged to—

MRS. LYNGE: But what about the scandal?

MRS. RUMMEL: Well, you see—it was the winter that Möller's theatrical company was here in town—

MRS. HOLT: Dorf and his wife were members of the company, you see. All the young men were mad about her.

MRS. RUMMEL: Heaven only knows what they saw in her! Well—one night Dorf came home very late—

MRS. HOLT: —quite unexpectedly—

MRS. RUMMEL: —and he found— No! I really don't think I can tell you!

MRS. HOLT: He didn't actually find anything, Mrs. Rummel. The door was locked on the inside.

MRS. RUMMEL: That's exactly what I was about to say: he found the door locked. And the man inside had to escape through the window.

MRS. HOLT: A top-floor window, too!

MRS. LYNGE: And it was Mrs. Bernick's brother?

MRS. RUMMEL: That's who it was!

MRS. LYNGE: And that's why he ran away to America?

MRS. HOLT: He had to run away, as you can well imagine!

MRS. RUMMEL: Then, later on, they discovered something else—something almost as bad: he'd made off with a sum of money belonging to the firm—

MRS. HOLT: We don't know that for certain, Mrs. Rummel. That may only have been a rumor.

MRS. RUMMEL: Well—I must say! You know quite well the whole town knew about it! Poor old Mrs. Bernick almost went bankrupt on account of it. Rummel told me so himself. However—far be it from me to say another word!

MRS. HOLT: Anyhow—the Dorf woman didn't get any of it, that's certain. After all, she—

MRS. LYNGE: Yes—what became of Dina's parents?

MRS. RUMMEL: Dorf deserted them—both wife and child. But the woman had the effrontery to stay on here a whole year. She didn't dare appear on the stage again, that's true enough. She supported herself by doing laundry work and mending—

MRS. HOLT: She even tried to start a dancing school.

MRS. RUMMEL: That failed, of course. Who would trust their child to a person of that sort? In any case she didn't hold out long; our fine lady wasn't accustomed to hard work, you see! She soon developed some sort of lung trouble and died.

MRS. LYNGE: What a dreadful story!

MRS. RUMMEL: It's been hard on the Bernicks I can tell you! As Rummel once expressed it: it's the one dark cloud on the sunshine of their happiness. So don't ever speak of these things in this house again, dear Mrs. Lynge.

MRS. HOLT: And don't, for heaven's sake, mention the step-sister either!

MRS. LYNGE: Oh, of course! Mrs. Bernick has a stepsister too, hasn't she?

MRS. RUMMEL: *Had*—fortunately. She no longer recognizes the relationship. *There* was an eccentric creature if you like! Can you believe it?—she had her hair cut short like a man's; and she actually wore men's boots—at least, in rainy weather.

MRS. HOLT: And when Mrs. Bernick's half brother—that disreputable person—had run away, and the whole town was up in arms over his behavior—what do you think *she* did? She up and followed him!

MRS. RUMMEL: And think of the scandal she caused before she left!

MRS. HOLT: Don't speak of it!

MRS. LYNGE: Heavens! Was there a scandal about her too?

MRS. RUMMEL: Yes! I think perhaps you'd better know about it, Mrs. Lynge. You see, Bernick had just become engaged to Betty Tönnesen; he escorted her to her aunt's house to announce the engagement—

MRS. RUMMEL: —and Lona Hessel rose up from her chair and gave Karsten Bernick—and you know what a delightful charming man he is—a sound box on the ear!

MRS. LYNGE: Well, I never—!

MRS. HOLT: Yes, that's what happened!

MRS. LYNGE: She must have had her eye on him herself.

MRS. RUMMEL: That's just it! She fully expected to marry him when he got back from Paris.

MRS. HOLT: Such presumption; just imagine! Bernick—a young man-of-the-world—such a perfect gentleman—the darling of all the ladies—

MRS. RUMMEL: And so high-principled, Mrs. Holt. A model of good behavior—

MRS. LYNGE: What became of this Miss Hessel in America?

MRS. RUMMEL: We'd best draw a veil over that, Mrs. Lynge —as my husband once expressed it.

MRS. LYNGE: How do you mean?

MRS. RUMMEL: Naturally the family has severed all connection with her; but everyone knows she's sung in cabarets for money—

MRS. HOLT:—and she's given public lectures—

MRS. RUMMEL: —and has published an utterly preposterous book, as well.

MRS. LYNGE: Just fancy!

MRS. RUMMEL: Yes; undoubtedly Lona Hessel is another cloud on the Bernicks' happiness. Now you know the whole story, Mrs. Lynge. Heaven knows I've only told you this to put you on your guard.

MRS. LYNGE: I'll be careful, I assure you— But that poor Dina Dorf! I'm really sorry for her.

MRS. RUMMEL: In the long run, it was actually a bit of luck for her. If she'd had to stay with her parents God knows what would have become of her! We all of us took charge of her, and tried to direct and guide her to the best of our ability. Finally Mrs. Bernick took her in—arranged for her to live here.

MRS. HOLT: But she's always been a difficult girl to deal with; the result of the life she led as a child, no doubt. She's not like one of us. We've simply had to make the best of her, Mrs. Lynge.

MRS. RUMMEL: Sh! Here she comes. (*In a loud voice*) Yes, Dina's really quite a clever girl; she— Oh! Is that you, Dina? We're just finishing up our work.

MRS. HOLT: That coffee smells delicious, Dina dear. There's nothing like a cup of coffee at this time of the morning!

MRS. BERNICK (*From the veranda*): Coffee's ready, ladies!
(MISS BERNICK *and* DINA *have been helping the servant
to bring in the coffee things. All the ladies go out on to the
veranda and sit down. They vie with each other in being
kind to* DINA. *After a while she comes back into the room
and looks for her sewing.*)

MRS. BERNICK (*Calls from the coffee table*): Dina, don't you
want some—?

DINA: No, thank you; I don't care for any.
(*She sits down to sew.* MRS. BERNICK *and* RÖRLUND *ex-
change a few words and a moment later he comes into the
room.*)

RÖRLUND (*Pretends to be looking for something on the table
and says in a low voice*): Dina.

DINA: Yes?

RÖRLUND: Why don't you want to sit out there?

DINA: When I brought the coffee in, I could see by the
strange lady's face that they'd been telling her about me.

RÖRLUND: Then you must have noticed too how very kind
she was to you.

DINA: That's just what I can't bear!

RÖRLUND: You have a very stubborn nature, Dina.

DINA: Yes, I dare say.

RÖRLUND: Why are you like that?

DINA: That's the way I'm made.

RÖRLUND: Couldn't you try to change?

DINA: No.

RÖRLUND: Why not?

DINA (*Looks up at him*): I belong to the "Fallen Women"
too, you see.

RÖRLUND: Why, Dina!

DINA: And so did mother.

RÖRLUND: Who's been talking to you about such things?

DINA: No one; they never talk. Why *won't* they! They handle me so gingerly—as though I'd fall to pieces if—Oh,
how I hate their kindness!

RÖRLUND: I understand you, Dina. I know you feel tied down here, but—

DINA: If I could only get away! I'd manage somehow— If only I didn't have to live with people who are so—

RÖRLUND: So what?

DINA: So proper and self-righteous.

RÖRLUND: Dina—I'm sure you can't mean that.

DINA: You know perfectly well what I mean. Hilda and Netta come here every day, and I'm expected to pattern myself on them. But I could never be as well-behaved as they are—and what's more, I don't *want* to be. If I could only get away from here, I believe I could be quite good too.

RÖRLUND: You *are* good, Dina dear.

DINA: Even if I am—what good does it do me here?

RÖRLUND: You keep saying you want to go away; are you thinking of it seriously?

DINA: I wouldn't stay here another minute if it weren't for you.

RÖRLUND: Tell me, Dina—why do you especially like to be with me?

DINA: You teach me so much that's beautiful.

RÖRLUND: Beautiful? You call what I have to teach you beautiful?

DINA: Yes. Or rather—you don't really *teach* me anything. But when you talk, you make me think of beautiful things; you make me see them.

RÖRLUND: What do you actually mean by beautiful things?

DINA: I don't know; I've never thought about it.

RÖRLUND: Then think about it now. When you say "beautiful things," what do you really mean?

DINA: To me—a beautiful thing is something great—and far away.

RÖRLUND: I feel such sympathy for you, Dina dear.

DINA: Is that all?

RÖRLUND: You know how inexpressibly dear you are to me.

DINA: If I were Hilda or Netta you wouldn't be so afraid of letting people see it.

RÖRLUND: Oh, Dina; you can't possibly realize all the different reasons that— When one is looked upon as a moral force in the community in which one lives—it's impossible to be too careful. If I were only sure my motives would not be misconstrued— But, be that as it may—you need a helping hand, and you shall have it! It's agreed between us, isn't it, Dina? that when I come—when circumstances permit my coming to you to offer you my hand—that you will accept it and become my wife? You promise that?

DINA: Yes.

RÖRLUND: Thank you, thank you! You see, for me too— Oh, Dina—I'm so very fond of you!— Sh! Someone's coming. Please—for my sake—go out and join the others.

(*She goes and joins the party at the coffee table. At the same moment* RUMMEL, SANDSTAD *and* VIGELAND, *followed by* BERNICK, *enter from* BERNICK's *office. He holds a bundle of papers in his hand.*)

BERNICK: The matter's settled, then.

VIGELAND: God willing—let us hope so.

RUMMEL: Of course it's settled, Bernick! Definitely settled. A Norseman's word is his bond—you know that!

BERNICK: And we stand firm against all opposition. No weakening—no turning back!

RUMMEL: We stand or fall together, Bernick!

HILMAR (*Comes in through the garden door*): What's this about falling? I presume you mean the railroad's fallen through?

BERNICK: On the contrary—it's going ahead.

RUMMEL: Full steam ahead, Mr. Tönnesen.

HILMAR (*Coming forward*): Really?

RÖRLUND: What?

MRS. BERNICK (*At the garden door*): But, Karsten—I don't understand—

BERNICK: It can't possibly interest you, my dear Betty. (*To the three men*) We'll draw up the prospectus at once—there's no time to lose. Our four names will head it, nat-

urally. As leaders of this community it's our duty to throw
our full weight into the scale.

SANDSTAD: Of course, Mr. Bernick—I quite agree.

RUMMEL: We'll swing it, Bernick. We've pledged ourselves
to that.

BERNICK: I've no fear of the outcome, I assure you. We must
all of us get to work, each in his own circle. Once the general interest of the community is thoroughly aroused, the
town officials will be obliged to do their share.

MRS. BERNICK: Karsten, you really must come out and tell
us all about it.

BERNICK: It's not a topic for ladies, my dear Betty.

HILMAR: You mean to say you're going to back the railroad
after all?

BERNICK: Of course I am.

RÖRLUND: But, Mr. Bernick, I thought last year you—?

BERNICK: Last year was quite another matter. At that time
the plan was to run a line along the coast—

VIGELAND: —which would have been totally superfluous, Mr.
Rörlund. We have steamships, haven't we?

SANDSTAD: Also it would have been outrageously expensive—

RUMMEL: —and it would have seriously interfered with certain vested interests here in town.

BERNICK: It would have failed to benefit the community at
large—that was the principal objection; it was for this
reason that I opposed it. And now the inland route has
been decided on.

HILMAR: But surely it won't touch any of the towns round
here?

BERNICK: It's going to touch *our* town, my dear Hilmar; for
we propose to build a branch line.

HILMAR: Aha! Then this is an entirely new idea.

RUMMEL: A brilliant idea, don't you think?

RÖRLUND: Hm—

VIGELAND: It's as though the terrain had been designed by
Providence on purpose to accommodate a branch line.

RÖRLUND: You really think so, Mr. Vigeland?

BERNICK: Providence certainly had a hand in that business trip I took this spring. I traveled by way of a valley I'd never been in before; and in a flash I saw that here was the ideal route through which to bring a branch line to our town. I sent out engineers immediately to make a survey of the region; here is their report. The preliminary calculations and estimates are highly satisfactory. There are no obstacles; nothing prevents our going ahead at once.

MRS. BERNICK (*Still standing with the other ladies at the veranda door*): Think of your keeping all this secret, Karsten dear!

BERNICK: My dear Betty, the situation was far too complex for you to grasp. Besides—I haven't said a word to a living soul until today. But the decisive moment is now at hand; the matter must come out into the open, and we must work with all our might to bring it to a successful conclusion. I'm determined to see it through, if it means risking everything I own.

RUMMEL: We're all with you, Bernick; you can count on that!

RÖRLUND: Do you really expect such great results from this undertaking, gentlemen?

BERNICK: We do indeed! Imagine the stimulating effect it will have on the whole community! It will open up vast tracts of forest land; enable us to exploit rich mineral deposits hitherto inaccessible; harness the numerous waterfalls— the possibilities for industrial expansion are incalculable!

RÖRLUND: And you have no fear of the demoralizing influence this contact with the outer world—?

BERNICK: I think you can be quite easy on that score, Mr. Rörlund. Thank God our busy little town is founded on sound moral principles. We've all of us helped to drain off the poisons—if I may so express it—and shall continue to do so, each in his own way. You, Mr. Rörlund, will continue to spread your beneficent influence in our schools and in our homes; and we practical businessmen will continue to support Society by spreading prosperity in ever-widening circles. And, as for our good women—come closer, ladies, this is for your ears!—our women, I say, our wives and daughters, will carry on their charitable works and continue to be a help and comfort to those near and dear to them, as my dear Betty and Marta are to me and Olaf—(*Looks round*) By the way, where *is* Olaf today?

MRS. BERNICK: It's almost impossible to keep him home during the holidays—

BERNICK: Down at the water front again, I suppose! He'll get into trouble one of these days, I warn you!

HILMAR: Nonsense! It's good for him to play down by the water; to come in contact with the elements of Nature—

MRS. RUMMEL: You're a real family man, aren't you, Mr. Bernick? It's very edifying!

BERNICK: Isn't the family the true basis of Society? A good home, a few dependable, honorable friends, a small intimate circle protected against the intrusion of all disturbing influences—

(KRAP *enters from the right with some letters and newspapers.*)

KRAP: The foreign mail, Mr. Bernick—and a cable from New York.

BERNICK (*Taking it from him*): Ah—from the owners of "The Indian Girl."

RUMMEL: The mail's in, is it? Then I must ask to be excused—

VIGELAND: I must get back to the office too.

SANDSTAD: Goodbye, Mr. Bernick.

BERNICK: Goodbye, gentlemen. Remember we have a meeting this afternoon at five o'clock.

ALL THREE: Yes; yes, of course. (*They go out right.*)

BERNICK (*Who has read the cable*): This is typically American! Positively outrageous!

MRS. BERNICK: Good gracious, Karsten—what's the matter?

BERNICK: Take a look at this, Mr. Krap.

KRAP (*Reading*): "Fewest possible repairs. Despatch Indian

Girl without delay. Weather favorable. Count on cargo keeping her afloat." Well, I must say—

BERNICK: "Count on cargo keeping her afloat"! If anything should happen, with that cargo she'd go to the bottom like a stone! These fine gentlemen are well aware of that!

RÖRLUND: This only goes to show what conditions are really like in these great nations we hear so much about!

BERNICK: You're right there. Human life means nothing when dollars are at stake. (*To* KRAP) Can "The Indian Girl" be put to sea in four or five days?

KRAP: Only if Mr. Vigeland will allow us to hold up work on "The Palm Tree."

BERNICK: Hm. He'll never agree to that. Just look through the mail, will you? By the way, did you see Olaf at the pier?

KRAP: No, Mr. Bernick. (*He goes into* BERNICK's *office.*)

BERNICK (*Looks at the cable again*): These gentlemen think nothing of risking eighteen lives—

HILMAR: Well—it's a sailor's job to brave the elements; it must be a highly stimulating sensation to have nothing but a thin plank between you and eternity—

BERNICK: I'd like to see one of *our* shipowners doing a thing like that! There's not *one* of them would do it! Not a single one! (*Catches sight of* OLAF) Ah, there he is! He's all right, thank God!

(OLAF, *with a fishing rod in his hand, comes running up the street and through the garden gate.*)

OLAF (*Still in the garden*): Uncle Hilmar! Uncle Hilmar! I've been down watching the steamer—

BERNICK: Have you been down at the pier again?

OLAF: No, Father; I went out in a boat. Uncle Hilmar—just think! A whole circus company came in on the steamer— with lots of horses and wild animals. And there were lots of passengers as well.

MRS. RUMMEL: Don't tell me we're to have a circus!

RÖRLUND: We? I most certainly hope not!

MRS. RUMMEL: Of course I didn't mean that *we*—!

DINA: I'd love to see a circus.

OLAF: So would I!

HILMAR: You little idiot! What's there to see in that? It's all forced training—artificial tricks. To watch the gaucho racing across the pampas on his snorting mustang—that would be something different! That'd be worth while! But what can you expect in these provincial towns—!

OLAF (*Tugging at* MISS BERNICK's *dress*): Look, Auntie—here they come!

MRS. HOLT: Yes, my goodness—look at them!

MRS. LYNGE: What *awful* people!

(*Many travelers and a whole crowd of townspeople are seen coming up the street.*)

MRS. RUMMEL: A bunch of mountebanks! You can tell it at a glance! Look at that woman in the gray dress, Mrs. Holt; she's actually carrying a knapsack on her back!

MRS. HOLT: It's slung on the handle of her parasol. She's the manager's wife, I suppose.

MRS. RUMMEL: And that man with the beard must be the manager. He's exactly like a pirate, isn't he? Don't look at him, Hilda!

MRS. HOLT: Nor you either, Netta!

OLAF: He's waving to us, Mother.

BERNICK: What's that?

MRS. BERNICK: What did you say, dear?

MRS. RUMMEL: Good heavens—the woman's waving too!

BERNICK: What impertinence!

MISS BERNICK (*With an involuntary cry*): Ah—!

MRS. BERNICK: What is it, Marta?

MISS BERNICK: Nothing—I only thought—

OLAF (*Shouting with delight*): Look! Here come the others with the horses and wild animals! And there are the Americans too. The sailors from "The Indian Girl"— (*"Yankee-Doodle" is heard accompanied by a drum and a clarinet.*)

HILMER (*Stopping his ears*): Ugh! Ugh!

RÖRLUND: I think we should withdraw a little, ladies. This kind of spectacle is not for us. Let us take up our work again.

MRS. BERNICK: Perhaps we'd better draw the curtains.

RÖRLUND: That's just what I was thinking.

(*The ladies take their places at the table;* RÖRLUND *shuts the garden door and draws the curtains; the room is now in semidarkness.*)

OLAF (*Peeping out*): Mother, the manager's wife is washing her face at the fountain.

MRS. BERNICK: What! In the middle of the street!

MRS. RUMMEL: And in broad daylight too!

HILMAR: If I were traveling in the desert and came upon a spring, I shouldn't hesitate to—Ugh! That ghastly clarinet!

RÖRLUND: I'm surprised the police don't step in.

BERNICK: Oh, come! One mustn't be too hard on foreigners. We can't expect them to share our sense of decency. Let them do as they please; it can't matter to us. This revolt against good taste and good manners finds no echo here— if I may so express it— What on earth is this!

(*A strange woman enters briskly from the right.*)

THE LADIES (*Alarmed, in low voices*): The circus woman! The manager's wife!

MRS. BERNICK: What does this mean?

MISS BERNICK (*Jumping up*): Ah—!

THE WOMAN: Good morning, my dear Betty! Good morning, Marta. Good morning, Brother-in-law!

MRS. BERNICK (*Cries out*): Lona!

BERNICK (*Falls back a step*): Good heavens—!

MRS. HOLT: Gracious me—!

MRS. RUMMEL: It can't be possible!

HILMAR: Well! Ugh!

MRS. BERNICK: Lona—! Is it really—?

LONA: Is it really *me?* It is indeed! So don't hesitate to embrace me!

HILMAR: Ugh! Ugh!

MRS. BERNICK: You've come back here as—?

BERNICK: You're actually going to *perform* here—?

LONA: Perform? What do you mean perform?

BERNICK: In the circus!

LONA: Ha, ha, ha! My dear Brother-in-law have you gone mad? Do you really think I've joined the circus? I've plied all sorts of trades—made a fool of myself in a wide variety of ways—

MRS. RUMMEL: Hm—

LONA: —but I haven't yet become an acrobat!

BERNICK: Then, you're not—?

MRS. BERNICK: Thank God for that!

LONA: No; we've returned as perfectly ordinary respectable people, I assure you; second-class, of course; but then we're used to that.

MRS. BERNICK: *We?*

BERNICK (*Takes a step nearer*): Who do you mean by *we?*

LONA: My boy and I, of course.

THE LADIES (*Cry out*): Your boy!

HILMAR: What!

RÖRLUND: Well, I must say—!

MRS. BERNICK: Who are you talking about, Lona?

LONA: Why John, of course. He's the only boy I have as far as I know; or, rather, Johan as you used to call him.

MRS. BERNICK: Johan—!

MRS. RUMMEL (*Aside to* MRS. LYNGE): The disreputable brother!

BERNICK (*Hesitating*): Is Johan with you?

LONA: Of course he is. I wouldn't dream of going anywhere without him. But why are you all looking so dismal? And why are you sitting here in the pitch-dark sewing on a lot of white stuff? There hasn't been a death in the family, has there?

RÖRLUND: My dear Miss Hessel, this happens to be a meeting of the Society for Fallen Women—

LONA (*Lowering her voice*): Don't tell me all these respectable-looking ladies are—?

MRS. RUMMEL: This is too much—!

LONA: Oh, I beg your pardon! I see! I understand!—Good heavens, it's Mrs. Rummel, isn't it? And Mrs. Holt too, I declare! We're none of us any younger since last we met. But, look here; let the Fallen Women wait, just for today. They'll be none the worse for it, I'm sure. This is an occasion for rejoicing—

RÖRLUND: A homecoming is not always an occasion for rejoicing.

LONA: Indeed? Is that how you read your Bible, Parson?

RÖRLUND: I am not a Parson.

LONA: You'll be one some day, I expect—Pah! These holier-than-thou garments smell like a lot of shrouds! I'm used to the wide open spaces now, remember!

BERNICK (*Mopping his brow*): It *is* rather oppressive here.

LONA: We'll soon fix that; we'll let some light into this dismal tomb. (*Draws back the curtains*) Things must be bright and cheerful when my boy arrives. He'll be all shiny and clean, you'll see—

HILMAR: Ugh!

LONA (*Opens the door and the windows*):—after he's had a good wash at the hotel. He got dirty as a pig on board that steamer—

HILMAR: Ugh! Ugh!

LONA: Ugh? Well, if it isn't—! (*Points to* HILMAR *and asks the others*) Does he still loaf about here saying "ugh!" to everything?

HILMAR: I don't loaf about. I'm obliged to stay here; doctor's orders.

RÖRLUND: Hm—ladies, I hardly think that—

LONA (*Catches sight of* OLAF): Is that your boy, Betty? Well! Give us your paw, fellow. Or maybe you're scared of your ugly old aunt!

RÖRLUND (*Putting his book under his arm*): Ladies, I'm afraid we're in no mood to continue work today. But we shall meet tomorrow, shall we not?

LONA (*As the visitors get up to say goodbye*): Splendid! Till tomorrow then. I shall be here!

RÖRLUND: *You?* My dear Miss Hessel—what can you possibly contribute to this Society of ours?

LONA: I can let in some fresh air, Parson!

CURTAIN

ACT TWO

SCENE: *Same as Act I.* MRS. BERNICK *is sitting alone at the worktable sewing. In a little while* BERNICK *enters from the right, with his hat and gloves on; he carries a cane.*

MRS. BERNICK: Home already, Karsten?

BERNICK: I have an appointment here.

MRS. BERNICK (*With a sigh*): Yes; I suppose Johan will be coming again today.

BERNICK: My appointment has nothing to do with him. (*Takes off his hat*) Where are all the ladies?

MRS. BERNICK: Mrs. Rummel and Hilda hadn't time to come.

BERNICK: Sent their excuses, did they?

MRS. BERNICK: Yes; they had too much to do at home today, they said.

BERNICK: I see. And the others can't come either, I suppose.

MRS. BERNICK: No; they were prevented too.

BERNICK: I could have told you that beforehand; where's Olaf?

MRS. BERNICK: I let him go out with Dina.

BERNICK: Dina—that little scatterbrain! The fuss she made over Johan yesterday—!

MRS. BERNICK: After all, Karsten dear, the poor girl knows nothing about—

BERNICK: Then Johan should have had tact enough to take no notice of her. Didn't you see the expression on Vigeland's face?

MRS. BERNICK (*Dropping her sewing into her lap*): Why do you suppose they've come home, Karsten?

BERNICK: Well—that farm he has over there doesn't seem to be too flourishing; you heard her say yesterday they were obliged to travel second-class—

MRS. BERNICK: Yes; I'm afraid it must be something of that sort. But I can't get over *her* coming with him. How could she! After the dreadful way she insulted you—!

BERNICK: Why hark back to that! That's such an old story!

MRS. BERNICK: How can I help it? He's my own brother, after all. But I'm not thinking of *him;* I'm thinking of the unpleasantness it will cause *you.* I'm so dreadfully afraid—

BERNICK: What are you afraid of?

MRS. BERNICK: Mightn't they arrest him? On account of that money your mother lost?

BERNICK: Nonsense! There's no way of proving there was any money missing.

BERNICK: The whole town knows, unfortunately, and you said yourself—

BERNICK: I never said a word about it. And the town knows absolutely nothing. The whole thing was a rumor.

MRS. BERNICK: You're so generous, Karsten!

BERNICK: Do stop dwelling on the past! Don't torment me by raking up all this sordid business! (*He paces up and down the room, and flings down his cane*) If only they hadn't come back *now*—just when I need the support of the whole community, as well as the good will of the Press. There are bound to be comments in all the newspapers in the surrounding districts. And whichever way I take them.

—amicably or resentfully—there'll be gossip and innuen-
does. People will start dragging up the past—just as you
do! In a little town like ours— (*Throws his gloves down on
the table*) And I haven't a single soul to talk to; no one I
can depend on for support.

MRS. BERNICK: No one at all, Karsten?

BERNICK: You know quite well I haven't—Why did they
have to choose *this* moment to descend on me! They're
certain to cause a scandal, one way or another. Especially
she. It's nothing short of a calamity to have connections of
that sort!

MRS. BERNICK: Well, *I* can't help it if—

BERNICK: What can't you help? Being related to them? No—
God knows, that's true enough.

MRS. BERNICK: I didn't *ask* them to come home, you know.

BERNICK: There you go again! "*I* didn't ask them to come
home; *I* didn't write them; *I* didn't try to drag them back"!
I know the whole damn rigmarole by heart!

MRS. BERNICK (*Bursts into tears*): How can you be so unkind—!

BERNICK: That's right! Now start crying—give the town
something *else* to talk about! Stop this nonsense, Betty!
Go out on the veranda; someone might come in here. Do
you want people to see you with red eyes? It'd be a fine
thing if the rumor got around that—Sh! I hear someone in
the hall. (*There's a knock at the door*) Come in!
(MRS. BERNICK *goes out to the veranda with her work.*
AUNE *comes in from the right.*)

AUNE: Good morning, Sir.

BERNICK: Good morning. I suppose you know why I want to
see you.

AUNE: The head clerk told me yesterday you didn't like—

BERNICK: I don't like *anything* about the way things are going at the yard, Aune. You're not getting anywhere with
the work down there. "The Palm Tree" should have been at
sea days ago. Mr. Vigeland does nothing but pester me
about it. He's a hard man to deal with.

AUNE: "The Palm Tree" can sail the day after tomorrow.

BERNICK: And about time too! But what about the American ship, "The Indian Girl"? She's been here over five weeks now—

AUNE: The American? I kind of thought you wanted us to get your own ship out of the way first.

BERNICK: I gave you no reason to think that. I wanted you to get ahead with the American ship too. But you've done nothing about her.

AUNE: Her hull's rotted right through, Sir. The more we try to patch her, the worse she gets.

BERNICK: That's not the real cause of the trouble, and you know it. Mr. Krap has told me all about it; the truth is you don't understand the new machinery I've had installed; or, rather, you refuse to understand it, and you won't work with it.

AUNE: I'm getting on for sixty, Mr. Bernick. From the time I was a boy I've been used to the old ways—

BERNICK: The old ways are no longer adequate. You mustn't think it's merely a question of profit, Aune. Fortunately I've no need to consider that. But I do have to consider the community in which I live, and the business of which I am director. If we want progress it must come from me, or we won't have it at all.

AUNE: I want progress too, Sir.

BERNICK: Yes, I know; for your own limited circle—for the working class. I understand you're quite a firebrand! Making speeches—stirring people up. But when you come face to face with progress in a tangible form—with new machines, new working methods—you'll have no part of it. You shy away, as though you were afraid.

AUNE: I am afraid, Sir. I'm afraid of what'll happen to the workingman; these machines take the bread out of his mouth. You talk about considering the community, but I think the community has its duties too. It should educate a new generation before it allows scientists and capitalists

to foist a lot of newfangled machines on us when we don't
know how to use them.

BERNICK: You read and think too much, Aune; that's your
trouble. That's what makes you dissatisfied with your
position.

AUNE: It's not that, Mr. Bernick. But I can't bear to see one
good workman after another turned away and left to starve
for the sake of these machines.

BERNICK: No doubt a lot of scribes were turned away and left
to starve when they invented printing.

AUNE: And if you'd been a scribe yourself in those days, Mr.
Bernick, would you have thought the printing press such
a good invention?

BERNICK: I didn't send for you to argue with you. I sent for
you to tell you that "The Indian Girl" must be ready to
sail the day after tomorrow.

AUNE: But, Mr. Bernick—

BERNICK: The day after tomorrow, do you hear? At the same
time as our own ship, not an hour later. I have my own
reasons—very good ones, I assure you—for insisting upon
this. If you've read this morning's paper you must have
seen the account of the latest disturbance involving the
Americans. Those ruffians have turned the whole town
upside down. Not a night goes by without fights breaking
out in the taverns, and even on the streets; as well as
other abuses too abominable to mention.

AUNE: They're a bad lot, that's certain.

BERNICK: And who's blamed for all this? I am! I'm the one
they hold responsible. The newspapers, in their sly way,
are insinuating that we've concentrated all our efforts on
getting "The Palm Tree" under way. I'll not put up with
it! I, who've devoted my whole life to setting a good example to my fellow citizens. I won't tolerate it. I can't
have these slurs on my good name.

AUNE: Nothing could hurt your good name, Mr. Bernick. No
need to worry about that.

BERNICK: Under ordinary circumstances I might agree with
you. But just now I'm involved in a most important undertaking, as you may have heard; I must be able to
count on the wholehearted support of my fellow citizens.
If certain malicious people should succeed in undermining
the absolute confidence I now command, I might run into
serious difficulties. These newspapermen must be silenced
at all cost. That's why I say "The Indian Girl" must sail
the day after tomorrow.

AUNE: You might just as well say she must sail today, Mr.
Bernick.

BERNICK: You mean I'm asking the impossible?

AUNE: Yes, with our present working crew—

BERNICK: Very good; then we'll have to look elsewhere.

AUNE: Are you going to lay off still more of the old hands?

BERNICK: No, I'm not thinking of that.

AUNE: Because if you do it'll cause bad blood, I'm afraid;
among the people as well as in the newspapers.

BERNICK: Quite possibly; that's why I shall avoid it. But if
"The Indian Girl" isn't cleared by the day after tomorrow,
I intend to dismiss *you*.

AUNE (*With a start*): Me! (*Laughing*) Now you're joking,
Sir.

BERNICK: I wouldn't count on that.

AUNE: You'd really think of dismissing *me*? My father, and
my grandfather too, worked in the shipyard all their lives,
and I myself—

BERNICK: Who's forcing me to it, may I ask?

AUNE: You're asking me to do something impossible, Mr.
Bernick.

BERNICK: Where there's a will there's a way. I want a firm
answer: yes or no. Otherwise I'll discharge you on the
spot.

AUNE (*Coming a step nearer*): Have you really thought what
it means, sir, to discharge an old workman like me? You
expect him to look for another job, and so he can; but
there's more to it than that. You should be in that man's

house the night he comes home after losing his job, and puts his tool chest away in the corner.

BERNICK: Do you think I like discharging you? I've always been a considerate employer, haven't I?

AUNE: That only makes it worse, Sir. The folks at home would never think of blaming *you;* they wouldn't say a word to me, of course—they wouldn't dare. But they'd look at me when my back was turned, and they'd think: he must have done something to deserve it. I couldn't bear that, you see. I may be a poor man, but I've always been master in my own house. My little home is a community too, in its way. I've been able to support it, and keep it going, because my wife believed in me, and my children believed in me. Now it'll fall apart.

BERNICK: In a case of necessity the lesser must give way to the greater; the individual must be sacrified for the good of the majority. I can give you no other answer: that's the way things are. You're a stubborn fellow, Aune! You're opposing me in this, not because you can't do otherwise, but because you refuse to furnish proof that machinery is superior to hand labor.

AUNE: And you're insisting on this, Sir, because you know the newspapers will take my dismissal as a proof of your good will.

BERNICK: What if that's so? I've told you what's involved: I can't have the papers attacking me just now. I'm engaged in an important venture that will be of incalculable benefit to the whole community, and I must have their support. What else can I possibly do under the circumstances? The crux of the matter is this: it's a choice between keeping your home going—as you express it—and sacrificing hundreds of new homes; hundreds of homes that can never exist, can never come into being, unless I succeed in my present enterprise. It's up to you to choose.

AUNE: If that's the way things are, I've nothing more to say, Sir.

BERNICK: Hm—my dear Aune, I'm sorry we have to part.

AUNE: We're *not* parting, Sir.

BERNICK: What do you mean?

AUNE: Even a common workman has to stand up for something in this world.

BERNICK: Quite true, quite true. So, you think you can promise me——?

AUNE: "The Indian Girl" will sail the day after tomorrow. (*He bows and goes out to the right.*)

BERNICK: Obstinate fellow! But I got the better of him. I'll put that down as a good omen——

(HILMAR TÖNNESEN, *with a cigar in his mouth, comes through the garden gate.*)

HILMAR (*On the veranda steps*): Good morning, Betty. Good morning, Bernick.

MRS. BERNICK: Good morning.

HILMAR: You've been crying, I see. You must have heard then.

MRS. BERNICK: Heard what?

HILMAR: That the scandal's in full swing! Ugh!

BERNICK: What does *that* mean?

HILMAR (*Comes into the room*): The two Americans are parading about the streets accompanied by Dina Dorf.

MRS. BERNICK: It's not possible, Hilmar——!

HILMAR: I'm afraid it is, unfortunately. Lona was tactless enough to call out to me; but, of course, I pretended not to hear.

BERNICK: People are bound to have noticed.

HILMAR: Yes, naturally. Everyone stopped and turned to stare at them. The news spread all over the town like wildfire—like one of those fires on the Western prairies. The windows were jammed with people waiting for the procession to go by; faces peered out from behind the curtains. Ugh! You must forgive me, Betty, for saying "ugh!" but all this makes me very nervous. If it goes on, I'll simply have to get away from here; go on a long trip, or something.

MRS. BERNICK: You ought to have talked to him; you ought to have explained—

HILMAR: Out in the open street? No, thank you—not I! How can this fellow dare to show himself here! But the papers'll soon put a muzzle on him, I expect.

BERNICK: The papers? Have you heard anything to that effect?

HILMAR: Yes—more or less. Yesterday evening, when I left here, I took a stroll over to the club—I wasn't feeling very well. There was a sudden silence when I came in, and I realized they'd been discussing the Americans. And then that editor fellow—Hammer, or whatever his name is—came up and congratulated me at the top of his voice on my rich cousin's return.

BERNICK: Rich—?

HILMAR: Yes, that's what he said. I gave him an icy stare, of course, and told him in no uncertain terms that if Johan Tönnesen was rich, I certainly was unaware of it. "That's funny," he said; "people generally make their fortune in America if they have some capital to start with. And we all know your cousin didn't go there empty-handed."

BERNICK: Please oblige me by not—

MRS. BERNICK (*Troubled*): There, you see, Karsten—

HILMAR: That blasted fellow! I had a sleepless night on his account. And he goes marching about the streets looking as though no one could possibly have anything against him! Why didn't he stay away for good? Some people are so tough, they refuse to be killed off; it's quite incredible!

MRS. BERNICK: Good heavens, Hilmar! What are you saying?

HILMAR: Nothing. But just think of it! He could have been killed by a railroad accident, eaten by wild bears in California, attacked by Blackfoot Indians—and he comes out of it unscathed; without even getting scalped! Ugh! Here they come!

BERNICK (*Looks down into the street*): Olaf's with them too!

HILMAR: Of course! They want to remind people they belong
to the first family in town. Look! All the loafers are stream-
ing out of the drugstore to stare at them and make remarks. This is really too much for my nerves! How can
anyone expect a man to keep the flag of the Ideal flying
under such circumstances—!

BERNICK: They're coming straight here. Now listen to me,
Betty. You're to treat them with all possible friendliness; I
particularly wish it.

MRS. BERNICK: May I really, Karsten?

BERNICK: Yes, of course. And you too, Hilmar. They probably won't be here for long—at least I hope not. And when
we're alone with them—I want no allusions to the past.
We mustn't hurt their feelings.

MRS. BERNICK: Karsten—how generous you are!

BERNICK: Never mind that.

MRS. BERNICK: But you must let me thank you. And forgive
me for being tiresome; you had every reason to—

BERNICK: That's enough, I say!

HILMAR: Ugh!

(JOHAN TÖNNESEN and DINA, *followed by* LONA HESSEL
and OLAF, *come up from the garden.*)

LONA: Good morning, dear friends!

JOHAN: We've been out visiting all the old haunts, Karsten.

BERNICK: So I hear. There've been a lot of changes, haven't
there?

LONA: There are proofs of your kindness and generosity everywhere. We went through the public gardens you presented
to the town—

BERNICK: Oh, did you go there?

LONA: "The gift of Karsten Bernick," as the inscription at
the entrance says. You're certainly the chief benefactor
around here.

JOHAN: And what splendid ships you have. I met the captain of "The Palm Tree"—an old school friend of mine—

LONA: You've built a new school, too. And they tell me you're
responsible for the gas and waterworks.

BERNICK: One has to contribute something to the community one lives in.

LONA: Your contribution has been a fine one, Brother-in-law; and it's a pleasure to see how you're appreciated. We talked to several people, and though I don't think I'm particularly vain, I couldn't resist reminding them that we belong to the family too.

HILMAR: Ugh!

LONA: That makes you say "ugh," does it?

HILMAR: No, I said "hm"—

LONA: You say what you like, poor creature. You seem to be all alone here today?

MRS. BERNICK: Yes; today we're quite alone.

LONA: We ran into a couple of those virtuous ladies up at the market place; but they seemed extremely busy. We haven't had a chance to really talk yet. Yesterday, what with the three railroad pioneers, and the Parson too—

HILMAR: The schoolmaster, you mean—

LONA: I call him the Parson. But what do you think of the result of *my* work, in these past fifteen years? Hasn't he grown into a stout fellow? You'd never think this was the black sheep that ran away from home?

HILMAR: Hm—!

JOHAN: Stop your boasting, Lona!

LONA: I don't care—I'm really proud of it. It's the only thing I've accomplished in the world, it's true; but it justifies my existence to some extent. When I think of how we started over there, Johan and I, with nothing but our four paws—

HILMAR: Hands.

LONA: I call them paws; they were grubby enough, God knows—

HILMAR: Ugh!

LONA: And empty too.

HILMAR: Empty! Well, I must say—!

LONA: What must you say?

BERNICK: Hm.

HILMAR: Ugh! (*He goes out by the garden door.*)

LONA: What's the matter with the man?

BERNICK: Never mind him; he's been very nervous lately. Wouldn't you like to look round the garden? You haven't seen it yet, and I happen to have an hour to spare.

LONA: Yes, I'd love to. I've so often joined you all in the garden, in my thoughts.

MRS. BERNICK: There have been great changes there too— you'll see. (BERNICK, MRS. BERNICK *and* LONA HESSEL *go down into the garden, where they are visible now and then during the following scene.*)

OLAF (*At the garden door*): Uncle Hilmar, do you know what Uncle Johan asked me? He asked me if I'd like to go to America with him.

HILMAR: You, you little duffer? You who are tied to your mother's apron strings—

OLAF: I shan't be much longer. You'll see, when I'm grown up—

HILMAR: Nonsense! You could never face the kind of discipline one needs to—(*They go down to the garden together.*)

JOHAN (*To* DINA, *who has taken off her hat and stands at the door to the right brushing the dust off her dress*): That walk made you warm, didn't it?

DINA: It was a lovely walk; the loveliest walk I've ever had.

JOHAN: Aren't you used to taking walks in the morning?

DINA: Yes; but only with Olaf.

JOHAN: I see. Which would you rather do—join them in the garden or stay here?

DINA: I'd much rather stay here.

JOHAN: So would I. Now, remember; we've agreed to take a walk together every morning.

DINA: No, Mr. Tönnesen, you can't do that.

JOHAN: Why not? You promised, didn't you?

DINA: Yes, but on second thoughts— You'd better not go out with me.

JOHAN: Why on earth shouldn't I?

DINA: You're a stranger here; you wouldn't understand. But, you see—

JOHAN: What?

DINA: I'd rather not talk about it.

JOHAN: Please do; you can talk to me about anything, you know.

DINA: Well—it's just that I'm different from the other girls; there's something—something about me. That's why you shouldn't be seen with me.

JOHAN: I don't understand a word of this. You've done nothing wrong, have you?

DINA: I haven't—no. I can't talk about it any more; you'll hear about it from the others soon enough.

JOHAN: Hm.

DINA: But there is something I'd like to ask you.

JOHAN: Yes? What?

DINA: Is it really so easy to amount to something in America?

JOHAN: It isn't always easy; it's sometimes tough going, and you have to be ready for hard work.

DINA: Oh, I wouldn't mind that—

JOHAN: You?

DINA: I'm not afraid of work; I'm strong and healthy, and Aunt Marta has taught me a lot.

JOHAN: Why the devil don't you come back with us, then?

DINA: You're just joking; you said that to Olaf, too. But there's something else I'd like to know; are people very— well—very virtuous over there?

JOHAN: Virtuous?

DINA: Yes; I mean—are they as proper and respectable as they are here?

JOHAN: They're not as bad as people over here think they are—that's certain. You needn't be afraid of that.

DINA: You don't understand. I was hoping they *weren't* so proper and respectable.

JOHAN: Really? What would you like them to be?

DINA: I'd like them to be natural.

JOHAN: You know—I believe that's exactly what they are.

DINA: Then that would be the place for me.

JOHAN: I'm sure it would! So, you see—you'd better come with us.

DINA: I couldn't go with you; I'd have to go alone. I'm certain I could manage; I'd get along all right—

BERNICK (*At the bottom of the veranda steps with the two ladies*): Stay where you are; I'll fetch it for you, Betty dear. You might catch cold. (*He comes in to the room and looks for his wife's shawl.*)

MRS. BERNICK (*From the garden*): You must come too, Johan. We're going down to the grotto.

BERNICK: No, let Johan stay here with me for a little while. Here, Dina; take my wife's shawl and go with them. I want to ask Johan some things about America.

MRS. BERNICK: Then join us later, will you? You know where to find us.

(MRS. BERNICK, LONA *and* DINA *go down through the garden and off left.*)

BERNICK (*Watches them for a moment, then shuts the second door on the left and goes up to* JOHAN, *takes both his hands and presses them warmly*): Now that we're alone, Johan, you must let me thank you.

JOHAN: Oh, nonsense!

BERNICK: I owe everything to you; my house and home, my domestic happiness, my position in the community—I owe it all to you.

JOHAN: I'm glad about it, Karsten; at least some good came out of that silly business.

BERNICK: Thank you, all the same! Not one in ten thousand would have done for me what you did then.

JOHAN: Don't even mention it! In those days we were both young and irresponsible. One of us had to take the blame.

BERNICK: Wasn't that up to the guilty one?

JOHAN: Not at all! It was up to the innocent one, under the circumstances. I was an orphan; I was free and independent; and I can't tell you what bliss it was to get away from that dreary office work! On the other hand, your old mother was still alive, and you'd just become secretly engaged to Betty who adored you. What would have become of her if she'd found out—?

BERNICK: All that's true, but—

JOHAN: And, after all, it was on account of Betty that you decided to break off that affair with Madame Dorf. That's why you were there that evening—

BERNICK: That fatal evening, yes! When that drunken brute came home—! It's true, Johan, it *was* for Betty's sake; but still—it was incredibly generous of you to turn appearances against yourself; and then, to go away—

JOHAN: Forget it, my dear Karsten. We agreed it was the only thing to do. You had to be saved—that was essential; and you were my friend. I was mighty proud of that friendship, I can tell you! There was I, plodding along at a routine job—a provincial stick-in-the-mud; and there were you, a distinguished gentleman, just back from your grand tour—London, Paris, and all the rest of it! And though I was four years younger than you were, you actually chose me as your friend! It was because you were courting Betty, I see that now; but, my goodness, how proud I was! And who wouldn't have been proud? Who wouldn't have been willing to sacrifice himself for your sake? Especially when it only involved a few weeks' gossip—and when it provided a glorious opportunity to get away—to escape and see the world!

BERNICK: To be frank with you, Johan, I'm afraid the incident is not forgotten yet.

JOHAN: What of it! As soon as I'm back over there, hard at work on my farm—!

BERNICK: You're going back then?

JOHAN: Of course.

BERNICK: Not too soon, I hope?

JOHAN: As soon as possible. I only came here to please Lona.

BERNICK: Indeed? How so?

JOHAN: Lona's not young any more, you know. These last few years she's begun to get a little homesick—though she'd

never admit it, of course. She wouldn't have dared go off
and leave me there alone; an irresponsible creature like me,
who got himself mixed up in a scandal while still in his
teens—!

BERNICK: Yes? Well?

JOHAN: I've got something to confess to you, Karsten; something I'm really ashamed of.

BERNICK: You haven't told her the whole story?

JOHAN: Yes, I have. It was wrong of me, I know, but I simply
couldn't help it. You can't imagine what Lona's been to me.
You never could stand her; but to me she's been a mother.
Those first years when we had such a tough time of it—
my God, how she worked! I was ill for quite a while, and
unable to earn anything; and though I tried to prevent her,
she actually started singing in cafés; then she gave lectures
that everybody laughed at; and then she wrote a book; she
laughs herself, and cries too, when she speaks of that now.
She did all this simply to keep my body and soul together.
I noticed last winter that she was pining for home; I
couldn't very well look on unmoved remembering all she'd
done for me. I said to her: go on home if you want to, Lona.
You needn't be afraid of leaving me here; I'm really not so
irresponsible. And then I told her everything.

BERNICK: How did she take it?

JOHAN: It seemed to her—and she was quite right—that
since I knew I was innocent there was no reason why I
shouldn't come home for a visit too. But don't be afraid;
Lona won't say anything. And in future I'll guard my
tongue more carefully.

BERNICK: Yes, I'm sure I can count on that.

JOHAN: Here's my hand on it. And now don't let's talk about
it any more. I should think it's the only scrape either of us
has ever been mixed up in. I mean to thoroughly enjoy the
few days I have left here. We had such a splendid walk
this morning. Who would ever have thought that little tot
who used to play "cherubs" in the theatre—! By the way—
what ever happened to her parents?

BERNICK: There's not much to tell you on that score; only what I wrote you just after you left. You got my two letters, I expect.

JOHAN: Yes, of course; I have them both. That drunken beast left her, didn't he?

BERNICK: And got killed in a drunken brawl.

JOHAN: And then she died soon afterwards? I suppose you did as much as you could for her; that is—without getting involved?

BERNICK: She was very proud; she never gave me away, but she would take nothing from me.

JOHAN: You did the right thing in taking care of Dina.

BERNICK: Yes; though actually it was Marta who was responsible for that.

JOHAN: Marta, was it? That reminds me—where *is* Marta today?

BERNICK: Oh, she's always busy; when she isn't working at the school, she goes round visiting the sick.

JOHAN: So it was really Marta who took charge of her.

BERNICK: Marta's always had a passion for educating people; that's why she took up this work at the City School. It was extremely foolish of her.

JOHAN: She looked worn out yesterday. I shouldn't think her health could stand it.

BERNICK: There's nothing the matter with her health. But it reflects on me; after all, I'm her brother—people might think I was unwilling to support her.

JOHAN: Support her? I thought she had money of her own—

BERNICK: Not a penny. After you left, Mother was in serious financial difficulties, if you remember. I was able to help her, and she managed for a time, but from my point of view the situation was far from satisfactory. I went into partnership with her in the firm—but that didn't work either; so I decided to take over the whole business and run it on my own. In examining the books we discovered that my mother's share was practically wiped out. Soon after that she died, and Marta was naturally left penniless.

JOHAN: Poor Marta!

BERNICK: Why poor? You don't suppose I let her want for anything? I think I may say I've been a good brother to her. She lives here with us, and naturally has all her meals here; her teacher's salary is ample for her clothes—what more does a single woman need?

JOHAN: Hm. We don't think that way in America.

BERNICK: I dare say not; in a revolutionary society of that sort—But here in our little town, which so far, thank heaven, has managed to avoid corrupt influences from without, women are content to play a modest, self-effacing role. As a matter of fact, it's entirely Marta's fault; if she'd wanted to she could have been provided for long ago.

JOHAN: You mean she could have married?

BERNICK: Yes, and married very well; she's had several excellent offers—strangely enough! A spinster without means, no longer young, and totally insignificant!

JOHAN: Insignificant?

BERNICK: Oh, I don't hold that against her. I wouldn't have her otherwise. It's a great convenience at times, in a big household like ours, to have a good steady person to rely on—someone who can take care of all sorts of tiresome little jobs.

JOHAN: But what about her *own* life?

BERNICK: What do you mean? She has many interests, I assure you. After all, she has me, and Betty, and Olaf, and —and *me*. It's bad for people to concentrate too much on themselves—especially women. Each of us has his own particular community, be it large or small, to support and work for. At any rate, that's what I do. (*Pointing to* KRAP, *who enters from the right*) I'll give you immediate proof of it! You think I devote my time to my own affairs? Far from it! (*Quickly, to* KRAP) Well?

KRAP (*Softly, showing him a sheaf of papers*): All the sales contracts are in order.

BERNICK: Splendid! Excellent! —Johan, I'm afraid you'll have to excuse me for a moment. (*In a low voice, shaking his*

hand) Thank you, thank you, Johan; and remember
—anything I can do for you—! Well—you understand.
—Come, Mr. Krap. (*They go into* BERNICK's *office.*)

JOHAN (*Looks after him for a while*): Hm— (*He turns to go
into the garden. At that moment* MARTA *enters from the
right with a little basket on her arm*) Well—Marta!

MISS BERNICK: Oh, it's you, Johan.

JOHAN: You've been out early too.

MISS BERNICK: Yes. The others'll be here soon, I expect—if
you want to wait a moment.

JOHAN: Why are you always in such a hurry?

MISS BERNICK: I?

JOHAN: You kept out of the way yesterday—I didn't have a
chance to say a word to you. And now today—

MISS BERNICK: Yes, but—

JOHAN: We're old playmates, remember. We used always to
be together—

MISS BERNICK: Oh, Johan—that's so many years ago.

JOHAN: It's exactly fifteen years ago; neither more nor less.
Do you think I've changed so very much?

MISS BERNICK: You? Yes; you've changed too, although—

JOHAN: What do you mean?

MISS BERNICK: Nothing.

JOHAN: You don't seem very pleased to see me!

MISS BERNICK: I've waited so long, Johan—*too* long.

JOHAN: Waited? For me to come?

MISS BERNICK: Yes.

JOHAN: What made you think I'd come?

MISS BERNICK: To atone for what you did.

JOHAN: I?

MISS BERNICK: Have you forgotten that a woman died in
shame and poverty because of you? Have you forgotten
that because of you the best years of a young girl's life
were filled with bitterness?

JOHAN: I can't bear to hear you say that! Hasn't your brother
ever—?

MISS BERNICK: Hasn't he what?

JOHAN: Hasn't he ever—? I mean, hasn't he ever said a word in my defense?

MISS BERNICK: You know how strict his principles are.

JOHAN: Hm—yes, of course; I know all about my old friend Karsten's principles. But this is really—! Well. I've just been talking to him. He's changed in many ways.

MISS BERNICK: How can you say that? Karsten's always been an admirable man.

JOHAN: That's not quite what I meant; but never mind— Hm; I realize now what light you've seen me in. You've been waiting for the prodigal's return.

MISS BERNICK: Listen, Johan; I'll tell you what light I've seen you in. (*Points down to the garden*) Look at that girl playing on the lawn with Olaf; that's Dina. Do you remember that confused letter you wrote me after you went away? You asked me to believe in you, and I have believed in you. When I heard people talk about all the wicked things you'd done, I kept telling myself that you had acted on the impulse of the moment—in the thoughtlessness of extreme youth—

JOHAN: What do you mean?

MISS BERNICK: You understand me well enough; don't let's talk about it any more. You naturally had to go away— begin afresh—start a new life. So your old playmate tried to take your place. The duties you forgot, or were unable to fulfill, I have fulfilled for you. I'm telling you this so that at least you need not reproach yourself on that score. I've been a mother to that poor unfortunate child; I've brought her up to the best of my ability—

JOHAN: And wasted your own life in doing it—

MISS BERNICK: It hasn't been a waste. But you were a long time coming, Johan.

JOHAN: Marta—if I could only tell you—! At all events let me thank you for your loyal friendship.

MISS BERNICK (*Smiles sadly*): Hm— Well, now we've talked things out, Johan. Sh! Someone's coming. Goodbye. I can't— No more now—

(*She goes out through the second door on the left.* LONA HESSEL *comes in from the garden, followed by* MRS. BERNICK.)

MRS. BERNICK (*Still in the garden*): Good gracious, Lona! What are you thinking of!

LONA: Let me alone. I'm going to talk to him, I tell you.

MRS. BERNICK: It would cause the most awful scandal! Oh, Johan; are you still here?

LONA: Out you go, my boy! I don't want you hanging about in stuffy rooms; go down into the garden and talk to Dina.

JOHAN: Just what I thought of doing.

MRS. BERNICK: But—

LONA: By the way, John; have you really taken a good look at her?

JOHAN: Yes, I think so.

LONA: Then look at her to some purpose, my boy. She's the very thing for *you!*

MRS. BERNICK: Really, Lona!

JOHAN: For me?

LONA: To look at, I mean. Go along now!

JOHAN: All right. I don't need much persuasion. (*He goes out into the garden.*)

MRS. BERNICK: Lona, you amaze me. You surely can't be serious?

LONA: Of course I am! She's young, and fresh, and healthy. She's just the wife for John. He needs someone like that with him over there; instead of an old stepsister.

MRS. BERNICK: Dina! Dina Dorf! But think of—!

LONA: All I care about is the boy's happiness; and I intend to help him get it. He's not much good at this kind of thing himself; he's never had much interest in women.

MRS. BERNICK: What? Johan hasn't—? It seems to me we've had proof enough, unfortunately—!

LONA: Oh, blast that stupid old story! Where's Bernick? I want to talk to him.

MRS. BERNICK: You simply mustn't do this, Lona!

LONA: I'm going to do it. If the boy likes her, and she likes

him, we'll make a match of it. Karsten's such a clever man;
we'll let him handle it—

MRS. BERNICK: Don't think these disgraceful American cus-
toms will be accepted here—

LONA: Rubbish, Betty—

MRS. BERNICK: You can't expect a man like Karsten, with his
strict moral principles—

LONA: Oh, come now! They're not as strict as all that, are
they?

MRS. BERNICK: You *dare* say that!

LONA: Yes; I dare to say that I don't think Karsten is much
more moral than other men.

MRS. BERNICK: You still hate him, don't you? Why did you
come here, since you've never been able to forget? I don't
see how you had the audacity to face him, after insulting
him the way you did.

LONA: I admit I behaved very badly, Betty.

MRS. BERNICK: Think how generously he forgave you! He's
never done you the slightest wrong. It wasn't *his* fault that
you fostered a lot of foolish hopes! And ever since—you've
hated *me* too. (*Bursts into tears*) You've always envied me
my happiness. And now you've come here to spoil it all—
to show the whole town the kind of family I've saddled
Karsten with. *I'm* the one who has to suffer for it—and
that's just what you want, I suppose. (*She goes out crying,
by the second door on the left.*)

LONA (*Looking after her*): Poor Betty!

(BERNICK *comes out of his office.*)

BERNICK (*Still in the doorway*): That's right, Mr. Krap; excellent. Send 400 crowns to the Benevolent Fund. (*Turns*)
Lona! (*Comes nearer*) Are you alone? Is Betty coming?

LONA: No. Shall I call her?

BERNICK: No, no; don't! I can't tell you how I've longed to
talk to you alone; to beg you to forgive me.

LONA: Don't let's be sentimental, Karsten; it doesn't suit us.

BERNICK: You *must* listen to me, Lona. I know you've heard
about Dina's mother, and that appearances are all against

me. But I swear it was only a passing infatuation. I did really love you once; deeply and sincerely.

LONA: Why do you think I've come home?

BERNICK: Whatever you may have in mind, I implore you to do nothing until I've cleared myself; for I can clear myself, Lona—or, at least, I can explain.

LONA: Now you're frightened. You say you loved me once. You told me so often enough in your letters. And perhaps it was true, in a way; at least as long as you were away from here—out in the great free world—where you found the strength and courage to think like a free man. The fact that I had more character, more will power, more independence of spirit than most of the people here at home appealed to you. And since we'd kept our love a secret, no one could make fun of your bad taste.

BERNICK: Lona, how can you think—?

LONA: But then, when you came back here, and saw how people ridiculed me, and laughed at what they called my eccentricities—

BERNICK: You *were* rather rash in those days.

LONA: Mostly because I enjoyed shocking the prudes—both male and female—that infested our little town. Then you met that fascinating young actress—

BERNICK: I was only showing off; that's all it was, I assure you. Believe me, only a fraction of the slander and gossip was really true—

LONA: That may be. But then Betty came home; she was young and pretty and adored by everyone. And then it became known that our aunt had left her all the money, and had left me nothing—

BERNICK: That's the crux of the whole matter, Lona. I want you to know the plain unvarnished truth. I didn't love Betty at that time; it wasn't fickleness that made me break with you—it was the money. I simply *had* to have it.

LONA: You say this to my face!

BERNICK: Yes, Lona. Listen to me—

LONA: And yet you wrote and told me you'd fallen madly in

love with Betty. You appealed to my generosity and
begged me, for Betty's sake, to say nothing about what had
been between us—

BERNICK: I *had* to, I tell you.

LONA: Then, by God, I don't regret behaving as I did!

BERNICK: Let me explain the situation to you coolly and
calmly: my mother was head of the firm, as you know; but
she was totally lacking in any business sense. Matters were
critical, and I was hurriedly called back from Paris to set
things right. I found myself faced with a business on the
verge of bankruptcy; this had to be kept secret, naturally.
Here was an old respected firm that had been in the family
for three generations, as good as ruined. What was I to do?
As the only son I felt it my duty to seek some way of saving it.

LONA: So you sacrificed a woman to the House of Bernick.

BERNICK: You know quite well that Betty loved me.

LONA: What about me?

BERNICK: Believe me, Lona—you would never have been
happy with me.

LONA: Was it out of consideration for my happiness that you
threw me over?

BERNICK: Do you think I acted as I did from selfish motives?
If I'd had only myself to think of I would gladly have
started over again—I had no lack of courage. But under
the pressure of responsibility a man becomes an integral
part of the business he inherits. The welfare of hundreds—
yes, thousands—of people depends on him. Do you realize
what a disaster it would have been to this whole community—this little town we both call home—if the House of
Bernick had gone bankrupt?

LONA: Is it also for the sake of the community, that for fifteen
years, you've been living a lie?

BERNICK: A lie?

LONA: What does Betty know about the circumstances of her
marriage? Of all that lies behind it?

BERNICK: Why should I wound her by telling her these things? What would be gained by it?

LONA: What would be gained? Well—you're a businessman; I suppose you know what's gainful and what isn't. But, look here, Karsten—now I'm going to talk coolly and calmly too: Tell me—are you really happy?

BERNICK: In my family life, you mean?

LONA: Of course.

BERNICK: Yes, Lona, I am; thanks to your self-sacrifice and friendship. I can honestly say I've grown happier each year. Betty has been a docile, loving wife. It's remarkable how she's learned to adapt her personality to mine—

LONA: Hm.

BERNICK: At first she had a lot of high-flown notions about love; she refused to see that time must inevitably transform it into the warmth and calm of friendship.

LONA: And now she's reconciled to that?

BERNICK: Completely. Her daily contact with me has naturally matured her. If one aspires to serve the community in which one lives, it's necessary to practice self-control and moderation. Betty has learned to realize this; and I'm happy to say our home is now a model to our fellow citizens.

LONA: But of course these fellow citizens know nothing about the lie?

BERNICK: The lie?

LONA: Yes; the lie you've been living for fifteen years.

BERNICK: You call that—?

LONA: A lie, yes; a threefold lie. First towards me; then towards Betty; then towards Johan.

BERNICK: Betty's never asked me to speak.

LONA: Of course not; she knows nothing.

BERNICK: And *you* won't ask me to? Out of consideration for her—you wouldn't?

LONA: No. I'm used to ridicule; I can take it—I have broad shoulders.

BERNICK: And Johan won't ask it either—he's promised that.

LONA: But what about you, Karsten? Is there nothing in you that longs to escape from all this lying?

BERNICK: Am I supposed to sacrifice my family of my own free will? Sacrifice my happiness, my position in society?

LONA: What right have you to that position?

BERNICK: I've earned some right to it, it seems to me, in fifteen years—through my way of life, through my work, through all that I've achieved.

LONA: It's true, you've worked hard, and achieved a great deal—both for yourself and others. You're the richest and most influential man in town. Everyone bows to your will— they daren't do otherwise. Your reputation is considered spotless; your home is considered a model home, your life a model life. But all this is founded on quicksand. A sudden move, a careless word, and you and all your splendor will collapse, unless you take steps to save yourself in time.

BERNICK: Lona, why did you come here?

LONA: I want to help you stand on solid ground again.

BERNICK: So that's it! You want revenge! I thought as much! But you won't succeed! There's only one man whose word would carry any weight, and he'll be silent.

LONA: Johan?

BERNICK: Yes, Johan. If anyone else accuses me I'll deny everything. If anyone tries to break me—I'll fight for my life—you'll see! You'll never succeed, I tell you! The one man who could destroy me will remain silent—and he'll soon be far away again.

(RUMMEL *and* VIGELAND *enter from the right.*)

RUMMEL: Good morning, my dear Bernick; you must come over to the Chamber of Commerce with us. There's a meeting on the railroad business.

BERNICK: I can't come now. It's quite impossible.

VIGELAND: You must come, Mr. Bernick—

RUMMEL: Yes, Bernick, you really must. A strong opposition has developed. That man Hammer, and several others who were in favor of the coast line, insist there are private interests behind our proposition.

BERNICK: You'll just have to explain to them—

VIGELAND: It's no use our explaining to them, Mr. Bernick.

RUMMEL: You've simply got to come yourself; no one would dare to question your integrity.

LONA: No indeed!

BERNICK: I can't go now, I tell you. I'm not feeling well—In any case—give me a few moments to collect myself.

(MR. RÖRLUND *enters from the right.*)

RÖRLUND: You must excuse me, Mr. Bernick; I'm very much upset—

BERNICK: What's the matter with you?

RÖRLUND: Let me ask you a question, Mr. Bernick. Is it with your knowledge and consent that a certain young girl who has found shelter under your roof shows herself in public with a man who—

LONA: What man, Parson?

RÖRLUND: With the one man in the world she should have least to do with.

LONA: Well, well!

RÖRLUND: Is it with your consent, Mr. Bernick?

BERNICK (*Looking for his hat and gloves*): I know nothing about it. Excuse me; I'm in a hurry; I'm due at the Chamber of Commerce.

HILMAR (*Comes in from the garden and goes over to the second door on the left*): Betty! Come here, will you?

MRS. BERNICK (*In the doorway*): Yes? What is it?

HILMAR: You'd better go into the garden and put a stop to the goings on down there. A certain person is flirting in an outrageous manner with that Dina Dorf. I couldn't bear to listen to it; it's quite upset my nerves!

LONA: Really? What did this "certain person" say?

HILMAR: Just that he wants her to go to America with him! Ugh!

RÖRLUND: It's not possible!

MRS. BERNICK: What's that you say?

LONA: I think that would be splendid.

BERNICK: You must have misunderstood him! It's impossible!

HILMAR: Here they come now. As him yourself; but kindly leave me out of it!

BERNICK (*To* RUMMEL *and* VIGELAND): Go on ahead. I'll join you in a moment—

(RUMMEL *and* VIGELAND *go out right.* JOHAN *and* DINA *come in from the garden.*)

JOHAN: Hurrah, Lona! She's coming with us!

MRS. BERNICK: Johan—you must be mad!

RÖRLUND: Is this true? What a dreadful scandal! What vile means did you use to—

JOHAN: Come, come man! Don't talk nonsense!

RÖRLUND: Dina, answer me? Is this really your intention? Did you decide this of your own free will?

DINA: I've got to get away from here!

RÖRLUND: But, with him—with *him!*

DINA: Do you know of anyone else with courage enough to take me?

RÖRLUND: That settles it; you'd better know who this man is.

JOHAN: Be quiet!

BERNICK: Not another word!

RÖRLUND: It is my duty to guard the moral well-being of this community; I should betray my trust by failing to point out to this young girl, in whose upbringing I've had a considerable part, and who is to me—

JOHAN: Be careful what you're doing!

RÖRLUND: She must be told! Dina, this is the man who was responsible for your mother's unhappiness and shame.

BERNICK: Mr. Rörlund—!

DINA: He! (*To* JOHAN) Is this true?

JOHAN: *You* answer her, Karsten.

BERNICK: Not another word! No more of this today!

DINA: It *is* true, then.

RÖRLUND: Of course it's true; and that's not all! This man in whom you were about to put your trust did not leave here empty-handed. There's the question of old Mrs. Bernick's money—Mr. Bernick can bear witness—

LONA: Liar!

BERNICK: Ah—!

MRS. BERNICK: Oh, God!

JOHAN (*Goes towards* RÖRLUND *with uplifted arm*): You dare to—!

LONA (*Holding him back*): Don't hit him, Johan.

RÖRLUND: You may attack me all you like, but the truth will out. And this *is* the truth—the whole town knows it; Mr. Bernick has vouched for it himself. So, Dina—now you know him for what he is.

(*A short silence.*)

JOHAN (*Softly, seizing* BERNICK'S *arm*): Karsten, what have you done!

MRS. BERNICK: Karsten, to think *I* should involve you in this shameful business!

SANDSTAD (*Enters hurriedly from the right, speaks with his hand still on the door handle*): You really must come immediately, Mr. Bernick. The whole railroad scheme is hanging by a thread.

BERNICK (*Absently*): What is it—? What am I to do—?

LONA (*Seriously and with emphasis*): Go along, Karsten. Go and rescue the community.

SANDSTAD: Yes, come at once. We need your moral support badly.

JOHAN (*Close to him*): Bernick, we two will have a talk tomorrow.

(*He goes out through the garden;* BERNICK *goes out to the right with* SANDSTAD, *like a man in a daze.*)

CURTAIN

ACT
THREE

SCENE: *The garden room in* BERNICK's *house.*
  BERNICK, *with a cane in his hand, enters in a towering rage
from the second door left, leaving it half open behind him.*

BERNICK: There! This time I think he'll realize I mean what I
  say. He's not likely to forget that thrashing. (*To someone
  in the other room*) What do you say? All *I* can say is
  you're an idiotic mother! Always making excuses for him;
  always condoning his bad behavior— Well, if you don't call
  that bad behavior, what *is* it, I'd like to know! Sneaking out
  of the house in the middle of the night; going to sea in a
  fishing smack; not coming home till late the next day, and
  causing me all this terrible anxiety! As if I didn't have
  enough worries without that. And now he threatens to run
  away—the little scoundrel! Just let him try it—! You? No,
  I dare say not. You don't seem to give a damn what becomes of him! Even if he were to get himself killed, I don't
  believe you'd—! Really! Well, I don't choose to lose my
  son; I need someone to carry on my work after me— Don't
  argue with me, Betty—just do as I say. He's not to leave
  his room, do you hear? (*Listens*) Sh! Don't let anyone notice anything.
  (KRAP *comes in by the door on the right.*)
KRAP: Can you spare me a moment, Mr. Bernick?
BERNICK (*Throwing down his cane*): Yes, certainly. Have you
  been to the shipyard?
KRAP: I've just come from there. Hm—
BERNICK: Well? There's nothing wrong with "The Palm
  Tree," I hope?

KRAP: "The Palm Tree" can sail tomorrow, but—

BERNICK: What about "The Indian Girl"? Don't tell me that pigheaded—

KRAP: "The Indian Girl" can sail tomorrow too; but—she won't get very far, I'm afraid.

BERNICK: What do you mean?

KRAP: Excuse me, Mr. Bernick; that door's ajar, and I believe there's someone in there—

BERNICK (*Shuts the door*): There we are. But why all the secrecy?

KRAP: It's just this: it looks as though Aune intends to send "The Indian Girl" to the bottom, crew and all.

BERNICK: Good heavens! You don't really think—?

KRAP: I don't see any other explanation, Mr. Bernick.

BERNICK: Just tell me briefly what—

KRAP: I will. You know how things have slowed up in the yard since we installed the new machinery, and brought in all those inexperienced workmen.

BERNICK: Yes, yes.

KRAP: Yet this morning when I went down there, I noticed that the repairs on the American ship had gone ahead at an extraordinary rate; the large gash in the hull—you know, where it had rotted right through—

BERNICK: What about it?

KRAP: It's completely repaired—to all appearances. Patched up; looks as good as new. I hear Aune worked on it himself all night—by lamplight.

BERNICK: Yes? Well?

KRAP: I thought I'd investigate a bit. The men were having breakfast, so I was able to look around, both outside and aboard, without anyone noticing. It wasn't easy scrambling about the hold with all that cargo; but I saw quite enough to convince me. There's some monkey business going on, Sir.

BERNICK: I can't believe it, Mr. Krap. I simply refuse to believe such a thing of Aune.

KRAP: I'm sorry, but I'm afraid it's true. There's some monkey

business, Mr. Bernick. As far as I could see not a scrap of
new lumber had been used. The hole had just been
plugged up; caulked and patched over with sheathing and
tarpaulin, and that sort of thing. It's all a sham! "The Indian Girl" 'll never reach New York. She'll go to the bottom
like a leaky bucket.

BERNICK: This is dreadful! What possible motive could he
have?

KRAP: Wants to discredit the new machines, I suppose; wants
to take revenge; wants the old hands taken on again.

BERNICK: And he's willing to sacrifice the lives of all these
men for that!

KRAP: Someone heard him say the other day that there *were*
no men aboard "The Indian Girl"—nothing but beasts.

BERNICK: That may be; but hasn't he given any thought to the
enormous loss of capital involved?

KRAP: Aune's not overfond of capital, Mr. Bernick.

BERNICK: True enough. He's a mischief maker; he's apt to stir
up trouble; but a dastardly trick like this—! I tell you
what, Mr. Krap: we must look into this matter further.
Meanwhile not a word to anyone. If this thing got about
it could do our yard a lot of harm.

KRAP: Of course, but—

BERNICK: You must manage to get down there again, during
the lunch hour. I must have absolute certainty.

KRAP: You shall have it, Mr. Bernick. But, excuse my asking—
what will you do then?

BERNICK: Report the case, of course. We can't be accessories
to a crime. I must keep my conscience clear. Besides, it'll
make a good impression on the Press, as well as the community at large, to see that I put all personal considerations
aside and let justice take its course.

KRAP: Very true, sir.

BERNICK: But first I must have absolute certainty. And, in the
meantime, silence!

KRAP: I won't say a word, Sir. And you shall have your certainty. (*He goes out through the garden and down the street.*)

BERNICK (*Half aloud*): Appalling! It's inconceivable! Impossible!

(*As he turns to go to his office,* HILMAR *comes in from the right.*)

HILMAR: Good morning, Bernick. You won a great victory at the Chamber of Commerce yesterday, I hear. Congratulations!

BERNICK: Thank you.

HILMAR: It was a splendid victory, they tell me. A victory of intelligent civic virtue over self-interest and prejudice—like a French military raid against a desert tribe. Amazing that you were able to pull it off, after that disagreeable scene here—

BERNICK: Never mind that.

HILMAR: But the main battle is still to come.

BERNICK: In the matter of the railroad, you mean?

HILMAR: Yes. I suppose you've heard what that editor fellow Hammer is cooking up?

BERNICK (*Anxiously*): No. What is it?

HILMAR: He's got hold of a rumor that's going round; he's writing an editorial on the subject.

BERNICK: What rumor?

HILMAR: About the buying-up of property along the branch line.

BERNICK: What are you talking about? Is there such a rumor?

HILMAR: It's all over town. I heard it at the club; I just happened to drop in. They say one of our local lawyers has been secretly commissioned to buy up all the forests, all the mineral deposits, all the water power—

BERNICK: Have they any idea who's behind all this?

HILMAR: They thought at the club some business concern from out of town must have got wind of your plans, and was trying to corner the property before prices begin to rise. Disgusting, isn't it? Ugh!

BERNICK: Disgusting?

HILMAR: Yes; that outsiders should poach on our preserves like that. And think of one of our own lawyers lending himself to such a scheme. Now all the profits will go to strangers.

BERNICK: But it's only a rumor, after all.

HILMAR: Everyone believes it. And tomorrow, or next day at the latest, Hammer will be ready to expose it as a fact. There was a great deal of indignation at the club. Several people said that if this rumor were true they'd withdraw from the whole enterprise.

BERNICK: Impossible!

HILMAR: You think so? Why do you think these petty mercenary souls were so anxious to support your scheme in the first place? Don't you suppose it was because they smelled a profit?

BERNICK: I tell you it's impossible! Our little town has too much civic pride—

HILMAR: Oh, come now! You're an optimist; you judge others by yourself. But I'm a pretty keen observer—and I tell you there's not one person here—with the exception of ourselves, of course—not *one*, I say, who keeps the flag of the Ideal flying. (*Goes up towards the back*) Ugh! There they are!

BERNICK: Who?

HILMAR: The two Americans. (*Looks out towards the right*) Who's that they're with? Good God, if it isn't the Captain of "The Indian Girl." Ugh!

BERNICK: What can they want with him?

HILMAR: It's fit company for them! They say he's been a slave trader, or a pirate; and heaven knows what those two have been up to all these years.

BERNICK: It's very wrong of you to think such things about them.

HILMAR: Yes—you're an optimist. I see they're about to descend on us again; I'll sneak out while I can! (*Goes towards the door on the left.*)

(LONA HESSEL *enters from the right.*)

LONA: Why, Hilmar! Am I driving you away?

HILMAR: Not all; I'm in a hurry; I've got to have a word with Betty. (*Goes out by the second door on the left.*)

BERNICK (*After a short pause*): Well, Lona?

LONA: Well?

BERNICK: What do you think of me today?

LONA: The same as yesterday. One lie more or less—

BERNICK: I must explain all this. Where's Johan?

LONA: He'll be here in a minute; he had to talk to someone— about something.

BERNICK: You must realize, from what you heard yesterday, that my position here would be completely ruined if the truth were to come out.

LONA: I realize that.

BERNICK: It's obvious, of course, that *I* was not guilty of the crime in question.

LONA: Yes, naturally. But then, who was the thief?

BERNICK: There was no thief. There was no money stolen. Not a penny was missing.

LONA: What do you mean?

BERNICK: No; not a cent, I tell you.

LONA: But what about the rumor? Why did people think that Johan—?

BERNICK: I believe I can talk to you quite frankly, Lona, as I can to no one else. I'll conceal nothing from you. I was largely responsible for that rumor.

LONA: You? How could you do this to Johan, after all he'd done for your sake—?

BERNICK: Before you judge me you must remember what the situation was at that particular time; I explained it to you yesterday. I came home to find my mother involved in a lot of foolish business enterprises; one calamity followed on another; we were hemmed in by difficulties of every sort; it looked as though the House of Bernick was on the verge of ruin. I was desperate—half out of my mind. I think it was mostly to forget my troubles that I got mixed up in the affair that led to Johan's going away.

LONA: Hm—

BERNICK: You can easily imagine the gossip that went on after you two had left. It was rumored that this was not the first time Johan had got into a scrape. Some said he paid Dorf a large sum of money to hold his tongue and go away. Others insisted it was to *her* he paid it. At the same time it became known that the House of Bernick was having trouble fulfilling its commitments. It was only natural that the scandal mongers should see a connection between these rumors. Madame Dorf stayed on here, and there was no doubt about her poverty, so they jumped to the conclusion that he'd taken the money with him to America. And as the rumor grew the sum became larger every day.

LONA: And you, Karsten—?

BERNICK: I saw salvation in that rumor, and I welcomed it.

LONA: And you helped to spread it?

BERNICK: I didn't contradict it. Our creditors had begun to threaten us; I had to quiet them. I couldn't allow them to suspect the business was in serious trouble; we had suffered a temporary setback, that was all. If they refrained from pressing us too hard—if they were willing to give us a little time—they would all be paid in full.

LONA: And were they?

BERNICK: Yes, Lona. That rumor saved our house; made me the man I am.

LONA: Then, what you are is founded on a lie.

BERNICK: Whom did it hurt at the time? It was Johan's intention never to come back here.

LONA: Whom did it hurt, you ask? Look into yourself. Haven't *you* been hurt by it? Tell me honestly!

BERNICK: Everyone has *something* to conceal. There's not a man alive who hasn't at least *one* black mark on his conscience.

LONA: And you call yourselves Pillars of Society!

BERNICK: Society has nothing better to uphold it.

LONA: Why should such a Society be upheld at all? What foundation has it? Lies and fraud—and nothing else! Here are you—the foremost man in town; happy and prosperous, powerful and respected. Yet you allowed an innocent man to be branded as a criminal!

BERNICK: Don't you think I feel, only too deeply, the wrong I've done him? Don't you suppose I'm ready to atone for it?

LONA: How? By speaking out?

BERNICK: You *can't* ask that!

LONA: How else *can* you atone for such a wrong?

BERNICK: I'm rich, Lona; Johan can demand of me anything he likes—

LONA: Yes, just you offer him money! I don't think you'd like his answer!

BERNICK: What are his plans? Do you know?

LONA: No. He hasn't said a word to me since yesterday. He's been like a boy up until now; but this whole business seems to have made a full-grown man of him.

BERNICK: I must have a talk with him.

LONA: Here he is.

(JOHAN TÖNNESEN *enters from the right.*)

BERNICK (*Going towards him*): Johan—!

JOHAN (*Waves him off*): Let me speak first! Yesterday morning I gave you my word—I promised to be silent.

BERNICK: You did.

JOHAN: But then I didn't know—

BERNICK: Just let me say two words—let me explain the circumstances—

JOHAN: There's no need. I understand the circumstances perfectly. Your business was going on the rocks; you could do what you liked with my name and reputation—— There was no one to protect it. Well, I don't blame you too much; in those days we were young and irresponsible. But now I need the truth, and now *you* must speak out.

BERNICK: And just at this moment I need all my authority, all the force of my integrity; it's impossible for me to speak out now!

JOHAN: I personally am not particularly troubled by all the lies you've told at my expense; but you must take the responsibility for the other thing. I want Dina for my wife; I intend to settle here in town with her and live here permanently.

LONA: Is that what you want to do?

BERNICK: Live here! With Dina as your wife?

JOHAN: Precisely. I intend to defy these liars and scandalmongers. But if I'm to win her, you must set me free.

BERNICK: If I admit the one thing, it will mean admitting all the rest as well—can't you see that? You may think I can prove by the books that there was no embezzlement; I can't do that. At that time our books were not kept very accurately. And even if I could, what would be gained by it? I'd stand revealed as a man who had made use of a lie to save himself; who had condoned that lie for fifteen years without making the slightest effort to expose it. You've forgotten what our Society is like, otherwise you'd know that this would utterly destroy me.

JOHAN: All I can say is, I intend to take Madame Dorf's daughter as my wife and live here in this town with her.

BERNICK: Please listen to me—both of you! I'm in very crucial circumstances just at this moment. If you strike this blow you will not only ruin me, but the future happiness and prosperity of this whole community as well; this little town where you were born and spent your childhood.

JOHAN: And if I don't strike now, I ruin my own future happiness.

LONA: Go on, Karsten.

BERNICK: Now, listen. It all concerns the railroad business, and that business is not as simple as you think. You've probably heard there was some question last year of running a line along the coast? That scheme had powerful advocates, here in town and in the surrounding districts, and especially in the Press. I managed to block it, however; I knew it would seriously damage shipping interests.

LONA: And you happen to be interested in shipping?

BERNICK: Yes. But no one would have dared suspect my motives in the matter; my good name and reputation protected me. As a matter of fact, I could quite well have borne the loss—but the town would have suffered greatly. Then they decided on the inland route. As soon as this was settled I made secret investigations to find out whether a branch line would be feasible.

LONA: Why "secret investigations," Karsten?

BERNICK: Have you heard rumors of the extensive buying-up of forests, mines and water power—?

JOHAN: They say it's some syndicate from out of town—

BERNICK: This vast property is at present in the hands of innumerable small landowners, and is practically worthless; they're willing to sell for next to nothing. If one had waited till word of the branch line had leaked out the prices would have gone sky-high.

LONA: Very likely. What about it?

BERNICK: Now we come to a matter which might be interpreted in several different ways; only a man looked up to by the whole community would have dared to embark on such a venture.

LONA: Well?

BERNICK: It is I who have bought up the property.

LONA: You?

JOHAN: On your own account?

BERNICK: On my own account. If the branch line goes through I'm a millionaire; if it doesn't I'm ruined.

LONA: A risky undertaking, Karsten.

BERNICK: I've staked my entire fortune on it.

LONA: I'm not thinking of your money; but when it becomes known that—

BERNICK: That's just the point. With the spotless reputation I now enjoy, I could carry through this whole transaction on my own, and say to my fellow citizens: I have risked this for the good of the community.

LONA: The community?

BERNICK: Yes; and not a soul would doubt my motives.

LONA: But there are other men here, it seems to me, who have acted more openly than you; with no thought of personal gain in mind; without regard for their own interests.

BERNICK: Who, for instance?

LONA: Rummel, Sandstad and Vigeland, of course.

BERNICK: In order to win their support I was obliged to let them in on the whole business.

LONA: And——?

BERNICK: They demanded a fifth of the gross profits.

LONA: Oh, these Pillars of Society!

BERNICK: Can't you see that it's Society itself that forces us into these devious ways? What would have happened if I hadn't acted secretly? Every Tom, Dick and Harry would have flung himself into the enterprise. It would have been frittered away, broken up into a hundred different factions; it would have been totally bungled and mismanaged. I'm the only man in town who can handle a transaction of this size. In this country it seems it's only we men of foreign stock who really understand big business. No! In this matter my conscience is quite clear. I know that I alone am capable of controlling this huge enterprise; of turning it into a permanent asset to the whole community and to the many thousands of workers whose well-being will depend on it.

LONA: I believe you, Karsten; I think you're right in that.

JOHAN: My life's happiness is at stake; the well-being of these "thousands" is no concern of mine.

BERNICK: The welfare of your native town is at stake too. If things should come out now that reflect on my past actions, my opponents will join forces and destroy me. A youthful indiscretion is never wiped out in our community. My whole career will be pitilessly examined; they'll rake up every little incident and weigh it in the light of these disclosures. I shall be crushed beneath the weight of all the rumors and slanders. I'll naturally have to withdraw from the railroad project, and, without me, the whole thing will fall apart. I shall lose my entire fortune and my position in Society as well.

LONA: After what you've just heard, Johan, you must keep silent and go away.

BERNICK: Yes, Johan, you must!

JOHAN: Very well; I'll go away for the present and keep silent. But I shall return, and then, I warn you I shall speak.

BERNICK: Stay over there for good, Johan. Only keep silent and I'll share everything with you.

JOHAN: Keep your money but give me back my good name and reputation.

BERNICK: And sacrifice my own!

JOHAN: You and your "community" must settle that between you. I am determined to have Dina for my wife. I sail tomorrow on "The Indian Girl"—

BERNICK: "The Indian Girl"?

JOHAN: Yes. The Captain has promised to take me along. I'm going over to sell my farm and settle my affairs. In two months I shall be back again.

BERNICK: And then you intend to speak?

JOHAN: Then the blame will be placed where it belongs.

BERNICK: But I'll also be blamed for a thing I never did; are you forgetting that?

JOHAN: Who has reaped the benefit of that shameful rumor, for the past fifteen years?

BERNICK: I warn you—I'm desperate! If you speak I shall deny everything. I'll say it's all a plot to ruin me; that you're blackmailing me out of revenge.

LONA: Shame on you, Karsten!

BERNICK: I'm desperate—I'm fighting for my life! I shall deny everything, I tell you; everything!

JOHAN: I have your two letters. I found them in my trunk among my other papers. I read them through this morning. They're clear enough.

BERNICK: And you'll produce them?

JOHAN: Yes; if I have to.

BERNICK: You'll be back here in two months?

JOHAN: I hope so. The wind is favorable. We should be in New York in three weeks—unless "The Indian Girl" goes down.

BERNICK (*With a start*): Goes down? Why should "The Indian Girl" go down?

JOHAN: Just what *I* think!

BERNICK (*Scarcely audible*): Goes down?

JOHAN: Well, Bernick, now you know what to expect; think it over in the meantime. Goodbye! Say goodbye to Betty for me, though I can't say she's treated me in a very sisterly fashion! But Marta I want to see myself. I must get her to tell Dina—she'll have to promise me— (*He goes out by the second door on the left.*)

BERNICK (*To himself*): "The Indian Girl"—? (*Rapidly*) You must prevent this, Lona!

LONA: I no longer have any power over him, Karsten—you can see that for yourself. (*She follows* JOHAN *into the room on the left.*)

BERNICK (*Perturbed*): Go down—?

(AUNE *enters from the right.*)

AUNE: I beg pardon, Mr. Bernick; may I speak to you a minute?

BERNICK (*Turning angrily*): What do you want?

AUNE: I'd like to ask you a question, Sir.

BERNICK: Very well; be quick then! What's it about?

AUNE I want to know if you're still determined—quite determined—to discharge me if "The Indian Girl" can't sail tomorrow?

BERNICK: Why do you ask? She *can* sail, can't she?

AUNE: Yes—she can. But suppose she couldn't—would you discharge me then?

BERNICK: What's the point of asking useless questions?

AUNE: I'd very much like to know, Sir. Please answer me. Would I be discharged?

BERNICK: I'm not in the habit of changing my mind, am I?

AUNE: Then tomorrow I should have been disgraced in my

own home, among those nearest to me; I should have lost my influence with the workmen; and I should have lost the power to do a bit of good among the poor and needy in this town.

BERNICK: Aune, we've discussed all that.

AUNE: Then "The Indian Girl" must sail.

(*A short pause.*)

BERNICK: Now, look here; I can't keep my eye on everything, and I can't be responsible for everything either—I suppose you're prepared to assure me that the repairs are entirely satisfactory?

AUNE: You didn't give me much time, Sir.

BERNICK: But the repairs *are* satisfactory, you say?

AUNE: It's summer, and the weather's good.

(*Another silence.*)

BERNICK: Have you anything else to say to me?

AUNE: I don't know of anything else, sir.

BERNICK: Then—"The Indian Girl" sails—

AUNE: Tomorrow?

BERNICK: Yes.

AUNE: Very well. (*He bows and goes out.*)

(BERNICK *stands for a moment irresolute; then he goes quickly towards the door as if to call* AUNE *back, but stops and hesitates with his hand on the doorknob. At that moment the door is opened from outside and* KRAP *enters.*)

KRAP: Aha, he was here, wasn't he? Has he confessed?

BERNICK: Hm—did you find anything?

KRAP: Is that really necessary, Mr. Bernick? You can see by his eyes what a bad conscience he has.

BERNICK: Nonsense—one can't *see* a thing like that. Did you find anything, I asked?

KRAP: It was too late; I couldn't get down there. They'd already started hauling the ship out of dock. But this very haste proves plainly enough—

BERNICK: It proves absolutely nothing. Has the inspection taken place?

KRAP: Of course, but—

BERNICK: There, you see? And they found nothing to complain of naturally?

KRAP: Mr. Bernick, you know how little these inspections mean; especially in a yard with as good a name as ours.

BERNICK: All the same, we're covered.

KRAP: Couldn't you tell by Aune's face, sir—?

BERNICK: I tell you Aune has completely reassured me.

KRAP: And I tell you I could swear that—

BERNICK: What's the meaning of all this, Mr. Krap? You obviously have a grudge against the man; if you want to attack him I advise you to choose some other opportunity. You know how vital it is to me—or rather, to the owners—that "The Indian Girl" should sail tomorrow.

KRAP: So be it then. But I doubt if we'll ever hear from her again—hm!

(VIGELAND *enters from the right.*)

VIGELAND: Good morning, Mr. Bernick. Have you a spare moment?

BERNICK: At your service, Mr. Vigeland.

VIGELAND: You agree with me, don't you, that "The Palm Tree" ought to sail tomorrow?

BERNICK: I thought that was definitely settled.

VIGELAND: The captain's just informed me that the storm signals are up.

KRAP: The barometer has fallen sharply since this morning.

BERNICK: Really? Is a storm expected?

VIGELAND: A stiff blow at all events; not a head wind though; quite the contrary—

BERNICK: Hm; what do you think yourself?

VIGELAND: I think—and I told this to the captain—that "The Palm Tree" is in the hands of Providence. Besides, she's only crossing the North Sea to begin with; and since freights are reasonably high just now in England—

BERNICK: It would mean a substantial loss if we delayed.

VIGELAND: The vessel's sound enough, and fully insured too. Now "The Indian Girl" is a much more risky business—

BERNICK: How do you mean?

VIGELAND: I understand she sails tomorrow too.

BERNICK: Yes; the owners gave us orders to rush matters, besides—

VIGELAND: Well, if that old tub can venture out—and with that crew into the bargain—it would be disgraceful if we couldn't—

BERNICK: Exactly. I suppose you have the sailing papers with you?

VIGELAND: Here they are.

BERNICK: Good; then if you'd be kind enough to go with Mr. Krap—

KRAP: This way, please. We'll soon have them in order.

VIGELAND: Thanks; and as to the outcome, Mr. Bernick, we'll leave that in the hands of the Almighty.

(*He follows* KRAP *into* BERNICK's *office.* MR. RÖRLUND *comes in from the garden.*)

RÖRLUND: Why, Mr. Bernick! Are you home at this hour of the day?

BERNICK (*Absent-mindedly*): As you see.

RÖRLUND: I stopped in to see your wife. I thought she might welcome a word of comfort.

BERNICK: I dare say she will. But I'd like to speak to you for a moment too.

RÖRLUND: With pleasure, Mr. Bernick. Is anything wrong? You look pale and upset.

BERNICK: Do I? That's not surprising. So many things seem to be crowding in on me. Besides my usual business—there's this matter of the railroad. Tell me something, Mr. Rörlund; let me ask you a question.

RÖRLUND: By all means, Mr. Bernick.

BERNICK: I've been turning something over in my mind. When one stands on the threshold of an important enterprise—one that would be of benefit to thousands—and it entails the sacrifice of one single individual—

RÖRLUND: How do you mean?

BERNICK: Take for example a man who is thinking of starting

a large factory. He knows only too well—for experience has taught him—that sooner or later, in the running of that factory, there will be a loss of human life.

RÖRLUND: That's all too probable.

BERNICK: Or supposing a man plans to operate a mine. He will naturally employ both fathers of families and young men in their prime. Isn't it a foregone conclusion that some of them will lose their lives in the undertaking?

RÖRLUND: Unfortunately, there's not much doubt of that.

BERNICK: Very well, then; such a man knows perfectly well beforehand that at one time or another his enterprise will lead to loss of life. But this enterprise is for the general good; each life lost will contribute to the welfare of many hundreds.

RÖRLUND: Ah—I understand. You're thinking of the railroad. Of the dangerous excavations, and the blasting, and all that kind of thing—

BERNICK: Yes—yes, of course; I'm thinking of the railroad. And, the railroad will inevitably lead to both factories and mines. But, don't you think that—?

RÖRLUND: My dear Mr. Bernick—I think you're overscrupulous. Believe me—place the whole matter in the hands of Providence—

BERNICK: Yes—the hands of Providence; of course—

RÖRLUND: Then your conscience will be clear. You can build your railroad with an easy mind.

BERNICK: Now let's take a specific case: Let's suppose a particularly dangerous piece of blasting is involved; but the building of the road depends upon it. Suppose the engineer knows, beyond the shadow of a doubt, that it will cost the life of the man who lights the fuse. Yet the job must be done, and it's the duty of the engineer to assign a man to do it.

RÖRLUND: Hm—

BERNICK: I know what you're about to say. It would be an act of heroism on the part of the engineer to light the fuse himself. But people don't do that kind of thing. So he must sacrifice one of his workmen.

RÖRLUND: You'd never get one of *our* engineers to do a thing like that.

BERNICK: No engineer in one of the big Nations would hesitate to do it.

RÖRLUND: The big Nations? No! I dare say not! But then they have no principles—no moral standards—!

BERNICK: They have their good points too.

RÖRLUND: You actually say that? When you, yourself, have—?

BERNICK: In big countries like that, a man, at least, has room for action; he's able to forge ahead and put his vision to some use. He has the courage to make sacrifices in a mighty cause. He's not tied down, as we are here, by petty considerations and narrow prejudice.

RÖRLUND: Is human life a petty consideration?

BERNICK: It is, when it interferes with the well-being of thousands.

RÖRLUND: These cases you've brought up are all quite inconceivable, dear Mr. Bernick. I don't understand you today. And you actually point to those big countries—! Human life is without value there; capital—money—is the all-important thing. But here, thank God, we look at things from quite a different standpoint. Take our good shipowners, for instance. There's not one of them who would dream of sacrificing a human life for gain! Compare them with those scoundrels in the big countries, who just for the sake of money, send out one unseaworthy ship after another—

BERNICK: I'm not talking about unseaworthy ships—!

RÖRLUND: No, but I am.

BERNICK: Why should you? It's quite beside the point—I'm sick of all these petty scruples! No doubt if one of our generals were to lead his men under fire and get some of them killed, he'd never sleep again of nights! Well, it's not like that in other places. You should hear what *he* has to say about it—(*Points to the door on the left.*)

RÖRLUND: He? Who? The American?

BERNICK: Of course. You should hear how people in America—

RÖRLUND: Is he in there? Why didn't you tell me? I must go in at once—

BERNICK: It won't do any good; you'll get nowhere with him.

RÖRLUND: We'll soon see. Ah, here he is.

(JOHAN TÖNNESEN *comes in from the room on the left.*)

JOHAN (*Calls back through the open doorway*): Very well, Dina. But, all the same, I'll never give you up. I'll come back—and then everything will be all right between us.

RÖRLUND: May I ask what you mean by that? What do you want here?

JOHAN: I want that girl to be my wife. The girl you turned against me yesterday.

RÖRLUND: Your—? You don't imagine that—?

JOHAN: She's going to be my wife.

RÖRLUND: In that case, you'd better know—(*Goes to the half-open door*) Mrs. Bernick, will you be kind enough to be a witness— You too, Miss Marta. And bring Dina with you. (*Sees* LONA) So—you're here too.

LONA (*In the doorway*): Shall I come in as well?

RÖRLUND: Yes, come in all of you; the more witnesses the better.

BERNICK: What are you going to do?

(LONA, MRS. BERNICK, MARTA, DINA *and* HILMAR *come out of the room on the left.*)

MRS. BERNICK: Mr. Rörlund, nothing I can say will stop him from—

RÖRLUND: I'll soon stop him, Mrs. Bernick. You're a thoughtless girl, Dina; but I don't blame you. You've been deprived too long of the kind of moral support you needed. I blame myself for not having given it to you sooner.

DINA: Don't speak about it now!

MRS. BERNICK: What is all this?

RÖRLUND: This is the time to speak about it, Dina; though your behavior yesterday and today has made it ten times harder for me. My only thought must be to save you. You remember that I gave you my word; and you must remember too what you promised to answer when I judged the time had come. Now I can hesitate no longer, and therefore— (*To* JOHAN) This young girl you've been pursuing with your attentions is engaged to me.

MRS. BERNICK: What's that you say!

BERNICK: Dina!

JOHAN: She! Engaged to—?

MISS BERNICK: No, no, Dina!

LONA: That's a lie!

JOHAN: Dina, is he telling the truth?

DINA (*After a short pause*): Yes.

RÖRLUND: I trust your powers of seduction have now been foiled. This decision, which I have made for Dina's sake, may now be announced to the entire community. I hope— indeed I'm positive—that it will not be misinterpreted. Now, Mrs. Bernick, I think we'd better take her away from here, restore her peace of mind, and give her an opportunity to regain her equilibrium.

MRS. BERNICK: Yes, come. Oh, Dina! What a lucky girl you are! (*She leads* DINA *out to the left;* MR. RÖRLUND *goes with them.*)

MISS BERNICK: Goodbye, Johan! (*She goes out.*)

HILMAR (*At the garden door*): Hm—well, I must say—!

LONA (*Who has followed* DINA *with her eyes*): Don't lose heart, my boy! I'll be here; I'll keep an eye on the Parson! (*She goes out to the right.*)

BERNICK: I suppose now you won't be sailing on "The Indian Girl."

JOHAN: Now more than ever.

BERNICK: But you surely won't be coming back?

JOHAN: I shall come back.

BERNICK: After this? Why should you want to come back now?

JOHAN: To revenge myself on all of you; and crush as many of you as I can.

(*He goes out to the right.* VIGELAND *and* KRAP *come in from* BERNICK'S *office.*)

VIGELAND: There, Mr. Bernick! The papers are all in order now.

BERNICK: Good—

KRAP (*In a low voice*): It's settled then: "The Indian Girl" is to sail tomorrow?

BERNICK: She's to sail.

(*He goes into his study.* VIGELAND *and* KRAP *go out to the right.* HILMAR TÖNNESEN *is about to follow them, when* OLAF *peeps cautiously out at the door on the left.*)

OLAF: Uncle! Uncle Hilmar!

HILMAR: Ugh, is that you? Why aren't you upstairs? You're supposed to stay in your room, you know.

OLAF (*Comes forward a step or two*): Sh! Uncle, have you heard the news?

HILMAR: I heard you got a good thrashing today.

OLAF (*With a threatening look towards his father's office*): He shan't hit me again. But do you know that Uncle Johan is sailing on the American ship tomorrow?

HILMAR: What's that to you? You'd better get upstairs again.

OLAF: Perhaps I'll go buffalo hunting after all, Uncle.

HILMAR: Rubbish! A little coward like you—

OLAF: Just you wait; you may get a surprise tomorrow!

HILMAR: Young idiot!

(*He goes out through the garden.* OLAF, *as he sees* KRAP *coming in from the right, runs back into the other room and shuts the door.*)

KRAP (*Goes up to* BERNICK'S *office and half opens the door*): Excuse my coming back, sir, but it's blowing up for a bad storm. (*He waits a moment; there is no answer.*) You're sure you still want "The Indian Girl" to sail?

BERNICK: "The Indian Girl" will sail in spite of it.

(KRAP *closes the study door and goes out to the right.*)

CURTAIN

ACT
FOUR

SCENE: *The garden room in* BERNICK'S *house. The work table has been removed. It is a stormy afternoon and already quite dark. The darkness increases during the following scene.*
   A manservant lights the chandelier; two maids bring in pots of flowers, lamps and candles which they place on tables and brackets along the walls. RUMMEL, *wearing a dress coat, white gloves and a white tie, stands in the room giving directions.*

RUMMEL (*To the servant*): Not all the candles, Jacob; just every other one. It mustn't look too festive; it's supposed to be a surprise, you know. What about all these flowers—? We might as well leave them; people will think they always have them there—
   (BERNICK *comes in from his office.*)
BERNICK (*In the doorway*): What's all this for?
RUMMEL: Oh dear, are you there? (*To the servants*) That'll do for now.
   (*The servants go out by the second door on the left.*)
BERNICK (*Comes into the room*): What's the meaning of all this, Rummel?
RUMMEL: It means that you're about to face the proudest moment of your life. The town has arranged a procession in honor of its leading citizen.
BERNICK: *What* do you say?
RUMMEL: A procession—with banners and a band too, if you please! There were to have been torches, but in this high wind we thought it might be dangerous. However, the

77

houses will be illuminated; that'll make a good impression
in the newspapers.

BERNICK: Listen, Rummel; I simply won't have this!

RUMMEL: It's too late now; they're due in half an hour.

BERNICK: Why on earth didn't you tell me?

RUMMEL: Because I was afraid you'd make objections. But I
took your wife into my confidence; she allowed me to make
a few arrangements, and she herself will see to the refreshments.

BERNICK (*Listening*): What's that? They surely can't be here
already! I heard singing.

RUMMEL (*At the garden door*): Singing? Oh, it's only the
Americans. "The Indian Girl" 's just getting under way.

BERNICK: Under way! Yes— No, I can't face it this evening,
Rummel; I'm not well.

RUMMEL: You don't look well; but you'll simply have to pull
yourself together. Come man! You've simply *got* to! Sandstad and Vigeland and I attach the greatest importance to
this affair. Our opponents must be crushed by an overwhelming expression of public confidence. There are rumors all over town; we must make a statement concerning
the purchase of those properties; we dare not hold back any
longer. This very evening—to the accompaniment of song
and speeches and the ring of glasses, when the festivities
have reached their height and everyone is in an expansive,
enthusiastic mood—you must announce the great risk you
have so generously taken for the good of the community.
When people are in a state of mellow enthusiasm it's amazing how easy it is to sway them. But the *mood* is essential.

BERNICK: Yes, yes—

RUMMEL: Particularly when dealing with a situation as tick-
lish and delicate as this. But with your good name I'm sure
there'll be no trouble; we'll pull it off! Now, listen; let me
explain the program: Hilmar Tönnesen has written verses
in your honor. They begin most beautifully with the words:
"Hoist the Ideal's flag on high." And we've commissioned

Mr. Rörlund to make the main speech of the evening. You'll have to reply to it, of course.

BERNICK: I can't do it this evening, Rummel. Couldn't you——?

RUMMEL: Much as I should like to, that's quite impossible. Naturally, for the most part, Rörlund's speech will be addressed to you; but he may possibly say a few words about the rest of us. I've talked to Sandstad and Vigeland about it. In your reply we thought you might propose a toast to the future prosperity of our community; then Sandstad would say a word about the harmonious co-operation between the different classes in our Society; Vigeland would express the hope that this new enterprise would in no way affect the moral well-being of our town; and I thought of saying, in a few well-chosen words, something about our women——whose activities, while on a more modest scale, are by no means insignificant. But you're not listening——

BERNICK: Yes, of course I am—— The wind's rising; do you think there's a very heavy sea?

RUMMEL: Ah, you're worried about "The Palm Tree." She's well insured, isn't she?

BERNICK: Yes, she's insured; but——

RUMMEL: And she's in good repair; that's the main thing.

BERNICK: Hm—— And even if anything should happen to the ship, it doesn't necessarily mean there'd be any loss of life. The ship and the cargo might be lost——people might lose their luggage and their papers——

RUMMEL: Good Lord! Papers and luggage don't matter much——

BERNICK: Not matter! No——I only meant——Sh! There's that singing again!

RUMMEL: That's aboard "The Palm Tree."

(VIGELAND *enters from the right.*)

VIGELAND: Well—"The Palm Tree" 's under way. Good evening, Mr. Bernick.

BERNICK: Tell me——as one who knows the sea——you still believe——?

VIGELAND: I believe in Providence, Mr. Bernick. Besides, I went aboard myself and distributed a few inspiring leaflets which will, I hope, have a most salutary effect.

(SANDSTAD *and* KRAP *come in from the right.*)

SANDSTAD (*Still in the doorway*): If they manage to pull *that* off, they can pull off anything. Well, well! Good evening!

BERNICK: Is anything the matter, Mr. Krap?

KRAP: I've nothing to say, sir.

SANDSTAD: The entire crew of "The Indian Girl" is drunk; if those fellows ever get over there alive, I'll be——!

(LONA *enters from the right.*)

LONA (*To* BERNICK): He asked me to say goodbye to you.

BERNICK: Is he on board already?

LONA: He will be soon, at any rate. We parted outside the hotel.

BERNICK: He's still determined?

LONA: Firm as a rock.

RUMMEL (*At one of the windows*): Blast these newfangled contraptions! I can't get these blinds down.

LONA: Do you want them down? I thought——

RUMMEL: Down at first, Miss Hessel. You know what's going on, of course?

LONA: Oh, yes indeed. Here, let me help you. (*Takes hold of the cord*) I'll draw the blinds down on my brother-in-law —though I'd rather raise them.

RUMMEL: You shall do that presently. When the garden is filled to overflowing with a joyous throng, we'll draw up the blinds, and disclose an amazed and delighted family. A worthy citizen need never fear glass houses!

BERNICK (*Seems about to say something, but turns abruptly and goes into his office.*)

RUMMEL: Now for a final conference. Come with us, Mr. Krap. There are a couple of facts we'd like you to corroborate.

(*All the men go into* BERNICK'S *office.* LONA *has pulled down the blinds on all the windows, and is about to close*

the ones on the glass door—which is open—when OLAF
*drops down onto the garden steps from above. He has a
traveling rug over his shoulder and a bundle in his hand.*)

LONA: Good heavens, child! You gave me such a fright!

OLAF (*Hiding the bundle*): Hush, Aunt Lona!

LONA: Why did you jump out of the window? Where are
you going?

OLAF: You won't tell, will you? I'm going to Uncle Johan—
only down to the pier, you know—just to say goodbye to
him. Good night, Aunt Lona! (*He runs out through the
garden.*)

LONA: Olaf! Wait a minute! Stop!

(JOHAN TÖNNESEN, *dressed for a journey, with a knapsack
on his back, comes cautiously through the door on the
right.*)

JOHAN: Lona!

LONA (*Turning*): What are you doing here?

JOHAN: I still have a few minutes. I must see her again. We
can't part like this.

(MISS BERNICK *and* DINA, *both wearing outdoor coats, and
the latter carrying a small traveling bag, come in from the
second door on the left.*)

DINA: I must go to him! I must!

MISS BERNICK: You shall go to him, Dina!

DINA: There he is!

JOHAN: Dina!

DINA: Take me with you!

JOHAN: What—!

LONA: You want to go?

DINA: Yes; take me with you! He's written to me; he says he
intends to announce it publicly this evening—

JOHAN: Dina—you don't love him?

DINA: I've never loved him. I'd rather throw myself into the
fjord than be engaged to him! I felt so humiliated yesterday! All that patronizing talk! As though he were raising
a fallen creature from the mud! I won't be looked down on
any more. I'll run away. May I come with you?

JOHAN: Yes, yes—a thousand times yes!

DINA: I shan't be a burden to you long. Just help me to get over there; help me to make a start—

JOHAN: Hurrah! Everything'll be all right now, Dina!

LONA (*Pointing to* BERNICK's *door*): Sh! Not so loud!

JOHAN: I'll take care of you, Dina, you'll see!

DINA: I won't let you do that. I'll be able to manage; I'm sure I'll be all right once I get away from here. Oh, all these women—you don't know what they're like! They sent me a letter today—exhorting me to appreciate my good fortune—pointing out the generosity of his behavior. Every single day from now on they'd be on the lookout; watching me to see whether I was worthy of it all. How I hate all this respectability!

JOHAN: Is that the only reason you're leaving, Dina? Do I mean nothing to you?

DINA: Oh, Johan; you mean more to me than anyone in the world.

JOHAN: Dina—!

DINA: They all tell me I should hate and despise you; that it's my duty; but I don't understand all this business about duty—I never could.

LONA: And you shan't either, my child!

MISS BERNICK: No, you shan't; that's why you're going to go with him as his wife.

JOHAN: Yes, yes!

LONA: I really must kiss you for that, Marta! I didn't expect *that* of *you*.

MISS BERNICK: I can well believe it; I didn't expect it of myself. But sooner or later something in me had to boil over! Oh, this tyranny of custom and convention! Rebel against it, Dina! Marry him! Show them it's possible to defy all their stupid rules and regulations!

JOHAN: What's your answer, Dina?

DINA: Yes; I will be your wife.

JOHAN: Dina!

DINA: But first I must work; make something of myself; be-

come a real person, just as you are. I don't want to be just
a thing you take along with you.

LONA: Quite right! That's as it should be!

JOHAN: Good. Then I shall wait and hope—

LONA: —and you'll win too, my boy! But now, on board!

JOHAN: Yes, on board! Lona—my *dear* sister—just one word
more; come here—(*He leads her towards the back and
talks to her rapidly.*)

MISS BERNICK: Dina, you lucky girl—let me look at you and
give you one last kiss; the very last.

DINA: Not the last! Dear, darling auntie! We'll meet again.

MISS BERNICK: Never, I'm afraid! Promise me never to come
back here, Dina. (*Seizes her hands and gazes at her*)
Now go to your happiness, my dearest child—over the sea.
How often have I sat in the schoolroom and longed to be
over there! It must be lovely there; the horizon must be
wider; the sky higher; the air freer overhead—

DINA: Aunt Marta, some day you'll join us.

MISS BERNICK: No, never. I have my work here, humble as it
is. And I believe, from now on, I'll have the courage to be
myself at last.

DINA: I don't know how I can part with you.

MISS BERNICK: One can part with a great deal, Dina. (*Kisses
her*) But you'll never have to go through that, my precious
child. Promise me you'll make him happy.

DINA: I won't promise anything. I hate promising things;
what must be shall be.

MISS BERNICK: Yes, you're right; just stay as you are—honest
and true to yourself.

DINA: I will, Auntie.

LONA (*Putting in her pocket some papers that* JOHAN *has
given her*): Good, good my dear boy. And now—be off
with you!

JOHAN: Yes, we've no time to lose. Goodbye, Lona. Thank
you for your loving care. Goodbye, Marta, and thanks to
you for your loyal friendship.

MISS BERNICK: Goodbye, Johan! Goodbye, Dina! And all
  happiness to you!
  (*She and* LONA *hurry them towards the veranda door.*
  JOHAN *and* DINA *go quickly out through the garden.* LONA
  closes the door and pulls down the blind.)

LONA: Now we're alone, Marta. You've lost her and I've lost
  him.

MISS BERNICK: You—him?

LONA: I'd already half lost him over there. I knew the boy
  was longing to be on his own; that's why I pretended to be
  homesick.

MISS BERNICK: Was that it? Now I understand why you returned. But he'll want you back, Lona.

LONA: An old stepsister—what would he want with her now?
  —Men don't mind what ties they break, when they see
  happiness ahead.

MISS BERNICK: Yes. That's sometimes true.

LONA: But we'll stick together, Marta.

MISS BERNICK: Can I mean anything to you?

LONA: Of course. Haven't we two foster mothers both lost
  our children? Now we are alone.

MISS BERNICK: Yes, we're alone. So, now—I want you to
  know this: I loved him more than anything in all the world.

LONA: Marta! (*Seizes her arm*) Is this true?

MISS BERNICK: My whole life is in those words. I loved him
  and waited for him. Each summer I expected him to come.
  And then he came—but he didn't see me.

LONA: You loved him! And yet you yourself gave him his
  happiness.

MISS BERNICK: Since I loved him, what else could I do? Yes,
  I've loved him. My whole life has been lived for him, ever
  since he went away. I suppose you wonder what grounds
  I had for hope? I had some grounds, I think. But when he
  came back—it was as though it had all been wiped out of
  his memory. He didn't see me.

LONA: Dina overshadowed you.

MISS BERNICK: It's good that she did. We were the same age

when he went away; but when I saw him again—oh, that awful moment—I realized I was ten years older then he. He'd been living out in the bright clear sunshine, breathing in youth and health with every breath; and I sat here in the shade, spinning and spinning—

LONA: —the thread of his happiness, Marta.

MISS BERNICK: Yes, a golden thread— No bitterness! We've been two good sisters to him, Lona, haven't we?

LONA (*Throws her arms round her*): Marta!

(BERNICK *comes out of his office.*)

BERNICK (*To the men inside*): Yes, yes; arrange things any way you like. When the time comes, I'll manage to— (*Shuts the door*) Oh, you're here, are you? You'd better change your dress, Marta. And tell Betty to do the same. Nothing elaborate, of course; a simple afternoon dress will do. But be quick about it.

LONA: And be sure and look cheerful, Marta. This is a joyful occasion, remember.

BERNICK: Olaf must come down too; I want him beside me.

LONA: Hm, Olaf—

MISS BERNICK: I'll go and tell Betty. (*She goes out by the second door on the left.*)

LONA: So the great and solemn hour has come.

BERNICK (*Paces restlessly up and down*): Yes, it has.

LONA: You must be feeling very proud and happy.

BERNICK (*Looks at her*): Hm!

LONA: The whole town is to be illuminated, I hear.

BERNICK: I believe that's the plan.

LONA: The various clubs and guilds will march here in procession with their banners; your name will blaze out in shining letters. The news will be telegraphed all over the country: "Surrounded by his happy family Karsten Bernick was hailed by his fellow citizens as a Pillar of Society".

BERNICK: That's how it will be. And everyone will shout "hurrah!" and I shall be forced to go out and face the crowd, and bow and thank them.

LONA: *Forced* to—?

BERNICK: Do you think I feel happy at this moment?

LONA: I shouldn't think you'd feel entirely happy, no.

BERNICK: You despise me, don't you, Lona?

LONA: No; not yet.

BERNICK: And you have no right to—no right to *despise* me! You have no idea how utterly alone I feel in this stunted, cramped community. I've gradually had to give up all thought of the great projects I once dreamed of; I've had to curb my ambition for a really full and satisfying life. When all is said and done what have I accomplished? Insignificant trifles—nothing else! Anything different, anything on a larger scale, would never be tolerated here. I should lose all my authority if I were to venture even one step beyond the current views and prejudices—narrow and restricting as they may be. Do you know what we really are, we so-called Pillars-of-Society? We're the *tools* of Society, nothing more!

LONA: Why has this never occurred to you before?

BERNICK: I've been thinking a lot lately—ever since you came home—and particularly this evening. Oh, Lona, if only I'd really known you then—in the old days.

LONA: What if you had?

BERNICK: I should never have given you up; if I'd had you, things would have been different.

LONA: What about her—the one you chose instead of me? Don't you think *she* might have meant something to you too?

BERNICK: I only know she's never been able to give me what I needed.

LONA: Because you never really shared your life with her. There's never been anything free or honest in your relationship. You've allowed her to suffer shame and humiliation by deliberately heaping disgrace on those belonging to her.

BERNICK: Yes; lies and false pretenses are at the bottom of it all.

LONA: Then why not get rid of them?

BERNICK: Now? It's too late, Lona.

LONA: Tell me, Karsten; what satisfaction do you gain from receiving all this honor and glory under false pretenses?

BERNICK: None— This social system of ours is rotten through and through; it's bound to vanish, and I shall vanish with it. But a new generation is growing up and will take over. I'm working for my son; I want to prepare the way for *him*. There'll come a time when human society will be based on truth; he'll have a happier life than his father ever had.

LONA: But it will still be founded on a lie. Think of the heritage you're leaving him.

BERNICK (*Controlling his despair*): The heritage I'm leaving him is a thousand times worse than you imagine. Surely, some day, this curse must pass away! And yet—and yet— (*Vehemently*) How could you bring all this down on my head! But it's done now. I must go on in spite of it. You won't succeed in crushing me!

(HILMAR TÖNNESEN, *with an open letter in his hand, comes in quickly from the right; he is obviously upset.*)

HILMAR: But this is quite—Betty, Betty!

BERNICK: What is it? Are they coming?

HILMAR: No, no; but I must speak to someone at once— (*He goes out by the second door on the left.*)

LONA: Karsten, you keep saying we came here to crush you. Now let me show you what stuff he's made of—this prodigal son that your smug little community shuns as though he had the plague. He doesn't need any of you; he's gone away.

BERNICK: But he'll come back—

LONA: Johan is never coming back. He's gone for good, and Dina has gone with him.

BERNICK: Not coming back? And Dina's with him?

LONA: She's going to marry him. They've given your precious Society a good slap in the face, as I did once— Ah, well!

BERNICK: Sailed. Both of them. On "The Indian Girl"—

LONA: No; he didn't dare trust such a precious cargo to those ruffians. He and Dina sailed on "The Palm Tree."

BERNICK: Ah! —Then it was all for nothing— (*Rushes to the door of his office, tears it open and calls in*) Krap, stop "The Indian Girl"! She mustn't sail tonight!

KRAP (*Inside the office*): "The Indian Girl"'s already standing out to sea, Mr. Bernick.

BERNICK (*Shuts the door and says dully*): Too late—and all for nothing—

LONA: What do you mean?

BERNICK: Nothing. Leave me alone—!

LONA: Hm. Listen, Karsten; Johan told me to tell you that he's leaving the name and reputation he once lent you in my charge, as well as the one you robbed him of while he was away. He won't say anything himself; and I can act in the matter or not—as I see fit. Look—here are your two letters; he left them with me.

BERNICK: You have them! And I suppose you'll—perhaps this very evening—just when the procession—

LONA: I didn't come back here to expose you; I hoped I'd be able to rouse you into speaking of your own accord. I've failed. So go on living your life of lies. Look: I'm tearing up your letters. Take the pieces; here they are. Now there's no proof against you, Karsten. Now you're safe; be happy too—that is, if you can.

BERNICK (*Profoundly moved*): Lona, why didn't you do this before! Now it's too late. Life is ruined for me now; I can't bear to go on living.

LONA: What's happened?

BERNICK: Don't ask about it— But I'll go on living all the same; I've *got* to, for Olaf's sake. He'll atone for everything— He'll put everything right—

LONA: Karsten—!

(HILMAR TÖNNESEN *enters again hurriedly.*)

HILMAR: Can't find anyone; all out; not even Betty!

BERNICK: What's the matter with you?

HILMAR: I daren't tell you.

BERNICK: What is it? Tell me! I insist!

HILMAR: Well, then—Olaf has run away; he's on "The Indian Girl."

BERNICK (*Staggering back*): On "The Indian Girl"! Olaf! No, no!

LONA: Why, of course; now I understand—I saw him jump out of the window.

BERNICK (*At the door of his office, calls out in desperation*): Krap, stop "The Indian Girl" at any price!

KRAP (*Comes into the room*): That's impossible, Mr. Bernick. We'd never be able to—

BERNICK: We've *got* to stop her! Olaf is on board!

KRAP: What!

RUMMEL (*Comes out of the office*): Olaf run away? Impossible!

SANDSTAD (*Enters from the office*): They'll send him back with the pilot, Mr. Bernick.

HILMAR: No, no; he left this note for me. (*Showing the letter*) He says he's going to hide in the hold till they're well out to sea.

BERNICK: I'll never see him again!

RUMMEL: Nonsense! A good stout ship, newly repaired—

VIGELAND (*Who has also come in*):—and in your own yard, too.

BERNICK: I'll never see him again, I tell you. I've lost him, Lona, and—I see it now—he never really belonged to me. (*Listens*) What's that?

RUMMEL: It's the band. The procession's coming.

BERNICK: I can't—I won't see anyone!

RUMMEL: What are you thinking of? That would never do!

SANDSTAD: You must see them, Mr. Bernick! Think of what you have at stake.

BERNICK: What does all that matter now! Whom have I to work for?

RUMMEL: How can you ask such a question! You have us and the community.

VIGELAND: Yes, that's right!

SANDSTAD: And you're surely not forgetting that we too—
(MISS BERNICK *enters by the second door on the left. The
band is heard playing in the distance, far down the street.*)

MISS BERNICK: Here comes the procession; but I can't find
Betty—she's not at home; I can't think where she—

BERNICK: Not at home! You see, Lona; I get no help from
her—either in joy or sorrow.

RUMMEL: Up with the blinds! Come and help me, Mr.
Krap; and you too, Mr. Sandstad. It's a dreadful pity the
family should be so scattered—just at the crucial moment!
It disrupts the entire program!
(*The blinds are pulled up from the windows and the door.
The whole street has been illuminated. On the house op-
posite is a large transparency with the words: "Long live
Karsten Bernick, the Pillar of our Society.*")

BERNICK (*Shrinking back*): Take it away! I don't want to
see it! Put it out! Put it out!

RUMMEL: With all due respect, are you out of your mind?

MISS BERNICK: What's the matter with him, Lona?

LONA: Hush! (*Speaks to her in a whisper.*)

BERNICK: Take that inscription away, I tell you! It's a mock-
ery! Put out those lights! It's all a farce, I say!

RUMMEL: Well, *really*—!

BERNICK: What do you know about it! But I, I—! They're
like funeral torches!

KRAP: Hm—

RUMMEL: Come, now! You're taking it much too hard.

SANDSTAD: The boy will have a trip across the Atlantic; you'll
soon have him back again.

VIGELAND: Put your trust in the Almighty, Mr. Bernick.

RUMMEL: And in the ship too, Bernick; she's not going to
sink, you know!

KRAP: Hm—

RUMMEL: Now, if she were one of those floating coffins, they
put to sea in the big countries—

BERNICK: My hair's turning white—I feel it—

(MRS BERNICK, *with a large shawl over her head, comes in through the garden door.*)

MRS. BERNICK: Karsten, Karsten, do you know——?

BERNICK: Yes, I know—but what about you? You, who see nothing. Who can't even guard him as a mother should—!

MRS. BERNICK: Listen to me—!

BERNICK: Why couldn't you keep watch over him! Now I've lost him. Now give him back to me, if you can!

MRS. BERNICK: I can, Karsten, I can! I have him!

BERNICK: You have him!

THE MEN: Ah!

HILMAR: I was sure of it.

MISS BERNICK: You see, Karsten—you have him back!

LONA: Now you'd better try to win him, too.

BERNICK: You have him! Are you telling me the truth? Where is he?

MRS. BERNICK: I won't tell you till you've forgiven him.

BERNICK: Good God! Forgiven——! But how did you find out——?

MRS. BERNICK: Do you think a mother has no eyes? I was desperately afraid you might hear about it. A couple of words he let slip yesterday—; and then his room was empty, and his knapsack and clothes were missing—

BERNICK: Yes, yes——?

MRS. BERNICK: I ran as fast as I could and got hold of Aune; we went out in his boat; the American ship was just about to sail. Thank God we arrived in time. We got on board—we searched the hold—and found him. Oh, Karsten, you mustn't punish him!

BERNICK: Betty!

MRS. BERNICK: Nor Aune either!

BERNICK: Aune? What do you mean? Is "The Indian Girl" under sail again?

MRS. BERNICK: No, that's just it—

BERNICK: Go on! Go on—!

MRS. BERNICK: Aune was just as upset as I was; it took us

some time to find the boy, and night was coming on; the
pilot started to make a fuss, so Aune took it upon himself
—in your name, you see—

BERNICK: Well?

MRS. BERNICK: To hold the ship back till tomorrow.

KRAP: Hm—

BERNICK: What a blessing, Betty!

MRS. BERNICK: You're not angry?

BERNICK: What an incredible, unbelievable blessing!

RUMMEL: You're really far too scrupulous, you know.

HILMAR: As soon as there's the slightest prospect of a battle
with the elements, then—ugh!

KRAP (*At the window*): Mr. Bernick, the procession is just
coming through the garden gate—

BERNICK: Let them come!

RUMMEL: The garden's full of people.

STANDSTAD: The street is jammed!

RUMMEL: The whole town's on the march, Bernick. This is
really an inspiring moment.

VIGELAND: Let us accept it in a spirit of humility, Mr. Rummel.

RUMMEL: Look at all those banners! What a procession!
There's our committee, headed by Mr. Rörlund.

BERNICK: Now, let them come, I say!

RUMMEL: But look here—in your present state of mind—

BERNICK: Yes? What about it?

RUMMEL: I'd be quite willing to speak on your behalf.

BERNICK: Thank you—no. Tonight I speak for myself!

RUMMEL: But you know what you have to say?

BERNICK: Don't worry, Rummel! Indeed I do know what I
have to say.

(*The band has stopped playing. The garden door is
thrown open and the committee, headed by* MR. RÖRLUND,
*enters, accompanied by two porters carrying a covered
basket. After them come townspeople of all classes—as
many as the room will hold. An immense crowd, with flags*

and banners, can be seen in the garden and along the street.)

RÖRLUND: My dear Mr. Bernick! I see by the amazement depicted on your countenance, that we are intruding, as unexpected guests, on a happy family circle; we surprise you at your peaceful hearth, surrounded by distinguished friends and public-spirited fellow citizens. But we obey an irresistible impulse in bringing you our heartfelt homage. We have often shown you our appreciation and respect, but never on such a comprehensive scale. We have frequently, in the past, expressed our thanks to you for the solid moral basis on which you have, so to speak, built up our community. Our chief purpose on this occasion is to hail you as a man of vision; a tireless, unselfish—I might even say self-sacrificing—citizen, who has dared to take the initiative in an enterprise which, in the opinion of all right-thinking men, must give a mighty impetus to the prosperity and well-being of our town.

VOICES AMONG THE CROWD: Bravo, bravo!

RÖRLUND: You have, sir, been for many years a shining example in our Society. I do not refer now to your exemplary domestic life; nor to the untarnished virtue of your conduct. Such things are better reserved for private tribute; one does not proclaim them from the housetops! No—I refer to the services you have rendered as a public figure; services apparent to the eyes of all. Well-appointed ships sail from your wharves, bearing our flag far and wide on all the oceans of the world. Hundreds of prosperous and contented workmen look up to you as to a father. By the creation of new industries you have brought happiness and comfort into countless homes. In other words, you are—in a very special sense—the true cornerstone of our community.

VOICES: Hear, hear! Bravo!

RÖRLUND: In these troubled times, the aura of unselfishness that surrounds your every action is particularly beneficent.

You are striving to procure for us—and I do not hesitate to call it by its prosaic, unromantic, name—a railroad.

MANY VOICES: Bravo, bravo!

RÖRLUND: And this undertaking is fraught with many difficulties, largely due to the narrow self-interest of unscrupulous men.

VOICES: Hear, hear!

RÖRLUND: It has become known that certain individuals, strangers to our community, have stolen a march on our hard-working citizens, securing for their own benefit advantages which should by rights have belonged to our own township.

VOICES: Yes, yes! Hear, hear!

RÖRLUND: And so, we salute in you tonight the ideal citizen —a man loyal both to town and state. May your undertaking be an enduring source of prosperity to our community. The railroad may—and we must face this possibility —be a means of bringing into our midst undesirable elements from without; but it will also provide a means of rapidly disposing of them. Even under present circumstances undesirable elements find a way of creeping in. I'm told we may congratulate ourselves on this most festive evening, on having been relieved—sooner and more rapidly than we had dared to hope—of certain elements of this description—

VOICES: Hush! Hush!

RÖRLUND: I regard this as a good omen for the enterprise. If I venture to bring up this matter *here*, it is because we know ourselves to be in a house where ethical considerations outweigh all thought of family ties.

VOICES: Hear! Hear! Bravo!

BERNICK (*Simultaneously*): Permit me—

RÖRLUND: Only a few words more, Mr. Bernick. We know that the great services you have rendered this community carried with them no thought of personal reward. But we hope you will not refuse a slight token of the appreciation and gratitude of your fellow citizens; especially at a time when—so men of practical experience assure us—we stand on the threshold of a new era.

MANY VOICES: Bravo! Hear, Hear!

(*He gives the porters a sign; they bring forward the basket; members of the committee take out and present, during the following speech, the articles referred to.*)

RÖRLUND: Therefore, it is my pleasure, Mr. Bernick, to present you with this silver coffee service. May it grace your board when, in the future as so often in the past, we have the good fortune to be received under this hospitable roof. And you too, gentlemen, who have so zealously supported the first citizen of our town, we beg you to accept a trifling souvenir. This silver goblet is for you, Mr. Rummel. Many a time, to the ring of wine glasses, your eloquent words have furthered the civic interests of our community; may you find many worthy occasions to raise and drain this cup— To you, Mr. Sandstad, I present this album, in which you will find photographs of many of your fellow citizens. Your well-known and highly appreciated philanthropy has placed you in the happy position of counting among your friends members of all sections of the community.

And to you, Mr. Vigeland, we offer as an ornament for your library, this volume of family prayers, printed on vellum and luxuriously bound. Under the mellowing influence of years you have come to look on life with gravity and wisdom. Your indefatigable industry, your scrupulous attention to the daily task at hand, have been sanctified and ennobled by thoughts of higher, holier things. (*Turns to the crowd*) And now, my friends, long live Karsten Bernick and his worthy colleagues! Hurrah for the Pillars of our Society!

THE ENTIRE CROWD: Long live Mr. Bernick! Long live the Pillars of Society! Hurrah, hurrah, hurrah!

LONA: Congratulations, Karsten!

(*An expectant silence.*)

BERNICK (*Starts to speak gravely and slowly*): My fellow

citizens—your spokesman has said that tonight we stand on the threshold of a new era—I hope it turns out to be so. But in order to bring this about, we must first dedicate ourselves to truth; and truth, up until this evening, has, unfortunately, been totally alien to this community.

(*Astonishment among the listeners.*)

BERNICK: I must begin by repudiating the praise with which, as is customary on such occasions, Mr. Rörlund has overwhelmed me. I do not deserve it, for until today I have not been a disinterested man. Even if I have not always had pecuniary gains in mind, I realize now that a desire for power, influence and prestige has been the motivating force behind all my actions.

RUMMEL (*Half aloud*): What on earth—?

BERNICK: As I stand here before you, my fellow citizens, I do not reproach myself for this; for I still think I have the right to consider myself one of our leading businessmen.

MANY VOICES: Yes, yes, yes!

BERNICK: But I do blame myself for being weak enough to stoop to crooked methods, simply because I knew and feared the tendency of our community to suspect dishonest motives in every enterprise a man might undertake. And now I come to a case in point.

RUMMEL (*Uneasily*): Hm—hm!

BERNICK: There are rumors of vast purchases of land along the proposed branch line. I am responsible for the purchase of this property; I—and I alone!

LOW MURMURS: What's he say? Bernick himself? Karsten Bernick?

BERNICK: At the present moment all of this vast property is in my hands. I have, of course, confided in my colleagues, Messrs. Rummel, Vigeland and Sandstad, and we have agreed to—

RUMMEL: That's not true! Prove it! Prove it!

VIGELAND: We've agreed to nothing!

SANDSTAD: Well, I must say—!

BERNICK: That is correct. What I'm about to propose we have not yet agreed on; but I have no doubt that these gentlemen will support me in the matter. I now propose—and I made up my mind this evening to follow this procedure—that a joint-stock company be formed for the exploitation of these properties; the shares will be placed on the open market, and will be available to all.

MANY VOICES: Hurrah! Long live Bernick!

RUMMEL (*In an undertone to* BERNICK): Of all the underhanded—

SANDSTAD (*Likewise*): A nice trick to play on us—!

VIGELAND: Well, I'll be damned! Good Lord—what am I saying!

THE CROWD OUTSIDE: Hurrah, hurrah, hurrah!

BERNICK: Silence, gentlemen, if you please! I have no right to this acclaim; at first my intentions in this matter were very different. I bought the land with the intention of keeping it myself; and I'm still of the opinion that the most efficient way to administer these properties would be to place them under the control of a single individual. However, it's up to you to choose. If you so decide, I'm willing to act as your representative and manage the enterprise for you to the best of my ability.

VOICES: Yes, yes, yes!

BERNICK: But first, I want my fellow citizens to know me for the man I really am. And if each one of you will in turn examine his own conscience, we may indeed be ready to embark on that new era of which Mr. Rörlund so eloquently spoke. Let us think of the past, with its false glitter, its hypocrisy, its sham respectability, its calculating cowardly spirit, as a museum—a kind of horror chamber—kept open only to remind us, and instruct us. And I think we might also donate to this museum—don't you agree, gentlemen? —the silver coffee service, the goblet, the album, and the volume of family prayers so exquisitely printed on vellum, and so luxuriously bound.

RUMMEL: Yes, by all means.

VIGELAND (*Mutters*): You've deprived us of all the rest, so—

SANDSTAD: Yes, yes—of course.

BERNICK: I come now to my main objective—which is to set my personal record straight with this community. "Undesirable elements," we have been told, left our town tonight. Now I'll tell you something you don't know: the man these words referred to did not leave alone; he was accompanied by the girl who intends to be his wife—

LONA (*In a loud voice*): Dina Dorf!

RÖRLUND: What!

MRS. BERNICK: What's that you say?

(*Great excitement.*)

RÖRLUND: Gone? Run away with him? Impossible!

BERNICK: She's to be his wife, I tell you. And I have more to add. (*In an undertone*) Betty, prepare yourself. This will be a shock. (*Aloud*) I say "all honor to that man"! He most generously took upon himself another's guilt. Fellow citizens, I must shake off this lie in which I've lived, and which has very nearly poisoned every fiber of my being. I want you to know the truth: fifteen years ago *I* was the guilty one.

MRS. BERNICK (*In a low trembling voice*): Karsten.

MISS BERNICK (*Likewise*): Oh, Johan—!

LONA: You've found your true self at last!

(*Speechless amazement among the onlookers.*)

BERNICK: Yes, my fellow citizens, I was the guilty one; it was the innocent one who went away. No human power can ever refute the rumors and the wicked lies that were circulated after his departure. But who am I to complain of them? It was on those very lies and rumors that I founded my career. It remains to be seen whether they will destroy me now. It is for each of you to decide this for himself.

RÖRLUND: What a bombshell! Our foremost citizen—! (*In an undertone, to* MRS. BERNICK) Oh, my dear lady, how I pity you!

HILMAR: What a confession! I must say—!

BERNICK: But don't decide tonight. I ask each one of you to go back to his home; to collect his thoughts; to examine his own heart. Then, when your minds are calm again, we shall see whether I have lost or gained by speaking out. Good night! I have still much, very much, to repent of; but that concerns my own conscience alone. Good night! And take away the decorations. I'm sure we all agree they no longer belong here.

RÖRLUND: There's no question of that! (*In a low voice to* MRS. BERNICK) Run away! So she was quite unworthy of me, after all! (*In a slightly louder tone, to the committee*) Well, gentlemen—after this we'd best withdraw in silence.

HILMAR: How's a man to keep the flag of the Ideal flying after this, I'd like to know! Ugh!

(*Word has been whispered from mouth to mouth. The members of the procession retire through the garden.* RUMMEL, SANDSTAD *and* VIGELAND *go off arguing violently, but in subdued voices.* HILMAR TÖNNESEN *slips out by the door on the right.* BERNICK, MRS. BERNICK, MISS BERNICK, LONA *and* KRAP *remain in the room in silence.*)

BERNICK: Can you forgive me, Betty?

MRS. BERNICK (*Looks at him and smiles*): Do you know, Karsten, you've made me feel happier and more hopeful than I've felt for many years!

BERNICK: How do you mean?

MRS. BERNICK: For many years I've thought that you were once mine, but that I'd lost you. Now I know that you were never really mine, but I intend to win you.

BERNICK (*Puts his arms round her*): Oh, Betty, you *have* won me. It's Lona who showed me what you *really* are! But, let Olaf come in now.

MRS. BERNICK: Yes, now you shall have him back—Mr. Krap—!

(*She whispers something to him in the background. He goes out by the garden door. During the following, the lights and the transparencies in the houses are gradually extinguished.*)

BERNICK (*Softly*): Thank you, Lona. You've saved what's best in me—what's best *for* me.

LONA: What else was I trying to do, do you suppose?

BERNICK: Well, was it that? Or wasn't it? I can't quite make you out.

LONA: Hm.

BERNICK: It wasn't hatred? Nor revenge? Then why did you come back?

LONA: Old friendship doesn't tarnish, Karsten.

BERNICK: Lona!

LONA: When Johan told me all this about the lie, I swore to myself: I must see the hero of my youth stand free and clear again!

BERNICK: A wretched creature like me! Lona—I don't deserve it!

LONA: Deserve! Heavens—if we women were always to insist on that—!

(AUNE *and* OLAF *come in from the garden.*)

BERNICK (*Going to him*): Olaf!

OLAF: Father, I promise you, I'll never—

BERNICK: Run away again?

OLAF: Yes; I promise, Father.

BERNICK: And I promise you'll never have cause to. From now on you'll be allowed to grow up for your own sake— not just to carry on my work. I want you to look forward to work of your own choosing.

OLAF: Will you really let me be whatever I want to be, Father?

BERNICK: Yes, I promise.

OLAF: Thanks! Well, I know one thing—I won't be a Pillar-of-Society!

BERNICK: Why not?

OLAF: I should think it would be awfully dull.

BERNICK: Just be yourself, Olaf; and let the rest take care of itself—And you, Aune—

AUNE: I know, Sir; I'm discharged.

BERNICK: We'll stick together, Aune; and please forgive me—

AUNE: How do you mean? The ship won't sail tonight.

BERNICK: And she won't sail tomorrow either. I gave you too little time. The job must be done thoroughly.

AUNE: It will be, Sir—and we'll use the new machines!

BERNICK: Splendid! But, mind you, thoroughly and honestly. There's quite a bit round here that needs a thorough, honest overhaul! Good night, Aune!

AUNE: Good night, Sir—and many thanks! (*He goes out to the right.*)

MRS. BERNICK: They've all gone now.

BERNICK: And we're alone. My name no longer blazes out in lights. The illuminations are extinguished.

LONA: Would you want them lit again?

BERNICK: Not for all the world! Where have I been all this time? You'd be horrified to know! It's as though I were just coming to my senses again, after being poisoned. But I'll soon be young and strong again—I'm sure of it! Come near—come close to me, all of you! Come, Betty! Come, Olaf, my boy! And you, too—Marta, I feel as though I hadn't seen you for years!

MISS BERNICK: I don't believe you have. You seem to live in a society of bachelors; you don't see women.

BERNICK: That's true; and for that very reason—it's settled, Lona, do you hear?—You're not to go away and leave Betty and me.

MRS. BERNICK: No, Lona—you mustn't!

LONA: I couldn't think of going away and leaving you young people, just as you're about to set up housekeeping! After all, I'm a foster mother too. We two old aunts, Marta— What are you looking at?

MISS BERNICK: The sky is clearing. It's growing light over the sea. "The Palm Tree" has good luck with her.

LONA: And happiness on board.

BERNICK: We have a long hard day's work ahead of us; I most of all. But let it come! So long as I have you beside me—you dear, loyal women. That's another thing I've learned these last few days: it's you women who are the Pillars of Society.

LONA: Then you've learned a piece of nonsense, brother-in-law! Don't you believe it! (*Puts her hand firmly on his shoulder*) Truth and the Spirit of Freedom—they're the *real* Pillars of Society!

                                                                              CURTAIN

The Wild Duck

A PLAY IN FIVE ACTS

CHARACTERS

WERLE, *a wholesale merchant and manufacturer*

GREGERS WERLE, *his son*

OLD EKDAL

HJALMAR EKDAL, *his son, a photographer*

GINA EKDAL, *Hjalmar's wife*

HEDVIG, *their daughter, a girl of fourteen*

MRS. SÖRBY, *Werle's housekeeper*

RELLING, *a doctor*

MOLVIK, *a former student of theology*

GRAABERG, *Werle's bookkeeper*

PETTERSEN, *Werle's servant*

JENSEN, *a hired waiter*

A FAT GENTLEMAN

A BALD GENTLEMAN

A NEARSIGHTED GENTLEMAN

SIX OTHER GENTLEMEN, *guests at Werle's party*

SEVERAL HIRED WAITERS

> *The first act takes place in Werle's house, the four following acts at Hjalmar Ekdal's.*

ACT
ONE

SCENE: *In* WERLE'S *house. A study richly and comfort-*
ably furnished; bookcases and upholstered furniture; a desk
covered with papers and documents stands in the center of
the room; several lamps with green shades give a subdued
light. In the back wall double doors stand open, with por-
tieres drawn back. Beyond them is seen a large elegantly
furnished room, brightly lighted with lamps and branched
candlesticks. A small baize door down right leads to WERLE'S
office. Down left a fireplace with a brightly burning coal fire,
and above this a double door to the dining room.

WERLE'S *servant* PETTERSEN, *in livery, and* JENSEN, *a hired*
waiter in black, are straightening up the room. In the large
room beyond, two or three other waiters move about tidying
up and lighting more candles. From the dining room comes
the hum of conversation, laughter, the sound of many voices;
a glass is tapped with a knife; silence follows, then a toast is
proposed. Shouts of "Bravo!" and then again the buzz of
conversation.

PETTERSEN (*As he lights a lamp on the mantlepiece and re-*
places the shade): Hear that, Jensen? The old boy's on his
feet again toasting Mrs. Sörby. Listen to him holding
forth!
JENSEN (*Pushing forward an armchair*): Is it true what peo-
ple say? That he's sweet on her, I mean?
PETTERSEN: Hell! How should I know!
JENSEN: I'll bet he was quite a chaser in his day!
PETTERSEN: I shouldn't wonder.
JENSEN: He's giving this party for his son, I hear.

PETTERSEN: Yes; he got home yesterday.

JENSEN: I never even knew Werle had a son.

PETTERSEN: He has a son all right. But he spends most of his time up at the Works, in Höjdal; he hasn't been back once; not in all the years I've worked here.

A WAITER (*In the doorway of the inner room*): Pettersen! There's an old fellow out here—says he wants—

PETTERSEN (*Muttering*): What is it *now!*

(OLD EKDAL *appears from the right in the inner room. He wears a threadbare overcoat with a turned-up collar; has on woollen mittens and carries a stick and an old fur cap. There is a brown paper parcel under his arm. He wears a dirty reddish-brown wig and has a small gray mustache.*)

PETTERSEN (*Going towards him*): What the devil are *you* doing here?

EKDAL (*In the doorway*): Got to get into the office, Pettersen.

PETTERSEN: The office was closed an hour ago—

EKDAL: I know—the porter told me. But Graaberg's still there, isn't he? Let me slip in this way, Pettersen—there's a good fellow! (*Points to the baize door*) Not the first time I've used this door, eh?

PETTERSEN: All right. (*Opens the door*) But when you leave, go out the other way—don't come back through here. We have company, you know.

EKDAL: Oh, yes—I know; I know. Hm! Thanks, Pettersen. Thanks, old man. You're a good friend. (*Mutters under his breath*) Ass! (*He goes into the office;* PETTERSEN *closes the door after him.*)

JENSEN: Does *he* belong to the office?

PETTERSEN: No! He just does a bit of copying now and then —when they're extra busy. Takes it home with him. Poor old Ekdal! Quite a swell in his day, he was.

JENSEN: He still has a way with him—

PETTERSEN: Yes, indeed! A military man he was. A lieutenant, no less.

JENSEN: A lieutenant! *Him?*

PETTERSEN: It's a fact. Then he went into business—something to do with timber, I believe. They say he once played Mr. Werle a very dirty trick. They were running the Höjdal Works together—they were partners then, you see. Oh, I know old Ekdal well. Many's the time we've drunk a bottle of ale at Mrs. Eriksen's; we've downed many a glass of bitters there together he and I.

JENSEN: Shouldn't think there was much chance of a treat from him!

PETTERSEN: Don't be a fool, Jensen! I'm the one who does the treating. It's as well to be kind to a gent like that who's come down in the world.

JENSEN: What happened? Did he go bankrupt?

PETTERSEN: Worse than that; he went to jail.

JENSEN: To jail!

PETTERSEN: Some kind of penitentiary, at any rate. (*Listens*) Sh! They're getting up from table.

(*The dining-room door is flung open from within by a couple of waiters.* MRS. SÖRBY *comes out talking to two gentlemen.* WERLE *and the other guests follow gradually. Finally* HJALMAR EKDAL *and* GREGERS WERLE *appear.*)

MRS. SÖRBY (*In passing*): You can serve the coffee in the music room, Pettersen.

PETTERSEN: Very well, Madam. (*She and the two gentlemen go into the inner room and off right.* PETTERSEN *and* JENSEN *go out the same way.*)

FAT GENTLEMAN (*To* BALD GENTLEMAN): Phew! That was hard work! Quite a meal!

BALD GENTLEMAN: With a little good will it's quite amazing what one can put away in three hours!

FAT GENTLEMAN: Oh, my dear fellow—I'm thinking of the aftermath!

A THIRD GENTLEMAN: They say coffee and liqueurs are being served in the music room.

FAT GENTLEMAN: Splendid! Perhaps Mrs. Sörby will play a tune for us.

BALD GENTLEMAN: If we aren't careful she may play us the wrong kind of tune someday!

FAT GENTLEMAN: Don't worry about Bertha! She's not the kind to go back on old friends!

WERLE (*In a low tone, dejectedly*): I don't think anyone noticed—did they, Gregers?

GREGERS (*Looks at him*): Noticed what?

WERLE: Then you didn't notice either?

GREGERS: No. What do you mean?

WERLE: We were thirteen at table.

GREGERS: Really? Were we?

WERLE (*With a glance towards* HJALMAR EKDAL): As a rule we're never more than twelve. (*To the others*) This way, gentlemen! (WERLE *and the others go out through the inner room to the right. Only* HJALMAR *and* GREGERS *remain.*)

HJALMAR (*Who has overheard*): Gregers—you shouldn't have invited me.

GREGERS: Don't be absurd! Not invite my best and only friend—? The party was given for me, wasn't it?

HJALMAR: Your father didn't approve, I'm afraid. I'm never asked to the house, you know.

GREGERS: So I gather. But I had to see you and have a talk. I'll be going away again soon—We've drifted so far apart since the old days at school. Do you realize it's sixteen or seventeen years since we last met?

HJALMAR: Is it really as long as that?

GREGERS: It is indeed! Well—how have you been? You're looking well. You've put on weight, I think; you've grown quite stout.

HJALMAR: I wouldn't exactly call it stout. I'm no longer a boy—if that's what you mean. I've filled out a bit—that's only natural.

GREGERS: Yes, of course. Well—outwardly you seem in splendid shape.

HJALMAR (*In a gloomy tone*): But inwardly—that's another story! I don't have to tell you all that I've been through. You know all about *that* catastrophe!

GREGERS: Yes. What's happened to your father? What's he doing now?

HJALMAR: Don't speak of it! The poor, miserable old man! I look after him, of course; he lives with me. He has no one else to turn to. But it's too painful to talk about—Tell me about yourself. Have you been getting on well—up at the Works?

GREGERS: I've been living in splendid isolation. I've had plenty of time for contemplation, I can tell you. Let's sit here and be comfortable. (*He sits down in an armchair by the fire, and pulls* HJALMAR *down to another one beside him.*)

HJALMAR (*Sentimentally*): As a matter of fact, Gregers, I'm very grateful that you asked me here today. It proves that you no longer have anything against me.

GREGERS (*Surprised*): Why on earth should you think I had anything against you?

HJALMAR: You had at first, you know.

GREGERS: At first? How do you mean?

HJALMAR: Directly after the—catastrophe. It was understandable enough. It was only by a miracle that your father escaped being dragged into all that ghastly business.

GREGERS: But that's no reason why I should have had anything against *you*. What put that into your head?

HJALMAR: I happen to know you did, Gregers. Your father told me so himself.

GREGERS: *Father* did? Well! Hm—Was that why I never heard from you? Why you never wrote to me?

HJALMAR: Of course.

GREGERS: You never even told me you'd decided to take up photography.

HJALMAR: I know. Your father advised me not to write to you at all.

GREGERS (*Gazes straight before him*): Well—well! Perhaps he was wise in that—But, tell me—are you happy in your work? Does it appeal to you, I mean?

HJALMAR (*With a sigh*): Yes—more or less; I really can't

complain. It all seemed very strange to me at first. I found myself in such totally different circumstances, you see. Father had lost absolutely everything—he was completely ruined. And then there was all the scandal—the disgrace—

GREGERS (*Moved*): Yes, yes. I understand.

HJALMAR: I naturally had to give up my studies—I was forced to leave the university. We hadn't a penny left—nothing but debts—mostly to your father, I believe.

GREGERS: Hm.

HJALMAR: I thought it best to break off all my former friendships—sever all my old connections. In fact it was your father who advised me to do so; and since he seemed to want to help me—

GREGERS: Father did?

HJALMAR: You must be aware of that. Where was *I* to get the money to learn photography, furnish a studio, and buy all the necessary equipment? It takes quite a bit of capital to make a start, you know.

GREGERS: You mean—*Father* provided that?

HJALMAR: Of course; didn't you know? I understood him to say he'd written you about it.

GREGERS: No—he never mentioned it. He must have forgotten, I suppose. Actually we've never exchanged anything but business letters. So it was *Father* who—!

HJALMAR: Yes, it was. He didn't want it generally known, he said—but it was he. He also made it possible for me to marry. Didn't you know that either?

GREGERS: No—I didn't. (*Shakes him by the arm*) My dear Hjalmar—I can't tell you how glad I am about all this. But I feel guilty, too. I've misjudged Father all these years—in some ways, anyhow. I thought he had no heart—no feelings. This proves me wrong. It's funny—one would almost think he was trying to atone for something—

HJALMAR: Atone?

GREGERS: Yes—it's as though he were suffering from a sense of guilt; I don't know *what* to call it. But I'm certainly delighted to hear all this about him. So you're married,

are you? You're a braver man than I am! How does it feel?
Are you content?

HJALMAR: Yes—I'm very happy, thank you. She's a thoroughly good wife—and very capable, as well. And, after
all—she's not *entirely* without education.

GREGERS (*Rather surprised*): No—I don't suppose she is—

HJALMAR: Life's the best education, when you come right
down to it. And, being so much with me, she— And I've
a couple of very brilliant friends who drop in almost every
day. She's learning—Gina's learning! You'd never recognize her.

GREGERS: Gina?

HJALMAR: Yes; Gina's her name—don't you remember?

GREGERS: *Whose* name is Gina? I don't know what you're—

HJALMAR: You must remember Gina! She worked here for a
while.

GREGERS (*Looks at him*): You don't mean Gina Hansen?

HJALMAR: Gina Hansen, yes—of course.

GREGERS: —who kept house for us those last few years—
when Mother was so ill?

HJALMAR: Yes, that's the one. But—my dear fellow—your
father wrote you all about it; I'm *positive* he did!

GREGERS (*Who has risen*): He wrote and told me you were
married, but not that— (*Walks about the room*) Wait,
though! On second thought—I think he may have—His
letters were always so very brief. (*Sinks down on the
arm of the chair*) Tell me, Hjalmar—this is most interesting—how did you happen to meet this Gina—your wife,
I mean?

HJALMAR: It was all quite simple. Gina didn't stay here long,
you know. Things were very upset here at the time—what
with your mother's illness; it was all too much for Gina, so
she left. It was the year before your mother died, I think;
or the same year, perhaps—I'm not quite sure.

GREGERS: It was the same year; I was away—up at the
Works. And then what happened?

HJALMAR: Gina went home to her mother—Mrs. Hansen; an

honest, hard-working woman who ran a little restaurant. They had a room to rent—a nice, comfortable room—

GREGERS: And I suppose you were lucky enough to acquire it?

HJALMAR: Yes. It was your father who recommended it. And, of course, there I got to know Gina very well.

GREGERS: And then you got engaged?

HJALMAR: Yes. It doesn't take young people long to fall in love—hm—

GREGERS (*Rises and paces about*): Tell me—was it *after* you became engaged that Father—I mean—was it after that, that you took up photography?

HJALMAR: Yes; I had to work at something; I was anxious to have a home of my own, you see. Your father and I agreed that a photographer's career would be practical and easy. And Gina thought so too—especially as she'd done a bit of retouching herself and knew quite a lot about it.

GREGERS: So it worked out very neatly, didn't it?

HJALMAR (*Rises, pleased*): Yes—wasn't it amazing? It really worked out very neatly!

GREGERS: No doubt of that! My father seems to have played the part of Divine Providence where you're concerned!

HJALMAR: He came to the rescue of his old friend's son. That shows what a kind heart he has!

(MRS. SÖRBY *enters arm in arm with* WERLE.)

MRS. SÖRBY: It's no use arguing, dear Mr. Werle! You mustn't stay in those bright lights another moment. It's bad for you!

WERLE (*Lets go of her arm and passes his hand over his eyes*): You know—I believe you're right.

(PETTERSEN *and* JENSEN *carry round trays of refreshments.*)

MRS. SÖRBY (*To the guests in the inner room*): Do come in here, gentlemen, and have some punch.

FAT GENTLEMAN (*Comes up to* MRS. SÖRBY): It can't be true! No smoking? You surely don't mean to deprive us of that precious prerogative!

MRS. SÖRBY: I'm afraid it can't be helped, Your Excellency! Smoking is not allowed in Mr. Werle's sanctum.

BALD GENTLEMAN: My dear lady! And when did you inaugurate this harsh decree?

MRS. SÖRBY: After our last dinner party, Mr. Balle. Several of our guests quite overstepped the mark.

BALD GENTLEMAN: Isn't it ever permitted to overstep the mark, dear Madam Bertha! Not even by an inch or two?

MRS. SÖRBY: Never! Under any circumstances, Mr. Balle. (*Most of the guests are now gathered in the study; servants hand round glasses of punch.*)

WERLE (*To* HJALMAR, *who is standing apart beside a table*): What are you so engrossed in, Ekdal?

HJALMAR: I was just looking at this album, Mr. Werle.

BALD GENTLEMAN (*Who is wandering about*): Ah, photographs! Of course—that's your line, isn't it?

FAT GENTLEMAN (*In an armchair*): I do hope you've brought some of your own!

HJALMAR: No, I'm afraid I haven't.

FAT GENTLEMAN: Too bad! It's good for the digestion to look at pictures after dinner.

BALD GENTLEMAN: And it provides entertainment, too.

NEARSIGHTED GENTLEMAN: All such contributions thankfully received!

MRS. SÖRBY: In other words, gentlemen, you mean a guest should sing for his supper!

FAT GENTLEMAN: Certainly, Mrs. Sörby—especially when the supper is so excellent!

BALD GENTLEMAN: Still—when it involves one's livelihood—

MRS. SÖRBY: Of course! I quite agree! (*They go on laughing and joking.*)

GREGERS (*Softly*): You ought to join in the conversation, Hjalmar.

HJALMAR (*Squirming*): What have *I* got to talk about?

FAT GENTLEMAN: Werle—I claim that Tokay is a comparatively mild wine; don't you agree?

WERLE (*By the mantlepiece*): Yes, I suppose so. I'll vouch for that Tokay you had today, at any rate. It's quite an exceptional vintage; an unusually good year—but I needn't tell *you* that!

FAT GENTLEMAN: I admit it had a most delicate bouquet.

HJALMAR (*Diffidently*): Is there a difference in the years, then?

FAT GENTLEMAN (*Laughing*): Come now! What a question!

WERLE (*Smiles, to* HJALMAR): Fine wines are lost on you it seems!

BALD GENTLEMAN: Wines are like photographs, Mr. Ekdal— they both need sunshine. Or am I mistaken?

HJALMAR: No—light is certainly important.

MRS. SÖRBY: What about court chamberlains? I hear they thrive on sunshine too!

BALD GENTLEMAN: Such sarcasm! Is that kind?

NEARSIGHTED GENTLEMAN: Mrs. Sörby will have her joke, you know!

FAT GENTLEMAN: Yes! And at our expense! (*Wags his finger at her*) Oh, Madam Bertha! Madam Bertha!

MRS. SÖRBY: Joking apart, however, Mr. Ekdal—wines differ greatly according to the year. Old vintages are nearly always best.

NEARSIGHTED GENTLEMAN: Am *I* an old vintage, Mrs. Sörby?

MRS. SÖRBY: Far from it, Excellency!

BALD GENTLEMAN: There! You see? How about me, dear Mrs. Sörby—?

FAT GENTLEMAN: And me! What would *my* vintage be?

MRS. SÖRBY: A most sweet vintage, Excellency! (*She sips her glass of punch. The men all laugh and flirt with her.*)

WERLE: Trust Mrs. Sörby to find a way out—when she wants to! Fill up your glasses, gentlemen! See to it, Pettersen—! Drink with me, Gregers, won't you? (GREGERS *doesn't move*) And you, Ekdal—won't you join us? There was no opportunity to drink with you at dinner.

(GRAABERG, *the bookkeeper, sticks his head in at the baize door.*)

GRAABERG: Excuse me, sir. I'm afraid I can't get out—

WERLE: Have they locked you in again?

GRAABERG: I'm afraid so, sir—Flakstad went off with the keys.

WERLE: Never mind—come through this way.

GRAABERG: But—I'm not alone, sir; there are two of us, sir.

WERLE: It doesn't matter; come along! The two of you!

(GRAABERG *and* OLD EKDAL *come out of the office.*)

WERLE (*Involuntarily*): Ugh!

(*The laughter and talk among the guests breaks off suddenly.* HJALMAR *starts at the sight of his father, puts down his glass and turns towards the fireplace.*)

EKDAL (*Without looking up, makes little bows to right and left as he passes through, murmuring*): Excuse me. Came in the wrong way. Door was locked. Door locked. Excuse me. (*He and* GRAABERG *go into the inner room and off right.*)

WERLE (*Between his teeth*): That blasted Graaberg!

GREGERS (*Stares open-mouthed; to* HJALMAR): Surely—that couldn't have been—!

FAT GENTLEMAN: What's going on? Who *was* that?

GREGERS: Nobody; just the bookkeeper, and someone with him.

NEARSIGHTED GENTLEMAN (*To* HJALMAR): Who *was* that man? Did you know him?

HJALMAR: No—I don't know—I didn't notice—

FAT GENTLEMAN (*Rising*): What the devil's happening? (*He joins another group, who are talking under their breath.*)

MRS. SÖRBY (*To* PETTERSEN *in a whisper*): Give him something to take home with him; something nice—you understand?

PETTERSEN (*Nods*): I'll see to it. (*Goes out.*)

GREGERS (*Softly, with emotion, to* HJALMAR): It really was he, then!

HJALMAR: Yes.

GREGERS: And you actually stood there and said you didn't know him!

HJALMAR (*In a vehement whisper*): But how could I—!

GREGERS: —acknowledge your own father?

HJALMAR (*Miserably*): If you were in *my* place, you—
(*The conversation among the guests, which has been carried on in a low tone, now swells into forced joviality.*)

BALD GENTLEMAN (*In a friendly manner approaches* HJALMAR *and* GREGERS): Aha! Reminiscing about old days at college, eh? Don't you smoke, Mr. Ekdal? May I give you a light? Oh—but of course!—it's not allowed!

HJALMAR: Thank you—I don't think I—

FAT GENTLEMAN: How about reciting a poem for us, Mr. Ekdal? You used to be so good at it.

HJALMAR: I'm afraid I don't remember any.

FAT GENTLEMAN: What a pity! Well—what can we find to do, Balle? (*They move away and go into the other room.*)

HJALMAR (*Gloomily*): I'm going, Gregers. When a man's been through what I've been through, you see— Say goodbye to your father for me.

GREGERS: Yes—of course. Do you think you'll go straight home?

HJALMAR: Yes—why do you ask?

GREGERS: I thought I might drop in a little later.

HJALMAR: No, don't do that—don't come to my place, Gregers; it's too sad and depressing there. Especially on top of all this splendour! We'll arrange to meet somewhere in town.

MRS. SÖRBY (*Comes over to them and speaks in a low voice*): Are you going, Ekdal?

HJALMAR: Yes.

MRS. SÖRBY: Remember me to Gina.

HJALMAR: Thanks.

MRS. SÖRBY: Tell her I'll drop in one of these days.

HJALMAR: Thanks—I will. (*To* GREGERS) Don't come with me. I'll slip out without being seen. (*He strolls across the room, into the inner room, and out to the right.*)

MRS. SÖRBY (*In a low voice to* PETTERSEN, *who has returned*): Did you give the old man something?

PETTERSEN: A nice bottle of brandy, Madam.

MRS. SÖRBY: You might have thought of something better than that!

PETTERSEN: Oh, no, Mrs. Sörby! He'd rather have that than anything!

FAT GENTLEMAN (*In the doorway, with a sheet of music in his hand*): How about playing a duet, Mrs. Sörby?

MRS. SÖRBY: Yes! That would be delightful!

GUESTS: Bravo! Bravo! (*She joins the guests in the inner room and they all go out to the right.* GREGERS *remains standing by the fireplace.* WERLE *pretends to be looking for something on the desk and seems to want* GREGERS *to go;* GREGERS *doesn't move,* WERLE *goes towards the door.*)

GREGERS: Can you spare a moment, Father?

WERLE: Yes; what is it?

GREGERS: I'd like to talk to you.

WERLE: Can't it wait till we're alone?

GREGERS: No, it can't; we may never be alone again, you see.

WERLE (*Comes towards him*): And what does *that* mean? (*During the following the sound of a piano is heard in the distance, from the music room.*)

GREGERS: Why has that family been allowed to go downhill like that?

WERLE: You're referring to the Ekdals, I presume.

GREGERS: Yes; I'm referring to the Ekdals. There was a time when you and Lieutenant Ekdal were close friends.

WERLE: Yes; too close for comfort—I've suffered for it for years. That friendship almost cost me my good name.

GREGERS: Was he the only guilty one? You're sure of that?

WERLE: What do you mean?

GREGERS: You were in that big timber deal together, weren't you?

WERLE: Ekdal was in charge of the entire transaction. He surveyed the land—he drew up the maps. How was I to know that they were fraudulent! He deliberately encroached on property belonging to the Government; he felled all that timber—acres of it!—belonging to the State. Lieutenant Ekdal acted entirely on his own responsibility. I never for a moment realized what he was up to.

GREGERS: Perhaps he didn't quite realize it himself.

WERLE: That may be. The fact remains that he was found guilty, and I was acquitted.

GREGERS: Yes; I know nothing was ever proved against you.

WERLE: An acquittal is an acquittal. But what makes you bring up that distressing business? God knows it turned my hair gray long before its time. Is that the kind of thing you've spent all these years brooding about up there? I assure you here in town it's been forgotten long ago—at least as far as *I'm* concerned.

GREGERS: But what about the Ekdals?

WERLE: What do you expect me to do for them? Ekdal came out of prison a broken man; he was beyond all help. There are certain people in this world who, given the slightest blow, dive straight to the bottom and never come up again. Believe me, Gregers, I did everything I could—short of exposing myself to suspicion and endless gossip—

GREGERS: Suspicion? Yes—I see.

WERLE: I've arranged for Ekdal to do some odd jobs for the office—copying and so forth—and I pay him ten times what the work is worth—

GREGERS (*Without looking at him*): I don't doubt *that* for a moment.

WERLE: Why do you laugh? Do you think I'm not telling you the truth? I admit there's no record of it on the books; I never enter payments of that sort.

GREGERS (*With a cold smile*): You're very wise.

WERLE (*Taken aback*): What do you mean?

GREGERS (*Summoning up his courage*): How about the money you gave Hjalmar Ekdal to learn photography? Is *that* entered on the books?

WERLE: Entered—how? I don't—

GREGERS: I know now it was you who paid for his tuition; I also know that it was you who set him up in business.

WERLE: And you call that doing nothing for the Ekdals! Those people have cost me plenty, I assure you!

GREGERS: And are *those* expenses entered on the books?

WERLE: Why do you ask me that?

GREGERS: I have my reasons. Now, tell me: when you evinced this sudden interest in your old friend's son—it was just before his marriage, wasn't it?

WERLE: Good heavens! You don't expect me—after all, it's years ago—!

GREGERS: You wrote me a letter at that time—a business letter, naturally—and you mentioned briefly, in a postscript, that Hjalmar Ekdal had married a Miss Hansen.

WERLE: Quite right. That was her name.

GREGERS: But you omitted the fact that this Miss Hansen was *Gina* Hansen—our former housekeeper.

WERLE (*With a slightly forced laugh of derision*): It never occurred to me you were so interested in our former housekeeper.

GREGERS: You're right; I wasn't. But—(*Lowers his voice*) I happen to know there were others in this house who were; *extremely* interested.

WERLE: What do you mean by that? (*Flaring up*) You're not referring to *me*, by any chance?

GREGERS (*Softly but firmly*): But I *am* referring to you.

WERLE: How *dare* you! How dare you presume to—! I'll teach that photographer fellow—ungrateful wretch! Spreading lies about me—!

GREGERS: Hjalmar hasn't said a single word about it. I'm certain he hasn't the faintest suspicion of such a thing.

WERLE: Then where did you get it from? Who put such ideas into your head?

GREGERS: It was poor Mother; it was she who told me about it; the very last time I ever saw her.

WERLE: Your mother! Yes—of course. I might have known. You and she—! You always held together. She turned you against me from the start.

GREGERS: That's not true; it was because of all she suffered —all she had to bear; till she broke down and went utterly to pieces.

WERLE: Nonsense! She had no more to bear, and she suffered no more, than the majority of women. But it's impossible to deal with sickly, hysterical people—I've learned that to my cost!—How could you harbor these suspicions—how could you bring yourself to rake up all these malicious rumors against your own father, Gregers? I don't understand it. I should think at your age you could apply yourself to something more constructive.

GREGERS: It's about time, isn't it?

WERLE: It would do you good; I'm sure you'd feel much happier. What do you expect to accomplish up there at the Works, slaving away year after year at a routine office job? Refusing to accept a penny above the regular wages? It's sheer madness!

GREGERS: Yes; well—I'm not so sure of that.

WERLE: I understand your reasons well enough; you don't want to owe me anything; you want to be completely independent—Now, it so happens, an excellent opportunity has opened up; one that would give you complete independence—full authority.

GREGERS: Indeed? What kind of opportunity?

WERLE: In my last letter—when I said it was essential for you to come back home at once—

GREGERS: Yes; what had you in mind? I've been waiting all day for you to tell me.

WERLE: What I had in mind was this: I propose to offer you a partnership.

GREGERS: In *your* firm? A partnership with *you?*

WERLE: It needn't be too *close* a partnership; we wouldn't necessarily have to work *together*. You could handle the business here, and I would move up to the Works.

GREGERS: To the Works? *You?*

WERLE: Yes; I no longer have the strength I used to have. It's time I started to let down a bit, you see. And I have to be careful of my eyes—they've been bad lately; I've had a lot of trouble with them.

GREGERS: That's nothing new; they've always troubled you.

WERLE: But not as they do now. There are other circumstances, too, that make it advisable for me to move up there—for a while, at any rate.

GREGERS: I certainly never expected anything like this.

WERLE: We've never been close—I know that, Gregers; but, after all, we *are* father and son. There must be some way we can come to an understanding.

GREGERS: In the eyes of the world, I suppose you mean.

WERLE: Well—at least that would be something, wouldn't it? Think it over, Gregers. I'm sure we can manage it. Don't you agree?

GREGERS (*Looks at him coldly*): What's your real motive in all this?

WERLE: My motive?

GREGERS: You're depending on me for something. You plan to make use of me somehow.

WERLE: It's only natural for a father to depend upon his son.

GREGERS: Yes—so they say.

WERLE: I'm most anxious that you should stay home with me a little while. I'm very lonely, Gregers. All my life I've been a lonely man—and one feels it more as one gets older. I need someone near me—someone who—

GREGERS: You have Mrs. Sörby, haven't you?

WERLE: That's true—I have; and I don't know what I'd do without her. She's good-natured and intelligent; and she's so cheerful too—that means a lot to me.

GREGERS: Then what more do you want?

WERLE: But it's an awkward situation—for her, I mean. I'm afraid it can't go on much longer. It puts her in a false position—there might be talk. And that kind of thing doesn't do a man any good either.

GREGERS: I think you can afford to risk it! As long as you go on giving the dinner parties you can give.

WERLE: But what about *her*, Gregers? I'm afraid she may find it impossible to accept the situation any longer. And even if her affection for me prompted her to stay—at the risk of talk and scandal and all the rest of it—would I be justified in—? You, with your high sense of integrity, tell me—?

GREGERS: You're thinking of marrying her, aren't you? Why not say so?

WERLE: And supposing I were? What then?

GREGERS: What then? Exactly!

WERLE: Would you be unalterably opposed to it?

GREGERS: By no means. Not at all.

WERLE: I wasn't sure. I thought perhaps—devotion to your mother's memory—

GREGERS: I'm not hysterical, you know.

WERLE: Well—whatever you may or may not be—you've taken a great weight off my mind. I'm delighted to know I can depend on your support.

GREGERS (*Looks at him intently*): Of course! *That's* how you plan to use me!

WERLE: Use you, indeed! What an expression!

GREGERS: Don't let's be fussy in our choice of words—not when we're alone, at any rate. (*With a short laugh*) Yes! Now I see! That's why it was so absolutely essential for me to come back here. We are to play the "Happy Family" in Mrs. Sörby's honor! The devoted father and the loving son! A touching picture! A new experience, indeed!

WERLE: Don't take that tone with me!

GREGERS: When was there ever a "Happy Family" in this house I'd like to know? Never—so far as *I* remember! But your plans require something of the sort. It'll make such a good impression—won't it? The beloved son rushing home to attend his dear old father's wedding! And what of all those ugly rumors about the miseries and torments the first wife had to bear? It'd be the end of them, wouldn't it? They'd be wiped out once and for all—and by her own son too!

WERLE: I don't think there's a man living you hate as much as you hate me.

GREGERS (*Softly*): I've seen you at close range.

WERLE: You've seen me through your mother's eyes. (*Low-*

ers his voice a little) You should remember that those eyes
were—shall we say "clouded," now and then?

GREGERS (*Trembling*): I know what you're implying. But who
was responsible for mother's tragic weakness? It was you,
and all your—! The last of them being that woman you
palmed off on Hjalmar Ekdal when you no longer—! Pah!

WERLE (*Shrugs his shoulders*): I hear your mother in every
word you say.

GREGERS (*Takes no notice of him*): Yes! And he's there now
—with that noble, trusting, childlike mind of his—living
under the same roof with that degraded creature—quite
unaware that what he calls his home is built on nothing
but a lie! (*Comes a step nearer*) When I look back on all
the wicked things you've done, I feel as though I were
gazing at some ghastly battlefield—strewn with shattered
corpses!

WERLE: I'm afraid the gulf between us is too wide to bridge.

GREGERS (*Bowing stiffly*): I share that opinion; so I shall take
my hat and go.

WERLE: Go? Leave the house, you mean?

GREGERS: Yes. My purpose in life is clear to me at last.

WERLE: What purpose, may I ask?

GREGERS: You'd only laugh if I told you.

WERLE: I don't know, Gregers; a lonely man doesn't laugh so
easily.

GREGERS (*Points toward the inner room*): Look, Father! Your
distinguished guests are playing blindman's buff with
Mrs. Sörby—Good night and goodbye.

(*He goes out by the back to the right. Sounds of laughter
and gay conversation from the guests, who are now seen
in the inner room.*)

WERLE (*Mutters contemptuously*): Ha—! He's not hysterical, eh? Poor fellow!

CURTAIN

ACT
TWO

SCENE: HJALMAR EKDAL's *studio. It is a good-sized room evidently on the top floor of the building. On the right a large studio window is let into the sloping roof; it is half covered by a blue curtain. In the right-hand corner at the back is the hall door. Farther downstage on the same side is a door leading to the sitting room. Two doors on the opposite side and between them an iron stove. At the back a wide double door with sliding panels. The studio is plainly but comfortably fitted out and furnished. Between the doors on the right, standing out a little from the wall, a sofa with a table and some chairs; on the table a lighted lamp with a shade; beside the stove an old armchair. Photographic instruments and equipment of different kinds lying about the room. Against the back wall, to the left of the double door, stands a bookcase containing a few books, boxes and bottles of chemicals, instruments, tools and other objects. Photographs and small articles such as camel's hair brushes, paper and so forth, lie on the table.*

GINA EKDAL *sits on a chair by the table sewing.* HEDVIG *is sitting on the sofa, with her hands shading her eyes and her thumbs in her ears, reading a book.*

GINA (*Glances at her a couple of times as if in secret anxiety*): Hedvig!

HEDVIG (*Doesn't hear her.*)

GINA (*Louder*): Hedvig!

HEDVIG (*Takes away her hands and looks up*): Yes, Mother?

GINA: You mustn't go on reading any longer, Hedvig dear.

124

HEDVIG: Oh, just a *little* longer, Mother! A *tiny* bit longer—please!

GINA: No; put your book down now—there's a good girl. Your father'd be angry. *He* never reads of an evening, you know.

HEDVIG (*Closes the book*): But Father doesn't care much for reading.

GINA (*Lays aside her sewing and takes up a pencil and a little account book from the table*): How much was the butter today—do you remember?

HEDVIG: One sixty-five.

GINA: That's right. (*Marks it down*) We certainly use enough butter in this house! Then there was the sausage, and the cheese—let's see—(*Puts it down*)—and then the ham—(*Adding up*) that comes to nearly—

HEDVIG: And don't forget the beer—

GINA: Oh, yes—of course. (*Puts it down*) It mounts up all right! Well—it can't be helped!

HEDVIG: But since Father was out to dinner, we saved a bit on that.

GINA: Yes, that's true. And I took in eight fifty for those photographs.

HEDVIG: Did you? As much as that!

GINA: Yes; eight fifty exactly.

(*A pause.* GINA *picks up her sewing again.* HEDVIG *takes a pencil and a piece of paper and starts to draw, shading her eyes with her left hand.*)

HEDVIG: It's fun to think of Father at Mr. Werle's; at that grand dinner party—isn't it?

GINA: But it wasn't really Mr. Werle who invited him—it was his son. (*After a pause*) We don't have nothing to do with Mr. Werle.

HEDVIG: I do hope Father'll come home soon; I'm looking forward to it. He promised he'd ask Mrs. Sörby to give him something nice for me.

GINA: They've plenty of good things to spare in *that* house!

HEDVIG (*Goes on drawing*): I'm beginning to be a bit hungry, too.

(OLD EKDAL *comes in by the hall door. He has a paper parcel under his arm, and another parcel in his coat pocket.*)

GINA: Why Grandfather! How late you are today!

EKDAL: They'd locked the office. Had to wait in Graaberg's room. Then had to go through—hm.

HEDVIG: Grandfather—did they give you some more copying to do?

EKDAL: All of this—look!

GINA: Good!

HEDVIG: And you've got a parcel in your pocket, too.

EKDAL: Never mind that! That's nothing. (*Puts his stick away in a corner*) This'll keep me busy quite a while, Gina—eh? (*Opens one of the sliding panels in the back wall a little*) Hush! (*Peeps inside the opening for a moment and slides the panel closed again*) He-he! They've all gone to sleep together. And she's gone into her basket of her own accord. He-he!

HEDVIG: You're sure she's not cold in that basket, Grandfather?

EKDAL: What nonsense! Cold? In all that straw? (*He goes towards the farthest door on the left*) Are there any matches in there?

GINA: On the chest of drawers.

(EKDAL *goes into his room.*)

HEDVIG: I'm glad Grandfather got all that copying to do.

GINA: Yes, poor old Grandfather. At least it'll mean a little pocket money for him.

HEDVIG: And it'll keep him from hanging round that horrid bar at Mrs. Eriksen's.

GINA: That's true, too.

HEDVIG: Do you suppose they're still sitting at the dinner table, Mother?

GINA: Lord knows; I shouldn't wonder.

HEDVIG: I expect Father's having some lovely things to eat! He'll be in an awfully jolly mood when he gets home. Don't you think so, Mother?

GINA: Yes. But I wish we could tell him that room was rented.

HEDVIG: Oh, we shan't need that this evening.

GINA: It'd be a real help, you know. And we don't use it.

HEDVIG: No—I meant we won't need it this evening, because he'll be in a good mood anyway. The news about the room'll come in handy another time.

GINA (*Looks up at her*): You like having a bit of good news to tell your father, don't you?

HEDVIG: It makes things pleasanter.

GINA (*Thinks this over*): There's something in that.

(OLD EKDAL *comes in again and starts towards the door down left.*)

GINA (*Half turning in her chair*): Do you want anything in the kitchen, Grandfather?

EKDAL: I just want— No! Don't get up! (*Goes out.*)

GINA: I hope he won't go messing about the stove. (*Waits a moment*) Better go and see what he's up to, Hedvig. (EKDAL *comes in again carrying a small jug of steaming hot water.*)

HEDVIG: Did you go to get hot water, Grandfather?

EKDAL: I did—yes. Need it for something. Got to do some writing; ink's as thick as porridge—hm.

GINA: But you'll eat your supper first—won't you, Grandfather? It's in there ready for you.

EKDAL: Can't be bothered with supper, Gina. Busy, I tell you. Don't want anyone coming in my room—not anyone—hm. (*He goes into his room.* GINA *and* HEDVIG *look at each other.*)

GINA (*Softly*): Wonder where he got the money.

HEDVIG: From Graaberg, I suppose.

GINA: No! Graaberg always sends *me* his money.

HEDVIG: Then he got it on credit, I expect.

GINA: Poor Grandfather, who'd give *him* credit?

(HJALMAR EKDAL, *wearing an overcoat and a gray felt hat, comes in from the hall door.*)

GINA (*Throws down her sewing and rises*): Why, Hjalmar! Are you back so soon?

HEDVIG (*Jumps up at the same time*): Fancy your being back already, Father!

HJALMAR (*Taking off his hat*): Most of the guests were leaving.

HEDVIG: So early?

HJALMAR: Well—it was an early dinner, after all. (*Starts to take off his overcoat.*)

GINA: Let me help you.

HEDVIG: Me too! (*They help him off with his coat;* GINA *hangs it up on a hook on the back wall.*)

HEDVIG: Were there a lot of people, Father?

HJALMAR: No, not many; about twelve or fourteen, I should think.

GINA: I suppose you had a chance to talk to all of them?

HJALMAR: Yes, of course. Though I must say Gregers took up most of my time.

GINA: Is he just as plain as ever?

HJALMAR: I can't say he's particularly handsome—Isn't the old man home yet?

HEDVIG: Yes; Grandfather's in his room. He's busy writing.

HJALMAR: Did he say anything?

GINA: What about?

HJALMAR: Then he didn't mention—? I heard something about his being with Graaberg, you see. I'll just look in on him a minute.

GINA: No—I don't think I'd do that—

HJALMAR: Why not? Did he say he didn't want to see me?

GINA: He doesn't want to see *anyone* this evening—

HEDVIG (*Signaling*): Hm—hm!

GINA (*Not noticing*): He fetched himself some hot water from the kitchen.

HJALMAR: You mean he's—?

GINA: Yes—I suppose so.

HJALMAR: Ah, well! Poor old man! My poor old father! Let him be—If it makes him a little happier—!

(OLD EKDAL, *in a dressing gown and smoking a pipe, comes in from his room.*)

EKDAL: Home, are you? Thought I heard your voice.

HJALMAR: I just got back.

EKDAL: You didn't see me, did you?

HJALMAR: No; but someone told me you'd passed through —; so I thought I'd come on after you.

EKDAL: Hm. Nice of you, Hjalmar— Who were all those people?

HJALMAR: Oh, I don't know—just people. There was Court Chamberlain Balle; and then there was Flor—and Kaspersen—they're court chamberlains too—honorary, of course. I don't remember all the others—but I know most of them had titles of some sort.

EKDAL: Titled people, eh? D'you hear that, Gina?

GINA: Yes. They're very grand over there these days.

HEDVIG: What did all these titled people do, Father? Did they sing—or give recitations?

HJALMAR: No; they just talked a lot of rubbish. They tried to persuade me to recite something—but, of course, I wouldn't hear of that.

EKDAL: Wouldn't hear of that, eh?

GINA: Oh—perhaps you should have, Hjalmar.

HJALMAR: Certainly not. One shouldn't cater to every Tom, Dick and Harry. (*Paces about the room*) I don't intend to, anyhow.

EKDAL: No; Hjalmar's not that kind.

HJALMAR: I see no reason why *I* should be expected to entertain the guests, on the rare occasions when I go into Society. That's up to those other fellows; they spend their lives going from one dinner table to another, gorging and guzzling day in and day out. It's only right they should do something to earn all that good food they eat.

GINA: I hope you didn't tell them that!

HJALMAR (*Humming*): Hm-hm-hm— I think I made my position clear.

EKDAL: To all those titled people, eh?

HJALMAR: Why not? (*Casually*) We also had a slight argument about Tokay.

EKDAL: Tokay! There's a fine wine!

HJALMAR: Yes—it *can* be. It's all according to the year, of course; vintages differ. It depends on the amount of sunshine the grapes have.

GINA: Hjalmar—I believe there's nothing you don't know!

EKDAL: They surely didn't dispute that?

HJALMAR: Oh—they tried to; but they were reminded that there was a difference in the vintage of court chamberlains too; their quality also varies according to the year—so they were told.

GINA: The things you think up, Hjalmar!

EKDAL: He-he! You really gave it to them, eh?

HJALMAR: Straight in their silly faces!

EKDAL: Hear that, Gina? All those titled people! Straight in their silly faces!

GINA: Straight in their silly faces! Fancy!

HJALMAR: I wouldn't want this to go any further, mind you. It's not right to repeat things like that; and it was all perfectly amicable, of course. They're nice friendly fellows; I wouldn't want to hurt their feelings.

EKDAL: But—straight in their silly faces, eh?

HEDVIG (*Ingratiatingly*): It's nice to see you in a dinner jacket, Father. It's so becoming to you!

HJALMAR: It is, isn't it? This one fits beautifully—almost as if it had been made for me— A little tight in the armholes, perhaps. Here—help me, Hedvig. (*Takes off the dinner jacket*) I'll put on my old house coat. Where is it, Gina?

GINA: Here it is. (*Brings him the coat and helps him on with it.*)

HJALMAR: There we are! See that Molvik gets his jacket back first thing in the morning.

GINA (*Laying it away*): I'll see to it.

HJALMAR (*Stretching himself*): Ah! That feels more comfortable! And, you know—I really think a loose, casual coat like this suits my figure even better. What do *you* think, Hedvig?

HEDVIG: Yes, Father—I believe you're right!

HJALMAR: Now—I'll tie my necktie in a loose knot, with flowing ends— There! See?

HEDVIG: That looks lovely with your mustache, and your long curly hair!

HJALMAR: I don't think I'd call it *curly;* wavy, perhaps.

HEDVIG: Yes. They're too big for curls.

HJALMAR: *Wavy*—definitely.

HEDVIG (*After a pause, tugs at his coat*): Father!

HJALMAR: Well—what is it?

HEDVIG: Oh! *You* know what it is!

HJALMAR: No, I don't—

HEDVIG (*Half laughing, half whimpering*): Father—please don't tease me any longer!

HJALMAR: I don't know what you mean.

HEDVIG (*Shaking him*): Of course you do! Oh, please, Father! Aren't you going to give them to me? All those nice things you promised to bring home?

HJALMAR: Good Lord!—I forgot about them!

HEDVIG: You're only teasing me! It's mean of you! Where are they?

HJALMAR: No, honestly—I really *did* forget. But, wait! I've brought you something else. (*He goes and looks in the pockets of the dinner jacket.*)

HEDVIG (*Jumps up and down, clapping her hands*): Oh, Mother, Mother!

GINA: You see; if you're just patient—

HJALMAR (*With a piece of paper*): Look—here it is.

HEDVIG: This? But it's just a piece of paper.

HJALMAR: It's the bill of fare, that's what it is—the entire bill of fare. Do you see—it says here: menu? That means bill of fare.

HEDVIG: Is that really all you brought?

HJALMAR: I told you—I forgot. But you just take it from me—all these fancy dishes are greatly overrated. Now you sit at the table and study the bill of fare, and I'll tell you what all the dishes taste like. Won't that be fun?

HEDVIG (*Gulping down her tears*): Thanks.

(*She sits down, but doesn't read the menu.* GINA *signals to her;* HJALMAR *sees her.*)

HJALMAR (*Pacing up and down the room*): The head of the family is expected to think of everything—it's quite amazing! If by chance he forgets the slightest thing, he's immediately surrounded by glum faces. Well—one has to get used to it, I suppose. (*Stops by the stove near the old man*) Have you taken a look in there this evening, Father?

EKDAL: You bet I have! She's in her basket!

HJALMAR: No! Is she really? Then she's beginning to get used to it.

EKDAL: Told you she would, didn't I? But there are still a couple of little things—

HJALMAR: A few improvements—yes.

EKDAL: They *must* be done, you know.

HJALMAR: Yes—let's just go over them. We'll sit here on the sofa.

EKDAL: All right. Hm. First I'll fill my pipe. Got to clean it, too. Hm. (*Goes into his room.*)

GINA (*Smiles, to* HJALMAR): His pipe, indeed!

HJALMAR: Leave him alone, Gina—never mind! Poor wretched old man!—About those improvements—yes. I think I'll have a go at them tomorrow.

GINA: You won't have time tomorrow, Hjalmar.

HEDVIG: Oh yes he will, Mother!

GINA: Those prints have got to be retouched; they've sent for them several times, you know.

HJALMAR: Oh do stop nagging me about those prints! I'll get them done. Anything happen today? Any new orders?

GINA: No; I'm afraid not. I have those two sittings for tomorrow, though.

HJALMAR: And that's all, eh? Of course—if no one makes the smallest effort—

GINA: But what more can I do? I've advertised in several papers—all we could afford.

HJALMAR: Advertising! A lot of good *that* does! And what about the room? I suppose nothing's happened about that either?

GINA: Not yet, no.

HJALMAR: What else can one expect? Rooms don't rent themselves! Everything requires a little effort, Gina!

HEDVIG (*Going towards him*): Would you like me to fetch your flute, Father?

HJALMAR: No thanks. No flute for me; no pleasures of any sort for *me*. (*Pacing about*) All I have to look forward to is *work*. As long as my strength holds out, I suppose I'll have to keep on working—!

GINA: Hjalmar dear—I didn't mean—

HEDVIG: Let me get you a nice bottle of beer, Father.

HJALMAR: No; not for me. I require nothing—(*Stops*) Beer?—Beer did you say?

HEDVIG (*Cheerfully*): Yes, Father. Nice, cool beer.

HJALMAR: Oh, very well—if you insist; you might bring in a bottle.

GINA: Yes, do. That would be very nice.

(HEDVIG *runs towards the kitchen door.*)

HJALMAR (*By the stove, stops her, puts his arm round her and draws her to him*): Hedvig! Hedvig!

HEDVIG (*With tears of joy*): Dear, *darling* Father!

HJALMAR: No—don't call me that. I sat there at the rich man's table—stuffing myself at that festive board—and I couldn't even—!

GINA (*Sitting at the table*): Oh, don't talk nonsense, Hjalmar!

HJALMAR: No—it's not nonsense! But don't be too hard on me. You know how much I love you—

HEDVIG (*Throws her arms round him*): And we love you too, Father! More than we can ever say!

HJALMAR: And remember—if I'm difficult at times—it's because I have so many problems—so many cares. There,
there! (*Dries his eyes*) No! No beer at a time like this—
give me my flute. (HEDVIG *runs to the bookshelf and
fetches it.*) Thanks! There! That's right—my flute in my
hand, and you two at my side—!

(HEDVIG *sits at the table near* GINA; HJALMAR *walks up
and down and starts to play with gusto; it is a Bohe-
mian peasant dance; his tempo is slow and plaintive and
his attack highly sentimental. He breaks off in the middle
of the tune, gives his left hand to* GINA *and says emotion-
ally*) Our rooms may be poor and humble, Gina—but
they're home all the same. And I can say from the bottom
of my heart: it's good to be here!

(*He starts to play again; soon after there is a knock at the
hall door.*)

GINA (*Rises*): Just a minute, Hjalmar. I think there's someone at the door.

HJALMAR (*Puts the flute back on the shelf*): What can it
be? How tiresome!

(GINA *goes and opens the door.*)

GREGERS: Excuse me—

GINA (*Takes a step back*): Oh!

GREGERS: Does Mr. Ekdal, the photographer, live here?

GINA: Yes, he does.

HJALMAR (*Going towards the door*): Gregers! So you came
after all. Well—come in then.

GREGERS (*Coming in*): I said I'd come to see you.

HJALMAR: Yes, but this evening—? Did you leave the party?

GREGERS: Both the party and my father's house— Good
evening; do you recognize me, Mrs. Ekdal?

GINA: It's not hard to recognize young Mr. Werle.

GREGERS: That's true—I'm very like my mother; you remember her, I expect?

HJALMAR: Left your father's house you say?

GREGERS: Yes; I've gone to a hotel.

HJALMAR: Have you really? Well—since you're here, sit down; take off your things.

GREGERS: Thanks. (*He takes off his overcoat. He has changed his clothes and now wears a plain tweed suit.*)

HJALMAR: Here—sit on the sofa. Make yourself at home. (GREGERS *sits on the sofa,* HJALMAR *on a chair by the table.*)

GREGERS (*Looking round*): So this is your home, Hjalmar. This is where you live.

HJALMAR: Yes; this is the studio, of course—

GINA: But it's such a nice large room—we nearly always sit here.

HJALMAR: We had a better place before; but this has great advantages; there's a lot of extra space—

GINA: And there's another room we can rent out—just down the passage.

GREGERS: Oh—you have lodgers then?

HJALMAR: Well—not just now. They're not so easy to find, you know; you have to keep your wits about you. (*To* HEDVIG) We might have that beer now. (HEDVIG *nods and goes out to the kitchen.*)

GREGERS: Is that your daughter?

HJALMAR: That's Hedvig, yes.

GREGERS: Is she your only child?

HJALMAR: Yes; she's the only one. She's our greatest joy, and—(*Lowers his voice*) our greatest sorrow too.

GREGERS: How do you mean?

HJALMAR: She's in danger of losing her eyesight, you see.

GREGERS: Of going blind!

HJALMAR: Yes; so far her eyes are not too seriously affected, and they may continue to be all right for a while; but eventually, the doctor says, it's bound to come.

GREGERS: What a dreadful thing! Has he any idea what caused it?

HJALMAR (*Sighs*): It may be hereditary, he thinks.

GREGERS (*With a slight start*): Hereditary?

GINA: Hjalmar's mother's eyes were bad, you see.

HJALMAR: So Father says; I don't remember her.

GREGERS: Poor child!—How does she take it?

HJALMAR: We naturally haven't told her anything about it; she suspects nothing. She's like a gay, carefree little bird, twittering away as it flutters towards the inevitable darkness. (*Overcome*) It's a terrible grief for me; it's heartbreaking to think of, Gregers.

(HEDVIG *brings in a tray with beer and glasses and puts it on the table.*)

HJALMAR (*Stroking her hair*): Thank you, Hedvig, thank you!

(HEDVIG *puts her arm round his neck and whispers in his ear.*)

HJALMAR: No—no sandwiches now. (*Looks at* GREGERS) Unless you'd like one, Gregers?

GREGERS (*With a gesture of refusal*): No—no thank you.

HJALMAR (*Still melancholy*): You might bring a few anyway—especially if there's a nice crusty piece of bread. And don't spare the butter, will you?

(HEDVIG *nods gaily and goes out to the kitchen.*)

GREGERS (*Who has been following her with his eyes*): She seems so strong and healthy otherwise.

GINA: There's nothing wrong with her apart from that, thank goodness.

GREGERS: She'll grow up to look like you—don't you think so, Mrs. Ekdal? How old is she now?

GINA: Nearly fourteen; her birthday's the day after tomorrow.

GREGERS: Tall for her age, isn't she?

GINA: She's shot up very fast in the past year.

GREGERS: It makes one feel old to see the youngsters growing up. How long is it now since you were married?

GINA: Let's see—we've been married nearly fifteen years.

GREGERS: Really! Is it as long as that?

GINA (*Becoming attentive; looks at him*): It is indeed.

HJALMAR: That's right. Fifteen years—all but a few months. (*Changing the subject*) They must have been long years for you, Gregers—up there at the Works.

GREGERS: They seemed long at the time; yet in looking back at them, they went by very quickly.

(OLD EKDAL *comes in from his room, without his pipe, but wearing his old military cap; his walk is a bit unsteady.*)

EKDAL: All right, Hjalmar my boy—I'm ready now to talk about those—hm. What was it we were supposed to talk about?

HJALMAR (*Goes to him*): Father—we have a visitor; Gregers Werle—I don't know if you remember him—

EKDAL (*Looks at* GREGERS, *who has risen*): Werle? The son is it? What does he want with me?

HJALMAR: Nothing; he came to see me, Father.

EKDAL: Oh. Then there's nothing wrong?

HJALMAR: Of course not.

EKDAL (*Waves his arms*): Not that I'm afraid, you know—but—

GREGERS (*Goes over to him*): I bring you greetings from your old hunting grounds, Lieutenant Ekdal.

EKDAL: Hunting grounds?

GREGERS: Yes—up by the Höjdal Works; remember?

EKDAL: Oh, up there. I was well known in those parts once.

GREGERS: You were a mighty hunter in those days.

EKDAL: I was; that's true enough! You're looking at my cap, I see. I ask no one's permission to wear it in the house. As long as I don't walk about the streets in it—

(HEDVIG *brings in a plate of sandwiches and sets it on the table.*)

HJALMAR: Sit down, Father; have a glass of beer. Help yourself, Gregers.

(EKDAL *mutters something and stumbles over to the sofa,* GREGERS *sits on the chair nearest to him, and* HJALMAR *on the other side of* GREGERS. GINA *sits slightly away from the table with her sewing;* HEDVIG *stands by her father.*)

GREGERS: Do you remember, Lieutenant Ekdal, how Hjalmar and I used to come up and visit you—in the summer, and at Christmas?

EKDAL: Did you? No—I don't remember that. Yes—I was a mighty hunter in my day. Shot bears too. Nine of them.

GREGERS (*Looks at him sympathetically*): I suppose you don't go hunting any more.

EKDAL: I wouldn't say that, my friend. I still get a bit of hunting now and then. Not *that* kind, of course. For the forest, you see—the forest—! (*Drinks*) Is the forest up there just as fine as ever?

GREGERS: Not as fine as it was in your time. It's been thinned out quite a bit.

EKDAL: Thinned out, eh? (*Softly, as though afraid*) That's a dangerous business. That brings trouble. The forest takes revenge, you see.

HJALMAR (*Filling his glass*): Have a little more, Father.

GREGERS: It must be hard on a man like you—a man used to the open—to live in a stuffy town, cooped up in a little room—

EKDAL (*Laughs and glances at* HJALMAR): Oh, it's really not so bad here. No. Not bad at all.

GREGERS: But don't you miss the open spaces—the cool sweep of the wind through the trees—and all the animals and birds—?

EKDAL (*Smiles*): Let's show it to him, Hjalmar.

HJALMAR (*Hastily, with some embarrassment*): No—not this evening, Father.

GREGERS: What is it he wants to show me?

HJALMAR: Oh, nothing—you can see it some other time.

GREGERS (*Goes on talking to the old man*): Do you know what I was thinking, Lieutenant Ekdal? Why don't you come up to the Works with me? I expect to be going back there soon. They'll have plenty of copying for you to do up there, I'm sure. This is no place for you. You've nothing here to cheer you up—or keep you interested.

EKDAL (*Looks at him in amazement*): Nothing here to keep me—!

GREGERS: You have Hjalmar here I know; but he has his own work to attend to. And a man like you—accustomed to an active outdoor life—

EKDAL (*Thumps the table*): Hjalmar—he's *got* to see it!

HJALMAR: This is a bad time, Father. It's dark, remember—

EKDAL: Nonsense! There's the moonlight, isn't there? (*Rises*) I tell you he *must* see it! Let me get by. Hjalmar—come and help me!

HEDVIG: Yes—*do*, Father!

HJALMAR (*Rising*): Oh—very well.

GREGERS (*To* GINA): What can it be?

GINA: It's nothing very wonderful—!

(EKDAL *and* HJALMAR *have gone to the back wall and each opens his side of the sliding door.* HEDVIG *helps the old man;* GREGERS *remains standing by the sofa;* GINA *continues sewing undisturbed. Through the opening one sees a large, deep, irregularly shaped attic, filled with nooks and corners; a couple of stovepipes run through it from the rooms below. There are skylights through which the moon shines brightly on parts of the big room—while other parts are in deep shadow.*)

EKDAL (*To* GREGERS): Come closer, if you like.

GREGERS (*Going over to them*): What is it I'm supposed to see?

EKDAL: Take a good look now! Hm.

HJALMAR (*Somewhat embarrassed*): All this belongs to Father—you realize that, of course.

GREGERS (*At the opening peers into the attic*): Oh! I *see*, Lieutenant Ekdal—you keep poultry!

EKDAL: I should say we *do* keep poultry! They've gone to roost now—but you should see our hens by daylight!

HEDVIG: And then there's—

EKDAL: Sh! Not a word about that yet!

GREGERS: And I see doves there, too.

EKDAL: Yes! There are doves there right enough! Their nesting boxes are up under the eaves. Doves like to roost high, you know.

HJALMAR: They're not a common variety, by any means; at least not all of them.

EKDAL: Common! No indeed! We have tumblers—and a pair of pouters too. And now—look here! You see that hutch over by the wall?

GREGERS: What's that used for?

EKDAL: That, Sir, is where the rabbits sleep at night.

GREGERS: Then you have rabbits, too?

EKDAL: I should damn well say we *do* have rabbits! He wants to know if we have rabbits, Hjalmar! Hm. But just you wait! We're coming to the *real* thing now! Out of the way, Hedvig! Now you stand here—that's it. And look down there— Do you see a basket there with straw in it?

GREGERS: Yes—and isn't there a bird there, too?

EKDAL: Hm. "A bird," he says—!

GREGERS: It's a duck, isn't it?

EKDAL (*Annoyed*): Yes—it's a duck; that's clear!

HJALMAR: But what *kind* of a duck do you think?

HEDVIG: It's not just an *ordinary* duck, you know—

EKDAL: Sh!

GREGERS: And it doesn't look like a Muscovy duck, either.

EKDAL: No—it's no Muscovy duck, dear Mr. Werle. It happens to be a *wild* duck, you see.

GREGERS: A wild duck! Is it really?

EKDAL: That's what it is! That "bird," as you called it, that is the wild duck. It's our wild duck, Sir.

HEDVIG: *My* wild duck. It belongs to me.

GREGERS: How does it manage in there? Is it all right?

EKDAL: It has its own trough of water, of course, to splash about in.

HJALMAR: And we change the water every other day.

GINA (*Turning towards* HJALMAR): It's getting to be freezing in here, Hjalmar dear.

HJALMAR: Let's close her up, then. Anyway—they don't like

to be disturbed at night. Go on, Hedvig—close her up!
(HJALMAR *and* HEDVIG *close the sliding doors.*)

EKDAL: You'll be able to see her better some other time.
(*Sits in the armchair by the stove*) Remarkable creatures
those wild ducks, I can tell you!

GREGERS: How did you manage to catch it, Lieutenant Ekdal?

EKDAL: I didn't catch it myself. There's a certain man here
in town, you see—we have him to thank for that.

GREGERS (*With a slight start*): That man wasn't my father,
by any chance?

EKDAL: Your father—that's it; he's the man. Hm.

HJALMAR: Strange that you should guess that, Gregers!

GREGERS: You were telling me how much you owed to Father—in many different ways, you said; so I thought, perhaps—

GINA: But Mr. Werle didn't actually give us the duck himself—

EKDAL: Still, Gina—Haakon Werle is the man we have to
thank for her. (*To* GREGERS) He was out shooting in a
boat. He fired at her and brought her down. But his sight
isn't too good now, you see—and so he only winged her.
Hm.

GREGERS: But she was wounded, I suppose?

HJALMAR: Oh yes—she had some shot in her.

HEDVIG: Her wing was broken, poor thing; she couldn't fly.

GREGERS: Did she dive to the bottom then?

EKDAL (*Sleepily, with thickened speech*): Course she did!
Always do that—wild ducks do. Make straight for the
bottom—as far as they can go. Then they get trapped
down there among the slimy roots and tangled reeds—and
they never come up again.

GREGERS: But *your* wild duck came up again, Lieutenant
Ekdal.

EKDAL: Had an amazingly clever dog, your father had. That
dog—he dived down after her and brought her back.

GREGERS (*Turning to* HJALMAR): And then they gave her to
you?

HJALMAR: No; not at once. First they took her to your father's house; but she started to pine away—so Pettersen was told to put an end to her—

EKDAL (*Half asleep*): That ass Pettersen—hm—

HJALMAR (*Lowers his voice*): And that's how we happened to get hold of her. Father knows Pettersen quite well, so when he heard about the wild duck he persuaded him to let *us* have her.

GREGERS: And the attic seems to agree with her, does it? She's doing well in there?

HJALMAR: Remarkably well—amazing, isn't it? She's grown quite plump, and she doesn't seem to miss her freedom. She's been there some time now, and I suppose she's forgotten all about it; that's what counts, you know.

GREGERS: I expect you're right; as long as she's kept away from the sky and the water—and has nothing to remind her— But I must be going now. Your father's gone to sleep, I think.

HJALMAR: Don't go on that account—

GREGERS: Oh, by the way—did you say you had an extra room? A room to rent, I mean?

HJALMAR: Yes, we have. Do you know anyone who—?

GREGERS: Would you let me have it?

HJALMAR: You?

GINA: Oh no, Mr. Werle, you—

GREGERS: If so, I'll move in first thing tomorrow morning.

HJALMAR: We'd be delighted!

GINA: But, Mr. Werle—it's not *your* kind of room—*really* it's not!

HJALMAR: What are you talking about, Gina?

GINA: I mean—it wouldn't be big enough, or light enough—

GREGERS: That doesn't matter, Mrs. Ekdal.

HJALMAR: It seems like a very nice room to me! And not badly furnished either.

GINA: How about those two fellows underneath?

GREGERS: What fellows?

GINA: There's one that says he's been a tutor—

HJALMAR: That's Molvik—Mr. Molvik—a B.A.

GINA: And the other one calls himself a doctor; his name's Relling.

GREGERS: Relling? I think I know him slightly. He had a practice up at Höjdal for a while.

GINA: Well—they're a no-good, rowdy lot! Out till all hours every night—drinking themselves silly—

GREGERS: I shan't mind them; I'll soon get used to it. I'll try to be as adaptable as the wild duck—

GINA: All the same—you'd better sleep on it.

GREGERS: You don't seem very anxious to have me as a lodger, Mrs. Ekdal.

GINA: Who, *me?* Why do you say that?

HJALMAR: I must say, Gina—you're being very odd about it. (*To* GREGERS) You plan to stay in town then—for the present?

GREGERS: That's what I've decided, yes.

HJALMAR: Not at your father's house, though? What do you plan to do?

GREGERS: I only wish I knew. When one has the misfortune to bear the name of "Gregers," followed by the name of "Werle"—a pretty hideous combination, don't you think?

HJALMAR: I don't think so at all.

GREGERS: Pah! I'd feel like spitting on a man with a name like that! But since I'm doomed to go on being Gregers Werle in this world—

HJALMAR (*Laughs*): Ha! Ha! Well—if you weren't Gregers Werle, what would you choose to be?

GREGERS: I think I'd choose to be a clever dog.

GINA: A dog!

HEDVIG (*Involuntarily*): Oh, no!

GREGERS: Yes, a very clever dog; the kind that plunges after wild ducks when they dive to the bottom, and get trapped down in the mud.

HJALMAR: That's beyond me, Gregers! What *are* you driving at?

GREGERS: Just nonsense; never mind. I'll move in early tomor-

row morning then. (*To* GINA) I won't be any trouble; I'm
used to doing things myself. (*To* HJALMAR) We'll discuss
details tomorrow— Good night, Mrs. Ekdal. (*Nods to* HED-
VIG) Good night!

GINA: Good night, Mr. Werle.

HEDVIG: Good night.

HJALMAR (*Who has lighted a candle*): Wait; I'll see you
out. The stairs are rather dark.

(GREGERS *and* HJALMAR *go out by the hall door*.)

GINA (*Sits with her sewing in her lap gazing before her*):
What a queer thing to say—that he'd like to be a dog.

HEDVIG: You know, Mother—I think he really meant something quite different.

GINA: What else *could* he have meant?

HEDVIG: I don't know; but it's almost as though everything he
said *really* meant something different.

GINA: Do you think so? Well—it seems very queer to me.

HJALMAR (*Comes back*): The lamp down in the hall was still
alight. (*Blows out the candle and puts it down*) Ah! Now,
perhaps we can have a bite to eat! (*Starts to eat the sandwiches*) You see, Gina, what happens when you keep your
wits about you—?

GINA: What do you mean—"wits about you"?

HJALMAR: We rented the room, didn't we? And to an old
friend like Gregers, too.

GINA: I don't know what to think of that.

HEDVIG: It'll be fun, Mother—you'll see!

HJALMAR: You really are amazing! I thought you were so
hipped on renting it—and now you behave as if you didn't
want to.

GINA: If it had only been to someone else— What will Mr.
Werle say I wonder.

HJALMAR: Old Werle? It's no business of his.

GINA: I expect they've been quarreling again; otherwise
young Werle would never have left home. You know
they've never been able to get on together.

HJALMAR: That may be, but still—

GINA: You never know; Mr. Werle may think it's all your doing.

HJALMAR: Well—let him! Mr. Werle's done a lot for me—
God knows I'm the first one to admit it—but he can't expect me to go on kowtowing to him for ever!

GINA: But—Hjalmar dear—he might take it out on Grandfather; he might tell Graaberg not to give him any more
copying to do.

HJALMAR: I could almost say: I wish he would! You don't
seem to understand how humiliating it is for a man like
me to see his old father treated like a servant. But some
day the pendulum will swing the other way; it won't be
long now—I feel it! (*Takes another sandwich*) I have a
sacred duty in life, and I intend to perform it to the full!

HEDVIG: You will, Father! I know you will!

GINA: Hush! Don't wake him!

HJALMAR (*Lowers his voice*): To the *full,* I say! There'll
come a day when— That's another reason why I'm glad
we've rented the room, you see. It'll make me a bit more independent. A man needs independence if he's to face the
task *I* have to face. (*By the armchair; with emotion*)
Poor white-haired old man!—Don't you be afraid—lean on
your Hjalmar; his shoulders are broad. They're strong, at
any rate. One of these fine days you'll wake up to see—
(*To* GINA) Don't you believe me?

GINA (*Rising*): Yes, of course I do. But let's get him to bed.

HJALMAR: Yes—very well.

(*They lift up the old man carefully.*)

CURTAIN

ACT
THREE

SCENE: HJALMAR EKDAL's *studio. It is morning; daylight streams through the large window in the slanting roof, and the curtain is drawn back.* HJALMAR *sits at the table busy retouching a photograph; several others lie before him. After a few moments* GINA *comes in through the hall door, wearing a hat and coat and with a basket on her arm.*

HJALMAR: Back already, Gina?

GINA: Yes; I've no time for dawdling.

HJALMAR: Did you look in at Gregers?

GINA: I certainly did! You should just see the mess in there! He's made a good start, he has!

HJALMAR: Why? What's he done?

GINA: Used to doing things for himself, says he! So he lights the stove, but leaves the damper shut: the whole room's filled with smoke. The smell in there's enough to—

HJALMAR: Oh, dear!

GINA: But that isn't the worst of it: he decides to put the fire *out* again; so what does he do but take the pitcher from his washstand and empty every blessed drop of water right into the stove! The floor's a mess!

HJALMAR: What a nuisance.

GINA: I got the porter's wife to come and clean it up for him —the pig! But it'll be afternoon before the place is fit to live in.

HJALMAR: What's Gregers doing now?

GINA: He went out for a bit.

HJALMAR: While you were gone, I stopped in to see him too.

GINA: I know; you've asked him to lunch, I hear.

146

HJALMAR: Not *lunch* exactly—more of a snack, you know. After all, it's his first day here—I didn't know what else to do. You must have something in the house.

GINA: I'll have to try and find something, I suppose.

HJALMAR: Don't be *too* skimpy, though. Relling and Molvik are coming too, I think. I ran into Relling on the stairs, and I couldn't very well—

GINA: Oh dear! Do we have to have *them* too?

HJALMAR: Good heavens—one more or less—what difference does it make?

EKDAL (*Opens his door and looks in*): Look here, Hjalmar— (*Sees* GINA) Oh.

GINA: Anything you want, Grandfather?

EKDAL: No, no. It doesn't matter. Hm! (*Goes into his room again.*)

GINA (*Picking up her basket*): Don't let him go out will you? Keep an eye on him.

HJALMAR: All right, all right—I will. Oh, Gina; some herring salad might be just the thing: Relling and Molvik were on a bit of a spree last night.

GINA: Just so long as they don't get here before I'm ready.

HJALMAR: Of course they won't. Just take your time.

GINA: Very well; meanwhile you can get a bit of work done.

HJALMAR: Work! I *am* working, aren't I? What more can I do?

GINA: I just meant—the sooner you get it done, the sooner it'll be over with. (*She takes the basket and goes out to the kitchen.* HJALMAR *sits for a few moments working reluctantly on the photograph.*)

EKDAL (*Peeps in, looks round the studio, and says softly*): Are you busy, Hjalmar?

HJALMAR: Slaving away at these blasted pictures—!

EKDAL: Well—never mind; as long as you're busy—Hm! (*He goes into his room again but leaves the door open.*)

HJALMAR (*Goes on working for some time in silence, then lays down his brush and goes over to the open door*): Are *you* busy, Father?

EKDAL (*In a low growl, from his room*): If *you're* busy then
I'm busy too. Hm.

HJALMAR: Yes; very well. (*Goes back to his work.*)

EKDAL (*Presently, coming to the door again*): Hm. Hjalmar,
I'm not as busy as all *that,* you know.

HJALMAR: I thought you were writing.

EKDAL: To hell with it! It's not a matter of life and death, after all. It won't hurt Graaberg to wait a day or two.

HJALMAR: No; and you're not his slave, either.

EKDAL: There's that job in there, you see—

HJALMAR: Just what *I* was thinking of. Would you like to go
in? I'll open up for you.

EKDAL: It mightn't be a bad idea.

HJALMAR (*Rises*): Then we'd have it all done, wouldn't
we?

EKDAL: And we've got to finish it before tomorrow morning.
It *is* tomorrow, isn't it? Hm?

HJALMAR: Of course it's tomorrow.

(HJALMAR *and* EKDAL *each pull open a side of the sliding
door. Inside the attic the morning sun pours through the
skylights; some doves are flying about, others sit cooing on
their perches; the clucking of hens can be heard farther
back in the attic.*)

HJALMAR: There! Now you can get to work, Father.

EKDAL (*Goes into the attic*): Aren't you coming too?

HJALMAR: Well, you know—Yes! I believe I— (*Sees* GINA
at the kitchen door) No, no! I can't—haven't time! Too
much work to do! How about our new invention, though?
(*He pulls a cord and a curtain drops inside the opening;
the lower part consists of an old piece of sailcloth, the
upper part of a piece of fishing net. The floor of the attic
is now concealed*) There! Now perhaps I can have a little
peace!

GINA: Must he go messing about in there again?

HJALMAR: Would you rather he'd run off to Mrs. Eriksen's?
(*Sits down*) What is it you want? I thought you said—

GINA: I wanted to ask—will it be all right to lay the table for lunch in here?

HJALMAR: Why not? There aren't any appointments, are there?

GINA: Just that engaged couple; you know—the two that want to be photographed together.

HJALMAR: Why the devil can't they be photographed together some *other* day?

GINA: It's all right, Hjalmar dear. I told them to come in the late afternoon; you'll be taking your nap by then.

HJALMAR: That's good; we'll eat in here then.

GINA: Very well; but there's no hurry—you can go on using the table for a good while yet.

HJALMAR: I'm using it—don't worry! I'm using it for all I'm worth!

GINA: Then, later on—you'll be free, you see. (*She goes into the kitchen. A short pause.*)

EKDAL (*In the doorway of the attic, behind the net*): Hjalmar!

HJALMAR: Well?

EKDAL: Afraid we'll have to move that water trough—

HJALMAR: I said so all along.

EKDAL: Hm-hm-hm. (*Goes away from the door again.* HJALMAR *goes on working a little, then glances towards the attic and starts to rise.* HEDVIG *comes in from the kitchen.*)

HJALMAR (*Sits down again hurriedly*): What do you want?

HEDVIG: Just to be with you, Father.

HJALMAR: What are you snooping about in here for? Were you told to keep an eye on me?

HEDVIG: Of course not.

HJALMAR: What's your mother up to now?

HEDVIG: She's busy making the herring salad. (*Goes over to the table*) Father—isn't there anything I can do to help?

HJALMAR: No, no. I'll carry on alone as long as my strength holds out. Never you fear, Hedvig; while your father keeps his health—

HEDVIG: Father! I won't have you say such awful things! (*She wanders about the room a little, stops by the doorway, and looks into the attic.*)

HJALMAR: What's he doing? Can you see?

HEDVIG: Making a new runway to the water trough, I think.

HJALMAR: He'll never manage that alone! And here I have to sit—*chained* to this—!

HEDVIG (*Goes to him*): Give me the brush, Father. I do it quite well, you know.

HJALMAR: Nonsense! You'd only hurt your eyes.

HEDVIG: No, I wouldn't—really! Please give me the brush.

HJALMAR (*Rises*): It'll only take a minute—

HEDVIG: What's the harm, then? (*Takes the brush*) There! (*Sits down*) I'll use this one as a model.

HJALMAR: Don't strain your eyes, do you hear? And remember, I'm not responsible; you're doing this on your own responsibility you understand!

HEDVIG (*Starts retouching*): Of course.

HJALMAR: You're very good at it. I'll only be a minute. (*He slips through the side of the curtain into the attic.* HEDVIG *sits at her work.* HJALMAR *and* EKDAL *are heard arguing.*)

HJALMAR (*Appears behind the net*): Hedvig—would you hand me those pincers on the shelf; and the chisel, too. (*Turning back to the attic*) You'll see, Father— Now just let me show you what I mean! (HEDVIG *has fetched the tools from the shelf and hands them in to him.*) Thanks. It's a good thing I got here when I did! (*Goes away from the opening; they can be heard carpentering and talking inside.* HEDVIG *stands watching them. A moment later there's a knock at the hall door; she doesn't hear it.*)

GREGERS (*Bareheaded and without an overcoat comes in and stops near the door*): Hm—!

HEDVIG (*Turns and goes towards him*): Good morning. Do come in.

GREGERS: Thanks. (*Looks toward the attic*) Have you workmen in the house?

HEDVIG: No; it's only Father and Grandfather. I'll call them.

GREGERS: No, don't. I'd rather wait a little. (*Sits down on the sofa.*)

HEDVIG: It's so untidy here— (*Starts clearing away the photographs.*)

GREGERS: Never mind—don't bother! Are those the prints that need retouching?

HEDVIG: Yes; I was just helping Father with them.

GREGERS: Don't let me disturb you.

HEDVIG: No—you won't. (*She gathers the things together and sits down to work;* GREGERS *watches her in silence.*)

GREGERS: Did the wild duck sleep well last night?

HEDVIG: Yes, thank you; I think so.

GREGERS (*Turning and looking towards the attic*): How different it looks by day; quite different than by moonlight.

HEDVIG: Yes—it changes all the time. In the morning it's not a bit the same as it is in the afternoon; and it looks quite different on rainy days from the way it looks when the sun shines.

GREGERS: You've noticed that, have you?

HEDVIG: Of course; how could I help it?

GREGERS: Do you spend much time in there with the wild duck?

HEDVIG: I go in whenever I can manage it—

GREGERS: I expect you're pretty busy. You go to school, I suppose?

HEDVIG: No—not any more; Father's afraid I'll hurt my eyes.

GREGERS: Does he give you lessons himself then?

HEDVIG: He promised to; but so far he hasn't had time.

GREGERS: Is there nobody else who could help you with your studies?

HEDVIG: There's Mr. Molvik; but he's not always—

GREGERS: Sober, you mean?

HEDVIG: Yes—I suppose that's it.

GREGERS: Then you've a good deal of spare time, haven't you? I should think it must be a world all to itself in there.

HEDVIG: Oh, it is! And it's full of the most wonderful things too!

GREGERS: Is it really?

HEDVIG: Yes. There are great big cupboards filled with books; and lots of them have pictures in them.

GREGERS: Aha!

HEDVIG: And there's an old desk with drawers and pigeon-holes; and a great big clock with figures that used to pop in and out. But the clock's stopped—so they don't work any more.

GREGERS: Time has ceased to exist in the wild duck's world.

HEDVIG: And there's an old paintbox too—and lots of other things; and all the books, of course.

GREGERS: And you read the books, I suppose?

HEDVIG: Whenever I can I do. But most of them are in English, and I don't understand English, you see. Still—I look at the pictures. There's one very large book—*Harrison's History of London* it's called—it must be a hundred years old, I should think. That has lots of pictures in it. On the front page there's a picture of death holding an hourglass —and he has a lady with him. That one's horrid, I think. But there are heaps of others; pictures of churches, and castles, and streets, and great ships sailing on the sea.

GREGERS: Where did all these wonderful things come from?

HEDVIG: An old sea captain lived here once, and he must have brought them home with him. They used to call him "The Flying Dutchman"; and that was funny, because he wasn't Dutch at all, you know.

GREGERS: Wasn't he?

HEDVIG: No. Then he went away, and never came back—and the things just stayed here.

GREGERS: Tell me—when you sit in there looking at those pictures—don't you ever long to travel, and see something of the world yourself?

HEDVIG: Oh, no! I want to stay home always and help Father and Mother.

GREGERS: To retouch photographs?

HEDVIG: No—not only that. Do you know what I'd *really*

like to do? I'd like to learn engraving; then I could make pictures like the ones in all those books.

GREGERS: Hm. What does your father say to that?

HEDVIG: He doesn't like the idea at all; Father's funny in some ways. He keeps talking about my learning basket weaving and wickerwork! I don't think that'd be much fun, do you?

GREGERS: No—I shouldn't think so.

HEDVIG: Still—in a way he's right; he says if I'd learned basketwork I could have made the wild duck its new basket.

GREGERS: That's true enough; you'd have been the logical one to do it, after all.

HEDVIG: Yes—because it's *my* wild duck, you see.

GREGERS: Of course it is.

HEDVIG: Yes, it belongs to me. But when Father and Grandfather want it, I don't mind lending it to them, you know.

GREGERS: What do they do with it?

HEDVIG: Oh, they look after it, and build things for it; all that sort of thing.

GREGERS: I'm not surprised; she's the most important creature in there!

HEDVIG: Indeed she is! After all, she's a *real* wild bird. And it must be so sad for her to be there all by herself.

GREGERS: She has no family, like the rabbits—

HEDVIG: No. And the hens, too; lots of them were hatched at the same time and were little chicks together. But she has no one belonging to her, poor thing. She's a complete stranger; no one knows where she came from—no one knows anything about her.

GREGERS: And then, too—she was rescued from the boundless deep, remember!

HEDVIG (*Glances at him swiftly and represses a smile*): What makes you call it the boundless deep?

GREGERS: What would you have me call it?

HEDVIG: Most people would say "from under the water" or "from the bottom of the sea."

GREGERS: But *I* prefer the boundless deep.

HEDVIG: It sounds funny to hear somebody else say that.

GREGERS: Why? What do you mean?

HEDVIG: Nothing. You'd only laugh at me.

GREGERS: Of course I wouldn't. Tell me—what made you smile? Go on!

HEDVIG: It's just that whenever I think of that place in there —suddenly—unexpectedly, you know—I think of it as the boundless deep. It *feels* like that, somehow. You must think me awfully silly!

GREGERS: No—don't say that!

HEDVIG: After all—it's only an old attic.

GREGERS (*Looks at her intently*): Are you so sure?

HEDVIG (*Astonished*): That it's an attic?

GREGERS: Yes. How can you be so certain?

(HEDVIG *is silent and looks at him open-mouthed.* GINA *comes in from the kitchen with a tablecloth.*)

GREGERS (*Rising*): I'm afraid I came too early.

GINA: You have to be somewhere, I suppose. We're nearly ready now. Clear off the table, Hedvig.

(HEDVIG *obeys; she and* GINA *lay the table during the following.* GREGERS *sits in the armchair looking through a photograph album.*)

GREGERS: I hear you've done quite a bit of retouching, Mrs. Ekdal.

GINA (*With a sidelong glance*): Yes, I have.

GREGERS: A lucky coincidence, wasn't it?

GINA: Why lucky?

GREGERS: Since Hjalmar's a photographer, I mean.

HEDVIG: And Mother can take pictures too.

GINA: I more or less *had* to take it up.

GREGERS: Then I suppose it's you who really runs the business?

GINA: When Hjalmar has too many other things to do, I—

GREGERS: I dare say his father takes up a good deal of his time.

GINA: Yes; and this is no fit job for Hjalmar anyway—wasting his time taking pictures of a lot of silly people!

GREGERS: I quite agree; but once having chosen it as his profession—

GINA: He's no *ordinary* photographer, mind you! I'm sure you understand that, Mr. Werle.

GREGERS: Yes, of course, but still—

(*A shot is heard from the attic.*)

GREGERS (*Starting up*): What's that?

GINA: There they go—at that shooting again!

GREGERS: Do you mean to say they shoot in there?

HEDVIG: They're out hunting, you see.

GREGERS: What! (*Goes to the door of the attic*) Are you out hunting, Hjalmar?

HJALMAR (*From inside the net*): Oh, you've come. I didn't know. I was so taken up with—(*To* HEDVIG) Why didn't you call us? (*Comes into the studio.*)

GREGERS: Do you mean to tell me you go shooting in the attic?

HJALMAR (*Showing a double-barreled pistol*): Only with this old thing.

GINA: You and Grandfather'll get into trouble one of these days—fooling with that gun.

HJALMAR (*Irritably*): How often have I told you—this weapon is a *pistol*.

GINA: I don't see that that makes it any better.

GREGERS: Well, Hjalmar—so you've become a hunter too!

HJALMAR: We do a little rabbit shooting now and then. It pleases the old man, you know.

GINA: Men are a queer lot! Must have their divergence!

HJALMAR (*Angrily*): Diversion—I suppose you mean!

GINA: That's what I said, isn't it?

HJALMAR: Well—! Hm. (*To* GREGERS) It works out very well; the attic's so high up, no one can hear the shooting. (*Lays the pistol on the top shelf of the bookcase*) Mind you don't touch the pistol, Hedvig. One of the barrels is still loaded; remember that.

GREGERS (*Peering through the net*): You have a rifle too, I see.

HJALMAR: It's an old gun of father's. But there's something wrong with the lock—it won't fire any more. It's fun to have it, though; we take it apart, grease it, give it a good cleaning—and then put it together again. That is—*Father* does; he likes puttering about with things like that.

HEDVIG (*Beside* GREGERS): Look! You can see the wild duck clearly now.

GREGERS: Yes—I was just looking at her. She seems to drag her wing a bit.

HJALMAR: That's not strange; that's the broken wing, you see.

GREGERS: And she's lame in one foot, isn't she?

HJALMAR: Yes—perhaps a little.

HEDVIG: That's the foot the dog caught hold of.

HJALMAR: But she's all right otherwise; it's quite amazing—considering she had a charge of shot in her, and the dog grabbed her with his teeth—

GREGERS (*With a glance at* HEDVIG): —and she was down in the boundless deep, as well.

HEDVIG (*Smiling*): Yes.

GINA (*Goes on laying the table*): That blessed wild duck! She gets enough fuss made over her!

HJALMAR: Hm— Will lunch be ready soon?

GINA: Yes, in a minute. Now, Hedvig—come and help me. (GINA *and* HEDVIG *go out into the kitchen.*)

HJALMAR (*In a low voice*): I wouldn't stand there watching Father; he doesn't like it. (GREGERS *moves away from the attic door*) I'd better close up before the others come. (*Claps his hands to drive the birds back*) Shoo! Get back there! (*Draws up the net and pulls the door panels together*) These contraptions are all my own invention. It's rather fun to fiddle about with things like that. Gina doesn't like the hens and rabbits to get into the studio, so it's important to keep all this in running order.

GREGERS: Yes, I see—It's your wife who really runs the business then?

HJALMAR: I leave the routine part of it to her. It gives me a chance to work on more important things; I use the sitting room, you see.

GREGERS: What kind of things?

HJALMAR: I'm surprised you haven't asked me that before. But you haven't heard about the invention, I suppose?

GREGERS: Invention? No.

HJALMAR: You haven't, eh? Of course—I know you've been living in the wilds—

GREGERS: Have you invented something?

HJALMAR: I haven't quite solved it yet; but I'm working on it constantly. I didn't become a photographer in order to spend my life taking commonplace pictures of commonplace people—I need hardly tell you that.

GREGERS: Just what your wife was saying.

HJALMAR: When I chose the photographic medium, I swore to myself that I would raise it to the level of a science and an art combined; so I set to work on this invention.

GREGERS: What kind of an invention is it? What does it consist of?

HJALMAR: My dear fellow, you mustn't try to pin me down to details yet; these things take time, you know. And, believe me, it's not a question of self-glorification—I'm not working on it for my own sake, I assure you! I have a fixed purpose in life—a sacred duty; and I consider this work part of it.

GREGERS: What is this "purpose in life" you speak of?

HJALMAR: Are you forgetting that white-haired old man in there?

GREGERS: Your poor father—yes. What exactly do you plan to do for him?

HJALMAR: I plan to give him back his self-respect by restoring the name of Ekdal to its former dignity and honor.

GREGERS: I see.

HJALMAR: Yes—I shall rescue him! Poor, broken old man!

Do you know that from the moment the trouble started—
from the very beginning—he went all to pieces, and he
seemed unable to recover. In those terrible days—all during the trial—he was so changed, I hardly knew him—
That pistol over there—the one we use to shoot rabbits
with—that played its part in the Ekdal tragedy too!

GREGERS: The pistol! Really?

HJALMAR: Oh, yes! When he was found guilty, and they
sentenced him to prison—he stood with that pistol in his
hand—

GREGERS: You mean—he was going to—?

HJALMAR: Yes. But his courage failed him; he dared not use
it. That shows you how broken and demoralized he was.
Imagine! He, a soldier! A great hunter with nine bears to
his credit. A man directly descended from two Lieutenant
Colonels—in successive generations, naturally—and yet
his courage failed him! Can you understand that, Gregers?

GREGERS: Yes; I understand that very well.

HJALMAR: I don't. But that pistol was to turn up again in the
Ekdal Saga. When I thought of him in his prison clothes
—under lock and key—in that gloomy prison cell—! Those
were agonizing days for me! I kept all the shades down in
my room. I'd look out now and then, and I couldn't understand how the sun could still be shining. I couldn't understand how people could still be walking through the
streets—laughing and chatting about trivial things. It
seemed to me as though the world had come to a stand-
still—as though life itself were under an eclipse.

GREGERS: I felt like that when Mother died.

HJALMAR: And there came a moment when Hjalmar Ekdal
seized that pistol and aimed it at his own breast.

GREGERS: You, too, thought of—!

HJALMAR: Yes.

GREGERS: But you didn't fire?

HJALMAR: No—I didn't fire. By a supreme effort I conquered
the temptation—and I went on living. It takes courage to
choose life under such circumstances, I can tell you.

GREGERS: That depends on how you look at it.

HJALMAR: No, my dear fellow—it's indisputable. And I'm glad I managed to find the necessary strength, for now I shall be able to finish my invention. And when it's ready, Dr. Relling thinks—and I agree with him—that Father may get permission to wear his uniform again. I shall demand that as my sole reward.

GREGERS: Does that mean so much to him—?

HJALMAR: It's his dearest wish. Oh, Gregers—my heart bleeds for him! Whenever we have a little family celebration— Gina's and my wedding anniversary, whatever it may be— in comes the old man wearing the lieutenant's uniform he wore in happier days. But if there's a knock at the door, or if he hears someone in the hall—back he runs to his room as fast as his poor old legs will carry him; for he dare not be caught wearing it in public. It breaks my heart to see him!

GREGERS: When do you expect to finish the invention?

HJALMAR: Good heavens—that's impossible to say! An invention is not a matter of routine, you know. It depends on inspiration—on a sudden intuition—on factors beyond one's immediate control.

GREGERS: But you're making progress with it?

HJALMAR: Of course I'm making progress! I wrestle with it every day—my mind is full of it. Every afternoon, as soon as I've had lunch, I lock myself in the sitting room in there, where I can work in peace. But it's no use *hounding* me about it; as Relling says, that does more harm than good!

GREGERS: What about all this business in the attic? Don't you find that distracting? Doesn't it waste a great deal of your time?

HJALMAR: On the contrary! You mustn't think that for a moment! I must have *some* relaxation, after all; something to relieve the strain of incessant concentration. And, anyhow, inspiration is quite unpredictable; when it comes it comes —that's all!

GREGERS: You know, Hjalmar—I think you and the wild duck have quite a lot in common.

HJALMAR: The wild duck! What on earth do you mean?

GREGERS: You dived to the bottom too, and got yourself trapped down there.

HJALMAR: You mean that I was wounded too—by the blow that almost killed my father?

GREGERS: No, not exactly. It's not that you're wounded, Hjalmar; but you've lost your way in a poisonous swamp. You've become infected with an insidious disease, and you've sunk to the bottom to die in the dark.

HJALMAR: Die in the dark? I? Really, Gregers—how can you talk such nonsense!

GREGERS: But don't worry—I'll bring you back. I have a purpose in life too, you see. One I discovered yesterday.

HJALMAR: That's all very well—but kindly leave *me* out of it! I assure you that—apart from a perfectly justifiable melancholy—I'm as content and happy as any man could be.

GREGERS: That's part of the illness, you see. It's all part of the poison.

HJALMAR: My dear Gregers—please don't go on about illnesses and poisons any more! I dislike that kind of talk. In my house no one ever speaks to me about unpleasant things.

GREGERS: That I can well believe.

HJALMAR: I dislike it and it's bad for me— And I don't care what you say—there are no swamps or poisons here! My surroundings may be modest—my home may be humble; but I'm an inventor and the breadwinner of a family, and I assure you this exalts me above any petty material concerns— Ah! Here comes lunch!

(GINA *and* HEDVIG *enter bringing bottles of beer, a decanter of brandy, glasses, etc. At the same time* RELLING *and* MOLVIK *enter from the hall, both without hats or overcoats;* MOLVIK *is dressed in black.*)

GINA (*Placing dishes on the table*): You're just in time!

RELLING: Molvik got a whiff of herring salad and there was no holding him!

HJALMAR: I'd like you to meet Mr. Molvik, Gregers; and doctor—oh, but you know Dr. Relling, don't you?

GREGERS: Slightly, yes.

RELLING: Mr. Werle Junior, of course. We had a few little skirmishes up at the Höjdal Works. Did you just move in?

GREGERS: This morning.

RELLING: Molvik and I live just below you; so if you should happen to need a doctor or a clergyman, you won't have far to go.

GREGERS: I might have to take you up on that: we were thirteen at table yesterday.

HJALMAR: I do wish you'd stop talking about unpleasant things!

RELLING: Your time hasn't come yet, Hjalmar! No need to worry!

HJALMAR: For the sake of my family I hope you're right. But let's sit down now—and eat, drink and be merry!

GREGERS: Shouldn't we wait for your father?

HJALMAR: No; he'll have lunch in his own room presently. Come on! (*The men seat themselves at table and start eating and drinking.* GINA *and* HEDVIG *go in and out waiting on them.*)

RELLING: Molvik was drunk as a Lord yesterday, Mrs. Ekdal.

GINA: Was he? Again?

RELLING: Didn't you hear him when I brought him home last night?

GINA: Can't say I did.

RELLING: Just as well; last night he was downright disgusting.

GINA: Is that true, Molvik?

MOLVIK: Let us draw a veil over last night's proceedings; they have no connection with my better self.

RELLING: He becomes like one possessed; then he insists on dragging me out with him. He's daemonic—that's what it is.

GREGERS: Daemonic?

RELLING: Yes; Molvik is daemonic.

GREGERS: Hm.

RELLING: And people with daemonic natures can't be expected to go through life on an even keel, you know. They're obliged to run amok now and then—they *have* to — Are you still slaving away at those horrible grimy Works?

GREGERS: I have been until now.

RELLING: Did you ever get anyone to honor that claim you made such a fuss about up there?

GREGERS: Claim? (*Understands him*) Oh, I see.

HJALMAR: Claim? What sort of a claim, Gregers?

GREGERS: Nothing. A lot of nonsense.

RELLING: Not at all! He carried on a regular crusade! He went from house to house preaching about something— what was it you called it?—the Claim of the Ideal?

GREGERS: I was young then.

RELLING: Yes! You were young all right! But did you ever get anyone to honor it? You hadn't while I was there, as I remember.

GREGERS: And not since, either.

RELLING: Have you perhaps learned to compromise a little?

GREGERS: Compromise? Never in dealing with a man who really *is* a man.

HJALMAR: No! I should hope not!— More butter, Gina.

RELLING: And a bit of pork for Molvik.

MOLVIK: Ugh! Not *pork!*
(*There's a knock at the attic door.*)

HJALMAR: Father wants to come out; open up for him, Hedvig. (HEDVIG *goes and slides the door open a little way;* EKDAL *comes in carrying a fresh rabbit skin;* HEDVIG *closes the door after him.*)

EKDAL: Good morning, gentlemen! Good hunting today! Shot a big one!

HJALMAR: And you skinned it without waiting for me—!

EKDAL: Salted it, too. Good *tender* meat, is rabbit meat. And sweet; tastes like sugar. Enjoy your lunch, gentlemen! (*Goes into his room.*)

MOLVIK (*Getting up*): Excuse me— I can't— I must get downstairs at once—

RELLING: Take some soda water, man!

MOLVIK: Ugh—Ugh! (*Hurries out by the hall door.*)

RELLING (*To* HJALMAR): Let's drink a toast to the old hunter.

HJALMAR (*Clinks glasses with him*): To the gallant old sportsman on the brink of the grave.

RELLING: To the old gray-haired—(*Drinks*) By the way, is his hair gray or white?

HJALMAR: A little of both, I think. As a matter of fact, he hasn't much hair left.

RELLING: Well—you can get on just as well in a wig! You know—you really are a lucky man, Hjalmar; you have a definite purpose in life to strive for—

HJALMAR: And, believe me, I *am* striving for it—!

RELLING: And there's your good, capable wife—padding about so quietly in her old felt slippers, making everything cozy and comfortable for you—

HJALMAR: Yes, Gina—(*Nods to her*) You're a good companion on life's journey, Gina dear.

GINA: Don't go making a fool of me!

RELLING: And then, there's your Hedvig, Hjalmar—

HJALMAR (*Moved*): Yes—best of all, my child! My Hedvig! Come here to me, my darling! (*Strokes her hair*) What day is it tomorrow, eh?

HEDVIG (*Shakes him*): Don't say anything about that, Father.

HJALMAR: It cuts me to the heart to think how meager it will be; just a little ceremony in the attic—

HEDVIG: But I like that best of all!

RELLING: Just you wait till the invention's finished, Hedvig!

HJALMAR: Yes!— *Then* you'll see! Your future will be taken care of; you shall live in comfort all your life—I shall make sure of that! I shall demand—well—something or other on your behalf. It will be the poor inventor's sole request.

HEDVIG (*In a whisper, her arms round his neck*): Dear, darling Father!

RELLING (*To* GREGERS): Isn't it pleasant for a change to sit here with this happy family—eating delicious food at a well-spread table?

HJALMAR: It's a joy to share a meal with such good friends!

GREGERS: Personally—I don't like the smell of poison.

RELLING: Poison?

HJALMAR: Oh, don't start *that* again!

GINA: I'd have you know, Mr. Werle, there's no smell of poison here; I air this room out every single day!

GREGERS: No amount of airing can ever get rid of the stench I mean.

HJALMAR: Stench!

GINA: Well—I must say—!

RELLING: Perhaps you brought the stench with *you*, from those mines of yours up there!

GREGERS: You *would* call what I have to bring a stench! That would be like you, Dr. Relling.

RELLING: Now listen, Mr. Werle Junior—! Unless I'm very much mistaken you're still obsessed by that blasted *Claim of the Ideal* of yours. I'll bet you have a copy on you now—hidden in some pocket.

GREGERS: You're wrong. I have it hidden in my heart.

RELLING: Well—wherever it is don't produce it here! Not while I'm around at any rate.

GREGERS: And what if I produce it all the same?

RELLING: Then I give you fair warning, I shall kick you downstairs head first.

HJALMAR (*Rising*): Why, Relling!

GREGERS: All right! Why don't you try it—!

GINA (*Coming between them*): Dr. Relling! Please! That's enough of that—! But I'd like to tell *you* something, Mr. Werle. After that filthy mess you made with your stove in there, you've no business to come talking about stenches and poisons to *me!*

(*There's a knock at the hall door.*)

HEDVIG: Mother, there's someone at the door.

HJALMAR: What *is* this! Now we're to be overrun with visitors, I suppose!

GINA: Never mind—I'll go. (*She goes and opens the door, starts and draws back*) Ah!— Oh, no!

(WERLE, *wearing a fur coat, steps into the room.*)

WERLE: I beg your pardon; I'm told my son is living here.

GINA (*With a gasp*): Why—yes.

HJALMAR (*Goes towards him*): Won't you do us the honor, Mr. Werle—

WERLE: Thank you; I merely wish to see my son.

GREGERS: I'm here; what is it?

WERLE: May we go to your room?

GREGERS: My room? Yes—very well—

GINA: Oh! But it's in no fit state—!

WERLE: Out here in the hall will do; but I'd like to speak to you alone.

HJALMAR: You can have this room to yourselves, Mr. Werle. Come, Relling—we'll go in here. (HJALMAR *and* RELLING *go into the sitting room;* GINA *takes* HEDVIG *with her into the kitchen.*)

GREGERS: (*After a short pause*): Well? Now that we're alone, what is it?

WERLE: I gather from something you said last night—and your moving here to the Ekdals seems to confirm it—that you're bent on causing me some mischief.

GREGERS: I intend to open Hjalmar Ekdal's eyes; he must be made to see his position in its true light.

WERLE: I suppose this is the "purpose in life" you spoke of yesterday?

GREGERS: You've left me no other.

WERLE: Why hold *me* responsible for your warped mind, Gregers?

GREGERS: I hold you responsible for the fact that my whole *life* has been warped. I'm not referring now to what happened to my mother— But I have you to thank for the burden of guilt that weighs on my conscience.

WERLE: So it's your conscience that torments you, is it?

GREGERS: I knew you were laying a trap for old Lieutenant Ekdal, and I should have been man enough to face you with it. I should at least have warned him. I guessed what you were up to.

WERLE: Then why didn't you speak out?

GREGERS: I was too much of a coward; I didn't dare. At that time I was so dreadfully afraid of you. I went on being afraid of you for years.

WERLE: But you're no longer afraid now, it seems.

GREGERS: No—thank God. I know the wrong done to old Ekdal—by me and others—can never be undone. But I can at least save Hjalmar. I can prevent his life from being ruined by a mass of lies.

WERLE: What good do you think that would do? You don't imagine you'd be doing him a service?

GREGERS: I know I would.

WERLE: And Hjalmar Ekdal will agree with you, you think? You actually believe he's man enough to *thank* you for it?

GREGERS: I know he is.

WERLE: Hm—we'll see.

GREGERS: Besides—if I'm to go on living—I must try to find a cure for my sick conscience.

WERLE: You'll never find a cure; your conscience has been sick, as you choose to call it, ever since you were a little child. That's a legacy from your mother, Gregers; that's all she had to leave you.

GREGERS (*With a scornful smile*): You haven't got over it yet, have you? You expected her to bring you a fortune when you married her—you've never recovered from the shock of having being mistaken!

WERLE: Let's stick to the point, shall we? You still insist on guiding young Ekdal back to, what is in your opinion, the right path?

GREGERS: That is my intention.

WERLE: Then I might have spared myself this visit; for I suppose it's no good. asking whether you'll change your mind and come back home again?

GREGERS: No.

WERLE: And you won't consider joining the firm either?

GREGERS: No.

WERLE: Very well. But, since I'm marrying again, I'll arrange to have your part of the estate transferred to you at once.

GREGERS: No—I don't want it.

WERLE: You don't want it?

GREGERS: My conscience won't allow me to accept it.

WERLE (*After a pause*): Are you going up to the Works again?

GREGERS: No; I've resigned from your employ.

WERLE: What do you plan to do?

GREGERS: I only want to fulfill my purpose in life—that's all.

WERLE: But what do you propose to live on?

GREGERS: I've saved up a little money from my wages.

WERLE: How long will *that* last!

GREGERS: Long enough for me, I expect.

WERLE: What does that mean?

GREGERS: I'll answer no more questions.

WERLE: Very well then, Gregers. Goodbye.

GREGERS: Goodbye.

(WERLE *goes out by the hall door.*)

HJALMAR (*Sticks his head round the sitting-room door*): Has he gone?

GREGERS: Yes.

(HJALMAR *and* RELLING *come in.* GINA *and* HEDVIG *come from the kitchen.*)

RELLING: That certainly put an end to the lunch party, didn't it!

GREGERS: Put on your things, Hjalmar. I want you to come for a long walk with me.

HJALMAR: All right, I'd be glad to. What did your father want? Was it anything to do with me?

GREGERS: Come along. We've got to have a talk. I'll go and get my coat. (*Goes out by the hall door.*)

GINA (*To* HJALMAR): I wouldn't go with him if I were you.

RELLING: No, don't! Stay where you are.

HJALMAR (*Getting his hat and overcoat*): What! When an old friend wants to pour out his heart to me in private—!

RELLING: But, damn it! Can't you see the fellow's mad? He's a crackpot—a lunatic!

GINA: You hear that, Hjalmar? His mother was a bit queer too at times.

HJALMAR: All the more reason his friend should keep a watchful eye on him. (*To* GINA) Be sure to have dinner ready in good time. Goodbye for the present. (*He goes out by the hall door.*)

RELLING: Too bad that fellow didn't fall right into Hell down one of the Höjdal mine shafts!

GINA: Good gracious! What makes you say that?

RELLING (*Mutters*): I have my reasons.

GINA: Do you think young Werle's really mad?

RELLING: No, worse luck; I don't suppose he's any madder than most people. But he's a sick man all the same.

GINA: What do you think's the matter with him?

RELLING: Well—I'll tell you, Mrs. Ekdal: I'd say he had integrity-fever—a particularly bad case of it.

GINA: Integrity-fever?

HEDVIG: Is that a kind of illness?

RELLING: Yes; it's a national disease, but it only breaks out sporadically. (*Nods to* GINA) Thanks for lunch. (*He goes out by the hall door.*)

GINA (*Pacing restlessly up and down*): Ugh! That Gregers Werle! He's always been a troublemaker.

HEDVIG (*Stands by the table, gives her mother a searching look*): Mother; this all seems very strange.

                                                              CURTAIN

ACT
FOUR

SCENE: HJALMAR EKDAL'S *studio. A photograph has just been taken; a camera covered with its cloth, a pedestal, two chairs and a console table stand forward in the room. It is late afternoon, the sun is setting; during the act dusk falls.* GINA *stands at the hall door with a slide and a wet photographic plate in her hand; she is talking to somebody outside.*

GINA: Without fail! Don't worry, I never break a promise. I'll have the first dozen ready for you Monday—Good afternoon. (*Someone is heard going down the stairs.* GINA *closes the door, slips the plate into the slide and puts it into the camera.*)

HEDVIG (*Comes in from the kitchen*): Have they gone?

GINA (*Tidying up*): Yes, thank God. I got rid of them at last.

HEDVIG: It's funny Father isn't back yet.

GINA: You're sure he's not in Relling's room?

HEDVIG: No, he's not there; I just ran down the back stairs to see.

GINA: And his dinner's getting cold too.

HEDVIG: It's funny—Father's never late for dinner.

GINA: He'll be here soon—you'll see.

HEDVIG: I wish he'd come: things seem so queer today.

GINA (*Calls out*): Here he is now!

(HJALMAR EKDAL *comes in by the hall door.*)

HEDVIG (*Runs to him*): We thought you'd *never* come back, Father!

GINA (*Gives him a sidelong look*): You were out a long time, Hjalmar.

HJALMAR (*Doesn't look at her*): A fairly long time, yes.

GINA: Did you have something to eat with Werle?

HJALMAR (*Hanging up his coat*): No.

GINA (*Going towards the kitchen*): I'll bring your dinner at once, then.

HJALMAR: Never mind about dinner. I don't want anything to eat.

HEDVIG (*Goes nearer to him*): Don't you feel well, Father?

HJALMAR: Well? Yes—well enough. We had a very tiring walk, Gregers and I.

GINA: You shouldn't have gone with him, Hjalmar. You know you're not used to long walks.

HJALMAR: There are many things one has to get used to in this world. (*He wanders about the room*) Has anyone been here while I was out?

GINA: Only that engaged couple.

HJALMAR: No new orders, I suppose?

GINA: No, not today.

HEDVIG: But tomorrow there are sure to be some, Father!

HJALMAR: Let's hope so. For tomorrow I mean to set to work in earnest.

HEDVIG: Tomorrow! Have you forgotten what day it is tomorrow, Father?

HJALMAR: Ah, yes—of course. The day after tomorrow, then. I intend to take personal charge of everything. From now on I shall do all the work myself.

GINA: Why should you bother to do that, Hjalmar? You know it only makes you miserable. I can take the pictures well enough; and that sets you free to work on your invention.

HEDVIG: And then there's the wild duck, Father—and all the hens and rabbits—

HJALMAR: I won't hear another word about that childish nonsense! From tomorrow on I shall never set foot in there again.

HEDVIG: But, Father, tomorrow you promised we'd have our celebration—

HJALMAR: Hm. Yes, that's true. From the day *after* to-morrow, then. As for that wild duck, I'd like to wring its neck!

HEDVIG (*Cries out*): The wild duck!

GINA: I never heard of such a thing!

HEDVIG (*Shakes him*): But, Father! It's *my* wild duck! You can't—!

HJALMAR: That's the only thing that stops me. I haven't the heart to do it, Hedvig—for your sake. But I ought to do it, I'm convinced of that. No creature that has been in that man's hands should be allowed to stay under my roof.

GINA: Good Lord—what if Grandfather did get it from poor old Pettersen—

HJALMAR: One has certain moral obligations; there are laws —one might call them the laws of the Ideal. A man may jeopardize his soul by failing to obey them.

HEDVIG: But the poor wild duck, Father! Think of the wild duck!

HJALMAR: I told you—I intend to spare it for your sake. Not a hair of its head—I mean—it shall be spared. I've other things to deal with—far more important things than that. Now that it's dusk, Hedvig, you'd better run along and take your walk as usual.

HEDVIG: Must I, Father? I don't much feel like going out.

HJALMAR: I think you'd better go. You seem to be blinking your eyes a lot—it's this foul air in here. It's bad for you.

HEDVIG: Very well. I'll go by the back stairs. My hat and coat—? They must be in my room. But, Father—promise me you won't hurt the wild duck while I'm gone?

HJALMAR: Not a feather on it shall be harmed, I promise you. (*Clasps her to him*) You and I, Hedvig—we two—! Run along now.

(HEDVIG *nods to her parents and goes out through the kitchen.*)

HJALMAR (*Walks about the room with downcast eyes*): Gina.

GINA: Yes?

HJALMAR: From tomorrow on—from the day *after* tomorrow, rather—I wish to take charge of the household accounts myself.

GINA: You want to look after the accounts as well?

HJALMAR: I intend to check all the receipts at any rate.

GINA: Lord knows *that* won't take you very long.

HJALMAR: I wonder. It seems to me our money stretches a surprisingly long way. (*Stops and looks at her*) How do you manage it?

GINA: It's because Hedvig and I use so very little, I suppose.

HJALMAR: What about Father's work for Mr. Werle? Is it true that he gets very generously paid for it?

GINA: I don't know how generous it is. I don't know what other people get, you see.

HJALMAR: Well—how much *do* they pay him? Tell me!

GINA: It varies; he gets enough to cover his expenses here, and maybe a little pocket money besides.

HJALMAR: Enough to cover his expenses! Why have you never told me this?

GINA: I didn't like to; I knew it made you happy to think he owed everything to you.

HJALMAR: And instead he owes it all to Mr. Werle!

GINA: Well, God knows, Mr. Werle can afford it.

HJALMAR: Light the lamp!

GINA (*Lighting the lamp*): Anyway—how do we know it *does* come from Mr. Werle? It might be Graaberg who—

HJALMAR: Don't try to evade matters by dragging Graaberg into this!

GINA: Well, I mean—I only thought—

HJALMAR: Hm!

GINA: I didn't get Grandfather that copying to do: it was Bertha—in the days when she still used to come and see us—

HJALMAR: Why is your voice trembling?

GINA (*Putting on the lamp shade*): My voice—?

HJALMAR: Yes; and your hands are shaking too. Don't tell me I'm mistaken!

GINA (*Firmly*): What's he been saying about me, Hjalmar? You might just as well come out with it.

HJALMAR: Is it true—*can* it be true, that—that there was something between you and Werle, while you were in service there?

GINA: No. It wasn't true then, at any rate. Mr. Werle wouldn't leave me alone, *that's* true enough. His wife got suspicious, and fussed and fumed and made a lot of scenes; made my life miserable, she did. And then I gave my notice.

HJALMAR: And after that?

GINA: Then I went home, and Mother—well, she wasn't the kind of woman you took her for, Hjalmar; she kept on at me all the time—you see Mr. Werle had become a widower by then.

HJALMAR: Well?

GINA: I suppose I'd better tell you; he gave me no peace until I let him have his way.

HJALMAR (*Clasps his hands together*): So this is the mother of my child! How could you hide this from me!

GINA: It was wrong of me, I know; I should have told you long ago.

HJALMAR: You should have told me at the very start; then I'd have known what kind of woman I was dealing with.

GINA: But if you'd known—would you have married me?

HJALMAR: What do you think? Of course not!

GINA: That's why I couldn't bring myself to tell you. I'd grown so fond of you, you see. I'd have been so miserable —I couldn't bear the thought of it.

HJALMAR (*Paces about*): So this is my Hedvig's mother! And to think that I owe all I possess—(*Kicks a chair*) my home and everything that's in it, to a man who was your former lover! To that damned scoundrel Werle!

GINA: Hjalmar, do you regret these years we've been together?

HJALMAR (*Stands in front of her*): Tell me! Haven't your days been filled with remorse at the thought of the web of

deceit you've spun around me? Answer me! Hasn't it been
a constant source of agony and shame to you?

GINA: Hjalmar dear—I've had so much to do. My days have
been so full—what with the house and all—

HJALMAR: So you've never even given a moment's thought
to your past life!

GINA: It's a long time ago—to tell you the truth I'd almost
forgotten the whole stupid business.

HJALMAR: It's this crude, sluggish content that I find so
shocking—so revolting! Not a twinge of remorse—incredible!

GINA: I'd like you to tell *me* something, Hjalmar; what would
have become of you if you hadn't found a wife like me?

HJALMAR: Like you—!

GINA: Yes. You know I was always more practical and more
efficient than you were; I suppose that's only natural—
I'm a couple of years older, after all.

HJALMAR: What would have become of *me!*

GINA: You were getting into some pretty wild habits when
you first met me. You can't deny that, can you?

HJALMAR: Wild habits! That's what you call them, do you?
But how could *you* understand what a man goes through
when he's on the brink of despair, as I was! Especially a
man with my ardent, sensitive nature.

GINA: Maybe that's true. Anyway—I don't hold it against
you; you made a real good husband once we got married
and settled down—— And things were beginning to be so
cozy and comfortable here. Hedvig and I were thinking
we might even start spending a bit more on ourselves—get
ourselves a few clothes, perhaps—and a little extra food.

HJALMAR: In this swamp of deceit, you could actually think
of things like that!

GINA: Oh, God! I wish that awful man had never set foot inside this house!

HJALMAR: I was happy here too; I loved my home. But it
was all a delusion! How I shall ever find the necessary inspiration now to bring my invention to fruition, heaven

knows! It will die with me, I expect. And it will be your fault—it will be your past, Gina, that will have killed it.

GINA (*On the verge of tears*): You mustn't say that, Hjalmar! Please don't say things like that! All I've ever wanted was to serve you—to do the best I could for you. You must know that!

HJALMAR: What's become of the poor breadwinner's dream now! As I lay in there on the sofa, incessantly brooding over my invention, I realized only too well that the effort of creation was fast sapping my strength. I had a premonition: I knew that the day when I finally held the patent in my hand—I knew that day would be my last! I saw you in my dream—the proud widow of the inventor —sad, but prosperous and grateful.

GINA (*Drying her tears*): Hjalmar, you *mustn't* say such things! God forbid that I should ever be a widow.

HJALMAR: It makes no difference now one way or the other. The dream is over now—all over!

(GREGERS WERLE *opens the hall door cautiously and looks in.*)

GREGERS: May I come in?

HJALMAR: Yes; come in.

GREGERS (*Comes forward, his face beaming with joy, and holds out both his hands to them*): Well, my dear friends —! (*Looks from one to the other and says to* HJALMAR *in a whisper*) Perhaps you haven't had your talk yet?

HJALMAR (*Loudly*): Yes—we have.

GREGERS: You *have?*

HJALMAR: I've just been through the bitterest moments of my life.

GREGERS: But, surely, the most uplifting too?

HJALMAR: Anyway—we've got it over with; at least for the time being.

GREGERS (*In great surprise*): But—I don't understand—

HJALMAR: What don't you understand?

GREGERS: This crisis was to have been a turning point; the basis for a whole new way of life. No more falsehood and deception, but a union based on confidence and truth—

HJALMAR: Yes, I know; I know all that.

GREGERS: I expected to find you both radiant—transfigured.
But you seem sad and gloomy—

GINA: Yes—well. (*Takes off the lamp shade*)

GREGERS: I don't expect you to understand me, Mrs. Ekdal.
It's only natural that you should need time to— But *you,*
Hjalmar? You must feel like a man newly dedicated to
higher things.

HJALMAR: Yes, of course I do. To some extent—that is.

GREGERS: Surely there can be no greater joy than to forgive
a poor erring creature; to rehabilitate her through love
and understanding.

HJALMAR: It's not so easy to recover from the bitter experience I've just lived through!

GREGERS: Perhaps not for an *ordinary* man; but for a man
like *you*—

HJALMAR: Yes—I realize that. But don't *hound* me about it,
Gregers. These things take time, you know.

GREGERS: There's a lot of the wild duck in you, Hjalmar.
(RELLING *enters through the hall door.*)

RELLING: Well, well! So we're on the subject of the wild
duck again!

HJALMAR: Yes: Mr. Werle's poor wounded victim—

GREGERS: Mr. Werle? Were you talking about *him?*

HJALMAR: Him—and *us;* yes.

RELLING (*To* GREGERS *in an undertone*): You damned inter-
fering fool!

HJALMAR: What did you say?

RELLING: Nothing. I was just expressing my feelings about
this quack here. (*To* GREGERS) Why don't you get out before you ruin both their lives?

GREGERS: Their lives won't be ruined, I assure you, Dr.
Relling. I needn't speak of Hjalmar—we know him. But I
feel sure that, fundamentally, she too possesses the necessary qualities of decency and loyalty—

GINA (*Almost in tears*): Then why couldn't you have let me be?

RELLING: May I ask you, Mr. Werle Junior, what you think you're doing in this house?

GREGERS: Laying the foundations of a true marriage. ✻

RELLING: I see; so you think the Ekdal's marriage wasn't good enough?

GREGERS: I suppose it was as good as the majority of marriages—unfortunately! But it certainly was never based on truth.

HJALMAR (*To* RELLING): I'm afraid you've never given much thought to the Ideal.

RELLING: Rubbish, my friend! Tell me, Mr. Werle—roughly speaking—how many true marriages have you encountered in your life?

GREGERS: Hardly any—now I come to think of it.

RELLING: Neither have I.

GREGERS: But I've seen all too many of the other kind. And I know only too well how harmful such marriages can be to both people concerned.

HJALMAR: A man's spiritual integrity can be totally destroyed—that's the appalling part of it!

RELLING: I've never actually been married—so perhaps I'm not competent to judge. But one thing I *do* know: the child is part of the marriage too; and I advise you to leave the child alone.

HJALMAR: Hedvig!—My poor Hedvig!

RELLING: Yes; you'd better damn well leave Hedvig out of this! You two are grown-up people; if you want to make a mess of your lives, that's up to you. But I warn you to be careful about Hedvig. You might cause her irreparable harm.

HJALMAR: Harm?

RELLING: Yes. Or she might try to harm herself—and others too.

GINA: What makes you think that, Relling?

HJALMAR: You mean——? There's no immediate danger to her eyesight, is there?

RELLING: I'm not talking about her eyesight! Hedvig's at a difficult age. Heaven knows *what* she might get into her head.

GINA: You're right——she's had some queer ideas of late. She's taken to messing about with the kitchen stove, for instance. Playing at "house-on-fire" she calls it. I've been afraid she might really set fire to the place one of these days.

RELLING: There, you see! I knew it.

GREGERS (*To* RELLING): But how do you explain that kind of thing?

RELLING (*Curtly*): Adolescence——Mr. Werle Junior.

HJALMAR: As long as she has her father——! As long as I'm this side of the grave——!

(*There's a knock at the door.*)

GINA: Hush, Hjalmar; there's someone in the hall. (*Calls out*) Come in!

(MRS. SÖRBY *enters; she wears a hat and a warm coat.*)

MRS. SÖRBY: Good evening!

GINA (*Goes towards her*): Why, Bertha! Is it you?

MRS. SÖRBY: Yes. I hope I'm not disturbing you?

HJALMAR: Good heavens, no! How could an emissary from *that* house——!

MRS. SÖRBY (*To* GINA): Actually——I'd hoped to find you alone, at this time of day. I just ran over to have a little chat with you, and say good-bye.

GINA: Good-bye? Are you going away?

MRS. SÖRBY: Early tomorrow morning——up to Höjdal. Mr. Werle left this afternoon. (*To* GREGERS, *casually*) He told me to say goodbye to you for him.

GINA: Well——fancy!

HJALMAR: So Mr. Werle's gone, has he? And you're going after him?

MRS. SÖRBY: Yes. What do you say to that, Ekdal?

HJALMAR: I say: be careful!

GREGERS: Let me explain; my father is going to marry Mrs. Sörby.

HJALMAR: Marry her!

GINA: Oh, Bertha! So it's really happened at last!

RELLING (*With a slight quiver in his voice*): This surely can't be true?

MRS. SÖRBY: Yes, dear Dr. Relling, it's true enough.

RELLING: You're really going to marry again?

MRS. SÖRBY: It looks like it! Mr. Werle got a special license, and we're to have a very quiet wedding, up at the Works.

GREGERS: Then let me be a dutiful stepson, and wish you happiness.

MRS. SÖRBY: Thanks very much—if you really mean it. I hope it will bring happiness to both of us.

RELLING: I don't see why it shouldn't. Mr. Werle never gets drunk, as far as I know—and, unlike the late-lamented horse doctor, he's not in the habit of beating his wives either.

MRS. SÖRBY: Oh, let poor Sörby rest in peace. He had his good points too.

RELLING: But I expect Mr. Werle has even better ones.

MRS. SÖRBY: At least he hasn't wasted all that was best in him; when a man does that, he must face the consequences.

RELLING: Tonight I shall go out with Molvik.

MRS. SÖRBY: Don't do that, Relling. Please—for my sake!

RELLING: What else is there to do? (*To* HJALMAR) If you feel like joining us, Hjalmar—come along!

GINA: No, thank you. Hjalmar doesn't go to places of *that* sort!

HJALMAR (*In an angry undertone*): Oh, do be quiet!

RELLING: Goodbye Mrs.—Werle. (*Goes out by the hall door.*)

GREGERS (*To* MRS. SÖRBY): You seem to be on very intimate terms with Dr. Relling.

MRS. SÖRBY: We've known each other for many years. At one time it looked as though something might have come of it.

GREGERS: It's just as well for you it didn't.

MRS. SÖRBY: Yes, you're right. But then, I've never been one to act on impulse. A woman can't afford to throw herself away.

GREGERS: Aren't you afraid I might say something to my father about this former friendship?

MRS. SÖRBY: I've naturally told him all about it.

GREGERS: Oh?

MRS. SÖRBY: Yes; I've told him everything that anyone could possibly find to say against me. The moment I realized what was in his mind, I made a point of doing so.

GREGERS: Then you're more than usually frank, it seems to me.

MRS. SÖRBY: I've always been frank. I think for a woman it's the best policy.

HJALMAR: What do you say to that, Gina?

GINA: We can't all be alike. Some women are one way, and some another.

MRS. SÖRBY: You know, Gina—I believe my way is best. And Mr. Werle has no secrets from me either. He can sit and talk to me quite openly—just like a child. It's the first time he's ever been able to do that. It's all wrong that a man of his type—full of health and vigor—should have had to spend the best years of his life listening to interminable lectures on his sins! And mostly imaginary sins too—as far as I can make out.

GINA: Lord knows *that*'s true enough!

GREGERS: If you ladies intend to pursue this topic, I think I'd better go.

MRS. SÖRBY: No—you needn't go; I shan't say any more. I just wanted you to know that my dealings have been honorable and aboveboard from the start. I dare say many people will envy me and think me very lucky—and in a way I am. But I shall give as good as I get, I promise you.

I shall never fail him. And now that he'll soon be helpless,
I'll be able to repay him by serving him and caring for him
always. I can do that better than anyone else, I think.

HJALMAR: What do you mean—helpless?

GREGERS (*To* MRS. SÖRBY): Don't say anything about that
here.

MRS. SÖRBY: It's no use trying to hide it any longer; he's going
blind.

HJALMAR (*With a start*): Blind? He's going blind you say?
That's very strange.

GINA: Lots of people do, unfortunately.

MRS. SÖRBY: You can imagine what that means to a man in
his position. I shall simply have to use my eyes for both of
us, and do the best I can— But I really can't stay any
longer—I have so much to do— By the way, I was to give
you a message, Mr. Ekdal: If there's anything Werle can
ever do for you, just mention it to Graaberg.

GREGERS: An offer that Hjalmar Ekdal will most certainly
refuse.

MRS. SÖRBY: Really? He didn't used to be so—

GINA: No, Bertha. Hjalmar doesn't need anything from Mr.
Werle now.

HJALMAR (*Slowly and forcefully*): Be so good as to give my
regards to your future husband, and tell him I intend to
call on Mr. Graaberg very shortly—

GREGERS: What! You don't mean you—?

HJALMAR: —call on Mr. Graaberg, I say, and demand a full
accounting of the money I owe to his employer. I intend to
pay this debt of honor—ha-ha-ha! debt of honor is a good
name for it!—but no more of that—I intend to pay it in
full with interest at 5 per cent.

GINA: But, Hjalmar dear—where will we ever get the money?

HJALMAR: You may tell your fiancé that I am forging ahead
with my invention. Tell him that I am sustained in this
laborious task by the desire to rid myself once and for all
of this painful debt. That is my chief motive in pursuing
the work on my invention so relentlessly. I plan to devote

the profits to freeing myself from all obligation to your future husband.

MRS. SÖRBY: What has been happening here?

HJALMAR: You may well ask!

MRS. SÖRBY: Well—I'll say good-bye. There were a couple of other things I wanted to talk to you about, Gina—but they must wait till some other time—Goodbye.

(HJALMAR *and* GREGERS *bow silently;* GINA *takes* MRS. SÖRBY *to the door.*)

HJALMAR: Not beyond the threshold, Gina!

(MRS. SÖRBY *goes out;* GINA *closes the door after her.*)

HJALMAR: There, Gregers! That burden of debt is off my mind!

GREGERS: It soon will be, at any rate.

HJALMAR: I think my behavior might be described as suitably correct?

GREGERS: Your behavior was admirable, as I knew it would be.

HJALMAR: There are times when one cannot possibly disregard the claim of the Ideal. But it will be a long hard struggle. It's not easy for a man without a penny to his name, and with a family to support, to pay off a long-standing debt of this sort—on which, one might say, the dust of oblivion has settled. But it must be faced; my integrity as a human being demands it.

GREGERS (*Puts his hands on* HJALMAR's *shoulders*): My dear Hjalmar—wasn't it a good thing that I came?

HJALMAR: Ye-es.

GREGERS: Don't you feel happier, now that you see your position clearly?

HJALMAR (*Somewhat impatiently*): Yes—of course I do. But there's one thing that offends my sense of justice.

GREGERS: What thing?

HJALMAR: It's just that—but perhaps I shouldn't speak of your father in this way—

GREGERS: Say anything you like as far as I'm concerned.

HJALMAR: It shocks me to think that he has succeeded

where I have failed. His marriage will be a *true* marriage, you see.

GREGERS: How can you say a thing like that!

HJALMAR: But it's so, isn't it? Your father's marriage to Mrs. Sörby is based on truth and mutual confidence. They've kept nothing back; they hold no secrets from each other. They've reached a complete agreement. It's as though they'd each confessed their sins and given each other absolution.

GREGERS: Well—what then?

HJALMAR: That's the whole point—don't you see? You said yourself that no true marriage could exist unless these problems had been faced and cleared away.

GREGERS: But this is quite different, Hjalmar. You surely don't compare yourself—or Gina here—with *those* two—? You know quite well what I mean.

HJALMAR: All the same—there's something about this that offends my sense of justice. If things like this are allowed to happen, there's obviously no such thing as a Divine Power ruling the Universe!

GINA: Hjalmar! For God's sake don't say such things!

GREGERS: Hm. Don't let's embark on that subject.

HJALMAR: Yet—now I come to think of it—it's possible to see the hand of Destiny at work in this: He's going blind.

GINA: But perhaps that isn't true.

HJALMAR: I'm positive it's true; if there *is* such a thing as Divine Justice it *must* be true. Look at all the unsuspecting people he's hoodwinked in his time—!

GREGERS: A great many, unfortunately.

HJALMAR: And now he's being made to pay for it by going blind himself: it's retribution.

GINA: You frighten me when you say such dreadful things.

HJALMAR: It's sometimes salutary to examine the darker sides of life.

(HEDVIG, *in her hat and coat, comes in by the hall door. She is breathless and excited.*)

GINA: Back already?

HEDVIG: Yes; I didn't want to stay out any longer. And it was just as well, because I met someone at the front door as I came in—

HJALMAR: That Mrs. Sörby, I suppose.

HEDVIG: That's right.

HJALMAR (*Pacing up and down*): I hope that's the last time you'll ever lay eyes on *her*.

(*A pause.* HEDVIG *glances from one to the other as if trying to gauge their mood.*)

HEDVIG (*Coaxingly, going up to* HJALMAR): Father.

HJALMAR: Well—what is it?

HEDVIG: Mrs. Sörby brought me something.

HJALMAR: Something for you?

HEDVIG: Yes—it's something for tomorrow.

GINA: Bertha always has some little present for you on your birthday.

HJALMAR: What is it?

HEDVIG: Oh, we're not supposed to see it yet. Mother's to bring it in to me early tomorrow morning.

HJALMAR: What *is* this? A conspiracy behind my back?

HEDVIG (*Rapidly*): No, of course not! You can see it if you like! Look—it's this great big letter. (*She takes it out of her coat pocket.*)

HJALMAR: So there's a letter too.

HEDVIG: That's all she gave me; the rest'll come later, I suppose. But, just think—a letter! It's the first one I've ever had. And there's "Miss" written on the envelope. (*Reads*) "Miss Hedvig Ekdal." Just think of it—that's *me!*

HJALMAR: Let me see that letter.

HEDVIG (*Hands it to him*): There you are.

HJALMAR: This is Mr. Werle's handwriting.

GINA: Are you sure, Hjalmar?

HJALMAR: Look for yourself.

GINA: I don't know about such things.

HJALMAR: May I open it, and read it, Hedvig?

HEDVIG: Of course, Father, if you want to.

GINA: Not this evening, Hjalmar; we're supposed to save it till tomorrow.

HEDVIG (*Softly*): Oh, let him read it, Mother. I'm sure it's something nice. Father will be pleased and things will be all right again.

HJALMAR: I may open it then?

HEDVIG: Yes, Father, do! It'll be such fun to see what's in it!

HJALMAR: Very well. (*He opens the envelope, takes out a paper, reads it through, and seems bewildered*) What does this mean—?

GINA: What does it say?

HEDVIG: Do tell us, Father dear!

HJALMAR: Be quiet. (*Reads it through again; he turns pale but speaks with self-control*) It's a deed of gift.

HEDVIG: Really? What do I get?

HJALMAR: Here—read it yourself. (HEDVIG *takes it and goes over to the lamp to read it.*)

HJALMAR (*In an undertone, clenching his hands*): The eyes! The eyes—and now, *this!*

HEDVIG: But—isn't this for Grandfather?

HJALMAR (*Takes the paper from her*): Gina—what do you make of it?

GINA: I wouldn't understand anything about it. Just tell me what it is.

HJALMAR: It's a letter to Hedvig from Mr. Werle, informing her that in the future her grandfather need trouble himself no further with any copying work; but, instead—he may draw on Mr. Werle's office for a hundred crowns a month.

GREGERS: Aha!

HEDVIG: A hundred crowns, Mother! That's what I thought it said!

GINA: That's nice for Grandfather.

HJALMAR: —a hundred crowns a month as long as he may need it; which means as long as he lives, of course.

GINA: Poor old man—so he's provided for at least.

HJALMAR: Wait. There's more to come. You probably didn't read this, Hedvig. Afterwards the gift reverts to you.

HEDVIG: To me! All that money to *me!*

HJALMAR: For the rest of your life you will receive a hundred crowns a month, he writes. Do you hear that, Gina?

GINA: Yes, I hear it.

HEDVIG: All that money, Father! Think of it! (*Shakes him*) Father, Father—aren't you glad?

HJALMAR (*Shakes her off*): Glad! (*Paces up and down*) God! What perspectives—what vistas all this opens up to me! So—it's Hedvig! Why should he shower gifts on her!

GINA: Well, I suppose—it's Hedvig's birthday after all—

HEDVIG: But it will all belong to you, Father! You know I'll give it all to you and Mother!

HJALMAR: To your mother, yes! Of course—that's as it should be!

GREGERS: Hjalmar—this is a trap he's laid for you.

HJALMAR: Another one of his traps, you think?

GREGERS: He said to me only this morning: Hjalmar Ekdal is not the man you take him for.

HJALMAR: Not the man—!

GREGERS: You'll soon find out, he said.

HJALMAR: So he wants to show you he can bribe me—

HEDVIG: Mother, what does all this mean?

GINA: Go and take off your things.

(HEDVIG *goes out through the kitchen, on the verge of tears.*)

GREGERS: Well, Hjalmar—? Was *he* right about you, or am I?

HJALMAR (*Slowly tears the paper in two and lays the pieces on the table*): There is my answer.

GREGERS: Just what I expected.

HJALMAR (*Goes over to* GINA *who is standing by the stove and says in a low voice*): I want no more lies, I warn you, Gina. If things were really over between you and Werle when you became "fond of me"—as you choose to put it— why did he make it possible for us to marry?

GINA: He perhaps thought he'd be able to come and go as he liked, here in our house.

HJALMAR: Was that all? Mightn't he have been afraid? Wasn't it something to do with your condition at the time?

GINA: I don't know what you mean.

HJALMAR: I must know— Has your child the right to live under my roof?

GINA (*Draws herself up; her eyes flash*): You ask *me* that!

HJALMAR: Answer me! Does Hedvig belong to me—or—? Well?

GINA (*Looks at him coldly and defiantly*): I don't know.

HJALMAR (*Trembling slightly*): You don't know?

GINA: No. How should I? A creature like *me*—?

HJALMAR (*Quietly, turning away from her*): Then I have nothing more to do in this house.

GREGERS: Consider what you're doing, Hjalmar!

HJALMAR (*Putting on his overcoat*): What is there to consider? For a man like me there can be no alternative.

GREGERS: There are many things to be considered. You three must stay together. How else can you start afresh in a spirit of forgiveness and self-sacrifice?

HJALMAR: I don't want to. Never, never! My hat! (*Takes his hat*) My home is nothing but a mass of ruins! (*Bursts into tears*) Gregers! I have no child!

HEDVIG (*Who has opened the kitchen door*): Father! What are you saying! (*Runs to him*) Father!

GINA: There, you see!

HJALMAR: Don't touch me, Hedvig! Keep away from me—I can't bear to look at you! Oh! Those eyes—! Good-bye. (*Starts towards the door.*)

HEDVIG (*Clings to him, screaming*): No! No! Don't leave me!

GINA (*Cries out*): The poor child, Hjalmar! Look at the child!

HJALMAR: I won't! I can't! I must get out of here—away from this! (*He tears himself away from* HEDVIG *and goes out through the hall door.*)

HEDVIG (*Her eyes full of despair*): He's going away from us, Mother! He's going away! He'll never come back—never!

GINA: Don't cry, Hedvig. Father will come back—you'll see.

HEDVIG (*Flings herself down on the sofa sobbing*): No he won't! He won't! He'll never come home to us any more!

GREGERS: I meant it all for the best, Mrs. Ekdal. You do believe that, don't you?

GINA: Yes—I suppose so. But God forgive you all the same.

HEDVIG: I shall die if he doesn't come back, Mother—I shall die! What have I done to him? Go and find him, Mother, and bring him home again!

GINA: Yes, darling—yes! Try and be calm now. I'll go and look for him. (*Puts on her outdoor things*) Perhaps he's down at Relling's. Don't cry any more—promise!

HEDVIG (*Sobbing convulsively*): I won't—I won't! I promise! If only he'll come back!

GREGERS: You don't think it would be better to let him fight it out alone?

GINA: Let him do that later! We must get the child quieted down first. (*Goes out by the hall door.*)

HEDVIG (*Sits up and dries her tears*): Please! What is it all about? You've got to tell me! Why doesn't Father want me any more?

GREGERS: You must wait till you're grown-up before asking about that.

HEDVIG: But I can't wait till I'm grown-up and go on being miserable like this!—I think I know what it's all about—Perhaps I'm not really Father's child.

GREGERS (*Uneasily*): How could *that* be?

HEDVIG: Mother may have picked me up somewhere; and Father's just discovered it. I've read about things like that.

GREGERS: But even if that were so—

HEDVIG: I don't see why he should stop being fond of me on that account; I should think he'd love me even more. The wild duck came to us as a present too—and I love it very dearly all the same.

GREGERS (*Switches the conversation*): The wild duck—yes! Let's talk about the wild duck for a while.

HEDVIG: Poor wild duck. He can't bear to look at her either any more. Just think—he said he'd like to wring her neck!

GREGERS: But I'm sure he'd never do it!

HEDVIG: He said he'd like to! I thought it was horrid of him. I say a prayer for the wild duck every night. I ask God to protect it from death and everything that's evil.

GREGERS (*Looking at her*): Do you say your prayers every night?

HEDVIG: Yes, I do.

GREGERS: Who taught you to do that?

HEDVIG: I taught myself. Father was terribly ill once—they had to put leeches on his chest. He kept saying death was staring him in the face.

GREGERS: Well?

HEDVIG: So that night when I went to bed, I said a prayer for him. And I've kept on with it ever since.

GREGERS: And now you pray for the wild duck too?

HEDVIG: Yes, I thought I'd better; she was so very weak at first, you know.

GREGERS: Do you say your prayers in the morning too?

HEDVIG: No—of course not!

GREGERS: Why not? Aren't morning prayers any good?

HEDVIG: Well—in the morning it's light, you see; there's nothing to be afraid of then.

GREGERS: And this wild duck you're so fond of— You say your father wanted to wring its neck?

HEDVIG: He said he'd *like* to—but that he'd spare her for my sake. That was kind of him, I thought.

GREGERS (*Coming a little nearer*): What if you were to offer up the wild duck as a sacrifice? For *his* sake?

HEDVIG (*Rises*): The wild duck!

GREGERS: Yes. Supposing you were to sacrifice to him the thing you love most dearly in the world?

HEDVIG: Would that do any good—do you think?

GREGERS: Try it, Hedvig.

HEDVIG (*Softly, with shining eyes*): Very well—I *will*.

GREGERS: Do you think you'll really have the courage?

HEDVIG: The wild duck! I'll ask Grandfather to shoot it for me.

GREGERS: Yes, do that. But don't say a word to your mother about it.

HEDVIG: Why not?

GREGERS: She doesn't understand us.

HEDVIG: The wild duck! I'll try and do it the first thing in the morning.

(GINA *comes in from the hall door*.)

HEDVIG (*Goes to her*): Did you find him, Mother?

GINA: No. But he went to fetch Relling, and they went out together.

GREGERS: Are you sure?

GINA: The porter's wife told me—she saw them. Molvik was with them too, she said.

GREGER:: That's strange! I should have thought he'd want to fight things out alone—!

GINA (*Taking off her things*): Men are queer creatures! God knows *where* Relling's dragged him off to. I ran over to Mrs. Eriksen's—but they weren't there.

HEDVIG (*Fighting back her tears*): What if he *never* comes back to us, Mother!

GREGERS: He'll come back. I'll send him word tomorrow. You'll see—he'll come. Go to sleep now, Hedvig—and don't worry. Good night. (*He goes out by the hall door*.)

HEDVIG (*Sobbing, throws herself into her mother's arms*): Mother! Mother!

GINA (*Pats her shoulder and sighs*): Ah, yes! Relling was right. That's what happens when people come around with all this crazy talk of claims and idols!

CURTAIN

ACT FIVE

SCENE: HJALMAR EKDAL's *studio. Cold gray morning light; patches of snow lie on the large panes of the studio window.*

GINA *enters from the kitchen wearing an apron with a bib and carrying a broom and a duster; she goes towards the sitting-room door. At the same moment* HEDVIG *comes in quickly from the hall.*

GINA (*Stops*): Well?

HEDVIG: Mother—you know, I think he's down at Relling's—

GINA: There, you see!

HEDVIG: —Because the porter's wife says there were two people with Relling when he came home last night.

GINA: Just what I thought.

HEDVIG: But what good does it do, if he won't come up to us?

GINA: At least I can go down and have a talk with him.

(OLD EKDAL *in his slippers and a dressing gown, and smoking his pipe, appears at the door of his room.*)

EKDAL: Oh, Hjalmar— Isn't Hjalmar home?

GINA: No, he's gone out.

EKDAL: What—so early? And in all this snow? Well—never mind. I'll take my morning walk alone.

(*He slides open the attic door;* HEDVIG *helps him; he goes in; she closes it after him.*)

HEDVIG: Mother—what will poor Grandfather do, when he hears that Father's going to leave us?

GINA: Nonsense! Grandfather mustn't know anything about it. Thank God he was out yesterday—during all the rumpus.

HEDVIG: Yes, but—

(GREGERS *comes in from the hall.*)

GREGERS: Well? Any news of him?

GINA: They say he's down at Relling's.

GREGERS: Relling's! Did he *really* go out with those two?

GINA: It looks like it.

GREGERS: How could he! When it was so important for him to be alone—to collect his thoughts in solitude!

GINA: Yes. That's what he should have done.

(RELLING *comes in from the hall.*)

HEDVIG (*Going to him*): Is Father down with you?

GINA (*Simultaneously*): Is he down there?

RELLING: Yes, of course he is.

HEDVIG: You might have let us know!

RELLING: Yes—I'm a swine, I know. But I had that other swine on my hands—our daemonic friend, I mean. And I got so tired, I fell into a stupor—

GINA: What has Hjalmar got to say today?

RELLING: Nothing whatever.

HEDVIG: Hasn't he said anything at all?

RELLING: Not a blessed word.

GREGERS: Well—that's understandable enough.

GINA: Then what's he doing?

RELLING: Lying on the sofa snoring.

GINA: Is he? He's a great one for snoring, Hjalmar is.

GREGERS: You mean—he's actually *asleep?*

RELLING: He certainly appears to be.

GREGERS: I expect it's only natural; after the spiritual crisis he's been through—

GINA: And then, he's not used to gadding about at night.

HEDVIG: It'll do him good to get some sleep, Mother.

GINA: That's what I think. We'd better not wake him up too early. Thanks, Relling. I'll see about getting the house cleaned up a bit—come and help me, Hedvig.

(GINA *and* HEDVIG *go into the sitting room.*)

GREGERS (*Turning to* RELLING): How would you explain this spiritual upheaval that Hjalmar Ekdal's going through?

RELLING: Damned if I saw anything resembling a spiritual upheaval—!

GREGERS: Come now! At a turning point like this? When he's about to start on a whole new way of life—? You must realize that a man of Hjalmar's character—

RELLING: Did you say *character*? Hjalmar? If he ever possessed a vestige of that rare attribute, it was crushed in him, I assure you—thoroughly extirpated—while he was still a child.

GREGERS: That seems hardly likely—considering the loving care with which he was brought up.

RELLING: By those doting, hysterical maiden aunts of his, you mean?

GREGERS: Let me tell you they were women who never lost sight of the Ideal—now, I suppose, you'll start jeering again!

RELLING: No—I'm in no mood for that. I happen to know a lot about these ladies; he's often waxed eloquent on the subject of his two "soul-mothers"—as he calls them! Hjalmar has had the great misfortune of always being looked on as a shining light in his own particular circle—

GREGERS: And don't you think he is? Deep down—I mean?

RELLING: I've certainly never noticed it. That his father should have thought so—that's understandable enough; the old lieutenant's always been somewhat of an ass.

GREGERS: He's a man who has never lost his childlike nature —that's what you fail to understand.

RELLING: All right—have it your own way! Then, when our dear sweet Hjalmar went to college, his fellow students looked on him as the great hope of the Future, too. He was handsome enough—the scoundrel! Pink and white—the kind the girls all go for. And then he had a facile mind, and a romantic voice which he used to good effect declaiming other people's poetry, and other people's thoughts—

GREGERS (*Indignantly*): It can't be Hjalmar Ekdal you're talking about like this—?

RELLING: Yes—with your permission. This is the truth about that idol of yours to whom you bow the knee.

GREGERS: It never occurred to me I could be quite *that* blind.

RELLING: You are though—pretty nearly. You're a sick man too, you see.

GREGERS: You're right about that, at least.

RELLING: Yes. Yours is a complicated case. First you've got that blasted Integrity-Fever to contend with; then—what's worse—you live in a constant delirium of hero worship; it's absolutely necessary for you to look up to and adore something outside yourself.

GREGERS: It would inevitably have to be something outside myself.

RELLING: But you make such ridiculous mistakes about these imaginary paragons of yours! Why do you persist in presenting your Claim of the Ideal to people who are totally insolvent?

GREGERS: Why do you spend so much time with Hjalmar Ekdal, if this is your opinion of him?

RELLING: I'm a doctor of sorts, you know—God help me! I feel obliged to look after the sick people who live under the same roof with me.

GREGERS: So you think Hjalmar Ekdal is sick too?

RELLING: Most people are sick, unfortunately.

GREGERS: May I ask what cure you're using in Hjalmar's case?

RELLING: My usual one. I try to discover the Basic Lie—the pet illusion—that makes life possible; and then I foster it.

GREGERS: The basic lie? Surely—I misunderstood—?

RELLING: No, no; that's what I said: the Basic Lie that makes life possible.

GREGERS: And what "basic lie" do you suppose Hjalmar to be suffering from?

RELLING: I don't betray secrets like that to quacks. You've made enough mess of the case for me already. But my

method is infallible; I've used it on Molvik too; I've convinced him he's daemonic—that did the trick for him.

GREGERS: You mean—he's *not* daemonic?

RELLING: What the Hell does it mean: to be daemonic?
It's a lot of nonsense I invented to make life possible for
him. Without that the poor harmless wretch would have
gone under years ago—in an agony of despair and self-
contempt. And what about the old lieutenant? But that's
different: he discovered the cure for himself, you see.

GREGERS: Lieutenant Ekdal? What do you mean?

RELLING: Just think of it! The mighty bear hunter shooting
rabbits in the attic. And there's no happier hunter in the
world than that old man fooling about in there in all
that rubbish. He's saved four or five withered old Christmas trees, and to him they're just as beautiful and green
and fresh as the whole of the great Höjdal forest. To
him the rooster and the hens are wild birds in the treetops;
and the rabbits that lope about the attic floor are the
bears he used to grapple with out in the wilds, when he
was young and vigorous.

GREGERS: Poor old Lieutenant Ekdal; he's gone a long way
from the ideals of his youth.

RELLING: While I think of it, Mr. Werle Junior—I wish you'd
stop using that foreign word: ideals. We have a perfectly
good one of our own: lies.

GREGERS: You seem to think the two things are related!

RELLING: They are: they're as alike as typhoid and malignant
fever.

GREGERS: I shall never give up until I've rescued Hjalmar
from your clutches, Dr. Relling.

RELLING: So much the worse for *him*. Rob the average man
of his basic lie and you rob him of his happiness as well.
(*To* HEDVIG *who comes in from the sitting room*) And now,
little wild-duck mother, I'll just run down and see how
your father's getting on; I expect he's lying there meditat-
ing on that wonderful invention. (*He goes out through
the hall door.*)

GREGERS (*Going up to* HEDVIG): You haven't done it yet, have you? I can see it in your face.

HEDVIG: What? Oh, you mean—about the wild duck? No.

GREGERS: When it actually came to the point, I suppose your courage failed you.

HEDVIG: No—it wasn't that. But when I woke up this morning and remembered what we'd talked about, it seemed queer to me somehow.

GREGERS: Queer?

HEDVIG: Yes; I don't know— Last night, right at the time, I thought it was a very beautiful idea; but I didn't think so much of it—after I'd slept on it, you see.

GREGERS: I see that growing up in the atmosphere of this house has unfortunately had its effect on you.

HEDVIG: I don't care about that—if only Father would come back to us—

GREGERS: If only your eyes had been opened to the true values in life; if you only had the joyous, courageous spirit of self-sacrifice, you'd see how quickly your father would come back to you—But I still have faith in you, Hedvig—don't forget that. (*He goes out into the hall.*) (HEDVIG *paces about the room; she is about to go into the kitchen when a knock is heard at the attic door;* HEDVIG *goes over and opens it a little way;* OLD EKDAL *comes out. She slides the door closed again.*)

EKDAL: Hm. Not much fun going for your morning walk alone.

HEDVIG: Didn't you feel like going hunting, Grandfather?

EKDAL: Weather's not right for hunting; it's so dark you can hardly see.

HEDVIG: Do you ever feel like shooting anything besides the rabbits?

EKDAL: Why? Aren't the rabbits good enough?

HEDVIG: Yes, of course; but, what about the wild duck?

EKDAL: Ho-ho! You're afraid I'll shoot your wild duck, are you? I'd never do that. Never.

HEDVIG: No. I don't suppose you could, could you? It's very difficult to shoot wild ducks, they say.

EKDAL: What do you mean I *couldn*'t? I should rather think I *could!*

HEDVIG: How would you go about it, Grandfather?—Not with *my* wild duck, of course; I mean with others?

EKDAL: I'd shoot at the breast, you see; that's the surest place. And then you must always shoot *against* the feathers, you understand—not *with* them.

HEDVIG: And then do they die, Grandfather?

EKDAL: They die all right—if you shoot properly. I'll go in and brush up a bit. Hm—you see—hm. (*Goes into his room.*)

(HEDVIG *waits a moment or two, glances towards the sitting room door, goes over to the bookcase, stands on tiptoe, takes the double-barreled pistol down from the shelf and looks at it.* GINA *carrying her broom and duster comes in from the sitting room.* HEDVIG *puts down the pistol hastily without being seen.*)

GINA: Don't stand there messing about with your father's things, Hedvig.

HEDVIG (*Going away from the bookcase*): I was just trying to tidy up a bit.

GINA: You'd better go in the kitchen and see if the coffee's keeping hot. I'll take a tray down to him when I go.

(HEDVIG *goes out;* GINA *begins sweeping and cleaning up the studio. After a while the hall door opens cautiously and* HJALMAR EKDAL *looks in; he wears his overcoat but no hat; he is unwashed and his hair is dishevelled and unkempt. His eyes are dull and heavy.*)

GINA (*Stands with the broom in her hand and looks at him*): Well now, Hjalmar—you came back after all.

HJALMAR (*Comes in and answers in a gloomy voice*): I've come back—but only to go away again immediately.

GINA: Yes—I suppose so. But, my goodness! What a state you're in!

HJALMAR: A state?

GINA: And it's your good overcoat too! That's done for, I'm afraid!

HEDVIG (*At the kitchen door*): Mother, shall I—? (*Sees* HJALMAR, *gives a cry of joy and runs towards him*) Father, Father!

HJALMAR (*Turns away with a gesture of repulsion*): Keep away from me! (*To* GINA) Keep her away, I tell you!

GINA (*In an undertone*): Go into the sitting room, Hedvig. (HEDVIG *silently obeys.*)

HJALMAR (*Making a show of being busy opens the table drawer*): I want my books—I'll need them with me. Where are my books?

GINA: What books?

HJALMAR: My scientific books, of course— All those technical periodicals I need for my invention.

GINA (*Looking in the bookcase*): Are they these things— without a binding?

HJALMAR: Yes—naturally.

GINA (*Lays a pile of magazines on the table*): Don't you want Hedvig to cut the pages for you?

HJALMAR: I want no pages cut for me.
  (*A short pause.*)

GINA: So you still intend to leave us, Hjalmar?

HJALMAR (*Rummaging among the books*): I should think that was obvious.

GINA: Well, well!

HJALMAR: I don't intend to stay here to be stabbed through the heart each hour of the day!

GINA: God forgive you for believing all those dreadful things about me!

HJALMAR: Then prove—!

GINA: I think you're the one who ought to prove!

HJALMAR: After a past like yours? There are certain claims— I'm tempted to call them claims of the Ideal—

GINA: What about Grandfather? What's going to happen to him—poor old man?

HJALMAR: I know my duty. The poor helpless old man shall go with me. I'll go out presently and make arrangements— Hm. (*Hesitating*) Did anyone find my hat on the stairs?

GINA: No. Have you lost your hat?

HJALMAR: I naturally had it on when I came in last night; there's no doubt about that. But this morning I couldn't find it.

GINA: Dear Lord! Where on earth did you go with those two good-for-nothings?

HJALMAR: Don't bother me with trifles. I'm in no mood to remember details.

GINA: I do hope you haven't caught cold, Hjalmar! (*Goes out into the kitchen.*)

HJALMAR (*Mutters to himself in a low angry tone as he empties the table drawer*): You're a scoundrel, Relling; an infamous, treacherous scoundrel! I wish to God someone would wring your neck!

(*He lays aside some old letters, catches sight of the torn document from the day before, picks it up and examines the two pieces; puts it down hurriedly as* GINA *enters.*)

GINA (*Puts a tray with coffee, etc. down on the table*): You might like a drop of something hot. And there's some bread and butter and a bit of that smoked tongue.

HJALMAR (*Glancing at the tray*): Smoked tongue, you say? No! Nothing under this roof! I haven't eaten a morsel of food for nearly twenty-four hours, that's true enough— but never mind! My notes! And the preliminary chapters of my autobiography! What has become of my diary—and all my important papers? (*Opens the door to the sitting room but draws back*) There she is again!

GINA: The poor child has to be somewhere!

HJALMAR: Come out. (*He stands aside.* HEDVIG, *terrified, comes into the studio.* HJALMAR, *his hand on the door knob, says to* GINA) During these last few moments in my former home I wish to be spared all contact with intruders —(*Goes into the sitting room.*)

HEDVIG (*Runs to her mother and says softly in a trembling voice*): Does he mean me?

GINA: Stay in the kitchen, Hedvig; or, no—perhaps you'd better go to your own room. (*Speaks to* HJALMAR *as she goes in to him*) Wait a minute, Hjalmar. Don't rummage about in all the drawers; *I* know where everything is.

HEDVIG (*Stands motionless for a moment, confused and terrified; she bites her lips to prevent herself from crying. Then she clenches her hands convulsively and says softly*): The wild duck!

(*She steals over and takes the pistol from the shelf, slides open the attic door a little way, creeps in, and draws the door closed after her.* HJALMAR *and* GINA *begin to argue in the sitting room.*)

HJALMAR (*Comes in with some notebooks and old loose sheets of paper and lays them on the table*): What's the good of that portmanteau! That won't hold anything—I've *hundreds* of things to take with me!

GINA (*Follows him carrying the portmanteau*): Why not leave everything here for the time being, and just take a clean shirt and a pair of extra underdrawers?

HJALMAR: Phew! These exhausting preparations—! (*He pulls off his overcoat and throws it on the sofa.*)

GINA: Look! Your coffee's getting cold!

HJALMAR: Hm. (*Drinks a gulp without thinking and then another.*)

GINA (*Dusting the backs of the chairs*): You'll have a hard time finding a big enough place for all those rabbits.

HJALMAR: Good God! You don't expect me to drag all those rabbits with me!

GINA: Grandfather could never get along without his rabbits.

HJALMAR: He'll just have to get used to it. After all *I'm* sacrificing far more important things than rabbits!

GINA (*Dusting the bookcase*): I'd better pack your flute, hadn't I?

HJALMAR: No. No flute for me. But I shall need my pistol.

GINA: Are you going to take that gun along?

HJALMAR: My loaded pistol—yes.

GINA (*Looks for it*): It isn't here. He must have taken it in there with him.

HJALMAR: Is he in the attic?

GINA: Of course he is.

HJALMAR: Hm. Poor lonely old man. (*He takes some bread and butter and smoked tongue, eats it, and finishes his cup of coffee.*)

GINA: If we hadn't rented that room, you could have moved in there.

HJALMAR: And go on living under the same roof as—! Never! Never!

GINA: I suppose you couldn't manage in the sitting room for a day or two? You could have it all to yourself; I'd see to that.

HJALMAR: No! I can't breathe inside these walls!

GINA: Why not down with Relling and Molvik, then?

HJALMAR: Never mention their names to me again! The very thought of them is enough to take away my appetite—No —I shall simply have to go out into the storm; go from house to house, seeking shelter for my old father and myself.

GINA: But you have no hat, Hjalmar! You've gone and lost it, you know.

HJALMAR: Those two scoundrels! Vicious, infamous brutes! I'll have to pick up a hat somewhere on the way. (*Takes some more bread and tongue*) Something'll have to be done about it; I've no desire to risk my life. (*Looks for something on the tray.*)

GINA: What are you looking for?

HJALMAR: Butter.

GINA: I'll get you some at once. (*She goes out into the kitchen.*)

HJALMAR (*Shouting after her*): Oh, never mind; dry bread is good enough for me.

GINA (*Bringing in a dish of butter*): There you are; it's freshly churned.

(*She pours him a fresh cup of coffee; he sits on the sofa, spreads more butter on the already-buttered bread, and eats and drinks for a while in silence.*)

HJALMAR: Would it be possible for me, without being annoyed by anyone—anyone at all—to stay in the sitting room in there, just for a day or two?

GINA: Why, of course. I only wish you would.

HJALMAR: I don't see how I can possibly get Father moved in such a hurry.

GINA: No. And then, you ought to prepare him too. Tell him you don't want to live here with us any more.

HJALMAR (*Pushing away his coffee cup*): Yes, there is that. It's awful to think of having to broach this difficult subject with him. I must have a breathing spell—a chance to think things out. I can't cope with all these problems in a single day!

GINA: Of course not; and it's such awful weather too.

HJALMAR (*Touching* WERLE's *letter*): I see that paper is still hanging about.

GINA: Yes. *I* haven't touched it.

HJALMAR: Well—it's no concern of mine—

GINA: *I* certainly never thought of using it.

HJALMAR: Still—there's no sense in throwing it away; in all the commotion of my moving, it might easily—

GINA: I'll take good care of it, Hjalmar.

HJALMAR: In the first place, the gift was made to Father; it's really up to him to decide whether he'll make use of it or not.

GINA (*Sighs*): Yes—poor old Father—

HJALMAR: Just as a matter of precaution, I think—have you any paste?

GINA (*Goes to the bookcase*): There's a pot of paste right here.

HJALMAR: And a brush?

GINA: Here's a brush too. (*Brings him the things.*)

HJALMAR (*Takes a pair of scissors*): Just a strip of paper on the back— Far be it from me to lay hands on other people's property—especially when it belongs to a penniless old man. And to—that other one as well. There! Leave it there for now, and when it's dry, put it away. I never want to lay eyes on that document again. Never!

(GREGERS WERLE *comes in from the hall.*)

GREGERS (*Somewhat surprised*): Oh—you're sitting in here, are you?

HJALMAR (*Rises hurriedly*): I just sat down for a moment; out of sheer exhaustion.

GREGERS: You seem to have had breakfast too.

HJALMAR: The body has its claims too, you know—occasionally.

GREGERS: Well—what have you decided?

HJALMAR: For a man like me there can be only one possible decision. I was busy gathering a few of my most important things together; but it's bound to take a little time.

GINA (*With a touch of impatience*): Which shall I do? Get the room ready, or pack your bag for you?

HJALMAR (*With an irritated look at* GREGERS): Pack the bag! —and get the room ready too!

GINA (*Picks up the portmanteau*): Very well; I'll just put in the shirt and those other things we spoke of. (*She goes into the sitting room and closes the door after her.*)

GREGERS (*After a short pause*): It never occurred to me that things would come to this. Is it really necessary for you to leave your home?

HJALMAR (*Wandering about restlessly*): What would you have me do? I wasn't made to bear unhappiness, Gregers. I need security; I must be surrounded by peace and comfort.

GREGERS: But you could find all that here, couldn't you? Why not try it? You have a splendid opportunity now to start afresh; why not begin again from here? And there's your invention to consider too; don't forget that.

HJALMAR: My invention! Don't even speak of that. That's a very doubtful proposition, I'm afraid.

GREGERS: Really? What do you mean?

HJALMAR: What on earth do you expect me to invent? Other people have invented practically everything already. It gets more difficult every day—

GREGERS: But I thought you'd worked so hard on it.

HJALMAR: It's all that damned Relling's fault!

GREGERS: Relling?

HJALMAR: Yes. He kept on telling me I had great inventive talent—that I would undoubtedly discover something to revolutionize photography.

GREGERS: I see! So it was Relling!

HJALMAR: But it's been a source of great happiness to me. Not so much the invention itself, but the fact that Hedvig had such faith in it. She believed in it as only a child can believe—unreservedly, whole heartedly—At least, I was fool enough to *think* she did.

GREGERS: Hedvig couldn't possibly deceive you—you *must* know that.

HJALMAR: I know nothing any more! She's the obstacle, you see. Hedvig's the one who's plunged my whole life into darkness.

GREGERS: Hedvig! Are you talking about *Hedvig?* How could she possibly plunge your life into darkness?

HJALMAR (*Without answering*): I've loved that child more than anything on earth. Each time I came back to this humble room, she would run to meet me—and it was such a joy to see her blinking up at me with those sweet little eyes of hers so full of happiness. I loved her with all my heart—fool that I was! And I imagined that she loved me just as deeply in return.

GREGERS: You *imagined* it, you say?

HJALMAR: What else *can* I say now? I can get nothing out of Gina. Besides—she's totally unaware of the part the Ideal plays in this whole business. But I must open my heart to you, Gregers: I'm tormented by the thought that perhaps Hedvig never really cared for me at all.

GREGERS: And supposing she were to give you a great proof

of her love? (*Listens*) What's that? It sounded like the wild duck—

HJALMAR: Yes—it's the wild duck quacking; Father's in the attic.

GREGERS: Is he! (*His face lights up with joy*) You'll see— you may soon have proof of how much your poor misunderstood Hedvig loves you.

HJALMAR: What proof could she possibly give me? I'd never dare believe any assurances of hers.

GREGERS: I'm positive Hedvig doesn't even know the meaning of deceit.

HJALMAR: I wouldn't count too much on that, Gregers. Heaven knows what Gina and Mrs. Sörby have sat here scheming and plotting. And Hedvig's no fool—she has sharp ears. That gift may not have been such a surprise to her after all. As a matter of fact, I thought I noticed something in her manner—

GREGERS: What's got into you, Hjalmar? What makes you say such things?

HJALMAR: I've had my eyes opened—that's all. You'll see— this deed of gift may be only the beginning; Mrs. Sörby has always had a great fondness for Hedvig, and now she's in a position to do anything she wants to for the child. They could snatch her away from me whenever they chose to do so.

GREGERS: Nonsense! Hedvig would never consent to leave you.

HJALMAR: Don't be so sure. Just think of all *they* have to offer her! And *I* who have loved her so deeply—! My greatest happiness would have been to take her hand and lead her through life, as one might lead a frightened child through a dark, empty room. But—I'm convinced of it now!—the poor photographer up in his garret has never meant anything to her at all. She was just being shrewd; trying to keep on the good side of him until something better came along.

GREGERS: Come, Hjalmar—you know you don't believe that yourself.

HJALMAR: I don't know *what* to believe—that's the dreadful part of it—and I shall *never* know. You rely too much on the Ideal, my dear Gregers—otherwise you couldn't possibly doubt the truth of what I say. If those others were to come—laden with all their riches—and call out to the child: Leave him! You'll have a better life with us—

GREGERS: Yes? What then?

HJALMAR: And if I were to ask her: Hedvig, are you willing to give up that better life for me? (*With a scornful laugh*) You'd find out soon enough what her answer would be! (*A pistol shot is heard in the attic.*)

GREGERS (*Loudly and joyfully*): Hjalmar!

HJALMAR: There! He's at his shooting again!

GINA (*Comes in*): Oh, Hjalmar—I wish Grandfather wouldn't bang away in there all by himself!

HJALMAR: I think I'll just look in—

GREGERS (*Eagerly, with emotion*): Wait, Hjalmar. Do you know what that was?

HJALMAR: Of course I do.

GREGERS: No you don't; but *I* know. That was the proof!

HJALMAR: What proof?

GREGERS: That was the child's sacrifice to you. She's persuaded your father to shoot the wild duck.

HJALMAR: The wild duck!

GINA: Good gracious!

HJALMAR: What's the point of that?

GREGERS: She's sacrificed the thing she loved best in the world to *you*. She thought, if she did that, you'd come to love her again, you see.

HJALMAR (*Tenderly, with emotion*): Poor child!

GINA: The things she thinks of!

GREGERS: All she wants is your love, Hjalmar. She can't live without it.

GINA (*Fighting back her tears*): You see, Hjalmar!

HJALMAR: Where is she, Gina?

GINA (*Sniffs*): She's in the kitchen, I suppose—poor little thing!

HJALMAR (*Tears open the kitchen door and says*): Hedvig, come! Come to me, Hedvig! (*Looks round*) No—she's not in here.

GINA: Then she must be in her room.

HJALMAR (*From outside*): She's not here either. (*Comes in again*) She must have gone out.

GINA: Well—you wouldn't have her anywhere about the house.

HJALMAR: I hope she'll come home soon—so that I can tell her— Everything's going to be all right now, Gregers. I believe we'll be able to start a new life after all.

GREGERS (*Quietly*): Thanks to the child; I knew it would be so.

(OLD EKDAL *appears at the door of his room; he is in full uniform and is busy buckling on his sword.*)

HJALMAR (*In astonishment*): Why, Father! Were you in there?

GINA: Don't tell me you've been shooting in your room?

EKDAL (*Approaching, resentfully*): So you go hunting by yourself now, do you, Hjalmar?

HJALMAR (*Anxious and bewildered*): I thought you were in the attic; wasn't it you who fired that shot in there?

EKDAL: Fired a shot? I? Hm.

GREGERS (*Calls out to* HJALMAR): She's shot the wild duck herself!

HJALMAR: What can it mean! (*Rushes to the attic door, tears it open, looks in, and cries out*) Hedvig!

GINA (*Runs to the door*): God! What's happened?

HJALMAR (*Goes into the attic*): She's lying on the floor!

GREGERS: What! Hedvig? (*Goes in to* HJALMAR.)

GINA (*Simultaneously*): Hedvig! (*Inside the attic*) No, no, no!

EKDAL: Ho-ho! Is she going shooting too?

(HJALMAR, GINA *and* GREGERS *carry* HEDVIG *into the*

studio; her right hand hangs down with the pistol still clasped tightly in its fingers.)

HJALMAR (*Distracted*): The pistol must have gone off— she's wounded herself! Call for help! Help!

GINA (*Rushes out into the hall and calls down the stairs*): Relling! Relling! Dr. Relling! Come quickly!

(HJALMAR *and* GREGERS *lay* HEDVIG *down on the sofa.*)

EKDAL (*Quietly*): The forest takes revenge.

HJALMAR (*On his knees beside her*): She's beginning to come to. She's coming to—yes, yes.

GINA (*Who has come in again*): Where is she wounded? I don't see anything—

(RELLING *comes in hurriedly followed by* MOLVIK; *the latter without his waistcoat and necktie, and with his coat open.*)

RELLING: What's happening here?

GINA: They say Hedvig has shot herself.

HJALMAR: Quickly! Help us!

RELLING: Shot herself! (*He pushes the table aside and starts to examine her.*)

HJALMAR (*Still kneeling, looks up at him anxiously*): It can't be serious, can it? Eh, Relling? She's hardly bleeding at all; it can't be serious?

RELLING: How did it happen?

HJALMAR: We don't know—!

GINA: She wanted to shoot the wild duck.

RELLING: The wild duck?

HJALMAR: The pistol must have gone off.

RELLING: Hm. I see.

EKDAL: The forest takes revenge. But I'm not afraid! Not I! (*Goes into the attic and slides the door shut after him.*)

HJALMAR: Relling—why don't you say something?

RELLING: The bullet entered the breast.

HJALMAR: Yes—but she's coming to—

RELLING: Can't you see that Hedvig's dead?

GINA (*Bursts into tears*): My child! My little child!

GREGERS (*Huskily*): In the boundless deep—

HJALMAR (*Jumps up*): She must live, she *must!* For God's sake, Relling—if only for a moment. Just long enough for me to tell her how deeply I've loved her all the time!

RELLING: The bullet pierced her heart. Internal hemorrhage. Death must have been instantaneous.

HJALMAR: Oh, God! And I drove her from me like a dog! She died for love of me: she crept into the attic, filled with grief and terror, and died for love of me! (*Sobs*) Never to be able to tell her! Never to be able to atone! (*Clenches his fists and looks upwards shouting*) You, up there—! If you *are* there—! Why have you done this thing to me!

GINA: Hush, hush! You mustn't go on like that! We didn't deserve to keep her, I suppose.

MOLVIK: The child is not dead; it sleepeth.

RELLING: Rubbish.

HJALMAR (*Becomes calm, goes over to the sofa, folds his arms, and looks down at* HEDVIG): She's so stiff—so still.

RELLING (*Tries to loosen the hand holding the pistol*): She's holding it so tightly—so very tightly—

GINA: No, Relling—don't force her fingers. Let the gun be.

HJALMAR: She shall take it with her.

GINA: Yes; let her. But the child mustn't lie here—on show like this. She shall go to her own room. Help me, Hjalmar. (HJALMAR *and* GINA *carry* HEDVIG *between them.*)

HJALMAR (*As they carry her*): Gina, Gina! How can you ever bear it!

GINA: We must try and help each other. At least *now* she belongs to both of us.

MOLVIK (*Stretching out his arms and muttering*): Blessed be the Lord; to earth thou shalt return; to earth thou shalt return—

RELLING (*In a whisper*): Shut up, you fool—you're drunk. (HJALMAR *and* GINA *carry the body out through the kitchen door.* RELLING *shuts it after them.* MOLVIK *slinks out into the hall.*)

RELLING (*Goes over to* GREGERS *and says*): No one will ever make me believe this was an accident.

GREGERS (*Who has been standing horrified, his face twitching*): How could this dreadful thing have happened. No one will ever know.

RELLING: The front of her dress was burned. She must have aimed the pistol at her heart and fired.

GREGERS: Hedvig has not died in vain. Didn't you see? His sorrow brought out all that is noblest in him.

RELLING: Most people are noble in the presence of death. One wonders how long this nobility of his will last.

GREGERS: Why shouldn't it last? Why shouldn't it increase and grow stronger with the years?

RELLING: The years! Before this year is out, little Hedvig will be no more to him than a theme on which to exercise his eloquence!

GREGERS: How dare you say that of Hjalmar Ekdal!

RELLING: We'll talk of this again when this year's grass has withered on her grave. You'll see: He'll be spouting about "the child snatched from her father's loving arms by an untimely death"; he'll be wallowing in a sea of self-pity and maudlin sentimentality. You wait. You'll see.

GREGERS: All I can say is—if *you* are right and *I* am wrong, then life is not worth living.

RELLING: Life would be quite pleasant all the same—if it were not for certain lunatics, certain fanatics, who hammer at our doors, insisting on some nonsense they call the Claim of the Ideal.

GREGERS (*Gazing before him*): Then I'm glad my fate is what it is.

RELLING: And what *is* it, may I ask?

GREGERS (*Starts to go*): To be thirteenth at table.

RELLING: The Hell it is. I wish I could believe it!

CURTAIN

The Lady from the Sea

A PLAY IN FIVE ACTS

1888

R WANGEL, *district physician*

LIDA WANGEL, *his second wife*

BOLETTE

HILDE, *a young girl* ⎫ *his daughters by his*
                       ⎭ *former marriage*

ARNHOLM, *a schoolmaster*

LYNGSTRAND

BALLESTED

A STRANGER

> *Young townspeople, tourists, etc.*

> *The action takes place in the summertime, in a small town beside a fjord in Northern Norway.*

ACT
ONE

SCENE: *Stage left.* WANGEL's *house, with a large veranda; surrounded front and side by a garden. Below the veranda a flagstaff. In the garden, stage right, an arbor with tables and chairs. In the background a hedge with a small gate. Beyond the hedge a road along the shore, lined with trees. Through the trees a glimpse of the fjord with high mountain peaks in the distance. It is a warm, sparkling summer morning.*

BALLESTED, *a middle-aged man wearing an old velvet jacket and a broad-brimmed artist's hat, stands at the foot of the flagstaff, arranging the rope. The flag lies on the ground. A little way from him stands an easel with a canvas on it. On a campstool beside it are brushes, palette and a paint box.*

BOLETTE *comes out onto the veranda through the door from the garden room, which stands open. She carries a large vase of flowers, which she places on the table.*

BOLETTE: Were you able to fix it, Ballested?

BALLESTED: Yes indeed, Miss Bolette—it was simple enough. I hope you don't mind my asking, Miss—are you expecting company today?

BOLETTE: Yes, we are. Professor Arnholm's coming; he arrived in town last night.

BALLESTED: Arnholm. You mean that man who used to be your tutor?

BOLETTE: That's the one.

BALLESTED: So he's come back for a visit, has he?

BOLETTE: That's why we want to raise the flag—to welcome him.

BALLESTED: Of course, of course! I see!

(BOLETTE *goes into the house again. A moment later* LYNG-
STRAND *enters on the road from the right. He stops at the
sight of the easel and the painting materials and looks
at them with interest. He is a spare, delicate young man,
poorly but neatly dressed.*)

LYNGSTRAND (*From the other side of the hedge*): Good
morning!

BALLESTED (*Turning*): What's that? Oh! Good morning!
(*Hoists the flag*) There! Up she goes! (*He ties off the rope
and busies himself at the easel*) I say good morning to you,
Sir, though I don't believe I've had the pleasure—

LYNGSTRAND: You're a painter, are you?

BALLESTED: Correct. Any objections?

LYNGSTRAND: Well—I mean—you must be a painter; I can see
that you are. Would it be all right if I came in a moment?

BALLESTED: Want to have a look?

LYNGSTRAND: I'd like to very much.

BALLESTED: There's not much to see yet—it's just a start. But
come in if you like—you're very welcome.

LYNGSTRAND: Thanks—then I will. (*He comes through the
garden gate.*)

BALLESTED (*Painting*): I'm trying to catch that bit of the
fjord—in between those islands.

LYNGSTRAND: Oh, yes—I see.

BALLESTED: Of course I still have to put the figure in. But it's
so hard to find models around here.

LYNGSTRAND: Oh—there's to be a figure, is there?

BALLESTED: Yes—a dying mermaid. I'm going to put her
here in the foreground—stretched out by that rock.

LYNGSTRAND: Why is she dying?

BALLESTED: Well, you see—she strayed inland and lost her
way; and she can't get back to the sea again. So she's pining away here in the shallows.

LYNGSTRAND: Oh, I see.

BALLESTED: I got the idea from Mrs. Wangel—the lady who
lives here, you know.

LYNGSTRAND: What will you call the picture when it's finished?

BALLESTED: I thought of calling it "The Mermaid's End."

LYNGSTRAND: Splendid. It should be a fine piece of work.

BALLESTED: Are you a fellow artist by any chance?

LYNGSTRAND: A painter, you mean?

BALLESTED: Yes.

LYNGSTRAND: No; no, I'm not. But I'm going to be a sculptor. My name is Lyngstrand—Hans Lyngstrand.

BALLESTED: A sculptor, eh? Well—that's a great art too; a fine, distinguished art. Haven't I passed you on the street now and then? How long have you been here?

LYNGSTRAND: About two weeks. I hope to spend the summer here—if I can manage it.

BALLESTED: A nice holiday by the seaside, eh?

LYNGSTRAND: I thought it might benefit my health.

BALLESTED: Not an invalid, I hope?

LYNGSTRAND: A bit on the delicate side—nothing serious. It's my lungs; I have difficulty in breathing.

BALLESTED: That's nothing much! Still—it might be wise to see a doctor.

LYNGSTRAND: I thought of consulting Dr. Wangel—someday when he's not too busy.

BALLESTED: A good idea. (*Looks off left*) Here comes another steamer—packed with people, too. It's amazing what a lot of tourists we've had these past few years.

LYNGSTRAND: It seems like a very busy place.

BALLESTED: It gets worse every summer. Too many visitors! I'm afraid our little town may lose its charm.

LYNGSTRAND: Were you born here?

BALLESTED: No; no, I wasn't. But through the years I've become thoroughly accla—acclimatized. I've become attached to the place. Time and habit, I suppose.

LYNGSTRAND: Have you lived here long?

BALLESTED: Around seventeen or eighteen years. I first came here with Skive's company—a theatrical troupe, you know.

There were financial difficulties, and the company disbanded.

LYNGSTRAND: And you stayed on here?

BALLESTED: Yes, I stayed on, and I can't say I've regretted it. You see, I was a scenic artist in those days.

(BOLETTE *comes out of the house carrying a rocking chair, which she places on the veranda.*)

BOLETTE (*Calls back into the house*): Hilde—bring Father's footstool, will you? You know—the embroidered one.

LYNGSTRAND (*Goes to the veranda and greets her*): Good morning, Miss Wangel!

BOLETTE (*At the balustrade*): Well! If it isn't Mr. Lyngstrand! How do you do! Excuse me a moment; I just have to— (*Goes into the house.*)

BALLESTED: I see you know the Wangels.

LYNGSTRAND: Not really. I've been introduced to the young ladies; and I had a nice talk with Mrs. Wangel at the last band concert. She said I might come and call on them.

BALLESTED: You should get to know them better; it'd be a good connection.

LYNGSTRAND: I had thought of dropping in—just to pay my respects, you know—if a suitable opportunity arose—

BALLESTED: "Suitable opportunity"! What nonsense—! (*Looks off left*) Damn it all! (*Gathers his things together*) The steamer's docked already. I'd better get to the hotel. Someone might need my services. I'm an expert hairdresser too, you know.

LYNGSTRAND: You must be very versatile.

BALLESTED: In a small place like this you have to learn to accla—acclimatize yourself to various professions. If you ever need anything in the hair-goods line—just ask for Ballested the dancing master.

LYNGSTRAND: Dancing master—?

BALLESTED: Or leader of the brass band if you prefer. By the way—we're giving a concert tonight up at Prospect Park! Well—goodbye! Goodbye!

(*He picks up his painting materials and goes out through*

the gate and off left. HILDE *comes out of the house carrying
the footstool.* BOLETTE *brings more flowers.* LYNGSTRAND
greets HILDE *from the garden.*)

HILDE (*At the railing. Does not return his greeting*): Bolette
told me you'd screwed up enough courage to come inside
the gate today.

LYNGSTRAND: I hope you don't mind—I did take the liberty—

HILDE: Been for your morning walk?

LYNGSTRAND: I can't say I've walked very far—

HILDE: Been for a swim?

LYNGSTRAND: I went in for a few minutes. I saw your mother
down at the beach. She was just going into her bathhouse.

HILDE: Who was?

LYNGSTRAND: Your mother.

HILDE: Well, well! (*She places the footstool in front of the
rocking chair.*)

BOLETTE (*Changing the subject*): Did you see Father's boat
by any chance?

LYNGSTRAND: There was a sailboat heading in for shore.

BOLETTE: That must have been Father. He had to visit a patient on one of the islands. (*She arranges a couple of things
on the table.*)

LYNGSTRAND (*Steps up onto the lowest step of the veranda*):
What a lot of lovely flowers!

BOLETTE: Yes—they're pretty, aren't they?

LYNGSTRAND: Beautiful! Is it some sort of celebration?

BOLETTE: It is indeed!

LYNGSTRAND: I thought it must be! Your father's birthday perhaps?

BOLETTE (*Warningly, to* HILDE): Hm-hm!

HILDE (*Pays no attention*): No—Mother's.

LYNGSTRAND: Oh! Your mother's!

BOLETTE (*In a low angry tone*): Stop it, Hilde!

HILDE (*Likewise*): Leave me alone, will you! (*To* LYNG-
STRAND) Isn't it about time for your lunch?

LYNGSTRAND (*Backs down the step*): Yes, I ought to eat something, I suppose.

HILDE: You must be living in the lap of luxury down at the hotel!

LYNGSTRAND: Oh—I don't live there any more; it was too expensive.

HILDE: Then where do you live now?

LYNGSTRAND: I'm boarding at Mrs. Jensen's.

HILDE: Mrs. Jensen? Which one?

LYNGSTRAND: You know—the midwife.

HILDE: Well! I must say—! Excuse me, Mr. Lyngstrand— I've really too much to do—I can't stand here—

LYNGSTRAND: Oh—I oughtn't to have said that.

HILDE: What?

LYNGSTRAND: Well—what I just said.

HILDE (*Gives him a withering look*): I don't know what you're talking about.

LYNGSTRAND: No; of course not. Well—I'll say good-bye for the present.

BOLETTE (*Comes forward to the top of the steps*): Good-bye, Mr. Lyngstrand. You really must forgive us—we're very busy today. Perhaps some other time—when you've nothing better to do—you'll stop in and see Father and—well—all the rest of the family.

LYNGSTRAND: Thank you. I'd like to very much. (*He bows and goes out by the garden gate. He turns and bows again before disappearing off left.*)

HILDE (*Under her breath*): Adieu, Monsieur! Give my love to Mother Jensen!

BOLETTE (*Softly, shaking her by the arm*): Hilde—! You dreadful child! He might hear you!

HILDE: Well—let him!

BOLETTE (*Looking off right*): Here comes Father.

(DR. WANGEL *enters on the path from the right. He has on traveling clothes and carries a small bag.*)

WANGEL: Well, little girls! Here I am home again! (*He comes through the gate.*)

BOLETTE (*Runs down into the garden to meet him*): It's wonderful to have you back!

HILDE (*Also runs to meet him*): All through for the day, Father?

WANGEL: Not quite; I'll have to go down to the office presently—just for a little while. Any news of Arnholm?

BOLETTE: He got in last night. We asked at the hotel.

WANGEL: You haven't seen him yet?

BOLETTE: No, not yet. He's sure to come and see us this morning, though.

WANGEL: Yes—I expect so.

HILDE (*Tugging at his arm*): Look, Father! Look over there!

WANGEL (*Turns and looks up at the veranda*): Well! Doesn't it look festive!

BOLETTE: We've done a fine job, haven't we?

WANGEL: You certainly have! Where is—? Are we alone here?

HILDE: Yes. She went—

BOLETTE (*Breaking in*): Mother went for a swim.

WANGEL (*Looks tenderly at* BOLETTE *and pats her head. With some hesitation*): It's lovely, children. But—you won't leave it like this all day, will you? I mean—the flag flying and all?

HILDE: Of course, Father! What do you suppose!

WANGEL: Well—it's just that—

BOLETTE (*Nodding and smiling at him*): Don't you see, Father! It's in honor of Arnholm! He's an old friend, and he hasn't been here for years—it's only natural!

HILDE (*Smiling and tugging at his arm*): After all—he was Bolette's tutor, Father!

WANGEL: You're full of mischief, both of you!—Still—it's understandable enough—her memory is very dear to us. All the same— Here, Hilde (*Gives her his bag*)—this goes to the office—I don't quite like it, children; it's the wrong way to go about it. The fact that every year the three of us—Well, what can one say! I suppose it can't be otherwise.

HILDE (*About to go off left through the garden with her father's bag, stops and turning points off stage*): Look! Someone's coming up the road. Do you suppose it's the professor?

BOLETTE (*Looking off*): That old man? You're crazy! That
can't be Mr. Arnholm!

WANGEL: Wait, children—I believe—Yes! Of course it's he!

BOLETTE (*Staring, in amazement*): Why—so it is!

(ARNHOLM, *smartly dressed, wearing gold spectacles and
carrying a light cane, appears on the road coming from the
left. He looks tired, as though overworked. He bows in a
friendly way and comes into the garden through the gate.*)

WANGEL (*Goes to meet him*): Welcome my dear Arnholm!
Welcome to your old haunts again!

ARNHOLM: My dear Doctor! Many thanks! It's good to see
you! (*They shake hands and come back through the
garden*) And are these—? The children! (*Gives them his
hands*) I never would have known them!

WANGEL: I'm sure you wouldn't!

ARNHOLM: Bolette, perhaps. Yes—I think I'd have known
her.

WANGEL: I doubt it. It's eight or nine years since you last
saw her. Many things have changed since then.

ARNHOLM: Oh, I don't know— The trees have grown a bit,
of course; and that summerhouse is new—

WANGEL: I didn't mean just outwardly—

ARNHOLM: And, of course, now you have a couple of mar-
riageable young ladies on your hands.

WANGEL: A couple! Come now! One, perhaps—

HILDE (*Under her breath*): *Dear* Father!

WANGEL: It's cooler on the veranda; you'll be more comfortable there.

ARNHOLM: Thank you, dear Doctor.

(*They go up the steps to the veranda.* WANGEL *gives*
ARNHOLM *the rocking chair.*)

WANGEL: Do sit down; you look quite tired after your journey.

ARNHOLM: Not really. Now that I'm here I'll soon—

BOLETTE (*To* WANGEL): Shall I fetch some lemonade, Father? We'd better have it inside. It's getting warm out here.

WANGEL: Lemonade would be very nice, I think; and perhaps a little cognac too.

BOLETTE: Cognac, Father?

WANGEL: Just a drop—for those of us who want it!

BOLETTE: Very well. Hilde—take Father's bag down to the office.

(BOLETTE *goes into the house and closes the door after her.* HILDE *takes the bag and goes off left through the garden.*)

ARNHOLM (*Who has followed* BOLETTE *with his eyes*): A charming girl! Both charming girls, Doctor.

WANGEL (*Sitting down*): They are, aren't they?

ARNHOLM: I can't get over Bolette. Hilde too, for that matter. But, what about you, dear Doctor? What are your plans? Do you intend to go on living here?

WANGEL: Yes, I suppose so. I was born and raised here, you see. And I've known great happiness here too. You remember my first wife, Arnholm? I was not allowed to keep her long. Her death was a great sorrow to us all.

ARNHOLM: I remember her well.

WANGEL: But I've been very fortunate in my second wife. She's made me very happy too. All in all, fate has been most kind to me.

ARNHOLM: Have you children by this marriage?

WANGEL: About two and a half years ago we had a little boy. We lost him when he was only five months old.

ARNHOLM: Isn't your wife home today?

WANGEL: She should be here any moment now. She went down to bathe. She never misses a day this time of year— no matter what the weather is.

ARNHOLM: She's quite well I hope?

WANGEL: Yes, I think so; though she's been a little nervous, on and off, these past few years; I can't quite make out what's wrong with her. But as long as she can get into the sea—! That seems to keep her well and happy.

ARNHOLM: She was always like that, as I remember.

WANGEL (*With a scarcely perceptible smile*): Of course— you knew her, didn't you? When you were teaching up at Skjoldvik?

ARNHOLM: That's right. I was living at the parsonage; she often used to visit there. And I nearly always caught a glimpse of her when I went to see her father at the lighthouse.

WANGEL: Those years at the lighthouse seem to have made a great impression on her. It's only natural, I suppose. The people round here don't understand her. They call her "The Lady from the Sea."

ARNHOLM: Do they?

WANGEL: Yes. That's why— Do talk to her about the old days, Arnholm; I've a feeling it would do her good.

ARNHOLM (*Looks at him doubtfully*): Are you sure? What makes you think so?

WANGEL: I'm certain of it.

ELLIDA'S VOICE (*Off stage in the garden*): Wangel! Are you there?

WANGEL (*Rising*): Yes, dear. I'm here.

(ELLIDA WANGEL, *wrapped in a large light cloak, enters through the trees by the summerhouse. Her wet hair hangs down over her shoulders.* ARNHOLM *rises.*)

WANGEL (*Smiles and holds out his hands to her*): Here comes the mermaid!

ELLIDA (*Goes quickly to the veranda and grasps his hands*): When did you get back? Thank heaven you're home again!

WANGEL: Just now—a few moments ago. (*Indicates* ARNHOLM) Here's an old friend waiting to see you.

ELLIDA: So you got here at last! Do forgive me for not being here to welcome you!

ARNHOLM: Don't mention it! No need to stand on ceremony with me!

WANGEL: How was the water? Cool and bracing?

ELLIDA: Flat and tepid! The water's never bracing here! It's not like the open sea. Here in the fjords the water always strikes me as unhealthy.

ARNHOLM: Unhealthy?

ELLIDA: Yes, unhealthy. And I believe it has an unhealthy effect on people too.

WANGEL (*Smiling*): A fine recommendation for a health resort!

ARNHOLM: Do you know what I think, Mrs. Wangel? I think there's a strange bond between you and the open sea— and everything connected with it.

ELLIDA: Perhaps. I've often thought that might be true— Well! Aren't you pleased? Look at all these decorations in your honor! The girls *have* been busy!

WANGEL (*Embarrassed*): Hm— (*Looks at his watch*) I think I'd better—

ARNHOLM: You mean—? All this is for me?

ELLIDA: Well—of course! We're not usually this festive. Uh! It's stifling here! (*Goes down in the garden*) Let's go and sit in the arbor. There's sometimes a little breeze out there. (*She settles herself in the arbor.*)

ARNHOLM (*Joins her*): It seems delightfully cool to me.

ELLIDA: You're used to city air. They say Christiania is dreadful in the summer.

WANGEL (*Who has also come down into the garden*): Ellida dear—will you look after our friend for a little while?

ELLIDA: Have you business to attend to?

WANGEL: I must just look in at the office. And then I'll change my clothes. I shan't be long—

ARNHOLM (*Sits down in the arbor*): Take your time, my dear Doctor. I'm sure we'll find plenty to talk about.

WANGEL: I'm sure you will. Well—goodbye for now! (*He goes off through the garden left.*)

ELLIDA: (*After a short pause*): It's quite pleasant here.

ARNHOLM: I find it *very* pleasant!

ELLIDA: They call this my summerhouse— I had it built, you see. Or rather Wangel did—to please me.

ARNHOLM: Is this where you usually sit?

ELLIDA: Yes, nearly always—in the daytime.

ARNHOLM: And, I suppose, the children keep you company?

ELLIDA: No—they usually stick to the veranda.

ARNHOLM: And Wangel?

ELLIDA: He divides his time between us. Sometimes he sits with me—sometimes with the girls.

ARNHOLM: Was that arrangement your idea?

ELLIDA: I think we all prefer it. We can always call across to each other—if, by chance, we've anything to say.

ARNHOLM (*After a reflective pause*): The first time I got to know you—up at Skjoldvik, I mean— How long ago that seems—!

ELLIDA: It's a good ten years ago.

ARNHOLM: Just about—yes. I can see you so clearly—standing by the Lighthouse. "The Heathen" our old priest used to call you; he said that when your father had you christened he gave you the name of a ship—not the name of a Christian!

ELLIDA: What did you start to say?

ARNHOLM: At that time the last thing I would have thought possible was to meet you here again as Mrs. Wangel.

ELLIDA: That was before Wangel was— The children's mother was still living then. Their real mother, I mean.

ARNHOLM: Yes, I know. But even if things had been different—even if he'd had no ties—I still would never have expected this.

ELLIDA: Neither would I. Not at that time.

ARNHOLM: Wangel is such a fine man—so honorable and kind—

ELLIDA (*Warmly*): Yes! Indeed he is!

ARNHOLM: But I can't help wondering what you could possibly have in common. You're such different kinds of people, it seems to me.

ELLIDA: You're right. We are.

ARNHOLM: Then—how did it happen? Tell me.

ELLIDA: Don't ask me about it, Arnholm. I don't think I can explain it. And even if I could—I don't believe you'd understand.

ARNHOLM: Hm. (*In a lower tone*) Does your husband know—? Have you ever told him how I felt about you at that time?

ELLIDA: Of course not! I've never mentioned it.

ARNHOLM: I'm glad. I should feel embarrassed if I thought—

ELLIDA: Well, you needn't. I told him what was true: that I was very fond of you, and that in those days you were the best and truest friend I had.

ARNHOLM: Thank you. I've often wondered—why did you never write to me after I went away?

ELLIDA: I thought it would make it easier for you—since I couldn't share your feelings.

ARNHOLM: Perhaps so.

ELLIDA: Why did *you* never write?

ARNHOLM (*Looks at her with a half-reproachful smile*): I couldn't take the initiative—you might have misunderstood my motives. You'd refused me with such finality—I didn't want to seem importunate.

ELLIDA: Yes—I see. But how is it you've remained single all these years?

ARNHOLM: I had no desire to marry. I preferred to stay true to my memories.

ELLIDA: Nonsense! It's high time you forgot them! You should have been happily married long ago.

ARNHOLM: I'm getting old, it's true! I'm nearly thirty-eight!

ELLIDA: You see! You'd better hurry up! (*Is silent a moment, then speaks in a low serious tone*) I'd like to tell you something, Arnholm—something I couldn't possibly have told you then.

ARNHOLM: What is it?

ELLIDA: When you asked me to marry you—I *had* to refuse you. I had no choice.

ARNHOLM: I understand. All you felt for me was friendship.

ELLIDA: But what you don't understand is this: At that particular time my heart, my mind—all of me—belonged to
someone else.

ARNHOLM: At that particular time, you say?

ELLIDA: Yes. Precisely.

ARNHOLM: But that's impossible! Surely you're mistaken. You
scarcely knew Wangel then.

ELLIDA: I'm not speaking of Wangel.

ARNHOLM: Not of——? But who else was there? I don't remember a single soul at Skjoldvik who could have meant anything to you.

ELLIDA: It would seem so, wouldn't it? It was all such madness!

ARNHOLM: Won't you tell me about it?

ELLIDA: No; there's no need. But I was not free at that time
—I did want you to know that.

ARNHOLM: You mean—if you had been free——?

ELLIDA: Well?

ARNHOLM: —your answer to me would have been different?

ELLIDA: It's hard to say; my answer to Wangel was different,
wasn't it?

ARNHOLM: But—I don't understand; what's the point in telling me this now——?

ELLIDA (*Rises and moves about in restless agitation*): I must
confide in someone! No—stay where you are!

ARNHOLM: You mean—your husband doesn't know——?

ELLIDA: I told him when he first asked me to marry him that
at one time I had been bound to someone else. He never
tried to find out any more about it, and since then we've
neither of us mentioned it. It was sheer madness in any
case. And then, it all ended so abruptly. In a way—that is.

ARNHOLM (*Rises*): Only in a way? Not entirely?

ELLIDA: Yes, yes—entirely, my dear Arnholm. I know what
you must be thinking—but it's nothing like that, I assure
you. It's hard to understand—I couldn't possibly explain it.
You'd either think me ill—or raving mad—

ARNHOLM: Ellida—Mrs. Wangel—you must tell me the whole story! I insist!

ELLIDA: Very well—I'll try. But you're such a sane, well-balanced man— You'd never be able to realize what— (*Looks off stage and breaks off suddenly*) Wait! Someone's coming. Some other time. (LYNGSTRAND *appears from the road left and enters the garden. He wears a flower in his buttonhole and carries a large bouquet wrapped in paper and tied with silk ribbons. He stops, hesitating by the veranda steps.*)

ELLIDA (*From the arbor*): Are you looking for the girls, Mr. Lyngstrand?

LYNGSTRAND (*Turning*): Oh—you're there, Mrs. Wangel. (*Bows and goes towards her*) No—as a matter of fact I wasn't. I was looking for you. You did give me leave to call on you, and—

ELLIDA: Of course I did. You're always welcome here.

LYNGSTRAND: Thanks. This seemed a good opportunity— since you're celebrating here today—

ELLIDA: So you know about it, do you?

LYNGSTRAND: Yes, indeed. That's why— May I offer you these flowers, Mrs. Wangel?

ELLIDA (*Smiles*): How lovely, Mr. Lyngstrand! How kind of you! But here's Professor Arnholm—you should give them to him. You see, it's in his honor—

LYNGSTRAND (*Looks from one to the other puzzled*): I'm sorry—I don't know this gentleman. It's just—I meant them as a birthday present, Mrs. Wangel.

ELLIDA: Birthday? You're mistaken, Mr. Lyngstrand. It's nobody's birthday here today.

LYNGSTRAND: Oh yes, it is! (*With a quiet smile*) I know all about it; but I didn't realize it was such a secret.

ELLIDA: Know all about what, Mr. Lyngstrand?

LYNGSTRAND: About your birthday—that today is your birthday, Mrs. Wangel!

ELLIDA: *My* birthday?

ARNHOLM (*Looks at her inquiringly*): Today? Surely not.

ELLIDA (*To* LYNGSTRAND): Whatever made you think that?

LYNGSTRAND: It was something Miss Hilde said. You see, I was here a little while ago, and I couldn't help asking about all the flowers—and why the flag was flying—

ELLIDA: Yes? Well?

LYNGSTRAND: And Miss Hilde said: "It's because of Mother's birthday."

ELLIDA: Ah—I see!

ARNHOLM (*Exchanges a glance with Ellida*): Well—since the young man's found out about it, Mrs. Wangel—

ELLIDA: Of course—since you've found out about it—

LYNGSTRAND (*Offers the bouquet again*): May I offer my congratulations—

ELLIDA (*Takes the flowers*): Many, many thanks. Do sit down a moment, Mr. Lyngstrand. (ELLIDA, ARNHOLM *and* LYNGSTRAND *sit down in the arbor*) This business of my birthday—was to have been kept secret, Mr. Arnholm.

ARNHOLM: So I see. We outsiders weren't supposed to know about it!

ELLIDA (*Lays the bouquet on the table*): That's right. Outsiders weren't supposed to know.

LYNGSTRAND: I won't say a word to anyone—I promise.

ELLIDA: Oh—it's not as important as all that. But tell me about yourself. I think you're looking better than you did.

LYNGSTRAND: I'm getting along very nicely, thank you. And next year—if I can manage to go South—

ELLIDA: The girls told me that's what you hope to do—

LYNGSTRAND: Yes. I have a patron in Bergen who is interested in helping me. He's promised to send me there.

ELLIDA: How did you run across him?

LYNGSTRAND: It was a great bit of luck. I happened to be employed on one of his ships, you see—

ELLIDA: Really? Did you want to be a sailor?

LYNGSTRAND: No; far from it! But when my mother died Father didn't want me hanging about the house—so he sent me to sea. On the voyage home we were shipwrecked in the English Channel. It was the best thing that could have happened to me.

ARNHOLM: How do you mean?

LYNGSTRAND: I was in the icy water for hours before they rescued me—and this trouble started in my chest. I was forbidden to go to sea again. It was a great bit of luck for me!

ARNHOLM: Is that the way you look at it?

LYNGSTRAND: Yes, of course. After all—this lung condition isn't dangerous; and now I'll be able to become a sculptor —I always dreamed of that. Modeling in clay is wonderful; to feel it taking shape under one's fingers!

ELLIDA: What do you want to model? Mermen and mermaids? Vikings, perhaps?

LYNGSTRAND: No—nothing like that. As soon as I can manage it, I plan to start on a big piece of work—a group, as they call it.

ELLIDA: I see. What sort of a group?

LYNGSTRAND: I want to try and express something I once experienced.

ARNHOLM: A good idea. Stick to the things you really know.

ELLIDA: But what is it to be?

LYNGSTRAND: The main figure is that of a young woman—a sailor's wife. She's sleeping, but it's a restless sleep—tormented by dreams. I believe I can make it quite clear that she's dreaming.

ARNHOLM: Is that all?

LYNGSTRAND: Oh, no. There's to be another figure—a sort of phantom, you might call it. It's her husband; she's been unfaithful to him while he was away—and now he's drowned.

ARNHOLM: You mean he—?

ELLIDA: Drowned?

LYNGSTRAND: Yes—drowned at sea. But the strange thing is that he's come home all the same. It's the middle of the night, and he stands there by the bed looking down at her.

The water is dripping from his hair and from his clothes. He should look as though he'd just been hauled out of the sea.

ELLIDA (*Leans back in her chair*): What a strange idea! (*Closes her eyes*) I can see it vividly.

ARNHOLM: But my dear Mr.—Mr.—I thought you said it was something you'd experienced?

LYNGSTRAND: So I have—in a way.

ARNHOLM: Seen a dead man come to—?

LYNGSTRAND: I didn't mean I'd actually experienced it—not literally, that is. But still—

ELLIDA (*With eager animation*): Tell me more about it! I'd like to understand it thoroughly.

ARNHOLM (*Smiles*): Quite in your line, isn't it? Anything to do with the magic of the sea!

ELLIDA: How did it happen, Mr. Lyngstrand?

LYNGSTRAND: Well, you see—we were sailing from a town called Halifax, and we had to leave our boatswain behind—laid up in a hospital. We took on an American instead. This new boatswain—

ELLIDA: The American?

LYNGSTRAND: Yes. One day he borrowed a whole lot of old newspapers from the captain; he wanted to learn Norwegian he said. He was always poring over them.

ELLIDA: Well?

LYNGSTRAND: One night there was a violent storm. All hands were on deck—all except the boatswain and me. He'd sprained his ankle and couldn't walk; I was sick and lying in my bunk. He sat there in the fo'c'sle, poring over one of the old newspapers as usual—

ELLIDA: Yes? Yes?

LYNGSTRAND: Suddenly he let out a kind of roar; I looked at him and his face was as white as chalk. Then he crumpled the paper in his hands and tore it into a thousand pieces. But he did it quietly; quite quietly.

ELLIDA: Did he speak? Did he say anything?

LYNGSTRAND: Not at first. But after a while he said, as if to himself: "Married. Married another man while I was away."

ELLIDA (*Closes her eyes and says half to herself*): He said that, did he?

LYNGSTRAND: Yes. And the strange thing is, he said it in perfect Norwegian. I remember thinking what a gift for languages he must have had.

ELLIDA: And after that? What happened then?

LYNGSTRAND: The strangest thing of all. I'll never be able to forget it. He added—and he said this very quietly too—: "She's mine and she always will be. I shall go back and find her. Even were I to drown I should rise up from the bottom of the sea to claim her; and she would have to follow me."

ELLIDA (*Pours herself a glass of water. Her hand trembles*): Pah! It's stifling here today!

LYNGSTRAND: And there was such intensity—such power—in the way he said this, I felt sure he was actually capable of doing it.

ELLIDA: What became of him? Do you know?

LYNGSTRAND: He's dead, Mrs. Wangel. I'm sure of that.

ELLIDA (*Rapidly*): What makes you think so?

LYNGSTRAND: It was just after this that we were wrecked in the Channel. I got off in the longboat with the captain and five others. The mate and another man went in the dinghy —and the American went with them.

ELLIDA: And nothing's been heard of them since?

LYNGSTRAND: Not a word, Mrs. Wangel. That's why I'd so much like to translate this story into a work of art: the unfaithful wife, and her husband who comes back from the depths of the sea to take revenge. I see them both so clearly.

ELLIDA: So do I. (*She rises*) Come— Shall we go inside? Or we might join Wangel. It's stifling here. (*She goes out of the arbor.*)

LYNGSTRAND (*Who has also risen*): I'm afraid I must be going. I only looked in for a moment to wish you a happy birthday.

ELLIDA: Well—if you must—(*Shakes hands with him*) Goodbye, and thanks for the flowers.

(LYNGSTRAND *bows and goes out through the gate and off left.*)

ARNHOLM (*Rises and joins* ELLIDA): I'm afraid this has upset you, Mrs. Wangel.

ELLIDA: Yes, in a way—although—

ARNHOLM: Still—it's no more than might have been expected.

ELLIDA (*Looks at him bewildered*): Expected?

ARNHOLM: So it seems to me.

ELLIDA: Expect someone to come back from the dead?

ARNHOLM: What do you mean? Don't tell me it's that absurd story—!

ELLIDA: Not so absurd, perhaps.

ARNHOLM: Is that what has upset you? This nonsense about a dead man? I thought of course—

ELLIDA: What did you think?

ARNHOLM: I thought you were just pretending to be moved by that because you were upset about this birthday celebration. It surely must distress you to find that your husband and his children still live in a world of memories in which you have no share.

ELLIDA: Oh, no. That can't be helped. Wangel doesn't belong to me alone; I've no right to expect it.

ARNHOLM: I think you have.

ELLIDA: I haven't; that's the point. I have my memories too. A life of memories in which *they* can have no share.

ARNHOLM: You! (*In a low voice*) Are you implying—? Don't you—Don't you really love your husband?

ELLIDA: Yes! I do! I've grown to love him with all my heart. That's what makes it all so dreadful—so confusing— so unthinkable!

ARNHOLM: Tell me what's troubling you. You *must* confide in me!

ELLIDA: I can't—I can't! Not now. Some other time, perhaps.

BOLETTE (*Comes out onto the veranda and down into the garden*): Here comes Father—he's back from the office. Couldn't we all go and sit inside?

ELLIDA: Yes, let's.

WANGEL (*Enters with* HILDE *round the house from the left; he has changed his clothes*): Now I'm a free man again! How about a nice cool drink?

ELLIDA: Just a moment. (*She goes back to the arbor and fetches the bouquet.*)

HILDE: What lovely flowers! Where did you get them?

ELLIDA: From Mr. Lyngstrand, Hilde dear.

HILDE (*With a start*): Lyngstrand!

BOLETTE (*Uneasily*): Was he here again?

ELLIDA (*With a half smile*): Yes, he came back to bring these. They're a birthday present.

BOLETTE (*With a glance at* HILDE): Oh—!

HILDE (*Mutters*): The little beast!

WANGEL (*In acute embarrassment, to* ELLIDA): You see, darling—it's just that—

ELLIDA: Come along, girls! Let's put my flowers in water with the others. (*She goes onto the veranda.*)

BOLETTE (*Softly to* HILDE): You see? She's really very kind.

HILDE (*Angrily. Under her breath*): It's all put on! She's playing up to Father!

WANGEL (*Who has followed* ELLIDA *to the veranda; presses her hand*): Thank you! Thank you, my dear!

ELLIDA (*Arranging the flowers*): Nonsense! It's only right that I should join you in celebrating—Mother's birthday!

ARNHOLM: Hm— (*He joins* WANGEL *and* ELLIDA. BOLETTE *and* HILDE *remain in the garden.*)

CURTAIN

ACT TWO

SCENE: *In Prospect Park; a wooded height behind the town. A cairn of stones stands in the background supporting a weather vane. Large stones for seats are placed round the vane and in the foreground. Far below in the background one sees the outer fjord, with islands and jutting promontories. The open sea is not visible. It is twilight on a clear summer night. The sky is tinged with orange over the mountain peaks in the far distance. The sound of singing is heard faintly from the lower slopes on the right.*

Young people from the town, ladies and gentlemen come in couples from the right, pass the vane conversing familiarly and go out to the left. Shortly afterwards BALLESTED *appears, acting as guide to a party of foreign tourists. He is loaded with the ladies' shawls and satchels.*

BALLESTED (*Points upward with his stick*): *Sehen Sie, meine Herrschaften*—over there *liegt eine andere* height. *Das willen wir* also *besteigen, und so herunter*—(*He continues in English and leads the party out to the right.*)
(HILDE *comes quickly up the slope on the right and looks backward. Presently* BOLETTE *comes up the same way.*)

BOLETTE: Hilde! Why do you insist on running away from Lyngstrand?

HILDE: That snail's pace drives me mad. Look at him! Look at him creeping up the hill!

BOLETTE: He's very ill, remember.

HILDE: Do you think it's really serious?

BOLETTE: I'm sure it is.

234

HILDE: Father examined him today. I wonder what he thought.

BOLETTE: He told me. It's hardening of the lungs or something. Father says he hasn't long to live.

HILDE: Is that what he said? I thought as much!

BOLETTE: Now don't go saying anything to *him!*

HILDE: Of course not! (*Drops her voice*) Look at little Hans crawling up the slope! Wouldn't you know he'd have a name like Hans? He looks just like it!

BOLETTE (*In a whisper*): Now behave yourself! I warn you! (LYNGSTRAND *enters from the right carrying a parasol.*)

LYNGSTRAND: I'm so sorry! I can't seem to keep up with you.

HILDE: You've taken to using a parasol I see.

LYNGSTRAND: It's your mother's. I'd forgotten my stick, so she lent me this instead.

BOLETTE: Are Father and the others still down there?

LYNGSTRAND: Yes; your father went into the restaurant a moment, and the others are outside listening to the music. They're coming up here a little later on your mother said.

HILDE (*Stands and stares at him*): You're quite exhausted, aren't you?

LYNGSTRAND: I am a little tired. I'd better sit down for a bit. (*Sits on a rock downstage right.*)

HILDE (*Stands in front of him*): There's to be a dance tonight down by the bandstand. Have you heard?

LYNGSTRAND: I heard it mentioned, yes.

HILDE: Do you like dancing?

BOLETTE (*Who is picking wild flowers*): Hilde! Do let Mr. Lyngstrand get his breath!

LYNGSTRAND: I don't know. I think I might like it very much.

HILDE: Haven't you ever learned?

LYNGSTRAND: As a matter of fact I haven't, but that isn't what I meant. I'm not allowed to—on account of my chest, you know.

HILDE: Oh yes! That "weakness" as you call it.

LYNGSTRAND: Yes—that's it.

HILDE: It must make you very unhappy, doesn't it?

LYNGSTRAND: No, not really. (*Smiles*) I think it's due to that, that people are so very kind to me.

HILDE: And, besides—it isn't really serious.

LYNGSTRAND: Not in the least. Your father didn't seem to think so either.

HILDE: All you need's that trip abroad—and then you'll be quite well again.

LYNGSTRAND: Quite well! I'm sure of that.

BOLETTE (*Brings him the flowers*): Here's a boutonniere for you, Mr. Lyngstrand.

LYNGSTRAND: Oh, thank you, Miss Bolette! How very kind of you.

HILDE (*Looking down off right*): Here they come now.

BOLETTE (*Also looking down*): I wonder if they know the path. No! They're going the wrong way.

LYNGSTRAND (*Rises*): I'll run down to the turn and call them back.

HILDE: You'll have to give a good shout or they won't hear you.

BOLETTE: Don't go! You'll get so tired again.

LYNGSTRAND: Going downhill's easy! (*He goes off right.*)

HILDE: "Downhill" says he! (*Watches him*) He's actually running! He forgets he'll have to climb all the way up again!

BOLETTE: Poor thing—

HILDE: If Lyngstrand proposed to you, would you accept him?

BOLETTE: Are you crazy?!

HILDE: I mean—if he didn't have this "weakness" in his chest? And if he weren't going to die so soon? Would you?

BOLETTE: I think I'll let you have him.

HILDE: No thank you! He can't even support himself. He hasn't a penny to his name.

BOLETTE: Why are you so interested in him, then?

HILDE: It's this "weakness" of his. It fascinates me.

BOLETTE: But you're not a bit sorry for him, are you?

HILDE: No, I'm not. But it intrigues me.

BOLETTE: What do you mean?

HILDE: It's fun to watch him; to make him say it isn't serious. I like to hear him tell about his plans; about going abroad and becoming a great sculptor. He's so confident—so pleased with everything. And all the time I know nothing will ever come of it; nothing can possibly come of it—because he won't live long enough. It's absolutely thrilling!

BOLETTE: Thrilling!

HILDE: Yes, thrilling! Why shouldn't I say so? I find it absolutely thrilling!

BOLETTE: What a beast you are, Hilde!

HILDE: That's what I want to be. Out of spite! (*Looks down*) Here they come at last! Look at Arnholm—he doesn't like climbing either! (*Turns around*) By the way—do you know what I noticed while we were having lunch?

BOLETTE: No—what?

HILDE: His hair's beginning to fall out! He's quite bald on top.

BOLETTE: What nonsense! That's not true!

HILDE: Oh yes it is! And he has awful wrinkles round his eyes. How could you ever have been in love with him, Bolette!

BOLETTE (*Smiling*): It does seem funny, doesn't it? I remember once crying my heart out because he said Bolette was an ugly name.

HILDE: You didn't! (*Looks down again*) Look! Just look at this! Arnholm and the Lady from the Sea! She seems very taken up with him. Do you suppose there's anything between them?

BOLETTE: You ought to be ashamed, Hilde—saying a thing like that! Just as we were getting along so well—

HILDE: Don't fool yourself, my girl! We'll never get along. She's not our sort—and she doesn't like us either. God knows what Father ever saw in her. I wouldn't be surprised if she went mad one of these days.

BOLETTE: Mad! Whatever put that into your head?

HILDE: It's quite possible, you know. After all, her mother died a lunatic—I know that for a fact.

BOLETTE: Where do you pick up such things? For God's sake keep your mouth shut! Try and behave—for Father's sake. Hilde! Do you hear?

(WANGEL, ELLIDA, ARNHOLM *and* LYNGSTRAND *come up the path from the right.*)

ELLIDA (*Pointing towards the background*): It's right out there!

ARNHOLM: Of course. It must be.

ELLIDA: That's where the sea is.

BOLETTE (*To* ARNHOLM): It's pretty up here, isn't it?

ARNHOLM: Beautiful! A glorious view!

WANGEL: Did you never come up here before?

ARNHOLM: No never. It was inaccessible in my time; there wasn't even a path, as I remember.

WANGEL: That's true—it was a wilderness then. All this has been developed in the last few years.

BOLETTE: The view's even finer over there. They call that Pilot's Peak.

WANGEL: How about going there, Ellida?

ELLIDA (*Sits down on a rock stage right*): You others go if you like. I think I'll stay here for a while.

WANGEL: Then I'll stay with you. The girls will show you around, Arnholm, if you care to see the sights.

BOLETTE: Would you like to, Mr. Arnholm?

ARNHOLM: I'd be delighted. Is there a path all the way to the top?

BOLETTE: Yes, a nice wide one.

HILDE: People can even walk arm in arm on it!

ARNHOLM (*Jokingly*): Can they indeed, Miss Hilde! (*To* BOLETTE) Let's see if she's right, shall we?

BOLETTE (*Repressing a smile*): If you like.

(*They go off left arm in arm.*)

HILDE (*To* LYNGSTRAND): Shall we go too—?

LYNGSTRAND: Arm-in-arm—?

HILDE: Why not? I've no objection.

LYNGSTRAND (*Takes her arm and laughs delightedly*): This *is* fun, isn't it?

HILDE: Fun?

LYNGSTRAND: It's almost as if we were engaged!

HILDE: Don't tell me it's the first time you've given your arm to a lady, Mr. Lyngstrand! (*They go out left.*)

WANGEL (*Stands upstage beside the landmark*): It's nice to be alone for a little while, Ellida.

ELLIDA: Yes. Come here and sit beside me.

WANGEL: How peaceful it is. Now we can talk.

ELLIDA: What about?

WANGEL: About you. About us. We can't go on like this, Ellida.

ELLIDA: How do you mean?

WANGEL: We must have faith in one another. We must be close—as we used to be.

ELLIDA: I wish that were possible—but I'm afraid it's not.

WANGEL: I believe I understand. From certain things you've said—I think I know what's wrong.

ELLIDA: You don't. You can't! Don't say you understand.

WANGEL: But I do. I know how honest, how loyal you are—

ELLIDA: Loyal—yes. That's true, I think—

WANGEL: The only relationship that could make you happy —that could make you feel secure—must be complete and perfect.

ELLIDA (*Looks at him intently*): Well?

WANGEL: Being a man's second wife is hard for you, Ellida.

ELLIDA: What makes you say that—just now?

WANGEL: I've often suspected it, and what happened today convinced me I was right. I know you were upset by that birthday celebration the children had arranged. You blamed me for it too, I think—and perhaps in a way you're right. It's hard for a man to wipe out old memories—at least it is for me. That's not my nature.

ELLIDA: I know. I know that very well.

WANGEL: But you're mistaken all the same. You know, Ellida —I believe the thought of the children's mother has become almost an obsession with you. You think of her as still alive; you feel her invisible presence in our midst; and

you're tormented because you imagine I divide my love
equally between you. You've come to see something almost
immoral in our relationship; that's why you can no longer
bring yourself to live with me as my wife.

ELLIDA: Is that how you see it, Wangel? You've come to that
conclusion?

WANGEL: Yes, I have. Today it all became quite clear to me.

ELLIDA: Quite clear, you say. No! You mustn't believe that.

WANGEL: Oh, I know there's more to it than that.

ELLIDA: What more?

WANGEL: I know you find these surroundings unendurable.
The mountains weigh on you and crush your spirit. The
light is not intense enough, nor the horizon wide enough.
The air here is not potent or bracing enough for you.

ELLIDA: It's true. Day and night, winter and summer, I can
never shake off this longing for the sea. I'm homesick for
it.

WANGEL: I know, Ellida dear. (*Lays his hand on her head*)
That's why I've decided to take my poor sick child back
home again.

ELLIDA: What do you mean?

WANGEL: We'll move away from here.

ELLIDA: Move away!

WANGEL: Yes; to the open sea—where you can have the sort
of home you long for.

ELLIDA: That's impossible! You mustn't think of that. You
could never be happy anywhere but here.

WANGEL: That's as it may be. Besides—do you think I could
ever be happy without you?

ELLIDA: But I'm here—and I shall go on being here. You
know I'm yours, Wangel.

WANGEL: Are you mine, Ellida?

ELLIDA: As for going away—you mustn't talk about that any
more. Your work is here; your life is here. This place means
everything to you!

WANGEL: We're moving all the same. My mind's made up,
Ellida.

ELLIDA: What would we gain by it?

WANGEL: You would regain your health and peace of mind.

ELLIDA: I wonder. And you? You must think of yourself. What would *you* gain by it?

WANGEL: I would regain you, my darling.

ELLIDA: You wouldn't, Wangel! You wouldn't! That's what's so pitiful—so heartbreaking!

WANGEL: We shall find out; for I insist on getting you away from here—the sooner the better. My mind's made up, I tell you!

ELLIDA: No! I won't have it! In that case—God help me—I'd rather tell you everything.

WANGEL: I wish you would, Ellida.

ELLIDA: I won't have your life made miserable on my account. And I assure you it would do no good.

WANGEL: Now tell me everything. You've promised!

ELLIDA: I'll try. I don't know if I can put it into words. Sit here beside me. (*They sit down on a rock.*)

WANGEL: Well, Ellida?

ELLIDA: Do you remember that day you came and asked me to be your wife? You spoke of your first marriage—very honestly and simply. You told me how happy it had been.

WANGEL: Yes. So it was.

ELLIDA: I know, dear. I only mention it because I want you to remember that I was honest with you too. I told you then about another man; a man I'd been engaged to—in a way.

WANGEL: In a way—?

ELLIDA: Yes. In a way. It lasted such a little while, you see. He had to leave—and shortly after that, I broke it off. I told you all about it.

WANGEL: Why do you speak of him now, Ellida? It had nothing to do with me. I've never even asked you who he was.

ELLIDA: That's true, you haven't. You've always spared my feelings.

WANGEL (*Smiles*): And, after all—it wasn't very difficult to guess his name.

ELLIDA: His name?

WANGEL: Yes. There weren't many to choose from up at Skjoldvik. There was actually only one man who—

ELLIDA: You think it was Arnholm, I suppose.

WANGEL: Well—wasn't it?

ELLIDA: No.

WANGEL: Not Arnholm? Then—I can't imagine—

ELLIDA: Do you remember one year late in the fall, a large American ship came into Skjoldvik harbor for repairs?

WANGEL: I remember very well; the captain was found murdered in his cabin. They wanted a post-mortem—they sent for me.

ELLIDA: Yes—so they did.

WANGEL: The second mate had killed him—so they said.

ELLIDA: But no one knew for certain. It was never proved against him.

WANGEL: There wasn't much doubt about it. Why else should he have drowned himself?

ELLIDA: He didn't drown himself. He sailed on another ship bound for the North.

WANGEL (*Amazed*): How do you know that?

ELLIDA (*With an effort*): Because he's the man I was engaged to.

WANGEL: What are you saying! That's impossible!

ELLIDA: All the same it's true. He was the man.

WANGEL: But how could you have done such a thing, Ellida? Become engaged to a man like that—an utter stranger! What was his name?

ELLIDA: He called himself Freeman then. But later, in his letters, he used the name of Johnston—Alfred Johnston.

WANGEL: Where was he from?

ELLIDA: He said he came from Finmark. But he was born in Finland and came across the border as a child—with his father, I think he said.

WANGEL: He was a Quinn, then.

ELLIDA: I believe that's what they're called.

WANGEL: What else do you know about him?

ELLIDA: Just that he went to sea when he was still a boy. He'd made many long voyages.

WANGEL: Nothing else?

ELLIDA: No. We didn't talk much about that sort of thing.

WANGEL: What did you talk about?

ELLIDA: Mostly about the sea.

WANGEL: Ah——! The sea!

ELLIDA: About storms and calms. Dark nights on the Ocean— and bright sunny days as well. But mostly about whales and porpoises, and the seals that bask on the reefs in the warm sunshine. And we talked about the sea birds too— the gulls and eagles. It was strange—as we talked I always felt that he was part of all these things.

WANGEL: How about you——?

ELLIDA: I felt somehow as though I were part of them too.

WANGEL: I see. And so you became engaged to him.

ELLIDA: Yes. He said I had to.

WANGEL: Had to? Had you no will of your own?

ELLIDA: Not while he was there. Then—afterwards—it all seemed so incredible.

WANGEL: Did you see him often?

ELLIDA: Not very often. He came out to have a look at the lighthouse—that's how I got to know him. After that we used to meet occasionally. But when the thing about the captain happened, he had to go away.

WANGEL: Tell me about that.

ELLIDA: Very early one morning—just before dawn—I got a note from him. He told me to come to him at Bratthammer —you know, the headland between Skjoldvik and the lighthouse.

WANGEL: Yes—I know it well.

ELLIDA: I was to come at once, he said. He had to talk to me.

WANGEL: And you went?

ELLIDA: I had to—I couldn't help it. Then he told me that during the night he'd stabbed the captain.

WANGEL: He told you that himself? He actually admitted it?

ELLIDA: Yes. But he'd only done what was right, he said.

WANGEL: What did he mean—right? What reason did he give?

ELLIDA: He wouldn't say. He said it would be wrong for me to hear about such things.

WANGEL: And you believed him?

ELLIDA: It never occurred to me not to. Still—he had to get away. And just as he was about to say good-bye to me— you'll never believe what he did then.

WANGEL: Tell me!

ELLIDA: He took a key ring from his pocket; then he took from his finger a ring he used to wear. I had a small ring on my finger; he slipped it off, put both rings onto the key ring—and said: "Now together we will be wedded to the sea."

WANGEL: Wedded—?

ELLIDA: That's what he said. Then, with all his might, he threw the key ring with our two rings on it far out into the deep water.

WANGEL: And you, Ellida? You agreed to this?

ELLIDA: Yes—can you believe it? I felt at the time as though it had to be. But then, thank God, he went away!

WANGEL: And once he'd gone—?

ELLIDA: I soon came to my senses then. I saw how utterly absurd—how meaningless it had all been.

WANGEL: But you said something about letters. Did you hear from him?

ELLIDA: Yes, I heard from him. Only a few lines the first time —from Archangel. He just said he was going to America. He told me where to write to him.

WANGEL: And did you write?

ELLIDA: At once. I simply said that it was all over between us. That he must no longer think of me—just as I would never think of him.

WANGEL: And he wrote again in spite of that?

ELLIDA: Yes, he wrote again.

WANGEL: What was his answer?

ELLIDA: He didn't refer to what I'd said. It was as though I'd

never broken off with him. He told me quite calmly that I
must wait for him. When he was ready for me he would
let me know, and then I was to go to him at once.

WANGEL: He wouldn't release you then?

ELLIDA: No. Of course, I wrote again. I repeated what I'd
said, almost word for word—but in even stronger terms.

WANGEL: And then did he give in?

ELLIDA: Oh no, far from it. He wrote quite calmly as before.
Not a word about my breaking off with him. Then I realized it was useless, and I never wrote to him again.

WANGEL: And you didn't hear from him either?

ELLIDA: Yes. I had three more letters from him after that. The
first was from California. The second was from China. The
last letter I had was from Australia. He said he was going
to the gold mines. I've not heard from him since.

WANGEL: He seems to have had great power over you, Ellida.

ELLIDA: Yes. He was a terrifying man!

WANGEL: Don't think about it any more. Never, dearest
Ellida! Promise me that. Once we get you away from the
fjords, out by the open sea, the tang of the salt air will cure
you—

ELLIDA: Don't even think of that, Wangel! Don't even speak
of it! It wouldn't be any use. It wouldn't help me to escape.

WANGEL: Escape from what? What do you mean, my dearest?

ELLIDA: My fear of him. The strange power he has over me—

WANGEL: But you escaped from that long ago—when you
broke off with him. It's all over long ago.

ELLIDA (*Jumps up*): But it's not over, you see!

WANGEL: Not over!

ELLIDA: No! It isn't over—and I'm afraid it never will be!

WANGEL (*In a choked voice*): You've never been able to forget this man?

ELLIDA: I had forgotten him. And then, suddenly, it was as
if he had come back again.

WANGEL: How long ago was that?

ELLIDA: About three years ago—a little more, perhaps. It was while I was carrying the child.

WANGEL: During that time! I see! That explains many things, Ellida.

ELLIDA: You're wrong, believe me! There *can* be no explanation for this thing that's taken hold of me.

WANGEL (*Looks at her sorrowfully*): To think that all these years you've loved another man!

ELLIDA: That's not true. I love no one but you.

WANGEL (*In a low voice*): Yet for a long time now, you've refused to be a wife to me. Why is that, Ellida?

ELLIDA: The thought of that strange man fills me with terror.

WANGEL: Terror?

ELLIDA: Yes, terror. I think only the Ocean could fill one with such an overwhelming dread. You see, Wangel—

(*The young people from the town come back from the left, bow, and go out right.* ARNHOLM, BOLETTE, HILDE, *and* LYNGSTRAND *follow them.*)

BOLETTE (*As they pass by*): You're still here, are you?

ELLIDA: It's been so cool and pleasant.

ARNHOLM: We're going down to dance.

WANGEL: Good. We'll join you later.

HILDE: Good-bye for now.

ELLIDA: Mr. Lyngstrand—wait a minute, will you?

(LYNGSTRAND *waits.* ARNHOLM, BOLETTE *and* HILDE *go off right.*)

ELLIDA (*To* LYNGSTRAND): Are you going to dance too?

LYNGSTRAND: No, Mrs. Wangel. I think I'd better not.

ELLIDA: That's right. You're wise. That weakness in your lungs—you haven't quite recovered yet.

LYNGSTRAND: Not quite—that's true.

ELLIDA (*With some hesitation*): How long ago is it since you were on that voyage—?

LYNGSTRAND: When this lung trouble began, you mean?

ELLIDA: Yes. When you were shipwrecked—

LYNGSTRAND: Let's see—a little over three years, it must have been.

ELLIDA: Three years.

LYNGSTRAND: Yes—just about. We left America in February and ran into the equinoctial gales. The wreck happened in March.

ELLIDA (*Looks at* WANGEL): You see—that was the time—

WANGEL: But, Ellida dear—?

ELLIDA: Don't let us keep you, Mr. Lyngstrand. Go and join the others. But don't dance, will you?

LYNGSTRAND: No. I'll just look on. (*He goes out right.*)

WANGEL: Why did you ask about that voyage, Ellida?

ELLIDA: Johnston was on that voyage. I'm certain of it.

WANGEL: What makes you think that?

ELLIDA (*Without answering*): That's when he found out I'd married someone else. That's when it first came over me.

WANGEL: The terror?

ELLIDA: Yes. At times—quite suddenly—he seems to stand before me. He stands a little to one side. He never looks at me. He just stands there.

WANGEL: How does he appear to you, Ellida?

ELLIDA: Just as he did last time I saw him.

WANGEL: Ten years ago?

ELLIDA: Yes, at Bratthammer. The thing I see most clearly is a bluish-white pearl—a scarfpin he always wore. It's like the eye of a dead fish. It seems to glare at me.

WANGEL: Ellida! For God's sake—! You're really ill, my darling. More ill than you know.

ELLIDA: Yes. Help me, Wangel! Help me if you can. I'm afraid this will destroy me.

WANGEL: And you've lived with this for three whole years. Lived with this secret torment. Why didn't you confide in me?

ELLIDA: I couldn't—don't you see? Not until now—not till it became necessary for your own sake. If I'd confided this much to you—I should have had to tell you about the most ghastly thing of all—ah! It's unspeakable!

WANGEL: Unspeakable—?

ELLIDA: Don't ask about it, Wangel! One more thing, and then

I've done: the child's eyes. How can we ever solve that mystery?

WANGEL: That was just your imagination, Ellida dear. The child's eyes were completely normal.

ELLIDA: That's not true! How could you fail to see it? His eyes changed color with the sea. They were blue and calm on sunny days—just like the water. And in a storm they became dark and troubled. You may not have seen it, but I did.

WANGEL (*Humoring her*): Well—supposing it were so? What then?

ELLIDA (*Softly—closer to him*): I've seen eyes like that before.

WANGEL: When? Where?

ELLIDA: Ten years ago. At Bratthammer.

WANGEL (*Steps back*): What do you—?

ELLIDA (*Trembling. In a whisper*): The child had his eyes. The strange man's eyes.

WANGEL (*Cries out involuntarily*): Ellida—!

ELLIDA (*Clasps her head in her hands in despair*): Now perhaps you understand why I cannot—why I *dare* not live with you as your wife! (*She turns suddenly and runs off down the hill to the right.*)

WANGEL (*Hurries after her, calling*): Ellida—Ellida! My poor, tragic Ellida!

CURTAIN

ACT
THREE

SCENE: *A remote corner of* DR. WANGEL'S *garden. It is a damp swampy place, overshadowed by large old trees. To the right is seen the edge of a stagnant pond. A low open fence separates the garden from the footpath and the fjord in the background. In the far distance beyond the fjord, a mountain range rises into peaks. It is late afternoon, almost evening.*

BOLETTE *sits on a stone bench stage left sewing. A couple of books and a sewing basket lie beside her on the bench.* HILDE *and* LYNGSTRAND, *with fishing rods, stand at the edge of the pond.*

HILDE: Look! There's a great big one! Do stand still!

LYNGSTRAND (*Looking*): Where?

HILDE: There! Can't you see? And, look over there! God's truth—there's another one! (*Looks off through the trees*) Drat it! Here he comes—just in time to frighten them away!

BOLETTE: Who is it?

HILDE: Your dear tutor, my pet!

BOLETTE: What do you mean, my—?

HILDE: God knows he was never *mine!*

   (ARNHOLM *enters from among the trees, right.*)

ARNHOLM: Don't tell me that pond has fish in it!

HILDE: Just the same old carp.

ARNHOLM: Are they still alive?

HILDE: They're tough old boys, they are! But it won't be long now! Some of them are about to meet their death!

ARNHOLM: I should think you'd have better luck in the fjord.

LYNGSTRAND: But there's something so mysterious about the pond!

HILDE: The pond is much more thrilling. Have you been in for a swim?

ARNHOLM: I just came from the bathhouse.

HILDE: You stay inside the ropes, I suppose.

ARNHOLM: Yes. I'm no great swimmer, I'm afraid.

HILDE: Can you swim on your back?

ARNHOLM: No.

HILDE: I can. (*To* LYNGSTRAND) Let's try over there on the other side.

(*They skirt the pond and go off right.*)

ARNHOLM (*Going closer to* BOLETTE): All by yourself, Bolette?

BOLETTE: I nearly always am.

ARNHOLM: Isn't your mother here?

BOLETTE: No. She went for a walk with Father.

ARNHOLM: How is she this afternoon?

BOLETTE: I really don't know. I forgot to ask.

ARNHOLM: What are your books?

BOLETTE: One's a book on plants; and the other's a geography.

ARNHOLM: Do you like that kind of reading?

BOLETTE: Yes, when I've time for it— My household duties come first, of course.

ARNHOLM: Doesn't your mother—your stepmother, I mean— help look after the house?

BOLETTE: No—that's my responsibility. I had to look after it during the two years Father was alone—and I've kept on ever since.

ARNHOLM: Then you're just as fond of reading as you used to be?

BOLETTE: Oh, yes. I read all the useful books I can lay my hands on. One should know something about the world, it seems to me. We're so isolated here—so cut off from everything.

ARNHOLM: You mustn't say that, Bolette dear.

BOLETTE: I can't help it. It's true. We live very much like those old carp there in the pond. In the fjord close by, great shoals of free fish sweep in and out, but the poor tame domestic fish know nothing about that; and they'll never be able to join in.

ARNHOLM: They probably wouldn't last long if they could.

BOLETTE: I don't see that that would matter much.

ARNHOLM: Besides this place is no longer isolated; not in the summer at all events. People from all over the world meet here—visitors are always passing through. It's become a kind of crossroads.

BOLETTE: You can afford to joke, seeing that you're a visitor yourself.

ARNHOLM: But I'm not joking!

BOLETTE: "Visitors from all over the world," "crossroads"— that's the sort of talk you hear in town; they're always saying things like that.

ARNHOLM: Yes—I must confess I've heard them!

BOLETTE: But there's not a word of truth in it! At least, it doesn't affect those of us who live here permanently. What difference does it make if "people from all over the world" pass through on their way to see the midnight sun? We never see it—there's no midnight sun for us! No! We're just stuck here in our carp pond!

ARNHOLM (*Sits beside her*): Bolette, dear—tell me—is there anything you really long to do?

BOLETTE: Yes—perhaps.

ARNHOLM: What is it?

BOLETTE: I long to get away from here.

ARNHOLM: That more than anything?

BOLETTE: I'd like the opportunity to study. I'd like to find out about all kinds of things.

ARNHOLM: I remember—when I was your tutor—your father often spoke of sending you to college.

BOLETTE: Poor Father! He says so many things—but when it actually comes to the point he— Father hasn't got much strength of character, you know.

ARNHOLM: You're right about that, I'm afraid. But have you never discusssed this with him? Have you never told him how you felt?

BOLETTE: As a matter of fact, I haven't.

ARNHOLM: You ought to—before it's too late, Bolette. Why haven't you told him?

BOLETTE: I suppose it's because I have no strength of character either. I take after him in that.

ARNHOLM: Aren't you being a bit unfair to yourself?

BOLETTE: No, I don't think so. Besides—Father has so little time for me. I don't think he particularly wants to think about my future. He seems to shy away from it. He's so completely taken up with Ellida, you see.

ARNHOLM: With—? How do you mean?

BOLETTE: He and my stepmother—(*Breaking off*) Father and Mother are completely engrossed in one another.

ARNHOLM: All the more reason for you to get away from here.

BOLETTE: But I couldn't leave Father; I don't think I have the right.

ARNHOLM: You'll have to leave him sometime, Bolette dear; why put it off?

BOLETTE: Of course, I realize I'll have to leave him sometime. And I suppose I should think a little more about myself—try to get a job, or something. When Father goes I'll have no one to depend on. But poor Father—I dread the thought of leaving him.

ARNHOLM: Dread—?

BOLETTE: Yes. I dread it for his sake.

ARNHOLM: But what about your stepmother? She'd be here with him.

BOLETTE: That's true enough. But she's not like Mother was. She's not capable of taking hold of things. There's so much she doesn't see—or doesn't want to see. Perhaps she just doesn't want to bother. I don't know which it is.

ARNHOLM: Hm—I think I understand.

BOLETTE: Poor Father—he's so weak in lots of ways. You may have noticed it yourself. He hasn't enough work to fill

up all his time. And she's certainly no help to him. That's
partly his own fault, I suppose.

ARNHOLM: In what way?

BOLETTE: Father wants to be surrounded by cheerful, happy
faces. The house must be filled with joy and sunshine, he
always says. So I'm afraid he very often allows her to take
medicine that's harmful to her in the long run.

ARNHOLM: You really think so?

BOLETTE: I can't think otherwise; she's so very queer at times.
(*Vehemently*) It does seem hard though, doesn't it, that I
should have to stay home here! Especially as it doesn't
really help Father at all. And, after all, I have a duty towards myself as well.

ARNHOLM: We must explore this whole matter very thoroughly, Bolette.

BOLETTE: Oh, what's the use! I suppose I'm destined to spend
the rest of my days here in my carp pond!

ARNHOLM: Nonsense! That's entirely up to you.

BOLETTE: You really mean that?

ARNHOLM: Most definitely. Your future lies in your own
hands.

BOLETTE: If only that were true—! You'd really be willing to
put in a good word for me with Father?

ARNHOLM: That too, of course. But the main thing is that I
should talk to you quite frankly—straight from the heart.
(*Looks off left*) Sh! Don't let them notice anything. We'll
go on talking presently. (ELLIDA *enters from the left. She
wears no hat but has a scarf over her head and shoulders.*)

ELLIDA (*With nervous agitation*): It's nice here! It's lovely
here!

ARNHOLM (*Rising*): Have you been for a walk?

ELLIDA: Yes; we had a wonderful walk—Wangel and I. Now
we're going for a sail.

BOLETTE: Won't you sit down?

ELLIDA: No thanks. I don't feel like sitting down.

BOLETTE (*Moves over on the bench*): There's plenty of room
here.

ELLIDA (*Walking about*): No, no! I can't sit down—I can't!

ARNHOLM: You seem much better; that walk has done you good.

ELLIDA: Yes! I feel marvellous! And I feel so happy! So safe. So safe and—(*Looks off left*) There's a big steamer coming in. What could it be?

BOLETTE (*Rises and looks off*): It must be the English ship.

ARNHOLM: They're dropping anchor by the buoy. Does she usually stop here?

BOLETTE: Only for half an hour; then she goes on farther up the fjord.

ELLIDA: And tomorrow out to sea again—out to the open sea. Right across the sea! Oh, to be able to sail on her! If one only could!

ARNHOLM: You've never been on a long sea voyage, have you, Mrs. Wangel?

ELLIDA: Never. Never in all my life. Only a few little trips in among the fjords.

BOLETTE (*With a sigh*): No! We have to stick to dry land, I'm afraid.

ARNHOLM: After all—that's where we belong.

ELLIDA: I don't believe that for a moment.

ARNHOLM: Why? We're surely land creatures, are we not?

ELLIDA: I don't believe it. I believe that if we had grown accustomed to live at sea—even in the sea, perhaps—we'd be much better people. Better and happier.

ARNHOLM: You really believe that?

ELLIDA: I'm convinced of it. I've discussed it with Wangel many times—

ARNHOLM: And what does *he* think?

ELLIDA: He thinks there might be something in it.

ARNHOLM (*Joking*): It's possible. But what's done is done. We chose the wrong path and became land beasts instead of sea beasts. I'm afraid it's too late to change it now!

ELLIDA: That's unfortunately true. I believe that people are instinctively aware of it; in an obscure way it weighs on them; fills them with sorrow—with a kind of anguish. Be-

lieve me—it's at the root of all our melancholy. I'm certain
of it.

ARNHOLM: But, my dear Mrs. Wangel—I don't think the majority of people are so melancholy. On the contrary, it seems
to me that most of them accept life cheerfully and easily—
with a deep, uncomplicated sense of joy.

ELLIDA: That's not so—I assure you. It's merely a surface joy
—the sort of joy one feels during the summer, when the
days are long and bright. Underneath there's always the
knowledge of the dark days to come. And that knowledge
clouds our joy—like the clouds that sail over the fjord; one
moment it's bathed in sunshine, then suddenly—

BOLETTE: Come now! Don't think such gloomy thoughts! Just
now you were so gay and cheerful.

ELLIDA: It's true, I was. All this—it's so stupid of me. (*Looks
round uneasily*) Why doesn't Wangel come? He promised
me he would—and now there's no sign of him. Perhaps he's
forgotten. Dear Mr. Arnholm, go and find him for me, will
you?

ARNHOLM: Of course I will.

ELLIDA: Tell him to come to me at once. I can't see him any
more—

ARNHOLM: Can't see him—?

ELLIDA: You wouldn't understand. When he's away from me
I often can't remember what he looks like. It's as though I'd
lost him— It's a dreadful feeling. Please go and find him!
(*She wanders over towards the pond.*)

BOLETTE (*To* ARNHOLM): I'll go with you. You might not
know—

ARNHOLM: There's no need. I'll manage—

BOLETTE (*Under her breath*): I'm worried. I'm afraid he
went aboard the steamer.

ARNHOLM: Why afraid?

BOLETTE: He usually goes to see if he can find any acquaint-
ances among the passengers. And there's a refreshment bar
on board—

ARNHOLM: Oh. We'd better go then.

(*He and* BOLETTE *go off left.* ELLIDA *stands a while gazing into the pond. From time to time she mutters a few
broken phrases to herself. A stranger in traveling clothes
enters from the left along the footpath beyond the fence.
He has bushy reddish hair, and has a beard. He wears a
Scotch cap and carries a traveling satchel slung across his
shoulder by a strap.*)

THE STRANGER (*Walks slowly along the fence and looks into
the garden. He catches sight of* ELLIDA. *He stops and looks
at her searchingly, intently; then says in a low voice*):
Good evening, Ellida!

ELLIDA (*Turns round and cries out*): Ah, my dear—there
you are at last!

STRANGER: Yes—at last.

ELLIDA (*Looks at him with astonishment and apprehension*):
Who are you? Are you looking for someone?

STRANGER: You know I am, Ellida.

ELLIDA (*With a start*): What's this? You called me by my
first name! Who are you looking for?

STRANGER: For you, of course.

ELLIDA (*Shaken*): Ah—! (*Stares at him, staggers backwards
with a half-smothered cry*) The eyes! The eyes!

STRANGER: I see you begin to recognize me. I knew you at
once, Ellida.

ELLIDA: The eyes! Don't look at me like that! I'll call for
help!

STRANGER: Sh! Don't be frightened. I won't harm you.

ELLIDA (*Covers her eyes with her hands*): Don't look at me
like that, I say!

STRANGER (*Leans his arms on the garden fence*): I came in
on the English steamer.

ELLIDA (*Gives him a frightened look*): What do you want
with me?

STRANGER: I promised to come as soon as I could—

ELLIDA: Go away! Go away again! You must never come here
any more! I wrote you that everything was over between
us! Everything! You know I did!

STRANGER (*Unperturbed; without answering her*): I wanted to come to you before. But I couldn't. At last I was able to manage it. And here I am.

ELLIDA: What do you want with me? What are you thinking of? What have you come for?

STRANGER: I've come to take you away with me, of course.

ELLIDA: Take me away! Is that why you've come?

STRANGER: Yes—naturally.

ELLIDA: But I'm married—surely you must know—

STRANGER: Yes—I know.

ELLIDA: And yet—in spite of that—you've come!

STRANGER: In spite of that.

ELLIDA (*Hides her head in her hands*): Oh, this is dreadful—! The Terror! Terror!

STRANGER: Don't you want to come with me?

ELLIDA (*Beside herself*): Don't look at me like that!

STRANGER: Don't you want to come with me, I asked you?

ELLIDA: No, no! I don't want to! Never! Never! I don't want to go with you, I tell you! I don't want to, and I can't. (*Lower*) I dare not, either.

STRANGER (*Climbs over the fence and comes into the garden*): Very well, Ellida. But I've one thing to say to you before I leave.

ELLIDA (*Tries to escape but cannot. She stands as though paralyzed with fear, leaning against a tree trunk by the pond*): Don't touch me! Don't come near me! Stay where you are! Don't touch me, I say!

STRANGER (*Cautiously takes a few steps towards her*): You mustn't be afraid of me, Ellida.

ELLIDA (*Puts her hands in front of her eyes*): Don't look at me like that!

STRANGER: Don't be afraid. Don't be afraid.

(DR. WANGEL *comes through the garden from the left. He speaks as he comes through the trees.*)

WANGEL: You've been waiting a long time—I'm sorry, darling!

ELLIDA (*Rushes to him and clings to his arm as she cries*

out): Oh, Wangel! Save me! Save me—if you can!

WANGEL: Ellida! In God's name—

ELLIDA: Save me! He's here, Wangel! Don't you see?

WANGEL (*Looks at the* STRANGER): Who is this man? (*Goes towards him*) Who are you? What are you doing in this garden?

STRANGER (*Indicates* ELLIDA): I came to talk to her.

WANGEL: Indeed. Then I suppose it was you who—? (*To* ELLIDA) They told me at the house a strange man had been asking for you.

STRANGER: Yes, it was I.

WANGEL: Why do you want to see my wife? (*Turns*) Do you know him, Ellida?

ELLIDA (*Softly, wringing her hands*): Do I know him! Yes! I know him!

WANGEL: Well?

ELLIDA: It is he, Wangel! It is he! The man I told you of—!

WANGEL: What's that you say? (*Turns*) Are you Johnston? Are you the man who—?

STRANGER: Call me Johnston if you like. That's not my name though.

WANGEL: Isn't it?

STRANGER: Not any more.

WANGEL: Why do you wish to see my wife? What do you want of her? You know of course that the lighthouse keeper's daughter married long ago. And you must know who her husband is.

STRANGER: I've known that for three years or more.

ELLIDA (*Intently*): How did you hear of it?

STRANGER: I was on my way home—home to you. I came across an old newspaper—a local paper from this part of the country. In it I found the announcement of your marriage.

ELLIDA (*Gazing in front of her*): My marriage— So that was how—

STRANGER: It seemed very strange to me, Ellida. For the ceremony of the rings—that was a marriage too.

ELLIDA (*Buries her face in her hand*): Ah—!

WANGEL: How dare you—!

STRANGER: Had you forgotten that?

ELLIDA (*Feeling his gaze on her*): Don't look at me like that!

WANGEL (*Confronting him*): Kindly address yourself to me. Since you know the circumstances, what possible reason can you have for coming here?

STRANGER: I promised Ellida I would come to her as soon as possible.

WANGEL: Ellida—! What! Again!

STRANGER: And Ellida promised faithfully to wait for me.

WANGEL: How dare you call my wife by her first name! It's unendurable!

STRANGER: Perhaps. But she belongs to me.

WANGEL: To you! Of all the—!

ELLIDA (*Shrinking behind* WANGEL): Ah—! He'll never let me go!

WANGEL: You say she belongs to you!

STRANGER: Did she tell you the story of the rings? My ring and hers?

WANGEL: Of course she did. What of it? She broke off with you—you're well aware of that. You received her letters, didn't you?

STRANGER: The ceremony of the rings was a valid marriage ceremony—Ellida and I were fully agreed on that.

ELLIDA: No, no! I won't have it—do you hear? I never want to see you again—I want nothing more to do with you!

WANGEL: Are you insane? You don't expect to base any claim whatever on that nonsense!

STRANGER: No. In your sense of the word, I have no claim on her.

WANGEL: Then what do you plan to do? You don't imagine you can take her away by force—against her will!

STRANGER: What would be the good of that? She must come of her own free will, if she's to come at all.

ELLIDA (*Starts and cries out*): My own free will—!

WANGEL: You don't suppose—!

ELLIDA (*To herself*): My own free will—!

WANGEL: You're behaving like a madman! Go away—leave us alone! We've nothing more to say to you.

STRANGER (*Looks at his watch*): I must get back to the ship —it's almost time. (*A step nearer*) Well, Ellida— I've kept my part of the bargain. (*Closer still*) I've kept my word to you.

ELLIDA (*Imploringly, shrinking away*): Oh—! Don't touch me!

STRANGER: I give you till tomorrow night to think it over.

WANGEL: What is there to think over? Now get out of here!

STRANGER (*Still to* ELLIDA): I have to go up the fjord now with the steamer. I'll be back tomorrow night, then I'll see you again. Wait for me here in the garden. I prefer to settle this matter with you alone. You understand?

ELLIDA (*Softly, in a trembling voice*): You hear that, Wangel?

WANGEL: Don't worry, dearest. I shall prevent this visit.

STRANGER: Goodbye for now, Ellida. Tomorrow night, then.

ELLIDA (*In a tone of entreaty*): No, no! Not tomorrow night! Never again!

STRANGER: And if by then you've decided to come with me—

ELLIDA: Don't look at me like that!

STRANGER: See that you're ready for the journey.

WANGEL: Go back to the house, Ellida.

ELLIDA: I can't. Help me! Save me, Wangel!

STRANGER: But just remember, if you don't come with me to-morrow—then it will be over.

ELLIDA (*Looks at him, trembling*): Over? Forever?

STRANGER (*With a nod*): Forever. I shall never come back here. You'll not see me any more, and you won't hear from me either. I shall be dead to you, Ellida. Gone forever.

ELLIDA (*Breathes uneasily*): Ah—!

STRANGER: Think it over carefully. Good-bye. (*He climbs over the fence, stops, and says*) Be ready for the journey tomorrow night, Ellida. I shall come for you. (*He goes slowly and calmly along the footpath and off right.*)

ELLIDA (*Looks after him a moment*): Of my own free will, he

said! Think of it. He said I was to go with him of my own
free will.

WANGEL: Keep calm, my darling. He's gone now. You'll never
see him again.

ELLIDA: How can you say that? He'll be here tomorrow night.

WANGEL: Let him come. He won't see you—I'll take good
care of that.

ELLIDA (*Shakes her head*): You won't be able to prevent him.

WANGEL: Of course I shall. Rely on me.

ELLIDA (*Musing—without listening to him*): And after he's
been here tomorrow night—? And after he's sailed away
over the ocean—?

WANGEL: What then?

ELLIDA: I wonder, will he never—never come back again?

WANGEL: You can be certain of that, Ellida dear. What
should he do here? He heard you say you would have
nothing more to do with him. The matter's ended.

ELLIDA (*To herself*): Then it's tomorrow night—or never.

WANGEL: And even if he should come here again—

ELLIDA: What then?

WANGEL: I'll know what to do. I'll make sure that he does no
further harm.

ELLIDA: How can you—?

WANGEL: I'll know what to do, I tell you! Unless he leaves
you alone, he'll have to answer for the murder of the captain.

ELLIDA: No, no! Not that! We know nothing about that murder! Absolutely nothing!

WANGEL: But he confessed to you himself!

ELLIDA: No! I won't have it! If you say anything about that I
shall deny it. He must never be caged in. His home is on
the sea. He belongs there!

WANGEL (*Looks at her and says slowly*): Ellida—oh, Ellida!

ELLIDA (*Clings to him passionately*): My dear, my faithful
one—save me from that man!

WANGEL (*Gently disengaging himself*): Come, my darling.
Come with me!

(LYNGSTRAND *and* HILDE, *both with fishing rods, enter along the pond from the right.*)

LYNGSTRAND (*Goes quickly to* ELLIDA): Mrs. Wangel—I've something remarkable to tell you!

WANGEL: Well—what is it?

LYNGSTRAND: Can you believe it—we've just seen the American!

WANGEL: The American?

HILDE: I saw him too.

LYNGSTRAND: He came from the footpath along the garden, and went aboard the English steamer.

WANGEL: Where did you know this man?

LYNGSTRAND: We were at sea together once. I was certain he'd been drowned. And there he was as large as life!

WANGEL: What more do you know about him?

LYNGSTRAND: Nothing much. Only I expect he came back to take revenge. His wife was unfaithful to him while he was at sea—

WANGEL: What's that you say?

HILDE: Mr. Lyngstrand plans to use the story for a statue.

WANGEL: What are you talking about?

ELLIDA: I'll tell you about it later.

(ARNHOLM *and* BOLETTE *come along the footpath from the left outside the fence.*)

BOLETTE (*Calls to them in the garden*): Do come and see! The English steamer's sailing up the fjord.

(*A large steamer glides slowly past in the distance.*)

LYNGSTRAND (*To* HILDE, *near the garden fence*): Tonight he'll suddenly appear before her.

HILDE (*Nodding*): You really think so? Before his faithless wife!

LYNGSTRAND: On the stroke of midnight—yes!

HILDE: How absolutely thrilling!

ELLIDA (*Gazing after the ship*): So—tomorrow—

WANGEL: And then—never again.

ELLIDA (*Softly and tremulously*): Oh, Wangel—save me from myself.

WANGEL (*Looks at her anxiously*): Ellida—I'm afraid. What's
   happened to you?

ELLIDA: I'm bewitched, Wangel.

WANGEL: Bewitched?

ELLIDA: That man is like the sea.

   (*She goes slowly through the garden out to the left, in
   deep thought.* WANGEL *walks beside her uneasily, observing
   her intently.*)

CURTAIN

ACT
FOUR

SCENE: *The garden room at* DR. WANGEL's. *Doors right and
left. In the back wall between the two windows a glass door
leading out to the veranda; it stands open. A part of the garden is seen below. A sofa and table downstage left. To the
right a piano and farther upstage a large flower stand. Stage
center a round table with chairs round it. On the table a rose
bush in bloom and other plants in pots about the room. It is
late morning.*

   BOLETTE *is seated on the sofa by the table, left, working on
a piece of embroidery.* LYNGSTRAND *sits on a chair at the upper end of the table.* BALLESTED *is seated in the garden painting.* HILDE *stands beside him looking on.*

LYNGSTRAND (*Sits for a while in silence, leaning his arms on
   the table watching* BOLETTE *work*): That work must be
   very difficult, Miss Wangel.

BOLETTE: It's not really so difficult; as long as you count correctly.

LYNGSTRAND: Do you have to count too?

BOLETTE: Yes—the stitches. Look—do you see?

LYNGSTRAND: Oh, of course! My goodness! It's quite an art, isn't it? Do you draw the design as well?

BOLETTE: No—I follow a pattern.

LYNGSTRAND: Oh—you need a pattern, do you?

BOLETTE: Yes.

LYNGSTRAND: Then it's not really an art after all.

BOLETTE: No; it's more of a knack, I suppose.

LYNGSTRAND: Still—you might perhaps learn to acquire an art.

BOLETTE: Even without talent?

LYNGSTRAND: Yes, you might. If you were to spend some time with a real artist—

BOLETTE: You think I could learn from him?

LYNGSTRAND: Perhaps "learn" is the wrong word for it. But you might absorb it by degrees—through a kind of miracle, Miss Wangel.

BOLETTE: What a strange idea!

LYNGSTRAND (*After a pause*): Have you given much thought to—? Have you thought at all—deeply and seriously I mean—about marriage, Miss Wangel?

BOLETTE (*Glances at him*): About—? Why, no.

LYNGSTRAND: I have.

BOLETTE: Really? Have you?

LYNGSTRAND: Yes, indeed. I often think a great deal about serious things; and particularly about marriage. And I've read a great many books about it too. I believe one should look upon marriage as a kind of miracle. The woman gradually undergoes a change; she comes to resemble her husband more and more.

BOLETTE: Acquires his interests, you mean?

LYNGSTRAND: Yes—that's it!

BOLETTE: And what about his gifts? His skills? His talents?

LYNGSTRAND: Who knows—? She might also—

BOLETTE: You believe a wife might gradually absorb her husband's knowledge? Her husband's way of thinking?

LYNGSTRAND: That too—yes. By degrees, of course. Through a kind of miracle. But this sort of thing could only happen in a *real* marriage—one founded on true love, and mutual happiness.

BOLETTE: I suppose it's never occurred to you that the husband too might undergo a change? Might come to resemble his wife, I mean?

LYNGSTRAND: The husband—? No. I've never thought of that.

BOLETTE: Why shouldn't it work both ways?

LYNGSTRAND: Well, you see—a man has a vocation—a fixed purpose in life. In that lies his strength. He has his work to live for.

BOLETTE: All men? Without exception?

LYNGSTRAND: No, perhaps not. I was thinking mainly of artists, you see.

BOLETTE: Do you think it's right for an artist to get married?

LYNGSTRAND: Most certainly. That is, if he finds someone he really loves—

BOLETTE: Even so—isn't it best for him to live for his art alone?

LYNGSTRAND: But marriage needn't interfere with that.

BOLETTE: Then what happens to her?

LYNGSTRAND: Her? Whom do you mean?

BOLETTE: The woman he marries, of course. What does *she* have to live for?

LYNGSTRAND: She must live for his art too. I should think that would be happiness enough for any woman.

BOLETTE: Hm—I'm not so sure—

LYNGSTRAND: Yes—believe me, Miss Wangel. It's not only a question of the honor and glory she would enjoy through him—that's the least part of it, perhaps. But to be able to help him to create—and to make his work easier for him; to take care of him and serve him, and make life comfortable for him. That would be a great joy for a woman, I should think.

BOLETTE: I've never heard of anything so selfish!

LYNGSTRAND: Selfish! You surely don't think *me* selfish, do you? You wouldn't say that if you really knew me! (*Leans closer towards her*) Miss Wangel—when I'm gone—and I shan't be here much longer—

BOLETTE (*Looks at him with compassion*): Don't think sad thoughts like that!

LYNGSTRAND: I don't see anything particularly sad about it.

BOLETTE: What do you mean?

LYNGSTRAND: I'll be leaving in a month. Home first, for a bit —and then off to the South.

BOLETTE: Oh, yes—I see. Of course.

LYNGSTRAND: Will you think of me, now and then, Miss Wangel?

BOLETTE: Yes; gladly.

LYNGSTRAND (*Happily*): You promise?

BOLETTE: Yes, I promise.

LYNGSTRAND: Your solemn word, Miss Wangel?

BOLETTE: My solemn word. (*In a different tone*) But— what possible difference can all this make? It can never lead to anything!

LYNGSTRAND: Don't say that—please! To know that you're here at home thinking of me—would make me very happy!

BOLETTE: And, after that? What then?

LYNGSTRAND: What then—? Well—I don't know exactly—

BOLETTE: No more do I. There are so many things against it. Everything in the world is against it, it seems to me.

LYNGSTRAND: Perhaps a miracle will happen—an unexpected turn of fate. Something of that sort. I'm a very lucky man, you know.

BOLETTE (*With animation*): Yes! You believe that, don't you?

LYNGSTRAND: I'm utterly convinced of it. You'll see—when I come back home again, in a few years, I'll be completely cured, and I'll be rich and famous!

BOLETTE: Yes. We must hope for that.

LYNGSTRAND: You can depend on it! Just so long as you keep

on sending me faithful, loving thoughts. And you've given
me your word—

BOLETTE: Yes, you have my word. (*Shakes her head*) But it
won't lead to anything all the same.

LYNGSTRAND: Oh, yes it will! It'll be a great help to *me;* in my
work, you know.

BOLETTE: You really mean that?

LYNGSTRAND: With all my heart. And think how exciting it'll
be for you! Even though you have to stay in this remote,
provincial place—you'll know that you're helping to create
my masterpiece!

BOLETTE: I see. But you—on your side?

LYNGSTRAND: I?

BOLETTE (*Looks out towards the garden*): Sh! Talk of something else. Here's Mr. Arnholm.

(ARNHOLM *is seen in the garden left. He stops and talks
to* BALLESTED *and* HILDE.)

LYNGSTRAND: You're fond of your old tutor, aren't you, Miss
Bolette?

BOLETTE: Fond of him?

LYNGSTRAND: Yes. I mean—you like him, don't you?

BOLETTE: Of course I do. He's such a wonderful friend—and
I value his advice. He's so kind and understanding.

LYNGSTRAND: It seems odd that he's never married.

BOLETTE: Why odd?

LYNGSTRAND: He's quite well off they say.

BOLETTE: Yes—so I've heard. He's never found anyone who'd
have him, I suppose. In his case I can see it might be difficult.

LYNGSTRAND: Why so?

BOLETTE: Well, the trouble is—he's been tutor to nearly all
the young girls he's ever known.

LYNGSTRAND: What difference would that make?

BOLETTE: Good Heavens! One would never think of marrying
one's tutor!

LYNGSTRAND: Why shouldn't a young girl fall in love with her
tutor? Is that impossible?

BOLETTE: Yes, quite. After she's grown up, I mean.

LYNGSTRAND: How very strange!

BOLETTE: Sh!

(*All during the above,* BALLESTED *has been collecting his things; he exits through the garden right.* HILDE *helps him.* ARNHOLM *comes onto the veranda and enters the room.*)

ARNHOLM: Good morning, dear Bolette. Good morning, Mr. —Mr.—Hm!

(*He looks annoyed and nods coldly to* LYNGSTRAND, *who rises and bows.*)

BOLETTE (*Rises and goes to* ARNHOLM): Good morning, Mr. Arnholm.

ARNHOLM: How's everything today?

BOLETTE: Fine, thank you.

ARNHOLM: Has your stepmother gone for her daily swim, as usual?

BOLETTE: No. She's up in her room.

ARNHOLM: Isn't she feeling well?

BOLETTE: I don't know. She's locked herself in.

ARNHOLM: Hm—has she?

LYNGSTRAND: I noticed yesterday she seemed upset; about that American, I mean.

ARNHOLM: What do you know of that?

LYNGSTRAND: I told Mrs. Wangel he was still alive; that I'd seen him on the path beyond the garden.

ARNHOLM: Oh—I see.

BOLETTE (*To* ARNHOLM): You and Father stayed up very late last night.

ARNHOLM: Fairly late—yes. We had quite a serious talk.

BOLETTE: Did you put in a good word for me?

ARNHOLM: No, Bolette dear. I didn't get a chance. He was too absorbed in other things.

BOLETTE (*With a sigh*): I'm afraid he always is!

ARNHOLM (*Gives her a significant look*): But in a little while, we'll continue yesterday's conversation—you and I. Where is your father now? He hasn't gone out, has he?

BOLETTE: I think he went to the office. I'll go and fetch him.

ARNHOLM: No never mind. I'll go and talk to him down there.

BOLETTE (*Hears something off left*): Wait a minute, Mr. Arnholm. I think I hear him on the stairs. He went up to see her, I expect.

(DR. WANGEL *comes in through the door left.*)

WANGEL (*Gives* ARNHOLM *his hand*): Arnholm! You're here already. It's good of you to come so early. There are still several things I want to talk to you about.

BOLETTE (*To* LYNGSTRAND): Let's join Hilde in the garden, shall we?

LYNGSTRAND: Yes, Miss Wangel, I'll be glad to.

(*They go out into the garden through the trees in the background.*)

ARNHOLM (*Who has followed them with his eyes, then turns to* WANGEL): Who is that young man? Do you know anything about him?

WANGEL: No. Nothing much.

ARNHOLM: He's always hanging about the girls. Do you think that's wise?

WANGEL: Is he? I hadn't noticed.

ARNHOLM: Don't you think you ought to keep an eye on him?

WANGEL: Yes—I suppose I should. But what's a poor man to do? The girls are so used to looking after themselves—they resent interference. They won't take anything from me; nor from Ellida either.

ARNHOLM: Won't they listen to her either?

WANGEL: No. And I can't very well ask her to bother about these things; she's not equipped for that. (*Breaking off*) But that's not what we're here to talk about. Tell me—the matter we discussed last night—have you given any further thought to it?

ARNHOLM: Ever since I left you, I've thought of nothing else.

WANGEL: Then what ought I to do?

ARNHOLM: Surely you're a better judge of that than I am? After all, you're a physician.

WANGEL: You don't know how hard it is for a physician to

treat someone he loves. And this is no ordinary illness. It's no case for an ordinary doctor—or for ordinary remedies.

ARNHOLM: How does she seem today?

WANGEL: I was just up to see her—she seemed to me quite calm. But under that reserve there's something that eludes me. And then she's so capricious—so unpredictable. Her mood changes constantly.

ARNHOLM: Part of her morbid condition, I suppose.

WANGEL: Not entirely. She was born like that, to some extent. She's a sea creature—that's where the trouble lies.

ARNHOLM: What precisely do you mean by that?

WANGEL: Have you never noticed that people who live by the sea are different from the rest of us? Their lives seem to reflect the ocean—with its waves and changing tides; it's as though their thoughts and feelings were controlled by it. And they can never be transplanted—I ought to have remembered that. It was wrong of me to drag Ellida away from there, and bring her inland.

ARNHOLM: You've really come to look at it like that?

WANGEL: Yes, I feel it more and more. I should have known it from the first—I *did* know it, I think. But I refused to face it. I was so very much in love with her, you see. I thought only of myself. I was unpardonably selfish!

ARNHOLM: Any man is apt to be selfish at a time like that—it's only natural. I don't think it's inherent in you, Doctor.

WANGEL: Oh, yes it is! I've been selfish all these years. I'm much older than she is, and I should have realized she needed guidance; I should have given her almost a father's care—helped her to develop spiritually and intellectually, and I've done nothing of the kind. I've been selfish and lazy; but, you see, I loved her so much just as she was. Then, gradually, she grew worse and worse, and I could think of nothing to do about it. (*Lower*) At last, in desperation, I wrote to you and asked you to come here.

ARNHOLM: Was *that* why you wrote to me?

WANGEL: Yes. But don't let anybody know that.

ARNHOLM: Why me? I don't understand why you should send for me?

WANGEL: There's no reason why you should; I was on the wrong track, you see. Ellida had been in love with you once, I thought—and perhaps still had a secret fondness for you. I thought it might do her good to talk to you again. That she might enjoy reminiscing about home— sharing old memories.

ARNHOLM: So when you wrote that there was someone here who missed me—and longed to see me—it was your wife you referred to?

WANGEL: Of course; who else?

ARNHOLM: Nothing—it's just that I didn't understand you.

WANGEL: No; how could you? I was on the wrong track, I tell you.

ARNHOLM: And you call yourself selfish!

WANGEL: I felt so guilty; it seemed to me I had so much to atone for. I was ready to do anything that might ease her mind a little.

ARNHOLM: About this strange man—and the power he evidently has over her—what explanation can you find for that?

WANGEL: I don't know. There are certain things about it that defy all explanation.

ARNHOLM: Do you think there's an element there beyond all explanation? Something that could never, under any circumstances, be explained?

WANGEL: It seems so—at the moment.

ARNHOLM: Do you believe there *are* such things?

WANGEL: I neither believe nor disbelieve. I just don't know. I can only suspend judgment.

ARNHOLM: Tell me something: that strange, uncanny conviction of hers, that the child's eyes were—

WANGEL: I don't believe a word of that! I simply won't believe it! That was pure imagination on her part—nothing else.

ARNHOLM: Did you notice the man's eyes when you saw him yesterday?

WANGEL: Yes, of course I did.

ARNHOLM: And you saw no resemblance?

WANGEL (*Evasively*): I don't quite know how to answer that. When I saw him it was growing dark. And I'd heard so much about the likeness from Ellida—I couldn't trust my judgment.

ARNHOLM: No—perhaps not. But about the other question: the fact that this restlessness—this sense of terror—came over her at the very time the man was on his homeward voyage?

WANGEL: I believe that's something she started to build up in her imagination two days ago, when Lyngstrand first told her about this man. When she heard that this Johnston, or Freeman, or whatever you want to call him, was on his way home three years ago in March—she hypnotized herself into believing there was a definite connection; that this mental state of hers dates from that very moment. Actually, of course, it came over her gradually. It didn't happen all at once.

ARNHOLM: But wasn't that about the time it started?

WANGEL: By no means. There had been definite symptoms long before that. She did happen to have a particularly violent attack three years ago in March, I must admit—

ARNHOLM: Ah! Then—you see!

WANGEL: But I felt that her physical condition at the time might well account for that. You see—it was just then that we—

ARNHOLM: Yes—one could interpret it both ways.

WANGEL (*Wringing his hands*): It's so dreadful not to be able to help her! To be utterly powerless! Not to be able to find some remedy—!

ARNHOLM: Would it do any good to move away from here? She might be happier somewhere else; somewhere that would remind her of her home, perhaps.

WANGEL: Do you think I haven't thought of that? I suggested

moving back to Skjoldvik—but she wouldn't hear of it.

ARNHOLM: Why not?

WANGEL: It wouldn't do any good, she said. She may be right in that.

ARNHOLM: What makes you think so?

WANGEL: In any case—on thinking the matter over—I doubt if I could manage it. It wouldn't be quite fair to the girls to ask them to live in such an out-of-the-way place. They must have the opportunity of meeting a few people now and then—of marrying and settling down some day.

ARNHOLM: Marrying? You've already given thought to that?

WANGEL: Well, naturally! I have to! —And yet, on the other hand, when I think of poor Ellida, I—! Oh, my dear Arnholm—I don't know what to do!

ARNHOLM: I don't think you need be too concerned about Bolette— (*Breaks off*) That reminds me; I wonder where she—where they went? (*Goes to the open door and looks out.*)

WANGEL (*Over by the piano*): I'd be ready to make any sacrifice for them—all three of them. But what? I don't know what to do!

(ELLIDA *enters from the door left.*)

ELLIDA (*Rapidly, to* WANGEL): You won't go out this morning, will you?

WANGEL: Of course not. I'll stay home with you. (*Points to* ARNHOLM *who comes towards them*) You haven't said good morning to our friend here.

ELLIDA (*Turns*): Oh, I didn't see you, Mr. Arnholm. (*Gives him her hand*) Good morning.

ARNHOLM: Good morning, Mrs. Wangel. Aren't you going for your swim today?

ELLIDA: No, not today—I couldn't! Won't you sit down a moment?

ARNHOLM: Thank you—not just now. (*Looks at* WANGEL) I promised the girls to join them in the garden.

ELLIDA: I hope you'll find them there. I never know where they're off to.

WANGEL: I expect they're by the pond.

ARNHOLM: I'll track them down! (*He nods, crosses the veranda down into the garden and off right.*)

ELLIDA: What's the time, Wangel?

WANGEL (*Looks at his watch*): Just past eleven.

ELLIDA: Just past eleven. And at eleven—half-past eleven tonight, the steamer will be here. If only it were over!

WANGEL (*Goes closer to her*): Ellida dear—there's one thing I'd like to ask you.

ELLIDA: Yes? What's that?

WANGEL: The day before yesterday, when we were talking up at Prospect Heights, you told me there had been times during the past three years when you thought this man appeared to you.

ELLIDA: He did. You must believe me when I tell you that.

WANGEL: How did he look?

ELLIDA: How did he look—?

WANGEL: Yes—what did he look like at these times?

ELLIDA: But you know what he looks like, Wangel; you saw him yourself yesterday.

WANGEL: And was that how he looked each time you thought you saw him?

ELLIDA: Yes, of course.

WANGEL: Exactly as he looked in real life yesterday?

ELLIDA: Exactly—yes.

WANGEL: Then how did you fail to recognize him?

ELLIDA (*With a start*): Did I—?

WANGEL: Yes. You said yourself at first you had no idea who he was.

ELLIDA (*Impressed*): I believe you're right! What a strange thing, Wangel. To think of my not knowing him at once.

WANGEL: You only recognized him by his eyes, you said.

ELLIDA: Yes—his eyes! His eyes!

WANGEL: Yet in our talk the other day you said when he appeared to you he always looked just as he did ten years ago—that day you parted.

ELLIDA: Did I say that?

WANGEL: Yes, you did.

ELLIDA: Then he can't have changed, I suppose.

WANGEL: He must have. For you described him quite differently the night before last as we were walking home. Ten
years ago he was clean shaven you said. His clothes were
quite different too. And that scarfpin you spoke of—the
one with the pearl—yesterday he wore nothing of that
sort.

ELLIDA: That's true; he didn't.

WANGEL (*Looks at her intently*): Think hard, Ellida dear.
Perhaps you no longer remember exactly how he looked,
when you said good-bye to him at Bratthammer?

ELLIDA: I don't remember very clearly. Today I don't seem
able to remember it at all. Isn't that strange!

WANGEL: Perhaps not so very strange. You've just seen him
as he really is; reality has blotted out the imaginary picture
you had of him in your mind, and now that's no longer
clear to you.

ELLIDA: You think so, Wangel?

WANGEL: Yes. Reality has blotted out illusion. It's a good
thing that he came.

ELLIDA: Good! You think it's good?

WANGEL: It may be your salvation.

ELLIDA (*Sits down on the sofa*): Wangel—come here and
sit by me. I want you to know all my thoughts.

WANGEL: Yes—Ellida dear. (*He sits down on a chair on the
other side of the table.*)

ELLIDA: You know—it was actually a great misfortune, for
us both, that we of all people should have come together.

WANGEL (*With a start*): What are you saying!

ELLIDA: Yes, it was. How could it be otherwise? When you
think of how it happened—it could lead to nothing but
unhappiness.

WANGEL: "How it happened"? What do you mean?

ELLIDA: Listen to me, Wangel—it's no good lying to ourselves—or to each other—any more.

WANGEL: We surely don't do that!

ELLIDA: Oh yes, we do; we conceal the truth at any rate. And the truth—the plain unvarnished truth is this: You came up to Skjoldvik and you bought me, Wangel.

WANGEL: Bought! How can you say such things!

ELLIDA: I was as much to blame as you were. I accepted the bargain; I consented to sell myself to you.

WANGEL: Ellida—how have you the heart to call it that!

ELLIDA: What else is there to call it? You wanted to find a new wife; you could no longer bear your loneliness—

WANGEL: I wanted to find a new mother for my children, too.

ELLIDA: Yes—that may have entered into it; though you never bothered to find out if I was fit to be a mother to them. You saw me a few times, talked to me once or twice, took a fancy to me and—

WANGEL: If it pleases you to call it that—!

ELLIDA: And I on my side—I was helpless, I had no one to turn to, I was utterly alone—it seemed only natural to accept you: you offered me security.

WANGEL: That isn't how I looked on it, Ellida. I asked you in all honesty if you would come and share with me, and with my children, what little I possessed.

ELLIDA: I know you did. All the same I shouldn't have accepted. No matter how little or how much you had to offer—I shouldn't have accepted! I should never have sold myself to you! Hard work—even abject poverty—anything would have been better; anything as long as it was of my own free will—by my own choice.

WANGEL (*Rises*): Then—to you—these years we've lived together have been wasted?

ELLIDA: No! You mustn't think that, Wangel! I've had a good life here with you. You've given me everything anyone could wish for. But I didn't come to you of my own free will, you see.

WANGEL (*Looks at her*): Not of your own free will!

ELLIDA: No. It was not of my own free will I married you.

WANGEL: That's the expression he used yesterday!

ELLIDA: And it's the key to everything; it explains everything; I see things clearly now.

WANGEL: What do you see?

ELLIDA: I see that our life together has never really been a marriage.

WANGEL (*Bitterly*): The life we lead together now is certainly no marriage—that's true enough.

ELLIDA: It never has been—never. Perhaps the first one might have been.

WANGEL: "First one"? What do you mean?

ELLIDA: Mine—with him.

WANGEL (*Looks at her in amazement*): It's impossible for me to understand you.

ELLIDA: Oh, my dear—don't let's lie to each other any more; and don't let's lie to ourselves!

WANGEL: Very well. What then?

ELLIDA: You see—there's no escaping it. A promise, given of one's own free will, is just as binding as a marriage.

WANGEL: But, what on earth—!

ELLIDA (*Rises impetuously*): You must let me leave you, Wangel!

WANGEL: Ellida—! Ellida—!

ELLIDA: Yes—you must! Believe me—sooner or later it will have to happen. We never really belonged together, you and I.

WANGEL (*Controlling his emotion*): Has it really come to this?

ELLIDA: It was inevitable. It had to.

WANGEL: You've never really belonged to me—in spite of our years together!

ELLIDA: Oh, Wangel! If I could only love you as I want to love you—as you deserve to be loved! But I know now that I never shall.

WANGEL: Then you want a divorce, I suppose. A formal, legal divorce—

ELLIDA: I wish I could make you understand me. I care nothing about formalities. Surely this is not a question of externals. Can't we simply agree to release one another—of our own free will?

WANGEL (*Bitterly. Nods slowly*): Cancel the bargain?

ELLIDA (*Eagerly*): Precisely—cancel the bargain!

WANGEL: And after that, Ellida? Afterwards? Have you thought of what will happen to us then? What will life hold for us? I mean for you, as well as me.

ELLIDA: It makes no difference. We must simply take life as it comes. Only one thing matters, Wangel: I beg you and implore you—let me go! Give me back my freedom!

WANGEL: You're asking a terrible thing of me, Ellida. Give me a little time! We must discuss this further. Give yourself time to think things over—to be absolutely certain of what you want to do!

ELLIDA: There's no time for thinking. You must set me free today.

WANGEL: Today! Why must it be today!

ELLIDA: Because tonight he will be here.

WANGEL: He! The stranger? What has he to do with this?

ELLIDA: When I see him tonight, I must be free to choose.

WANGEL: What do you mean to do?

ELLIDA: I can't take refuge in belonging to another man. I must be in a position to choose freely. Otherwise my decision will be worthless.

WANGEL: "Choose" you say! How can you speak of choice in such a case?

ELLIDA: I must be free to choose—one way or the other. Either to let him go away alone—or to go with him.

WANGEL: Go with him! Do you understand what that would mean, Ellida? You'd be putting your whole future in his hands!

ELLIDA: I once put my whole future in your hands—without giving it a thought.

WANGEL: That may be. But this man—! You know nothing about him! He's a total stranger to you!

ELLIDA: I knew even less about you, perhaps. Yet I went with you all the same.

WANGEL: At least you had some idea of the kind of life you'd have with me; but in this case—! Think of what you're doing! You don't know who he is—or what he is!

ELLIDA: That's true. That's what makes it so terrifying!

WANGEL: Terrifying indeed!

ELLIDA: And for that very reason I feel I have no right to run away from it.

WANGEL: Because it's terrifying?

ELLIDA: Yes—precisely.

WANGEL: Ellida—what do you actually mean by "terrifying"?

ELLIDA: I mean something that is frightening—yet fascinating too.

WANGEL: Fascinating?

ELLIDA: Above all, fascinating—perhaps.

WANGEL: You are like the sea, Ellida.

ELLIDA: That's terrifying too.

WANGEL: Yes—frightening and fascinating, just as you are.

ELLIDA: Is that how you think of me, Wangel?

WANGEL: I've never really known you—not fully, at any rate. I see that now.

ELLIDA: Then set me free! Release me, Wangel! You're right —you've never known me. I'm not the person you thought I was. We can part now, of our own free will—with perfect understanding.

WANGEL: I realize it might be best for us to part; but, all the same, I can't bring myself to do it! To me it is you who are "terrifying," Ellida—and, above all, fascinating!

ELLIDA: I don't know how you can say that.

WANGEL: We must try and live through this day prudently and calmly. I dare not release you and let you go today. For your own sake, Ellida—I dare not! I have both a duty and a right. I intend to use them to protect you.

ELLIDA: Protect me? What against? There's no question here of force or violence. No one is threatening me, Wangel. It's

not as simple as all that. The struggle lies within me—in
my mind. The struggle between the terror and the fascination. You can't help me in that.

WANGEL: I can! I can give you strength, and help you to resist.

ELLIDA: Yes—if to resist were really what I wanted.

WANGEL: But—isn't it, Ellida?

ELLIDA: I don't know! Can't you see—! That's just what I
don't know myself.

WANGEL: Tonight will decide everything, Ellida.

ELLIDA: Tonight! Just think—so soon! It's a question of my
life—

WANGEL: And then tomorrow—

ELLIDA: Tomorrow! Perhaps, by then, I shall have betrayed
my destiny—the life I was truly meant for.

WANGEL: Your destiny—?

ELLIDA: Yes. A life of truth and joy and freedom—lost to me
forever. And to him too, perhaps.

WANGEL (*In a lower tone, seizing her by the wrists*): Ellida—
do you love this man?

ELLIDA: Love—? How do I know! I only know he is both
terrifying and fascinating to me, and that—

WANGEL: Yes?

ELLIDA (*Tears herself away*): —and that I've a feeling I belong with him.

WANGEL (*Bows his head*): I begin to understand.

ELLIDA: What possible help have you to offer? What remedy
is there to suggest?

WANGEL (*Looks at her sadly*): Tomorrow—when he's gone,
and you are out of danger, I promise to release you and let
you go. Then we will cancel the bargain.

ELLIDA: But, Wangel—! Tomorrow—that will be too late—!

WANGEL (*Glancing towards the garden*): The children! At
least for the present—they must be spared!

(ARNHOLM, BOLETTE, HILDE *and* LYNGSTRAND *are seen in
the garden.* LYNGSTRAND *takes leave of them and goes
out to the left. The others enter the room.*)

ARNHOLM: We've been making all sorts of plans—

HILDE: We're going to sail up the fjord this evening and—

BOLETTE: No, Hilde! Don't tell!

WANGEL: We've been making a few plans too.

ARNHOLM: Really? Have you?

WANGEL: Yes. Ellida's going away tomorrow; she's decided to go to Skjoldvik for a while.

BOLETTE: She's going away—?

ARNHOLM: That strikes me as a very sensible idea, Mrs. Wangel.

WANGEL: Ellida wants to go home again; home to the sea.

HILDE (*Rushing wildly to Ellida*): You're going away? You're leaving us?

ELLIDA (*Startled*): Why, Hilde! What's the matter?

HILDE (*Controls herself*): Nothing. Nothing at all. (*Mutters as she turns away*) Go! For all I care!

BOLETTE: Father! Are you going to Skjoldvik too?—I believe you are! I can see it in your face!

WANGEL: No—of course not! I may go up for a visit now and then—

BOLETTE: But you'll come home to us—?

WANGEL: Yes—I'll come home to you—

BOLETTE: Just now and then, I suppose!

WANGEL: My dear child, it can't be helped. (*He walks away.*)

ARNHOLM (*To* BOLETTE *in a whisper*): We'll talk about this later. (*He goes over and joins* WANGEL. *They stand in the doorway talking in low tones.*)

ELLIDA (*Softly to* BOLETTE): What was the matter with Hilde? She seemed dreadfully upset!

BOLETTE: You don't know—you haven't noticed, I suppose, what Hilde's always longed for?

ELLIDA: Longed for?

BOLETTE: Yes. Ever since you first came to this house.

ELLIDA: No. What could that be?

BOLETTE: A word of tenderness from you; a word of love.

ELLIDA: Ah—! Is it possible—? Could I be needed here?

(*She stands motionless, her hands clasped to her head, a*

prey to conflicting thoughts and emotions. WANGEL *and*
ARNHOLM *come forward talking in low tones.* BOLETTE *goes
and looks off into the room right. Then throws the door
wide open.)*

BOLETTE: Dinner's ready, Father dear—if you—

WANGEL (*With forced composure*): Splendid, Bolette! Arnholm—come along! We must drink a toast—a parting
toast to "the Lady from the Sea."
(*They go towards the door right.*)

CURTAIN

ACT
FIVE

SCENE: *The remote corner of* DR. WANGEL's *garden by the
carp pond. Deepening summer twilight.* ARNHOLM, BOLETTE,
LYNGSTRAND *and* HILDE *in a boat are punting along the
shore from the left.*

HILDE: Here's a good place! Let's jump ashore.

ARNHOLM: No, no! Don't try that! Please!

LYNGSTRAND: I'm afraid I'm no good at jumping, Miss Hilde.

HILDE: How about you, Arnholm? Are you good at jumping?

ARNHOLM: I'd rather not attempt it.

BOLETTE: We'd much better land at the steps by the bathhouse.
(*They punt off towards the right. At the same moment
BALLESTED appears on the footpath from the right, carrying
some music and a French horn. He greets those in the*

*boat, turns and talks to them. The answers are heard far-
ther and farther off.*)

BALLESTED: What's that you say? Yes, that's right—in honor
of the English steamer. It's her last trip of the season. You'd
better hurry if you want to hear the music. (*Shouts*)
What? (*Shakes his head*) I can't hear you!

(ELLIDA, *with a scarf over her head, comes in from the left
followed by* DR. WANGEL.)

WANGEL: There's ample time, Ellida dear, I assure you.

ELLIDA: No, no. You're wrong! He might be here any moment.

BALLESTED: (*Outside the garden fence*): Good evening,
Doctor! Good evening, Mrs. Wangel!

WANGEL (*Becomes aware of him*): Oh—good evening,
Ballested. There's to be another concert tonight is there?

BALLESTED: Yes. The brass band is to perform. At this time
of year there's no lack of entertainment. We're playing in
honor of the English steamer.

ELLIDA: Has she been sighted yet?

BALLESTED: No, not yet. But she creeps in between those
islands, and before you know it she's lying at the pier.

ELLIDA: Yes—that's true.

WANGEL (*Partly to* ELLIDA): Her last trip of the season. She
won't be back again this year.

BALLESTED: A sad thought, Doctor, isn't it? That's why we
want to honor her, you see. Well, well! The happy summer
days are nearly over. We shall soon be icebound: "Trapped
in an icy prison," as the old melodrama puts it.

ELLIDA: "Trapped in an icy prison"—yes.

BALLESTED: A depressing thought. We've basked in the
golden summer months like happy children! It'll be hard to
reconcile ourselves to the dark days ahead. At first—
that is. People learn to alcli—acli—acclimatize themselves,
Mrs. Wangel. They do indeed! (*He bows and goes out
left.*)

ELLIDA (*Looking out over the fjord*): This dreadful suspense! The agony of this last half hour of waiting.

WANGEL: You still insist on talking to him yourself?

ELLIDA: I must talk to him myself. I must be free to choose.

WANGEL: You have no choice, Ellida. You won't be allowed
to choose. I won't allow it.

ELLIDA: No one can prevent my choosing, Wangel. If I should
choose to go with him, you can prevent my leaving; you
can keep me here by force, against my will—that's true
enough. But you can't control my mind. If I feel I should
and must choose him instead of you, you may forbid it—
but the choice would still remain; and nothing you can do
would alter it.

WANGEL: You're right; I've no way of controlling that.

ELLIDA: And then—I have no real reason to resist. What is
there here at home to hold me back? I have no roots in
this house, Wangel. The children are not mine; they
never have been mine—not in their hearts, I mean. When
I go away—if I go away, that is—either tonight with him,
or tomorrow to Skjoldvik—I shall have no keys to hand
over, no instructions of any sort or kind to give. I have no
roots in your house, I tell you. I've never been anything but
an outsider here.

WANGEL: That was the way you wanted it.

ELLIDA: Not really. I had no wishes one way or the other; I
simply left things as they were when I arrived. That was
the way *you* wanted it—you, and no one else.

WANGEL: I did what I thought was best for you, Ellida.

ELLIDA: I know, Wangel—I know only too well! And now all
that has to be paid for. I have no real ties here—no anchor;
nothing to give me the help and strength I need. We have
no common treasure—of memories shared—of experiences
cherished through the years. There's no compelling force to
hold me here.

WANGEL: I understand, Ellida. And tomorrow, I promise to
give you back your freedom; you shall live your own life
from then on.

ELLIDA: "My own life" you call it! I'm afraid I betrayed that
when I married you. (*Clenches her hands in fear and*

agitation) And now—tonight—in half an hour—he will be here. The man I failed; the man I should have felt irrevocably bound to—as he felt bound to me. He'll give me one last chance tonight to start afresh; to find my life again —that terrifying, fascinating life! Of my own free will, how can I let it go?

WANGEL: For this very reason I must insist on acting for you. As your husband, and as your doctor too.

ELLIDA: Yes, Wangel—I know you're right. I've often thought what peace and safety I should find if I could only cling to you—you must know that! If I could defy once and for all these terrifying, fascinating powers. But I can't! I can't bring myself to do it!

WANGEL: Come, Ellida—let's walk a little while.

ELLIDA: I should like to—but I dare not. This is where he said I was to wait.

WANGEL: Come along; you've still plenty of time.

ELLIDA: Are you sure?

WANGEL: Ample time, I tell you.

ELLIDA: Let's walk a little then.

(*They go off downstage right. At the same time* ARNHOLM *and* BOLETTE *enter along the upper back of the pond.*)

BOLETTE (*Catching sight of the others as they go out*): Look over there—!

ARNHOLM (*Softly*): Sh! Let them go.

BOLETTE: What's been happening between them lately?

ARNHOLM: Why? Have you noticed something?

BOLETTE: Have I noticed—!

ARNHOLM: Anything in particular, I mean?

BOLETTE: All kinds of things! What about you?

ARNHOLM: Well—I don't know—

BOLETTE: Oh yes, you do. Only you won't admit it.

ARNHOLM: I think it'll be a good thing for your stepmother to take this little trip.

BOLETTE: You think so?

ARNHOLM: It might be a good thing for all concerned for her to get away from time to time.

BOLETTE: If she goes home to Skjoldvik, she'll probably never come back again.

ARNHOLM: What makes you say that, Bolette dear?

BOLETTE: I'm certain of it. You wait and see! She won't come back. Not while Hilde and I are home at any rate.

ARNHOLM: You can get away if you really want to. You can study to your heart's content, become familiar with all the things you long to know about—live a fuller, happier life. What do you say to that?

BOLETTE (*Claps her hands*): It sounds too wonderful! Oh— but it's quite impossible. Since Father can't see his way to —I've no one else to turn to.

ARNHOLM: Perhaps you'll allow your old—well—let's say your former tutor—to lend a helping hand.

BOLETTE: You, Mr. Arnholm? You mean you'd really—?

ARNHOLM: Stand by you? Of course—with all my heart! You can depend on me. What do you say? Do you consent?

BOLETTE: Do I consent! I'd do anything to get away from here—to see the world—to study and improve myself— do all the things I've dreamed of, and that always seemed impossible—!

ARNHOLM: All this can come true—if you really want it.

BOLETTE: It would be almost too much happiness! You say you'll really help me? But—would it be right to accept this from a stranger?

ARNHOLM: Surely you can accept it from *me*, Bolette. You know you can accept anything from me.

BOLETTE (*Seizes his hands*): Yes, I really believe I can! I don't know why it is, but— (*In an outburst of emotion*) I'm so happy! I feel like laughing—and I feel like crying too! So—after all—I'll have a chance to live! I was beginning to be so afraid that life would pass me by.

ARNHOLM: You need never be afraid of that, Bolette dear. Now—tell me frankly—you're quite free, aren't you? You've no ties here at home?

BOLETTE: Ties? No—none at all.

ARNHOLM: You're sure?

BOLETTE: Yes, quite. That is—of course I'm tied to Father, in a way—and Hilde too, but—

ARNHOLM: Sooner or later you'll have to leave your father— and Hilde will have a life of her own someday; all that's just a question of time. But, apart from that, you say you have no ties? You're not engaged in any way?

BOLETTE: No. As far as that goes, I'm quite free to leave.

ARNHOLM: Then you shall come with me, Bolette dear.

BOLETTE: It's too wonderful to think of!

ARNHOLM: You trust me, don't you?

BOLETTE: Of course I do!

ARNHOLM: And you've no doubts—you're quite willing to place your future in my hands?

BOLETTE: Of course! Why shouldn't I? How can you ask? You're my old tutor, aren't you? Or my old-time tutor, perhaps I should say.

ARNHOLM: That's not the point—we needn't dwell on that. But since you're free—and have no ties of any sort—do you think you could—? Do you think you could see your way to—? Well—I'd like to ask you to join your life to mine, Bolette.

BOLETTE: Good heavens! What are you saying?

ARNHOLM: Will you join your life to mine, Bolette? Will you marry me?

BOLETTE (*Half to herself*): It's impossible! Utterly impossible!

ARNHOLM: Why should it be impossible—?

BOLETTE: Mr. Arnholm! You can't mean what you say! (*Looks at him*) Or— Perhaps— Was this what you had in mind when you offered me your help?

ARNHOLM: Bolette—listen to me a moment! This comes as a surprise, I realize that—

BOLETTE: Indeed it does! What else could you expect? A thing like that—coming from you—!

ARNHOLM: You're right. Of course you didn't know—how could you—that I came here for your sake.

BOLETTE: For my sake!

ARNHOLM: Yes, Bolette. This spring I had a letter from your father. I got the impression, from certain things he said, that your feelings for me were—well—a good deal warmer than mere friendship.

BOLETTE: How could Father write a thing like that!

ARNHOLM: It was all a mistake; that wasn't at all what he meant, you see. But I didn't know that at the time. So I built up in my imagination the picture of a young girl whose thoughts were full of me, and who waited eagerly for my return—No! Don't interrupt me, Bolette, please! Now, when a man is past the first flush of youth, as they call it, such a belief—or illusion if you prefer—makes a very strong impression. I started to think of you with tenderness and gratitude, and made up my mind to come and tell you that I shared your feelings—the feelings I imagined you had for me.

BOLETTE: Well—now you know it isn't true. You were mistaken!

ARNHOLM: That may be; but, all the same—it's too late now to change the picture of you I've built up in my heart. Can't you understand that, Bolette?

BOLETTE: How can such a thing be possible? I should never have believed it!

ARNHOLM: But now that you know it *is* possible—what do you say, Bolette? Won't you consent to be my wife?

BOLETTE: It seems quite inconceivable to me, Mr. Arnholm. After all—you were my tutor. I can't think of you in any other way.

ARNHOLM: Well—if you really feel you can't— However— this will in no way affect our friendship.

BOLETTE: How do you mean?

ARNHOLM: My offer stands, of course. I'll see that you get away from here; I'll help you to go on with your studies, and in the future I shall guarantee your security and independence; I promise you that. You can depend on me as a true and faithful friend.

BOLETTE: But, Mr. Arnholm—you've made all that impossible!

ARNHOLM: Is that impossible too?

BOLETTE: Of course! After what you've said to me—and after what I answered you— I couldn't possibly accept these things. I can take nothing from you now!

ARNHOLM: I see. Then you'd rather stay here and let "life pass you by"?

BOLETTE: That's such a dreadful thought!

ARNHOLM: You say you want to see something of the world; you long to take part in an active life; yet now that the opportunity is offered to you, you refuse it. How can you resign yourself to this meager, cooped-up life—knowing what infinite possibilities are open to you? Think seriously, Bolette.

BOLETTE: Yes, Mr. Arnholm; I know you're right.

ARNHOLM: And then, when your father is no longer with you, you'll be alone in the world—without any protection. You might find yourself obliged to marry some other man; a man whom you—quite conceivably—might not be able to care for, any more than you care for me.

BOLETTE: Everything you say is quite true, Mr. Arnholm; but—all the same—! — And yet, perhaps—

ARNHOLM: Well, Bolette?

BOLETTE: Perhaps it might not be so utterly impossible, after all—

ARNHOLM: You mean you might be willing to—? Or, at least, you'll accept my help—my friendship?

BOLETTE: No, no! That I could never do! That would be quite out of the question. But I might consent to—

ARNHOLM: Oh, Bolette! Will you—?

BOLETTE: Yes— I believe—I think I will.

ARNHOLM: You'll be my wife?

BOLETTE: Yes, if you'll still have me.

ARNHOLM: If I'll still have you—! (*Seizes her hand*) Thank you, thank you, Bolette dear! And as for the things you said—don't worry about them. Those doubts of yours don't trouble me. I shall know how to win your heart—you'll see. Oh, Bolette! How I shall cherish you!

BOLETTE: But you *will* take me away from here? You promised I should have a free and happy life.

ARNHOLM: Yes, and I'll keep my word.

BOLETTE: And you will allow me to go on with my studies?

ARNHOLM: I'll be your tutor, as I was before. Do you remember the last year you were my pupil—?

BOLETTE: I can't believe it! To be free—to have a chance to see the world! And not to have to think about the future; not to have to worry about money any more!

ARNHOLM: No; you needn't waste a thought on that. That, in itself, is something, isn't it?

BOLETTE: My goodness, yes! It is indeed!

ARNHOLM: We shall get on splendidly, Bolette! We'll have such a happy, peaceful life together.

BOLETTE: Yes. I'm beginning to think—perhaps we might make a go of it. (*Looks off right and disengages herself hastily*) Please don't say anything to anybody yet!

ARNHOLM: What is it, dear?

BOLETTE: Poor thing! (*Points*) Just look at him!

ARNHOLM: Is it your father—?

BOLETTE: No; it's that young sculptor. He's over there with Hilde.

ARNHOLM: Oh, Lyngstrand. What of him?

BOLETTE: Well—you know how ill he is; how delicate.

ARNHOLM: It's probably all put on.

BOLETTE: Oh, no—it's real enough. He hasn't long to live. But perhaps in a way it's best for him.

ARNHOLM: What makes you say that?

BOLETTE: Because—well—because I don't think his work will ever come to much—Let's go before they come.

ARNHOLM: Yes—let's, Bolette dear.

(HILDE *and* LYNGSTRAND *appear beside the pond.*)

HILDE: Hi! Hi there! Won't you condescend to wait for us?

ARNHOLM: We'll go on ahead.

(*He and* BOLETTE *go off left.*)

LYNGSTRAND (*Laughs quietly*): It's delightful—have you noticed? Everybody seems to be walking about in pairs these days.

HILDE (*Looking after them*): I'm willing to bet he's making love to her.

LYNGSTRAND: Really? What makes you think so?

HILDE: It's easy enough to tell—if you keep your eyes open.

LYNGSTRAND: But she won't have him; I'm sure of that.

HILDE: No. She thinks he's too old; and she's afraid he's going bald.

LYNGSTRAND: It's not because of that. She wouldn't have him anyway.

HILDE: How can you possibly know?

LYNGSTRAND: Because she's promised to think of someone else.

HILDE: Only to think about them?

LYNGSTRAND: While he's away—yes.

HILDE: I suppose you mean yourself. So she's to think about you, is she?

LYNGSTRAND: Possibly.

HILDE: Did she promise?

LYNGSTRAND: Yes, she did. She promised. But for heaven's sake don't tell her that you know.

HILDE: Don't worry. I'm as silent as the grave.

LYNGSTRAND: It was awfully nice of her I thought.

HILDE: Then, when you come home again, you'll get engaged I suppose. Do you intend to marry her?

LYNGSTRAND: No; I'm afraid that won't work out. I couldn't think of marrying for several years—not till my reputation is established; and by that time she'd probably be too old for me.

HILDE: Yet you expect her to go on thinking of you all the same!

LYNGSTRAND: Why not? It would be tremendously helpful to me as an artist. And what difference can it make to her? She has no vocation in life, you see. Still—I must say it was nice of her.

HILDE: You really believe, if Bolette went on thinking about you, it would make a difference in your work?

LYNGSTRAND: Yes, I believe it would. The fact that a young attractive woman was thinking of me—dreaming of me in secret— It would be positively—I don't know how to put it into words.

HILDE: Do you by any chance mean *thrilling?* Positively thrilling?

LYNGSTRAND: Yes—that's it! Thrilling! At least I think that's what I mean. (*Looks at her a moment*) You're so clever, Miss Hilde; really extraordinarily clever. By the time I come home again, you'll be about the same age your sister is now, won't you? And perhaps you'll have grown to look quite like her; and you may grow more like her in disposition too. You'll perhaps be a sort of combination of yourself and her—

HILDE: Would you like that?

LYNGSTRAND: I'm not quite sure. I rather think I would. But —for the moment—I prefer you as you are. Just exactly as you are.

HILDE: You like me like this, do you?

LYNGSTRAND: I like you very much like this.

HILDE: Hm. Tell me—as an artist—do you think I'm right to wear light colors?

LYNGSTRAND: Yes, I do indeed.

HILDE: You think they're becoming to me?

LYNGSTRAND: Most becoming.

HILDE: But, tell me—you who are an artist—how do you think I'd look in black?

LYNGSTRAND: Black isn't exactly right for summer. However I'm sure you'd look very well in it; especially with your figure.

HILDE: In black from head to toe—a black ruffle—black gloves—and a long black veil.

LYNGSTRAND: If I saw you dressed like that, Miss Hilde, I'd wish to be a painter. I'd paint a splendid picture of a beautiful young widow.

HILDE: Or a young girl grieving for her lost lover perhaps.

LYNGSTRAND: That would be even better. But you surely wouldn't want to dress like that?

HILDE: I don't know; it might be awfully thrilling.

LYNGSTRAND: Thrilling?

HILDE: Anyhow—it's thrilling to think about. (*Suddenly points off left*) Oh, look!

LYNGSTRAND: The English steamer! She's already docked! (WANGEL *and* ELLIDA *appear by the pond.*)

WANGEL: My dear Ellida, you're mistaken I assure you. (*Sees the others*) Oh—you're here, are you? She's not been sighted yet, has she, Mr. Lyngstrand?

LYNGSTRAND: You mean the English steamer?

WANGEL: Yes—of course!

LYNGSTRAND: She's already at the pier.

ELLIDA: Ah—! I was right!

WANGEL: So—she's come!

LYNGSTRAND: Like a thief in the night, Doctor. She crept in without a sound.

WANGEL: I expect Hilde would like to hear the music. Take her down to the pier, will you? You'd better hurry!

LYNGSTRAND: We were just going there, Doctor.

WANGEL: We may perhaps join you later. We'll be there in a little while.

HILDE (*To* LYNGSTRAND *in a whisper*) Another pair for you! (*She and* LYNGSTRAND *go off through the garden left. The sound of a brass band is heard in the distance through the following.*)

ELLIDA: He's come! He's here—I feel it!

WANGEL: Go into the house, Ellida; let me talk to him alone.

ELLIDA: No—that's impossible! Quite impossible, I tell you! (*Gives a cry*) Ah! There he is!

(*The* STRANGER *enters from the left, and stops on the path outside the garden fence.*)

STRANGER (*Bows*) Good evening. I told you I'd come back tonight, Ellida.

ELLIDA: Yes— This is the moment.

STRANGER: Are you ready for the journey? Or are you not?

WANGEL: No! Of course she isn't! You can see that for yourself.

STRANGER: I'm not speaking of traveling clothes, or trunks —nothing of that sort. There's everything she needs on board. I've engaged a cabin for her too. (*To* ELLIDA) Are you ready to come with me, Ellida? Of your own free will?

ELLIDA (*Imploringly*): I beg of you, don't tempt me! Don't ask me that!

(*A steamer bell is heard in the distance.*)

STRANGER: That's the first warning. You must decide now— yes or no!

ELLIDA: Decide! My whole life depends on this decision! I'll never have another chance to choose.

STRANGER: Never! Another half hour, and it will be too late.

ELLIDA: Why are you so ruthless? Why do you refuse to let me go?

STRANGER: We belong together; you know that.

ELLIDA: You mean—because we promised?

STRANGER: Men and women are not bound by promises. I refuse to let you go because I can't.

ELLIDA (*Softly, tremulously*): Why didn't you come back before?

WANGEL: Ellida!

ELLIDA (*In an outburst*): What is this thing that beckons me and tempts me—and drags me towards the unknown? It has all the power and seduction of the sea!

(*The* STRANGER *climbs over the garden fence.*)

ELLIDA (*Shrinking behind* WANGEL): What is it! What do you want?

STRANGER: You will choose me, Ellida! I know it. I can hear it in your voice.

WANGEL: My wife has no choice to make. I'm here to choose for her, and to protect her—yes, protect her! I warn you to get out! Get out of this country—and stay out! You know you're wanted here.

ELLIDA: Wangel! Not that!

STRANGER: What will you do to me?

WANGEL: I shall have you arrested immediately as the criminal you are. You won't have a chance to get away. I know all about that murder up at Skjoldvik.

ELLIDA: Wangel—how can you—!

STRANGER: I was prepared for that. (*Takes a revolver out of his breast pocket*) That's why I brought this with me.

ELLIDA (*Flings herself in front of* WANGEL): No! Not him! Rather kill me!

STRANGER: Don't be afraid. I won't harm either of you. I intend to live and die as a free man. I brought this for myself.

ELLIDA (*With increasing agitation*): Wangel! I must tell you this again—and I want him to hear it. I know you have the power to keep me here by force, and you intend to use it. But you can't control my mind. You can't prevent my thoughts, my longings and desires, from reaching out into that mysterious world of the unknown to which I belong, and that you have barred against me.

WANGEL: I understand, Ellida. I see you slipping further and further away from me. And I'm afraid this craving for a vague shadowy world of unreality will gradually destroy your mind—until it is blotted out in darkness.

ELLIDA: I feel it too, Wangel. It's like dark silent wings hovering over me.

WANGEL: Pray God it may not come to that. There's only one possible way of saving you; I can think of nothing else to do. Ellida! Here and now I release you from our bargain. You're free! I set you free. Now you can choose.

ELLIDA (*Looks at him for a moment as though speechless*): Is this true? Really true? You say this from your heart?

WANGEL: From my heart, Ellida.

ELLIDA: You'd really do this? You'd dare to do it?

WANGEL: Yes, I dare. Because I love you.

ELLIDA (*Softly and tremulously*): Have I become so close to you? So very dear?

WANGEL: Our years of marriage have made you so.

ELLIDA: And I never saw it! How blind I've been!

WANGEL: Your thoughts were filled with other things, Ellida.
Now—I've released you. You're no longer bound to me
by anything. Your life is yours again. You must act on your
own responsibility; you're free to choose!

ELLIDA (*Puts her hands to her head and gazes fixedly towards* WANGEL): Free to choose!— My own responsibility!
— This changes everything!

(*The steamer bell rings again.*)

STRANGER: That's the last bell, Ellida. We must go.

ELLIDA (*Turns toward him, looks at him fixedly, and says in
a determined voice*): I can never go with you after this.

STRANGER: Not go with me!

ELLIDA (*Clings to* WANGEL): Now I can never leave you.

WANGEL: Ellida—Ellida!

STRANGER: Is it all over then?

ELLIDA: All over.

STRANGER: What is it here that's stronger than my will?

ELLIDA: Your will can never touch me any more. You're
like a dead man to me now. A dead seaman who came
home out of the sea—and now goes back to it. You no
longer terrify me—nor fascinate me either.

STRANGER: Goodbye, Mrs. Wangel! (*He vaults over the
fence*) I've lived through many shipwrecks—I shall doubt-
less live through this one. I shall not think of you again.
(*He goes out to the left.*)

WANGEL (*Looks at her a while*): Ellida—your mind is like
the sea; it ebbs and flows. What made you change?

ELLIDA: Don't you see? Everything changed—was bound to
change—when you set me free to choose.

WANGEL: The unknown—it no longer fascinates you then?

ELLIDA: It neither frightens me nor fascinates me any more.
I was free to gaze into it—to plunge into it if need be. I
was free to choose it—and so I was able to reject it.

WANGEL: Gradually I begin to understand you. You see
things in images—in symbols. I believe now, your longing
for the sea—the fascination this strange man held for you

—was only the expression of a growing need for freedom on your part.

ELLIDA: I've no way of knowing if that's true. But you've been a good doctor to me, Wangel. You found—and dared to use—the only remedy. The one thing that could save me.

WANGEL: In matters of life and death, we doctors have to dare! —Are you coming back to me, Ellida?

ELLIDA: Yes, my very dear—my faithful Wangel! I'm coming back to you. And this time—of my own free will.

WANGEL (*Looks at her tenderly*): Ellida! Ellida! We'll live wholly for each other from now on—

ELLIDA: And we'll share our memories; yours—as well as mine.

WANGEL: Yes, my darling!

ELLIDA: And we'll care for our two children—

WANGEL: Ours! You call them ours!

ELLIDA: I know they're not mine yet—but I shall try and win them.

WANGEL: Ours—! (*Kisses her hands rapidly and joyfully*) That one word makes me so happy.

(HILDE, BALLESTED, LYNGSTRAND, ARNHOLM *and* BOLETTE *come from the left into the garden. At the same time a number of young townspeople and summer visitors pass along the footpath.*)

HILDE (*Aside to* LYNGSTRAND): You'd think they were in love with each other, wouldn't you?

BALLESTED (*Who has overheard*): It's still summertime, you know.

ARNHOLM (*Glancing toward* WANGEL *and* ELLIDA): The English steamer's under way.

BOLETTE (*Going to the fence*): You can see her best from here.

LYNGSTRAND: Her last trip of the season.

BALLESTED: Yes. We shall soon be icebound: "Trapped in an icy prison," as the old melodrama says. A sad thought, Mrs. Wangel. And you're leaving too, I hear. You're off to Skjoldvik in the morning.

WANGEL: She's not going after all. We've changed our minds, you see.

ARNHOLM (*Looks from one to the other*): Really! Have you?

BOLETTE (*Coming forward*): Father—is this true?

HILDE (*Going to* ELLIDA): You're staying with us?

ELLIDA: Yes—if you'll have me, Hilde dear.

HILDE (*Struggling between tears and joy*): Have you! Heavens! How can you ask—!

ARNHOLM: This is quite a surprise, Mrs. Wangel.

ELLIDA: Well, you see, Mr. Arnholm— Do you remember the conversation we had yesterday?— Once you've decided to become a land creature, it's hard to find your way back to the sea again—

BALLESTED: That's like my mermaid, isn't it?

ELLIDA: Yes—very like.

BALLESTED: Only, of course, the mermaid dies of it. People on the other hand, are usually able to acclam—acclimatize themselves. I assure you, Mrs. Wangel—they do acclimatize themselves!

ELLIDA: Especially if they're free to choose.

WANGEL: And if they're allowed to act on their own responsibility, Ellida.

ELLIDA (*Quickly gives him her hand*): That's it—precisely! (*The great steamer glides noiselessly down the fjord. The music is heard close inshore.*)

CURTAIN

Little Eyolf

A PLAY IN THREE ACTS

1894

CHARACTERS

ALFRED ALLMERS, *landed proprietor, man of letters, formerly an assistant teacher in the secondary schools*

RITA ALLMERS, *his wife*

EYOLF, *their child, nine years old*

ASTA ALLMERS, *Alfred's younger half sister*

BORGHEJM, *an engineer*

THE RAT-WOMAN

The action takes place on Allmers' estate, on a fjord, twelve or fourteen miles from the town.

ACT
ONE

SCENE: *A beautiful and richly appointed garden room. Lavishly furnished, and filled with plants and flowers. In the back wall glass doors open onto the veranda. A splendid view over the fjord. Wooded hillsides in the distance. A door in each side wall. The one on the right a double door placed far upstage. Downstage on the right a sofa with cushions and rugs. Beside the sofa a small table and chairs. Downstage left a larger table with several armchairs. On the table stands an open traveling bag. It is an early summer morning, with warm sunshine.*

RITA ALLMERS *stands by the table, facing towards the left, unpacking the bag. She is a beautiful, rather tall, well-developed blonde about thirty years old. She wears a light-colored housedress.*

In a few moments MISS ASTA ALLMERS *enters from the door on the right, wearing a light-brown summer dress, with hat, jacket and parasol. Under her arm she carries a large locked portfolio. She is slim, of medium height, with dark hair and dark, serious eyes. Twenty-five years old.*

ASTA (*At the doorway*): Good morning, Rita dear!

RITA (*Turns her head and nods to her*): Oh, it's you, Asta! How did you get all the way out here so early! You must have got up at dawn!

ASTA (*Takes off her things and puts them on a chair by the door*): I felt so restless this morning, somehow. I simply *had* to come out and see how little Eyolf was getting on. And you too, of course. (*Puts the portfolio down on the table by the sofa*) I came over by the steamer.

RITA (*Smiles*): Did you happen to meet any particular friend on board? Just by chance, I mean?

ASTA (*Quietly*): No. I didn't meet anyone I knew. (*Sees the traveling bag*) What's that, Rita?

RITA (*Goes on unpacking*): It's Alfred's bag. Don't you recognize it?

ASTA (*Joyfully, going nearer*): What! Is Alfred home?

RITA: Yes—he arrived last night by the late train; got back quite unexpectedly.

ASTA: I must have had a premonition! *That*'s why I felt I had to come out here today!—Didn't he write you he was coming? Not even a postcard?

RITA: Not a single word.

ASTA: Didn't he even send a telegram?

RITA: I got one an hour before he arrived. Very short, very curt. (*Laughs*) Just like him, isn't it?

ASTA: Yes; he never makes a fuss.

RITA: The surprise made his coming home even more wonderful.

ASTA: I can imagine!

RITA: Two whole weeks before I expected him!

ASTA: How is he? Well? Not depressed any more?

RITA (*Snaps the bag shut and smiles at her*): He's like a new man.

ASTA: Not even tired?

RITA: Oh yes, he was tired—very tired, in fact. But then, poor dear, he came most of the way on foot.

ASTA: And perhaps the mountain air may have been a bit too keen for him.

RITA: No it wasn't—I'm sure of that. He's not coughing at all.

ASTA: How splendid! What a good thing the doctor persuaded him to take this trip.

RITA: Yes; especially now that it's safely over. But it's been dreadful for me, Asta. I haven't said much to you about it. Anyhow you came out here so seldom—

ASTA: I know; it wasn't very nice of me. But—

RITA: Oh, I understand—I know how busy you are at the school. (*Smiles*) And of course our engineering friend—our road builder—he was away too, wasn't he?

ASTA: Stop it, Rita!

RITA: Very well. We'll say no more about the road builder! But I can't tell you how awful it's been here without Alfred! Such an empty feeling! I felt so lonely and deserted. The house seemed like a tomb—!

ASTA: Good heavens—it's only been six or seven weeks, after all!

RITA: Alfred's never been away from me before, you see. In all the ten years we've been married he's never left me—not even for a day—

ASTA: Then it was probably high time he got off by himself a bit. He ought to have gone for a tramp in the mountains every summer. It would have done him good.

RITA: It's all very well for you to talk. If I were as sensible as you are, perhaps I might have let him go before. But I simply couldn't, Asta! I had a feeling that I'd lose him; that he'd never come back to me again. But you don't understand that, I suppose.

ASTA: No. Probably because I have nobody to lose.

RITA (*With a teasing smile*): Nobody? Are you sure? Nobody at all?

ASTA: Not that I know of. (*Changing the subject*) Where's Alfred now, Rita? Is he still asleep?

RITA: Good heavens, no. He was up at his usual time.

ASTA: He can't have been so very tired, then.

RITA: He was last night when he arrived. Eyolf's with him now; he's been in his room over an hour.

ASTA: Poor little Eyolf! He shouldn't be forced to do all those lessons. His little face looks so white and strained!

RITA (*Shrugs her shoulders*): Alfred insists on it. You know how he is.

ASTA: You ought to put your foot down, Rita.

RITA (*Somewhat impatiently*): I don't want to get involved in it. Alfred understands these things much better than I

do. And Eyolf has to do *something*, after all. You know
perfectly well he can't go out and play like other children.

ASTA (*Firmly*): I shall have a talk with Alfred.

RITA: Yes do, dear; I wish you would—Ah! Here he is—
(ALFRED ALLMERS, *wearing a light summer suit, comes in
from the left, leading* EYOLF *by the hand. He is a slim,
delicately built man of thirty-six or thirty-seven years old,
with gentle eyes, and thin brown hair and beard. His face
is thoughtful and serious.* EYOLF *wears a suit cut like a
uniform, with gold braid and gilt military buttons. He is
lame, and walks with a crutch under his left arm. His leg
is paralyzed. He is undersized and looks delicate, but has
beautiful intelligent eyes.*)

ALLMERS (*Drops* EYOLF's *hand and goes to* ASTA *with a joyful expression, hands outstretched*): Asta! My dear Asta!
Fancy your being here! How splendid to see you again so
soon!

ASTA: I *had* to come here today—I had a feeling! Welcome
home again.

ALLMERS (*Shaking her hands*): Thank you for coming.

RITA: He looks well, doesn't he?

ASTA (*Looks at him intently*): Wonderful! Really wonderful!
His eyes are so much brighter. Did you do much writing
while you were away? (*With an outburst of joy*) I
shouldn't be surprised if you'd finished the whole book!

ALLMERS (*Shrugs his shoulders*): Oh, the book—! Well—!

ASTA: I kept thinking to myself: Now that he's off on his own,
he'll finish it in no time.

ALLMERS: I thought so too; but it didn't turn out that way;
I'm afraid I didn't write a single word.

ASTA: What! You didn't write at all?

RITA: So that's why all that paper was still in your bag untouched.

ASTA: Then—what have you been doing all this time?

ALLMERS (*Smiles*): I walked, and I did a lot of thinking. I
thought, and thought, and thought.

RITA: (*Puts her arm round his neck*): Did you have a
thought to spare for *us* once in a while?

ALLMERS: Of course! I thought of you every single day.

RITA (*Releases him*): Then everything's as it should be.

ASTA: I can't get over your not doing any writing! And yet you look so happy and contented. You're not usually like that—when you can't get on with your work, I mean.

ALLMERS: No—you're right. But I've been foolish up to now, you see. Thinking is what brings out the best in one. It doesn't really matter what you put on paper.

ASTA (*Exclaiming*): Not matter!

RITA (*Laughing*): Why, Alfred! Have you gone mad!

EYOLF (*Looks up at him confidingly*): What *you* write matters, Papa; it matters a great deal.

ALLMERS (*Smiles and strokes his hair*): Well—if *you* think so, then— But, you'll see—someone will come after me, who will do it all much better.

EYOLF: Who do you mean, Papa? Please tell us!

ALLMERS: Be patient. We shall recognize him when he comes.

EYOLF: Then what will *you* do, Father?

ALLMERS (*Seriously*): I shall go back to the mountains—

RITA: Alfred! Don't be so unkind!

ALLMERS: Back to the Wilds; up to the very highest peaks.

EYOLF: Papa—don't you think I'll soon be well enough to go there with you?

ALLMERS (*Sadly, with emotion*): Yes, little one—perhaps.

EYOLF: It would be such fun if I could go mountain climbing too.

ASTA (*Changing the subject*): I must say, Eyolf—you look very smart today!

EYOLF: Do you think so, Auntie?

ASTA: Yes, indeed. Did you put on those new clothes in honor of Papa?

EYOLF: Yes; I asked Mother if I might. I wanted Papa to see me in them.

ALLMERS (*In a low voice to* RITA): You shouldn't have given him a suit like that.

RITA (*In an undertone*): He'd set his heart on it. He kept on begging me—gave me no peace.

EYOLF: Papa—I forgot to tell you: Borghejm brought me a bow and arrows; and he's taught me how to shoot with it.

ALLMERS: Good! I should think you'd like that, Eyolf.

EYOLF: Yes. And next time he comes I shall ask him to give me swimming lessons.

ALLMERS: Swimming lessons! What makes you want to learn to swim?

EYOLF: All the other boys at the beach can swim. I'm the only one who can't.

ALLMERS (*Deeply moved, takes him in his arms*): You shall learn anything you like! Anything and everything!

EYOLF: Do you know what I'd like best of all, Papa?

ALLMERS: No; tell me.

EYOLF: I'd like best of all to learn to be a soldier.

ALLMERS: Oh, Eyolf! There are so many other things much better than that.

EYOLF: But, Papa—when I grow up I'll *have* to be a soldier; you know that.

ALLMERS (*Clenching his hands*): Well—we'll see.

ASTA (*Sits down at the table on the left*): Come over here a minute, Eyolf; I want to tell you something.

EYOLF (*Goes up to her*): What is it, Auntie?

ASTA: Just think, Eyolf—I've seen the Rat-woman!

EYOLF: Seen the Rat-woman! You *haven't*, Auntie—you're only making fun of me!

ASTA: No, it's true. I saw her yesterday.

EYOLF: Where did you see her?

ASTA: On the road—just outside the town.

ALLMERS: I saw her too; way out in the country somewhere.

RITA (*Who is sitting on the sofa*): Someday, Eyolf, perhaps *we* shall see her too.

EYOLF: Don't you think it's strange, Auntie, that she should be called the Rat-woman?

ASTA: They call her that because she wanders all over the country driving out the rats.

ALLMERS: I seem to remember hearing her real name is Miss Varg.

EYOLF: Varg? That means a wolf, doesn't it?

ALLMERS (*Patting him on the head*): Fancy your knowing that!

EYOLF (*Thoughtfully*): Then perhaps it's true, after all, that at night she turns into a werewolf. Do you think that could be true, Papa?

ALLMERS: No—I don't think so—You'd better go out now and play in the garden for a bit.

EYOLF: Shouldn't I take some books with me?

ALLMERS: No—no more books just now. Would you like to go down to the shore and see the other boys?

EYOLF (*Shyly*): No. I don't want to see the other boys today.

ALLMERS: Why not?

EYOLF: Because I've got this suit on.

ALLMERS (*Frowning*): Do you think they might make fun of —of your new clothes?

EYOLF (*Evasively*): They wouldn't dare. I'd beat up anyone who did.

ALLMERS: Well, then—why—?

EYOLF: They're such rude boys, you see. They keep on saying I can never be a soldier.

ALLMERS (*With suppressed indignation*): What makes them say that, do you think?

EYOLF: They're jealous of me, I expect. They're so terribly poor, Papa. They haven't even got any shoes—they have to walk barefoot.

ALLMERS (*Softly, in a strangled voice*): Oh, Rita—all this breaks my heart!

RITA (*Soothingly, rising*): There, there!

ALLMERS (*Threateningly*): They should be taught a lesson! I'll show them who's master around here!

ASTA (*Listening*): Wasn't that someone knocking?

EYOLF: It must be Borghejm.

RITA: Come in!

(THE RAT-WOMAN *comes in softly and noiselessly from the door on the right. She is a small, thin, shrunken figure, old and gray-haired, with keen piercing eyes. She wears an*

old-fashioned flowered dress, a black cape with a hood.
She carries a large red umbrella, and a black bag hangs on
her arm by its string.)

EYOLF (*Softly, clutching* ASTA's *skirt*): There she is, Auntie!
It must be she!

RAT-WOMAN (*Curtsying at the door*): I humbly beg your
Honors' pardon. Have your Honors noticed anything
scratching or gnawing around the house?

ALLMERS: No—I don't think so.

RAT-WOMAN: If so, I'd be only too glad to help get rid of it.

RITA: Yes—we understand; but there's nothing of that sort
here.

RAT-WOMAN: What a pity! I'm just starting off on my rounds,
you see. Lord knows when I'll be in this part of the country
again—Oh! how tired I feel!

ALLMERS (*Points to a chair*): Yes—you look tired.

RAT-WOMAN: You'd never think a person would get tired of
doing good to those poor little creatures; people hate them
and persecute them so cruelly. But it does take a lot out of
you.

RITA: Won't you sit down and rest a while?

RAT-WOMAN: Many thanks. (*Sits down on a chair between
the door and the sofa*) I've been hard at work all night.

ALLMERS: Have you really?

RAT-WOMAN: Yes; over on the Islands. (*Cackles with laughter*) They finally had to send for me. They didn't like it—
but there was nothing else for them to do. They had to eat
humble pie, you see. (*Looks at* EYOLF *and nods*) Humble
pie, little master. Humble pie.

EYOLF (*Involuntarily, rather timidly*): Why did they have
to—?

RAT-WOMAN: What?

EYOLF: Eat it?

RAT-WOMAN: Because the rats and all the tiny rat-babies were
devouring everything they had. That's why, little master.

RITA: Poor people! Were there *that* many?

RAT-WOMAN: They were teeming and swarming everywhere.

(*Laughs with quiet glee*) They crept and crawled in the beds at night. They plopped about in the milk pails. They went slithering and squeaking all over the house.

EYOLF (*Softly, to* ASTA): I shall never go to the Islands, Auntie.

RAT-WOMAN: But then *I* came, you see—with my assistant. We took them all away with us, the dear sweet little creatures. We made an end of them—every single one.

EYOLF (*Gives a shriek*): Papa—look, look!

RITA: Good heavens, Eyolf!

ALLMERS: What's the matter?

EYOLF (*Pointing*): Look at her bag! There's something wriggling in it!

RITA (*Backing away towards the extreme left of the room, shrieks*): Ugh! Send her away, Alfred!

RAT-WOMAN (*Laughs*): There's nothing to be afraid of, pretty lady! My little friend won't hurt you.

ALLMERS: But what, in God's name, *is* it?

RAT-WOMAN: it's only my little Pug-boy. (*Loosens the string of the bag*) Come along, then! Come up out of the dark, my precious little friend. (*A little dog with a broad black snout pokes his head out of the bag.*)

RAT-WOMAN (*Nods and beckons to* EYOLF): Don't be afraid. Come over here, my little wounded warrior. He won't bite you. Come and see him. Come along!

EYOLF (*Clinging to* ASTA): No; I don't dare!

RAT-WOMAN: Come along, young master! Have you ever seen such a sweet, lovable face?

EYOLF (*Points, in astonishment*): *His* face, you mean?

RAT-WOMAN: *His* face—exactly.

EYOLF (*In an undertone, staring fixedly at the dog*): I think he has the ugliest, most awful face I've ever seen.

RAT-WOMAN (*Closing the bag*): It'll come—you'll see—it'll come.

EYOLF (*Drawing nearer in spite of himself; then he goes right up to the bag and strokes it*): Still—he *is* lovely. He's lovely all the same.

RAT-WOMAN (*In a cautious tone*): But, just now, he's so tired
—so weary. So *very* tired, poor little thing. (*Looks at*
ALLMERS) That kind of game takes a lot out of you, you
see, Sir.

ALLMERS: What kind of game?

RAT-WOMAN: The luring-game.

ALLMERS: Luring? You mean it's the dog that lures the rats?

RAT-WOMAN (*Nods*): We lure them together, little Pug-boy
and I. It's all very simple—or so it seems. I tie a string
through his collar and lead him round the house three
times. Then I play on my pipes. And when they hear *that*
—out they come. All those blessed little creatures come out
of their holes and hiding places. Up from the cellars and
down from the attics they come!

EYOLF: And does the little dog bite them to death?

RAT-WOMAN: Oh, no! Not at all! We lead the way to the
boat, he and I. And they follow us; the big rats and all
the rat babies too.

EYOLF (*Eagerly*): And then? What happens then?

RAT-WOMAN: Then we push out from land. I row with one
hand and play my pipes with the other. And my Pug-boy
swims after the boat. (*With glittering eyes*) And all those
creepy-crawly creatures follow us; they follow us far out
into the deep water. They *have* to, you see.

EYOLF: Why do they *have* to?

RAT-WOMAN: Just because they don't want to. They *have* to
plunge into the water—just because they're so afraid of it.

EYOLF: And then do they drown?

RAT-WOMAN: Every single one. (*Softly*) Yes—the lovely
little things find peace in the quiet and the darkness.
They're not hated or persecuted any more. They go sound
asleep down there—a long blissful sleep. (*Rises*) In the
old days I didn't need my little Pug-boy. I did all the
luring myself—I alone.

EYOLF: What did you lure then?

RAT-WOMAN: Men. One man in particular.

EYOLF (*Eagerly*): Who was he? Tell me!

RAT-WOMAN (*Laughing*): He was my own beloved—you little charmer!

EYOLF: And where is he now?

RAT-WOMAN (*Harshly*): Down among the rats! (*Resuming her milder tone*) But I must be moving on—I've work to do. (*To* RITA) You're sure you have no use for me today, pretty lady? I could clear things up for you quite easily, as long as I'm here.

RITA: Thank you; there's no need.

RAT-WOMAN: Well—you never know, pretty lady. If you should ever notice anything nibbling and gnawing—or creeping and crawling—just send for me and little Pug-boy here— Goodbye, and many thanks. (*She goes out by the door on the right.*)

EYOLF (*Softly and triumphantly, to* ASTA): Just think, Auntie —*I've* seen the Rat-woman too!

(RITA *goes out onto the veranda, fanning herself with her handkerchief. In a few moments* EYOLF *slips out cautiously, and unnoticed, through the door on the right.*)

ALLMERS (*Picks up the portfolio from the table by the sofa*): Is this your portfolio, Asta?

ASTA: Yes; there are some of the old letters in it.

ALLMERS: Ah—the family letters—

ASTA: You asked me to sort them out while you were away— remember?

ALLMERS (*Pats her head*): And you actually found time for that!

ASTA: I went through some of them here—and some at my rooms in town.

ALLMERS: Thanks, dear— Did you find anything interesting?

ASTA (*Casually*): You nearly always find *something* interesting among old papers. (*In a low serious tone*) These, in the portfolio, are letters to my mother.

ALLMERS: You'll keep those yourself, of course.

ASTA (*With an effort*): I'd like you to have a look at them too, Alfred; sometime—later on— I haven't got the key with me today.

ALLMERS: It doesn't matter, Asta dear. In any case I'd never dream of reading your mother's letters.

ASTA (*Fixing her eyes on him*): Then, sometime or other—some quiet evening—I'll let you know what's in them.

ALLMERS: Yes—that's a good idea. But you should certainly keep them. You have little enough to remind you of her. (*He hands* ASTA *the portfolio. She takes it and puts it on the chair under her coat.* RITA *comes back into the room.*)

RITA: That horrible old woman! She's filled the whole house with a smell of corpses!

ALLMERS: She was rather horrible, I must admit.

RITA: She made me feel quite sick.

ALLMERS: Still—I think I understand that strange power she was talking about. There's a similar magic in the solitude of the wild empty spaces—up among the mountain peaks.

ASTA (*Looks at him attentively*): What is it that's happened to you, Alfred?

ALLMERS (*Smiling*): To me?

ASTA: Yes, something's happened to you. Something's changed you. Rita noticed it too.

RITA: I noticed it the moment you arrived. I hope it's a *good* change, Alfred?

ALLMERS: It *ought* to be. I feel it must be.

RITA (*In an outburst*): You had some kind of an adventure while you were away. Don't deny it! I can tell!

ALLMERS (*Shakes his head*): No, not really. Nothing specific, anyway. But—

RITA (*Eagerly*): But—?

ALLMERS: I did go through a sort of inner revolution.

RITA: Good heavens—!

ALLMERS (*Soothingly, patting her hand*): All for the good, Rita. I promise you.

RITA (*Sits on the sofa*): You must tell us about it at once—tell us everything!

ALLMERS (*Turns towards* ASTA): Very well. Let's sit down too, Asta—I'll try and tell you. As well as I can, that is.

(*He sits on the sofa beside* RITA. ASTA *pulls forward a chair and sits down near him.*)

RITA (*Looks at him expectantly*): Well—?

ALLMERS (*Gazing straight before him*): When I look back at the pattern of my life, during these past ten or eleven years, it all seems like a fairy tale—a dream. Don't you think so too, Asta?

ASTA: Yes—in many ways I do.

ALLMERS (*Continuing*): When I think of what we were, you and I; two penniless orphans—

RITA (*Impatiently*): But all that was years ago!

ALLMERS (*Not listening to her*): And now—here I am living in the lap of luxury. I've been able to follow my vocation— to work and study, just as I'd always longed to. (*Stretches out his hand*) And all of this unheard-of, this incredible good fortune—I owe to you, Rita my dearest.

RITA (*Half teasingly, half angrily, slaps his hand*): Do stop talking nonsense!

ALLMERS: I mention it only as a sort of introduction—

RITA: Well—skip the introduction, then!

ALLMERS: It wasn't the doctor's advice, Rita, that drove me to the mountains.

ASTA: Wasn't it, Alfred?

RITA: Then—what was it?

ALLMERS: I could no longer find peace in my work. I felt troubled and disturbed.

RITA: Disturbed! By whom?

ALLMERS: By no one—outside myself. But I had a feeling I was simply wasting time—making the wrong use of my powers; wasting my talents and my energy.

ASTA (*Wide-eyed*): You felt this while you were working on the book?

ALLMERS (*Nods*): It didn't seem *enough,* somehow. I felt I must be capable of doing other things as well.

RITA: So *that* was what was weighing on your mind!

ALLMERS: Yes—mostly.

RITA: And that was why you seemed so discontented; not only with yourself, but with all the rest of us. You *were* discontented, weren't you, Alfred?

ALLMERS (*Gazing in front of him*): I sat there writing hour after hour—sometimes far into the night. Writing away at that great tome that was to be called *Human Responsibility*. Hm!

ASTA (*Putting her hand on his arm*): But that book is to be your lifework, Alfred!

RITA: You've said so often enough.

ALLMERS: Yes, and I believed it. Ever since I grew up it's filled my thoughts. (*Looks at* RITA *tenderly*) Then, thanks to you, I was able to devote all my time to it, Rita, dear.

RITA: Oh, nonsense!

ALLMERS (*Smiles at her*): You—with your "gold and your green forests"—

RITA (*Half laughing, half annoyed*): If you don't stop that nonsense, I'll be really angry!

ASTA (*Looks at him sadly*): But what about the book, Alfred?

ALLMERS: It drifted further and further away from me. And instead, I've become increasingly aware of other claims— of more important duties.

RITA (*Radiant, seizing his hand*): Alfred!

ALLMERS: I'm thinking of Eyolf, Rita.

RITA (*Disappointed, lets go his hand*): Oh—of Eyolf!

ALLMERS: Yes—poor little Eyolf. He's grown so part of me. Ever since that fall of his—and, especially, ever since we've known his case to be incurable—

RITA (*Insistently*): But, Alfred—you've done everything you can for him!

ALLMERS: I've been a schoolmaster to him, not a father. I shall be a father to him from now on.

RITA (*Looks at him and shakes her head*): I don't quite understand you.

ALLMERS: I want to do everything in my power to make his deformity as painless—as easy to bear as possible.

RITA: Well—there's one good thing: I don't really think he feels it very much.

ASTA (*Deeply moved*): Oh yes, Rita—he does!

ALLMERS: He feels it very deeply, I assure you.

RITA (*Impatiently*): But what more can you possibly do for him, dear Alfred?

ALLMERS: I want to help him to develop the rare qualities that lie dormant in his childish nature. Foster all that's noblest in him; nurture it and cultivate it so that it may blossom and bear fruit. But there's something even more important: If he is ever to achieve an inner harmony of spirit, he must learn to limit his desires and aspirations to things within his power. At present, what attracts him most are the very things that will always be denied him. He must make this necessary adjustment—and I must help him. In spite of his misfortune, I must try and create in him a sense of happiness.

RITA: You let these things upset you too much, Alfred!

ALLMERS: Eyolf shall go on with my book—that is if he wants to. Or, if he prefers, he can choose a subject of his own—that might be even better—I've decided to give it up in any case.

RITA: But why shouldn't you go on with your own work, and work with Eyolf too?

ALLMERS: No, I can't do that. I should find that impossible. In a case like this I can't divide my powers. I'll step aside. I want Eyolf to grow into a complete human being—an example of all that's finest in the human race. I shall devote my life to bringing this about.

ASTA (*Rises and goes to him*): It must have been very hard for you to come to this decision.

ALLMERS: It was hard. If I'd stayed here I don't think I could have managed it; I should never have reached the point of complete renunciation; never—here at home.

RITA: Was that why you went away this summer?

ALLMERS (*His eyes shining*): Yes! I was able to lose myself in

that vast solitude. I watched the dawn—the sun glistening
on the mountain peaks. I felt, somehow, closer to the stars.
It was almost as though I understood them—became one
with them. Then I found the strength.

ASTA (*Looks at him sadly*): But your book, Alfred! *Human
Responsibility*. You really mean you'll never finish it?

ALLMERS: Never, Asta. I can't divide my powers, I tell you—
But I shall try and *practice* human responsibility—in my
own life.

RITA (*With a smile*): Are you sure you'll be able to do that
here at home? Live up to such high principles?

ALLMERS (*Takes her hand*): With your help I'm sure I can.
(*Stretches out his other hand*): And yours too, Asta—
of course.

RITA (*Draws her hand away*): With both of us—I see! So,
after all, you *can* divide yourself.

ALLMERS: Why Rita—darling—! (RITA *moves away from him
and stands at the veranda door. There is a light rapid
knock at the door right.* BORGHEJM, *the engineer, enters
briskly. He is a young man of about thirty. He has a
bright, cheerful expression, and holds himself very erect.*)

BORGHEJM: Good morning, Mrs. Allmers. (*He stops with an
expression of pleasure on seeing* ALLMERS) What's this!
Home again already, Mr. Allmers?

ALLMERS (*Shakes his hand*): I got back last night.

RITA: (*Gaily*): His leave was up, Mr. Borghejm.

ALLMERS: Now you know that's not true, Rita—

RITA (*Approaching*): Of course it's true. His furlough had run
out.

BORGHEJM: I see you keep a tight rein on your husband, Mrs.
Allmers.

RITA: I insist on my rights. Besides—everything must come to
an end, you know.

BORGHEJM: Oh, not everything—at least, I hope not. Good
morning, Miss Allmers.

ASTA (*Aloof*): Good morning.

RITA (*Looks at* BORGHEJM): Not everything, you say?

BORGHEJM: There are *some* things in life that don't come to an end; I'm quite convinced of that.

RITA: What sort of things? Are you thinking of love, perhaps?

BORGHEJM (*Warmly*): I'm thinking of so many beautiful things—

RITA: —that never come to an end? Very well, let's think of them—hope for them—all of us.

ALLMERS (*Goes towards him*): Your work on the new road is nearly finished, I suppose.

BORGHEJM: It *is* finished. We finished yesterday. We've been at it long enough! Thank heaven, at least that's something that *did* come to an end!

RITA: And you're radiantly happy about it, are you?

BORGHEJM: I am indeed.

RITA: Well—I must say—!

BORGHEJM: What, Mrs. Allmers?

RITA: That's not particularly nice of you.

BORGHEJM: Really? What do you mean?

RITA: I mean—from now on you won't be coming out here very much.

BORGHEJM: That's true. I hadn't thought of that.

RITA: But all the same—I hope you'll drop in and see us now and then.

BORGHEJM: I'm afraid I won't be able to do that for quite some time.

ALLMERS: Indeed? Why not?

BORGHEJM: I'm starting on a new job almost at once. A very important piece of work.

ALLMERS: How splendid! (*Shakes his hand*) I'm so glad for you.

RITA: Congratulations, Mr. Borghejm!

BORGHEJM: Sh! I'm not really supposed to talk about it yet. But I couldn't resist telling you!— It's a colossal job—up North. We have to tunnel through mountains—there are endless difficulties! (*In an outburst of joy*) What a glorious world this is! And how glorious it is to be able to build roads in it!

RITA (*Gives him a teasing smile*): You're in unusually high spirits, it seems to me. Is that all due to the new job?

BORGHEJM: Not entirely. It's just that life seems so bright and full of promise.

RITA (*As before*): Perhaps you have an even more delightful secret!

BORGHEJM (*Glancing towards* ASTA): Who knows! They say one bit of luck brings on another. (*Turns to* ASTA) Shall we take our usual walk, Miss Allmers?

ASTA (*Quickly*): No—no, thank you. Not now. Not today.

BORGHEJM: Oh, please come—won't you? Just a little walk. There's so much I want to talk to you about before I go.

RITA: Something *else* you're not supposed to talk about, perhaps?

BORGHEJM: That depends—

RITA: You could always say it in a whisper. (*In an undertone*) Go with him, Asta! You really *must*!

ASTA: But—Rita, dear—

BORGHEJM (*Pleading*): Please, Miss Asta!— It'll be our last walk for a long, long time, you know!

ASTA (*Takes up her hat and parasol*): Very well. We'll just walk round the garden for a bit.

BORGHEJM: Oh—thank you!

ALLMERS: And while you're out there, you might see what Eyolf's doing.

BORGHEJM: Eyolf—of course! Where is he today? I've brought something for him.

ALLMERS: He's out playing—somewhere in the garden.

BORGHEJM: Out playing, is he? He's usually indoors—with his nose stuck in a book.

ALLMERS: We're going to put a stop to that. He'll be a regular outdoor boy from now on.

BORGHEJM: Splendid! It's only right that he should get out into the fresh air too. This wonderful world was made to have fun in. *I* think it's fun just to be alive!— Shall we go, Miss Asta?

(BORGHEJM *and* ASTA *go out on the veranda and down through the garden.*)

ALLMERS (*Stands looking after them*): Rita—have you noticed? Is there anything between them?

RITA: I don't know what to say. I was beginning to think so; but Asta has been so strange of late—I can't quite make her out.

ALLMERS: Strange? Since I've been away, you mean?

RITA: These last couple of weeks, I've noticed it particularly.

ALLMERS: Then—she doesn't care for him, you think?

RITA: Not deeply, not seriously—not unreservedly, at any rate. (*Gives him a searching look*) Would you be against it if she did?

ALLMERS: No, not really. I'd feel a bit concerned, of course.

RITA: Concerned?

ALLMERS: Remember, I'm responsible for Asta— Anything that affects her happiness naturally concerns me.

RITA: Responsible! Well—really! Asta's of age, isn't she? I should think she was quite capable of choosing for herself.

ALLMERS: Let's hope so, Rita.

RITA: And as far as I know there's nothing *wrong* with Borghejm.

ALLMERS: No—I don't suppose there is—quite the contrary. But, still—

RITA (*Continuing*): For my part I'd be delighted to see them make a match of it.

ALLMERS (*Annoyed*): Why should you be?

RITA (*With growing excitement*): Because then she'd go away with him—go far away! She wouldn't be coming out here all the time!

ALLMERS (*Looks at her in amazement*): Are you saying you want to get rid of Asta, Rita?

RITA: Yes! Yes, I am!

ALLMERS: But—why on earth—?

RITA (*Flings her arms round his neck passionately*): Because then, at last, I'd have you to myself! And yet, I wouldn't really. Not entirely—not even then! (*Bursts into convulsive sobs*) Oh, Alfred, Alfred—I can *never* let you go!

ALLMERS (*Gently releasing himself*): My dearest Rita—do be reasonable!

RITA: I won't be reasonable—I don't want to be! All I want is
   you! In the whole world all I want is you! (*Throws her
   arms round him again*) You, you, you!

ALLMERS: Let me go—you're strangling me—!

RITA (*Lets him go*): I only wish I could! (*Looks at him with
   flashing eyes*) If you only knew how I've hated you—!

ALLMERS: Hated me!

RITA: Yes—when you shut yourself up in your room—slaving
   away at that book of yours till all hours of the night.
   (*Plaintively*) Such long hours, Alfred! Such *late* hours!—
   I *hated* your work, I tell you!

ALLMERS: Well—all that's over now.

RITA (*With a sarcastic laugh*): Yes, I dare say! Only now
   you'll be absorbed in something even worse.

ALLMERS (*Shocked*): Worse! You surely don't mean the
   child?

RITA (*Violently*): Yes, I do. It *will* be worse if *he's* to come
   between us. The book was different—but the child's alive
   —a living human being! (*With increasing violence*) But I
   won't tolerate it, Alfred! I won't—I warn you!

ALLMERS (*Looks at her steadily, and says in a low voice*):
   Sometimes I'm almost afraid of you.

RITA (*Gloomily*): Sometimes I'm almost afraid of myself.
   You mustn't rouse the evil in my nature.

ALLMERS: Do I do that?

RITA: Yes, you do! When you trample on all that's most sacred
   in our relationship.

ALLMERS: Think of what you're saying, Rita! It's your own
   child—our only child you're speaking of.

RITA: The child is only half mine. (*In another outburst*) But
   I want *you* to myself alone. You must be all mine, do you
   hear? I demand it of you! It's my right!

ALLMERS (*Shrugs his shoulders*): It's no use *demanding* anything, Rita; things must be given freely.

RITA (*Looks at him anxiously*): And you no longer feel you
   can do that, from now on?

ALLMERS: No, I can't. I must belong to both of you.

RITA: Supposing Eyolf had never been born? What then?

ALLMERS (*Evasively*): Then things would have been different. I'd have only you to care for.

RITA (*Softly, her voice quivering*): I wish he *hadn't* been born, then.

ALLMERS (*Vehemently*): Rita! You don't know what you're saying!

RITA (*Trembling with emotion*): His birth cost me unspeakable agony. But I bore it all gladly for your sake.

ALLMERS (*Warmly*): Yes—I know, I know.

RITA (*Decisively*): It should have ended there. I want to live my life with *you*. Only with you. I refuse simply to be Eyolf's mother. Just that, and nothing more. I won't stand it, I tell you. I *can't* stand it. I want to be *everything* to you, Alfred. Everything!

ALLMERS: So you are, Rita. And, through our child, we—

RITA: That's just talk—vapid, sickening talk. I won't be put off with phrases. I was able to *bear* the child—but I'm not able to be a mother to it. You must take me as I am.

ALLMERS: But you used to be so fond of Eyolf.

RITA: I felt sorry for him. You left him entirely to himself; except for making him read, and slave over a lot of lessons. You hardly ever saw him.

ALLMERS (*Nods slowly*): I was blind, I know. I wasn't ready for it—

RITA (*Looks at him*): But now you are.

ALLMERS: Yes—at last. I see that my most important task in life is to be a true father to Eyolf.

RITA: And what about *me*? What will you be to *me*?

ALLMERS (*Gently*): I shall always go on caring for you. With deep tenderness. (*He tries to take her hands.*)

RITA (*Evades him*): You can keep your deep tenderness—I don't want it! I want you to belong to me—utterly and completely—to me alone! I want you to belong to me as you did in those first wonderful days we were together. (*Violently and harshly*) I'll never be satisfied with leftovers, Alfred! Never!

ALLMERS (*Conciliatory*): I should have thought we could find great happiness together—the three of us.

RITA (*Scornfully*): Then it doesn't take much to make you happy. (*Sits down at the table on the left*) Now listen to me, Alfred.

ALLMERS (*Goes towards her*): Yes? What is it?

RITA (*Looks up at him languidly, with burning eyes*): Last night, when I got your telegram—

ALLMERS: Yes?

RITA: I dressed myself all in white—

ALLMERS: I noticed you had on a white dress when I arrived.

RITA: I had let down my hair—

ALLMERS: Your fragrant, lovely hair—

RITA: It curled about my neck and on my shoulders—

ALLMERS: I saw it. I saw it, Rita. You looked so beautiful.

RITA: I'd put rose-tinted shades on both the lamps. And we were quite alone, Alfred. Everyone else in the house was fast asleep; and I had champagne ready on the table.

ALLMERS: But I didn't drink it.

RITA (*Looks at him bitterly*): No, that's true enough; you didn't drink it. (*With a harsh laugh*) "You were offered champagne, but you tasted it not"—as the poet says. (*She rises from the armchair, walks over to the sofa wearily, sits down on it, half reclining.*)

ALLMERS (*Crosses the room and stands beside her*): My mind was full of serious thoughts, Rita. I was determined to talk to you about our future. And especially about Eyolf.

RITA (*Smiles*): And that is precisely what you did.

ALLMERS: No—you wouldn't listen. You started to undress.

RITA: Yes—and all the while you talked of Eyolf. Don't you remember? You kept asking me questions about the state of little Eyolf's stomach.

ALLMERS (*Gives her a reproachful look*): Rita—!

RITA: And then you got into your bed, and slept soundly until morning.

ALLMERS (*Shakes his head*): Rita—Rita!

RITA (*Lies full length on the couch and looks up at him*): Alfred?

ALLMERS: Yes?

RITA: "You were offered champagne, but you tasted it not."

ALLMERS (*Almost harshly*): No. I didn't taste it. (*He walks away from her and stands at the garden door.* RITA *remains lying motionless with closed eyes.*)

RITA (*Jumps up suddenly*): But I'll tell you one thing, Alfred.

ALLMERS (*Turns in the doorway*): What?

RITA: I wouldn't be too sure of yourself, if I were you.

ALLMERS: Sure of myself?

RITA: Yes. Don't become *too* indifferent. Don't take me too much for granted.

ALLMERS (*Coming towards her*): What do you mean by that?

RITA (*Her lips trembling*): I've never been untrue to you— not even in my thoughts. Never for a moment. You know that, don't you?

ALLMERS: Of course I do. I know you so well, Rita.

RITA (*With glowing eyes*): But if you treat me with disdain, and turn away from me—

ALLMERS: Disdain! What are you talking about?

RITA: There's no telling what lengths I might go to, if—

ALLMERS: If—?

RITA: If I were to discover that you no longer cared. No longer loved me as you used to.

ALLMERS: But, Rita—my darling! Human relationships are bound to change with time. This must happen to us too— as it does to everyone.

RITA: Not to me! Never! I won't have it happen to you either! I couldn't bear it. I want to keep you all to myself always, Alfred. Always!

ALLMERS (*Looks at her with concern*): Why must you be so jealous?—so possessive?

RITA: I can't help it. That's the way I'm made. (*Threateningly*) If you try to make me share you with anyone—with anyone at all—then—

ALLMERS: Then—?

RITA: I shall take my revenge, that's all.

ALLMERS: Your revenge? How?

RITA: I don't know— Yes, I do! Of course I know.

ALLMERS: Well?

RITA: I shall simply throw myself away—

ALLMERS: Throw yourself away?

RITA: Yes. I'll throw myself into the arms of—of the first man that comes along.

ALLMERS (*Looks at her tenderly and shakes his head*): You'd never do that. You're too honorable, too proud, too loyal.

RITA: (*Puts her arms round his neck*): Who knows what I might become—if you—if you didn't want me any more.

ALLMERS: Not want you, Rita? How can you say such foolish things!

RITA (*Half laughing, lets him go*): What about that engineer —that road builder? I might start using my wiles on him.

ALLMERS (*Relieved*): Thank God—I see you're only joking.

RITA: No, I'm not. He'd do as well as any other man.

ALLMERS: He seems to be engaged elsewhere, however.

RITA: So much the better! It'd be more fun to take him away from someone else. It's no more than Eyolf's done to me.

ALLMERS: How can you accuse Eyolf of such a thing!

RITA (*Pointing her finger at him*): You see! You see! The moment Eyolf's name is mentioned your voice trembles— you're all tenderness! (*Threateningly, clenching her hands*) I'm almost tempted to wish that—oh, well!

ALLMERS (*Looks at her anxiously*): To wish what, Rita—?

RITA (*Vehemently, goes away from him*): Nothing! I won't tell you! Never—never!

ALLMERS (*Goes towards her*): Rita! I implore you—for both our sakes—don't give way to evil thoughts.

(BORGHEJM *and* ASTA *come up from the garden. They both show signs of restrained emotion. They look serious and dejected.* ASTA *stays out on the veranda.* BORGHEJM *enters the room.*)

BORGHEJM: Well—Miss Allmers and I have gone for our last walk together.

RITA (*Looks at him in surprise*): What! Isn't the walk to be followed by a journey?

BORGHEJM: It is, for me.

RITA: For you alone?

BORGHEJM: For me alone.

RITA (*Gives* ALLMERS *a dark look*) You hear that, Alfred? (*Turns to* BORGHEJM) I've a feeling someone must have put the Evil-eye on you.

BORGHEJM: Evil-eye?

RITA (*Nods*): The Evil-eye, yes.

BORGHEJM: Do you believe in the Evil-eye, Mrs. Allmers?

RITA: I've begun to believe in it, just lately. Especially when the Evil-eye is a child's eye.

ALLMERS (*In a shocked whisper*): Rita—how can you—!

RITA (*In an undertone*): It's you that brings out the evil in me, Alfred.

(*Confused cries and shouts are heard in the distance, from the direction of the beach.*)

BORGHEJM (*Goes to the glass door*): What's all that noise—?

ASTA (*In the doorway*): Look at all those people running towards the pier!

ALLMERS: What can it be? (*Looks out for a moment*) I suppose it's those street urchins again—up to some mischief.

BORGHEJM (*Leans over the veranda railing and calls out*): Boys! You boys down there! What's happened?

(*Several voices are heard confusedly, all talking at once.*)

RITA: What are they saying?

BORGHEJM: They say a child's been drowned.

ALLMERS: A child drowned?

ASTA (*Uneasily*): A little boy, they say.

ALLMERS: Nonsense! They all know how to swim.

RITA (*Cries out in terror*): Eyolf! Where is Eyolf?

ALLMERS: Keep calm, darling! Eyolf is playing in the garden.

ASTA: No, he wasn't in the garden—

RITA (*Her arms upstretched*) Not Eyolf! Don't let it be Eyolf!

BORGHEJM (*Listens a moment, then calls down*): Whose child do you say it is?

(*A jumble of voices is heard.* BORGHEJM *and* ASTA *give a low cry and rush down into the garden.*)

ALLMERS (*In an agony of fear*): It can't be Eyolf! It *can't* be Eyolf, Rita!

RITA (*On the veranda, listening*): Sh! Be quiet! I'm trying to hear! (*She rushes back into the room with a loud cry.*)

ALLMERS (*Follows her*): What did you hear? What was it?

RITA (*Sinks down beside the armchair on the left*): They said the crutch was floating!

ALLMERS (*As though paralyzed*): No! No! No!

RITA: Eyolf! Eyolf! They *must* save him!

ALLMERS (*Half distraught*): They *must!* Such a precious life! So very precious! (*He rushes down into the garden.*)

CURTAIN

ACT TWO

SCENE: *A small wooded glen on* ALLMERS' *property, near the shore. The branches of lofty old trees form an arch overhead. A brook runs down the slope in the background and loses itself among the rocks at the edge of the wood. A path winds along beside the brook. To the right one sees the fjord between the trunks of some large trees. In the foreground is the corner of a boathouse. A boat is drawn up beside it. Under the old trees on the left stands a table with a bench and a couple of chairs made of rough birchwood. It is a gloomy, damp day, wreathed in mist.* ALFRED ALLMERS, *dressed as before, sits on the bench, his arms leaning on the table. His hat lies on the table in front of him. He sits motionless, star-*

ing vacantly out over the water. In a few moments ASTA
ALLMERS *comes along the path through the woods. She
carries an open umbrella.*

ASTA (*Approaches him quietly and cautiously*): You shouldn't
be sitting out here in this damp weather, Alfred.

ALLMERS (*Nods slowly, but doesn't answer.*)

ASTA (*Closes her umbrella*): I've been looking for you for
hours.

ALLMERS (*Expressionless*): Thanks.

ASTA (*Moves a chair and sits down near him*): Have you
been sitting here long? Have you been here the whole
time?

ALLMERS (*Doesn't answer. At last he says*): I can't grasp it.
It can't have happened; it's impossible.

ASTA (*Lays her hand on his arm, compassionately*): Poor Alfred.

ALLMERS (*Stares at her*): Is it really true, Asta? Or have I
gone mad? Or am I simply dreaming? How wonderful it
would be to wake up, and find that it had all been a nightmare.

ASTA: I only wish you could!

ALLMERS (*Gazes out over the water*): How pitiless the fjord
looks today—ominous and drowsy. Slate blue, with flecks
of gold—and the reflection of the clouds.

ASTA (*Imploringly*): Alfred! Don't sit there gazing at the
fjord!

ALLMERS (*Not listening to her*): It looks so calm on the surface. No one would suspect the violence of the undertow.

ASTA (*Anxiously*): For God's sake don't think about that,
Alfred!

ALLMERS (*Looks at her gently*): I suppose you think he's still
lying somewhere close to shore. He's not, you know. The
current's very swift here, you must remember. It sweeps
right out to the open sea.

ASTA (*Buries her face in her hands, sobbing*): Oh, God! Oh,
God!

ALLMERS (*Heavily*): Little Eyolf must be far away by now—far away from all of us.

ASTA (*Looks up at him pleadingly*): Don't talk about it, Alfred!

ALLMERS: You can work it out for yourself easily enough. Let me see— In twenty-eight hours—twenty-nine hours at the most—

ASTA (*Stops her ears and cries out*): Alfred!

ALLMERS (*Clenches his hands on the table*): What sense is there in all this? Do you know?

ASTA (*Looks at him*): In what?

ALLMERS: In this thing that has been done to Rita and me.

ASTA: Sense?

ALLMERS (*Impatiently*): Yes. There must be some sense in it —some reason for it. Surely life, existence, destiny—surely all that can't be entirely meaningless.

ASTA: These things are beyond our understanding, Alfred dear.

ALLMERS (*With a bitter laugh*): That's true enough! Perhaps there *is* no meaning. Perhaps life just goes along at random—like a ship that's lost its rudder. That's the way it is, I expect. At least, it seems so.

ASTA (*Thoughtfully*): It may seem so to us, but—

ALLMERS (*Violently*): But what? Does it make sense to *you?* Are *you* able to fathom it? I assure you *I* can't! (*More gently*) Eyolf was on the threshold of life. A life full of possibilities—splendid possibilities, perhaps. He would have lived to be an endless source of happiness and pride to me. And a crazy old woman comes along—shows him a little dog she carries in a bag—

ASTA: But we don't actually know how the thing happened, Alfred.

ALLMERS: Yes, we do. The boys saw her rowing out onto the fjord. They saw Eyolf standing all alone at the far end of the pier. He was gazing after her. Suddenly he seemed to grow dizzy; it was then that he fell into the water—and disappeared.

ASTA: Yes, but even so—

ALLMERS: She lured him out into the deep water. I'm certain of it.

ASTA: But, Alfred dear—why should she?

ALLMERS: Yes—that's the point! Why should she? It couldn't have been a question of retaliation—of revenge. Eyolf had never done her any harm. He'd never made fun of her, or thrown stones at her dog. He'd never even laid eyes on her, or the dog, till yesterday. It can't have been revenge. It just doesn't make sense. There's no possible reason for it. And yet, somehow—the Order of the Universe required it.

ASTA: Have you talked about these things to Rita?

ALLMERS (*Shakes his head*): It's easier for me to talk to you about them. (*Takes a deep breath*) It's always easier to talk to you.

(ASTA *takes some sewing things and a little paper parcel out of her pocket.* ALLMERS *sits watching her absently.*)

ALLMERS: What have you got there, Asta?

ASTA (*Picks up his hat*): Just some black crepe.

ALLMERS: What's the use of that?

ASTA: Rita asked me to get it. May I?

ALLMERS: Certainly—as far as I'm concerned. (*She sews the crepe on his hat.*)

ALLMERS (*Sits and looks at her*): Where is Rita?

ASTA: She's taking a little walk in the garden, I think. Borghejm is with her.

ALLMERS (*Slightly surprised*): Really? Is he out here again today?

ASTA: Yes. He came out by the noon train.

ALLMERS: I didn't expect that.

ASTA (*Sewing*): He was so fond of Eyolf.

ALLMERS: Borghejm is a faithful soul, Asta.

ASTA (*With quiet warmth*): He is indeed! That's certain!

ALLMERS (*Fixing his eyes on her*): And yet, you can't make up your mind to—?

ASTA (*Interrupting*): Dear Alfred—please don't talk about it!

ALLMERS: Why not? Why can't you seem to—?

ASTA: Don't, Alfred! Please! Don't ask me about it. It upsets me— There! Your hat's done now.

ALLMERS: Thanks.

ASTA: Now for the left arm.

ALLMERS: Do I have to wear an arm band too?

ASTA: That's the custom.

ALLMERS: Very well—just as you like. (*She moves closer to him and begins to sew.*)

ASTA: Keep your arm still. I don't want to prick you.

ALLMERS (*With a faint smile*): This is like the old days, isn't it?

ASTA: Yes—it is.

ALLMERS: You used to mend my clothes like this, when you were a little girl.

ASTA: I wasn't much good at it, but I did the best I could.

ALLMERS: I remember the first thing you ever sewed for me; that was black crepe too.

ASTA: Was it?

ALLMERS: On my student's cap. It was when Father died.

ASTA: Could I sew then? I don't remember.

ALLMERS: No. You were such a little thing!

ASTA: Yes—I was very little then.

ALLMERS: And then, a couple of years later, you sewed a wide crepe band on my sleeve. That was when your mother died.

ASTA: I thought it was the right thing to do.

ALLMERS (*Pats her hand*): And so it was— And then, when we were left all alone in the world, we two— Finished already?

ASTA (*Collects her sewing things*): Those were good times, Alfred. When we were just the two of us.

ALLMERS: Yes, they were. No matter how hard we had to work.

ASTA: *You* had to work, you mean.

ALLMERS: Oh—you did your share!—(*Smiles*) My dear, faithful—Eyolf.

ASTA: That silly nonsense about the name! You shouldn't remind me of it!

ALLMERS: Well—if you'd been a boy, your name would have been Eyolf.

ASTA: Yes—*if*. But when you went to college— (*Smiles in spite of herself*) I can't think how you could have been so childish!

ALLMERS: Was *I* the childish one?

ASTA: I think so—now that I look back on it. You were ashamed because you had no brother—just a sister.

ALLMERS: No—*you* were the one! *You* were ashamed.

ASTA: Perhaps I was a little too. I felt sorry for you, somehow—

ALLMERS: You did, didn't you? And you dug up some old clothes of mine—clothes I'd worn when I was still a boy—

ASTA: Your best clothes—your Sunday clothes, they were. Do you remember that blue shirt, and that pair of knickerbockers?

ALLMERS (*His eyes dwelling on her*): I remember exactly how you looked in them.

ASTA: Of course I only wore them when we were at home alone.

ALLMERS: How serious we were—how delighted with ourselves. And I always called you Eyolf.

ASTA: I hope you've never told this to Rita, Alfred?

ALLMERS: I think I did tell her about it once.

ASTA: Alfred! How could you!

ALLMERS: Well—you tell your wife practically everything, you know.

ASTA: Yes—I suppose you do.

ALLMERS (*As though suddenly awakened, clutches his forehead and jumps up*): How can I sit here, and—!

ASTA (*Rises and looks at him sadly*): What's the matter?

ALLMERS: I lost him for a moment—completely lost him!

ASTA: Eyolf!

ALLMERS: I sat here, reliving old memories—and he had no part in them.

ASTA: He did, Alfred—Little Eyolf was there all the time.

ALLMERS: He wasn't, I tell you. He slipped out of my mind—out of my thoughts. I completely lost sight of him as we sat here talking. I actually forgot him.

ASTA: You mustn't let your sorrow overwhelm you. It's only right that you should get away from it from time to time.

ALLMERS: No, no—I can't, I mustn't! I haven't the right to do that. And I haven't the heart for it, either. (*In great excitement starts towards the right*) I must be out there with him.

ASTA (*Follows him and holds him back*): Alfred—Alfred! Don't go to the fjord!

ALLMERS: I must be near him! Let me go, Asta! I'll take the boat.

ASTA (*Terrified*): Don't go to the fjord, I say!

ALLMERS (*Giving in*): Very well, I won't. But please leave me alone.

ASTA (*Leads him back to the table*): You must try and rest your thoughts. Come and sit down.

ALLMERS (*Starts to sit on the bench again*): Just as you say.

ASTA: No—not there.

ALLMERS: Yes—let me.

ASTA: No, don't! You'll only stare out at the fjord again—(*Forces him down in a chair with his back towards the right*) There. That's much better. (*Sits down on the bench*) And, now—let's go on with our talk.

ALLMERS (*Draws a deep, audible, breath*): It was good to get away from it all—just for a moment.

ASTA: You *must*, Alfred.

ALLMERS: Don't you think I'm very weak—very unfeeling—to be able to do so?

ASTA: Of course not. You can't go on dwelling on that one thought incessantly.

ALLMERS: It's true; I don't seem to be able to, at least. Before you joined me just now—I was sitting here in an agony of grief—

ASTA: Yes?

ALLMERS: And suddenly—you'll never believe it, Asta—

ASTA: Well?

ALLMERS: I suddenly caught myself wondering what we were going to have for dinner.

ASTA (*Soothingly*): Well—anything that rests your mind—

ALLMERS: You know—it's funny—it *did* seem to rest me, somehow. (*Holds out his hand to her across the table*) It's so good to have you with me, Asta. It makes me happy—even in the midst of grief.

ASTA (*Looks at him with a serious expression*): You should feel happy that you have Rita, Alfred.

ALLMERS: Yes, of course. But then Rita and I are not related. Nothing can take the place of a sister, after all.

ASTA (*Intently*): You mean that?

ALLMERS: And, don't forget, *our* family was always something special. (*Half jokingly*) All the first names in our family had to start with vowels—do you remember how we used to laugh at that? And all the members of our family were poor; and we had exactly the same eyes—every one of us.

ASTA: Do you think my eyes are—?

ALLMERS: No—but then you're the image of your mother; you don't take after us. You're not a bit like Father. But, even so—

ASTA: Even so—?

ALLMERS: You and I have a certain family resemblance; it's living together, I suppose. We bear the same stamp, somehow. It's an inner thing.

ASTA (*Warmly, with emotion*): If that's so—then I've taken my stamp from you. I owe everything to *you*, Alfred. Everything that's good, I owe to you.

ALLMERS (*Shaking his head*): You owe me nothing, Asta. Quite the contrary—

ASTA: I tell you I owe you *everything*. You must know that. No sacrifice has ever been too great for you—

ALLMERS (*Interrupting*): What nonsense! How can you talk of sacrifice! I've always loved you, Asta; ever since you

were a little child. (*After a short pause*) And then I felt I
had to make up to you for a great deal of injustice.

ASTA (*Astonished*): Injustice! You!

ALLMERS: Not so much on my own account, but—

ASTA (*Intently*): But—?

ALLMERS: On Father's.

ASTA (*Half rising from the bench*): Father's? (*Sits down
again*) What do you mean?

ALLMERS: Father was never really kind to you.

ASTA (*Vehemently*): Oh, don't say that!

ALLMERS: It's true. He never really loved you; at least, not
as he should have.

ASTA (*Evasively*): He didn't love me as he loved *you*, of
course. But that was only natural.

ALLMERS (*Continuing*): And he behaved very harshly to
your mother, too. In the last few years, at all events.

ASTA: Mother was so much younger than he was; don't forget that.

ALLMERS: Do you think, perhaps, they weren't really suited
to each other?

ASTA: It's possible.

ALLMERS: Still—all the same— In other ways, Father was so
gentle and warm-hearted. He was usually so kind to everyone—

ASTA (*Quietly*): Perhaps Mother didn't always behave as
well as she should have, either.

ALLMERS: Your mother!

ASTA: Perhaps not always.

ALLMERS: Towards Father, do you mean?

ASTA: Yes.

ALLMERS: I never noticed that.

ASTA (*Rises, struggling with her tears*): Dear Alfred, they're
gone now—let them rest. (*She starts towards the right*)

ALLMERS (*Rising*): Yes, let them rest. (*Wrings his hands*)
But it's those who are gone that won't let *us* rest, Asta.
Never—day or night.

ASTA (*Looks at him warmly*): Time will make everything seem easier, Alfred.

ALLMERS (*Looks at her helplessly*): Yes—you do believe that, don't you?— But how shall I live through these terrible first days? (*Hoarsely*) I don't see how I can.

ASTA (*Imploringly, laying her hands on his shoulders*): Go to Rita now. *Please* do!

ALLMERS (*Vehemently, drawing away from her*): No! Don't ask me to do that. I *can't*, I tell you! (*More calmly*) Let me stay here with you.

ASTA: I won't leave you.

ALLMERS (*Seizes her hand and holds it tightly*): Thank you! (*Looks over the fjord for a moment*) My little Eyolf! Where is he now, I wonder. (*Smiles at her sadly*) Can you tell me *that*—my big, wise Eyolf? (*Shakes his head*) No one in the whole world can tell me that. I'm only sure of one horrible fact: that he is lost to me.

(MRS. ALLMERS *and* BORGHEJM *come down the path through the woods. She leads the way; he follows her. She wears a dark dress and has a black veil over her head. He carries an umbrella under his arm.*)

ALLMERS (*Goes to meet her*): How are you feeling, Rita?

RITA (*Walks past him*): Don't ask me about that.

ALLMERS: Why have you come here?

RITA: I was looking for you. What have you been doing?

ALLMERS: Nothing. Asta's been here with me.

RITA: Yes, but before that. You've been away from me all morning.

ALLMERS: I was sitting here looking out over the water.

RITA: Ugh! I don't see how you can!

ALLMERS: I'm better off alone just now.

RITA (*Moves about restlessly*): And I don't see how you can bear to sit still, either! Stay in the same place all the time!

ALLMERS: Where would you have me go?

RITA: I can't seem to settle anywhere. Least of all here—so near the fjord.

ALLMERS: It's just because the fjord *is* near—

RITA (*To* BORGHEJM): Don't you think he should come back to the house with us?

BORGHEJM (*To* ALLMERS): I think it would be better for you.

ALLMERS: I'd rather stay where I am.

RITA: Then I'll stay with you, Alfred.

ALLMERS: Very well— You stay too, Asta.

ASTA (*To* BORGHEJM *in a whisper*): We'd best leave them alone!

BORGHEJM (*With an understanding look*): Miss Allmers— shall we take a little walk along the shore? Just one last time?

ASTA (*Picks up her umbrella*): Yes. Let's do that.

(ASTA *and* BORGHEJM *go out together past the boathouse.* ALLMERS *wanders about. Then he sits down on a rock under the trees on the left.*)

RITA (*Goes up to him and stands in front of him; her folded hands hang down limply*): To think that we've lost Eyolf, Alfred! Can you bear to face the thought?

ALLMERS (*Sadly, his eyes fixed on the ground*): We must force ourselves to face it.

RITA: I can't. I simply can't! And then—that ghastly sight!

ALLMERS (*Looks up*): What sight? What did you see?

RITA: I didn't see it myself. They told me about it. Oh—!

ALLMERS: What? Tell me!

RITA: I got Borghejm to take me to the pier—

ALLMERS: What did you want down there?

RITA: I wanted to find out from the boys just how it happened.

ALLMERS: But, we already know.

RITA: We found out something else.

ALLMERS: Well?

RITA: They told us at first that he'd disappeared immediately. But that's not true.

ALLMERS: Is that what they say now?

RITA: Yes. They say they saw him lying at the bottom—deep down in the clear water.

ALLMERS (*Clenching his teeth*): And they didn't try to save him!

RITA: I don't suppose they could.

ALLMERS: They can all swim—all of them!— How was he lying? Did they say?

RITA: Yes. They said he was lying on his back. With his eyes wide open.

ALLMERS: Open? But he was absolutely still?

RITA: Yes. Quite still. Then, suddenly, he was swept away. By the undertow, they said.

ALLMERS (*Nods slowly*): So that was the last they saw of him.

RITA (*Choked with tears*): Yes.

ALLMERS: And no one will ever see him again. Never!

RITA (*Moaning*): I shall always see him lying there.

ALLMERS: With his eyes wide open.

RITA (*Shuddering*): His eyes wide open, yes. I see them! I shall *always* see them!

ALLMERS (*Rises slowly and looks at her silently, threateningly*): And—were they *evil*, Rita?

RITA (*Turning pale*): Evil—!

ALLMERS (*Comes close to her*): Yes. Were those eyes that looked up through the deep, clear water—evil eyes?

RITA (*Shrinks away from him*) Alfred—!

ALLMERS (*Following her*): Answer me! Were they the evil eyes of a child, perhaps?

RITA (*Cries out*): Alfred! Alfred!

ALLMERS: Things have turned out just as you wished—haven't they, Rita?

RITA: What do you mean? What did I wish?

ALLMERS: That Eyolf wasn't here.

RITA: I *never* wished that—never! I didn't want him to come between us—that was all!

ALLMERS: He can never come between us now.

RITA (*Softly, gazing straight before her*): Now—perhaps more than ever. (*With a sudden shudder*) Oh, that ghastly, *horrible* sight!

ALLMERS (*Nods*): The child's evil eyes, yes.

RITA (*Recoils from him in terror*): Leave me alone, Alfred!
I'm afraid of you! I've never seen you look like this before.

ALLMERS (*Gives her a cold harsh look*): Sorrow brings out
the evil in one.

RITA (*Frightened, yet defiant*): Yes—I feel that too.
(ALLMERS *goes over to the right and looks out over the
fjord.* RITA *sits down at the table. A short pause.*)

ALLMERS (*Turns his head towards her*): You never really
loved him. Never!

RITA (*With cold self-control*): He would never allow me to
get close to him.

ALLMERS: Because you didn't want to.

RITA: That's not true. I did want to—very much. But there
was always someone in the way.

ALLMERS (*Turns round*): You mean me?

RITA: No. Certainly not at first.

ALLMERS (*Goes nearer to her*): Who, then?

RITA: His aunt.

ALLMERS: Asta?

RITA: Yes. Asta always stood between us.

ALLMERS: How can you say that, Rita!

RITA: She did. Ever since he had that—that unlucky fall, she
took complete possession of him.

ALLMERS: If she did, she only did it out of love.

RITA (*Vehemently*): That's just it! And I refuse to share people I love with anyone.

ALLMERS: We should have shared him in love, Rita.

RITA (*Looks at him scornfully*): We? The truth is you never
really loved him either.

ALLMERS (*Looks at her in amazement*): I didn't—!

RITA: No. You were too taken up with that book of yours.

ALLMERS (*Forcibly*): I was—it's true. But I sacrificed that
for Eyolf's sake.

RITA: Not out of love for him, though.

ALLMERS: Then why, do you suppose?

RITA: Because you had begun to doubt yourself. You'd completely lost faith in that vocation you used to talk so much about.

ALLMERS (*With a searching look*): You observed that, did you?

RITA: Yes—of course I did. It came over you little by little—quite gradually. And then—you needed a *new* interest to fill your life. *I* was no longer enough for you.

ALLMERS: The Law of Change, Rita.

RITA: So you decided to turn poor little Eyolf into an infant prodigy.

ALLMERS: I decided no such thing. I wanted him to be a happy human being. That, and nothing else.

RITA: Not out of love for him, though. Why not be honest with yourself! (*With a certain shyness*) Why not face the underlying cause—the basic reason?

ALLMERS (*Unable to meet her eyes*): There's something you're trying to avoid.

RITA: And so are you.

ALLMERS (*Looks at her thoughtfully*): If what you say is true, then Eyolf never really belonged to either of us.

RITA: No. Not in love, at any rate.

ALLMERS: Then why are we so filled with grief at losing him?

RITA (*Bitterly*): It's curious, isn't it? To be filled with grief at the loss of a little boy, who was no more than a stranger.

ALLMERS (*In an outburst*): Oh, you mustn't call him that!

RITA (*Sadly, shaking her head*): We neither of us succeeded in winning his love, Alfred.

ALLMERS (*Wringing his hands*): And now it's all too late!

RITA: Yes—and all so hopeless!

ALLMERS (*With sudden anger*): You're the one who's guilty, Rita!

RITA (*Rising*): *I!*

ALLMERS: Yes, *you!* It was your fault that he became—what he was! It was your fault that he couldn't save himself when he fell into the water.

RITA (*As though warding off a blow*): Alfred—I won't *have* you lay the blame on me!

ALLMERS (*More and more beside himself*): But I *do!* You *were* to blame! It was due to your neglect; you left him lying on the table—unguarded, unprotected—a helpless infant!

RITA: He seemed perfectly safe; he was lying on the pillows fast asleep. And you'd promised to look after him.

ALLMERS: Yes, I had. (*Lowers his voice*) But you came and lured me away from him; enticed me into going with you.

RITA (*Looks at him defiantly*): And you forgot the child, and everything else—why not admit it?

ALLMERS (*With suppressed rage*): It's true. (*In a lower tone*) I forgot him—in your arms!

RITA (*Outraged*): This is intolerable of you, Alfred!

ALLMERS (*In a low voice, shaking his clenched fists in her face*): So, you see, it was *you* who sent little Eyolf to his death.

RITA (*Wildly*): It was as much your fault as mine—if what you say is true!

ALLMERS: Yes—you have every right to accuse me. We were both guilty—both of us— Eyolf's death was a kind of retribution, after all.

RITA: Retribution?

ALLMERS (*With more self-control*): It was a judgment on us both. We have been justly punished. I suppose that's why we shrank from him while he was still alive; we were tormented by a secret shame—a cowardly sense of remorse. We couldn't bear to see him dragging himself about on that —that *thing*—

RITA (*In a whisper*): The crutch.

ALLMERS: Yes. And what we call our grief, is nothing but the pangs of conscience, Rita. Nothing else.

RITA (*Gazes at him helplessly*): We shall be driven to despair —driven into madness. There's no possible way that we can ever make amends.

ALLMERS (*In a calmer mood*): I dreamed of Eyolf last night. I saw him returning from the pier; and he was playing and running about just like the other boys. Nothing at all had ever happened to him. I thought to myself: all the torment and the agony has been nothing but a dream—a nightmare. I found myself blessing and thanking— (*Checks himself*) Hm—

RITA (*Looks at him*): Whom?

ALLMERS (*Evasively*): Whom—?

RITA: Yes. Who did you bless and thank?

ALLMERS (*Evading the question*): I was only dreaming, as I said—

RITA: A God in whom you have no faith?

ALLMERS: It was a sudden impulse; I was asleep, you see—

RITA (*Reproachfully*): You were wrong to rob me of my faith, Alfred.

ALLMERS: I couldn't let you go on cluttering up your mind with all that superstitious nonsense.

RITA: It would have been better for me. I'd have had something to cling to. I shouldn't be completely lost, as I am now.

ALLMERS (*Observing her closely*): Supposing you were given the choice— Supposing you could follow Eyolf; rejoin him where he is now, I mean?

RITA: Yes? What then?

ALLMERS: Supposing you were absolutely sure of finding him again? Of knowing him, and understanding him—?

RITA: Yes? Well?

ALLMERS: Would you be willing—quite deliberately—to follow him? Would you give up everything here—leave your present life—and join him of your own free will? Would you, Rita?

RITA (*Softly*): You mean—now? At once?

ALLMERS: Yes; immediately—this very day. Answer me. Would you?

RITA (*Hesitating*): I don't know, Alfred—No; I think I'd have to stay on here with you a little while.

ALLMERS: For my sake?

RITA: Only for your sake—yes.

ALLMERS: But, later? Would you then? Why don't you answer me!

RITA: I don't know what to answer. I can't ever leave you, Alfred. Never! Never!

ALLMERS: But supposing *I* were to go to Eyolf. And you had absolute assurance that you would meet both of us there? Then—would you come?

RITA: I'd want to! Yes! I'd want to! But—

ALLMERS: Well?

RITA (*Moaning softly*): I don't believe I could; I feel it. No —I'm sure I couldn't! Not even if I were promised all the joys of Heaven!

ALLMERS: Neither could I.

RITA: No. You couldn't either, Alfred, could you?

ALLMERS: No. We human beings belong here—on earth.

RITA: Yes. Here, on earth, is the only happiness we understand.

ALLMERS (*Darkly*): Oh, happiness—happiness—!

RITA: You mean—we shall never know happiness again? (*Looks at him inquiringly*) But supposing—? (*Vehemently*) No—I dare not say it. I dare not even think it.

ALLMERS: Yes—say it, Rita.

RITA (*Hesitantly*): Couldn't we try to—? Couldn't we possibly—forget him?

ALLMERS: Forget Eyolf?

RITA: Forget the anguish and remorse, I mean.

ALLMERS: You really wish that?

RITA: Yes. If it were only possible. (*In an outburst*) Because I won't be able to bear this forever, Alfred! Isn't there anything that could help us to forget?

ALLMERS (*Shakes his head*): What, for instance?

RITA: Couldn't we go away somewhere—far away from here?

ALLMERS: Leave your home? You know you're never happy anywhere but here.

RITA: Then—couldn't we surround ourselves with people— give a lot of parties? Anything that would dull the pain and help us to forget!

ALLMERS: I could never endure that kind of life— No— rather than that, I might try taking up my work again.

RITA (*Sharply*): Your work? But your work has always been a barrier between us!

ALLMERS (*Slowly, with a fixed stare*): There must always be a barrier between us from now on.

RITA: Why must there—?

ALLMERS: Perhaps because of a child's wide-open eyes, that watch us day and night.

RITA (*Softly, with a shudder*): Alfred—what a dreadful thought!

ALLMERS: Our love has been like a devouring flame. But now it must be quenched—

RITA (*Moves towards him*): Quenched!

ALLMERS (*Harshly*): It already is—in one of us.

RITA (*As though turned to stone*): You *dare* say that to me!

ALLMERS (*More gently*): Our love is dead, Rita. But we are bound to each other by a common sense of guilt; a common desire to make atonement. Perhaps, someday, our love will be reborn—on a purer, higher level.

RITA (*Violently*): Do you think I could ever be satisfied with that!

ALLMERS: Rita!

RITA: I'm a human being; I have blood in my veins, not water! (*Wrings her hands*) And now, I'm a prisoner for life; a prey to anguish and remorse. And I must share my prison with someone who is no longer mine! Mine, *mine!*

ALLMERS: It had to end like this, some time or other, Rita.

RITA: End like *this?* Our love that began with such a rush of ecstasy.

ALLMERS: That was not the way I felt for you at first.

RITA: Then—what *did* you feel for me?

ALLMERS: Fear.

RITA: I see. I understand. But I was able to win you over, all the same. How did I do that?

ALLMERS (*In a low voice*): You were so devastatingly beautiful, Rita.

RITA (*Gives him a searching look*): Was that the only reason? Tell me, Alfred. Was it?

ALLMERS (*Controlling himself*): No. There was something else.

RITA (*In an outburst*): I can guess what that was easily enough! It was my "gold and my green forests," as you call it. That was it, Alfred—wasn't it?

ALLMERS: Yes.

RITA (*Looks at him with deep reproach*): How could you! Oh!— How could you!

ALLMERS: I had Asta to think of.

RITA (*Vehemently*): Asta, yes! (*Bitterly*) Then it was really Asta that brought us two together.

ALLMERS: She knew nothing about it. To this day she doesn't know.

RITA (*With a gesture of dismissal*): But it was Asta, all the same! (*Smiles and glances at him scornfully*) Or rather— it was little Eyolf. Eyolf! Don't you remember?

ALLMERS: Eyolf—?

RITA: Yes. You used to call her Eyolf, didn't you? It seems to me you told me that—once, when we were very close. (*Goes close to him*) Do you remember that moment, Alfred? That wonderful, magical moment?

ALLMERS (*Recoils as though in horror*): I remember nothing! I don't *want* to remember!

RITA (*Follows him*): It was the very moment—when your other little Eyolf became a cripple!

ALLMERS (*Dully, leaning against the table*): Retribution!

RITA (*Menacingly*): Yes, retribution!

(ASTA *and* BORGHEJM *return from the direction of the boathouse. She carries some water lilies in her hand.*)

RITA (*Controlling herself*): Well, Asta—have you and **Mr.** Borghejm talked things out?

ASTA: Yes, more or less. (*She puts down her umbrella, and lays the flowers on a chair.*)

BORGHEJM: Miss Asta didn't seem to feel like talking. She was in a silent mood.

RITA: Was she indeed? Well—Alfred and I have talked things out thoroughly enough—

ASTA (*Looks at them both intently*): Is anything the matter—?

RITA: —enough to last us a whole lifetime, I should think. (*Breaking off*) But, let's go up to the house—all four of us. We must be surrounded by people from now on. It would never do for Alfred and me to be alone.

ALLMERS: You two go ahead. (*Turning*) I want to talk to Asta for a moment.

RITA (*Looks at him*): Oh?—Very well. You come with me then, Mr. Borghejm.

(RITA *and* BORGHEJM *go out by the path through the woods.*)

ASTA (*Anxiously*): Alfred—what's the matter?

ALLMERS (*Somberly*): I can't possibly go on staying here.

ASTA: Not stay here! You mean—with Rita?

ALLMERS: Yes. Rita and I can't live together any longer.

ASTA (*Shakes him by the arm*): Alfred! That's a dreadful thing to say!

ALLMERS: I can't help it. We'll destroy each other if we stay together.

ASTA (*Deeply moved*): I never would have believed that such a thing could happen!

ALLMERS: I didn't realize it myself—until today.

ASTA: So you want to—! Alfred, what do you really want to do?

ALLMERS: I want to get away from here. As far away as possible.

ASTA: You want to be completely on your own?

ALLMERS: Yes. Just as I used to be.

ASTA: But it's not good for you to be alone.

ALLMERS: Oh, yes it is. It was before, at any rate.

ASTA: Yes, but before—you had me with you.

ALLMERS (*Tries to take her hand*): And I want to come home to you again.

ASTA (*Evades him*): Home to me! That's quite impossible, Alfred.

ALLMERS (*Looks at her sadly*): I suppose Borghejm stands between us.

ASTA: No, no—he doesn't! You're mistaken, I assure you!

ALLMERS: Very well—then I'll come home to you. Home to my beloved sister. I *must* come home to you. I need to be cleansed. I need to be reclaimed—after my life with—

ASTA (*Shocked*): Alfred—you're doing Rita a great wrong.

ALLMERS: I *have* done her a great wrong, it's true—though not in this. Think back on our life together, Asta. How pure and good it was. Those were blessed days.

ASTA: They were indeed, Alfred. But they're over. We can't have them again.

ALLMERS: Why not? Has my marriage changed me so?

ASTA: No—not that.

ALLMERS: Then it's settled; we'll live together, as we used to.

ASTA (*Decisively*): We *can't*, Alfred. I tell you it's impossible.

ALLMERS: Of course we can—why shouldn't we? The love between a brother and sister, it seems to me—

ASTA (*Intently*): Well?

ALLMERS: —is the one relationship that is never subject to the Law of Change.

ASTA (*Softly, tremulously*): But supposing we were not—

ALLMERS: Were not—what?

ASTA: Supposing we were *not* related in this way?

ALLMERS (*Stares at her in astonishment*): What do you mean?

ASTA: I'd better tell you. You've got to know.

ALLMERS: Yes—tell me!

ASTA: Those letters to my mother—the ones in the portfolio—

ALLMERS: Well?

ASTA: You must read them, Alfred—when I've gone.

ALLMERS: Why must I?

ASTA: Because then you'll realize that—

ALLMERS: Go on!

ASTA: That I have no right to bear your father's name.

ALLMERS (*With a backward start*): Asta! What are you saying!

ASTA: Read the letters. Then you'll know. Then you'll understand. And perhaps you'll be able to forgive my mother, too.

ALLMERS (*Clutches his forehead*): I can't take it in. I can't grasp it. You mean, then, that you're not—?

ASTA: You are not my brother, Alfred.

ALLMERS (*Quickly, half defiantly, looking at her*): Still— why should this change anything between us? It makes no difference, after all—

ASTA (*Shakes her head*): It changes everything. We're not brother and sister, Alfred. We're not related.

ALLMERS: Our relationship is just as sacred as it ever was. It always will be.

ASTA: Yes. But now it's subject to the Law of Change. Don't you remember what you said?

ALLMERS (*Looks at her inquiringly*): You mean by that, that—?

ASTA (*Quietly but with warm emotion*): Don't talk any more now, Alfred—my dear Alfred. (*Picks up the flowers from the chair*) You see these water lilies?

ALLMERS (*Nods slowly*): Yes. They're the kind that shoot up from a great depth.

ASTA: I picked them in the stream—at the place where it flows into the fjord. (*Holds them out to him*) Would you like them, Alfred?

ALLMERS (*Takes them*): Thanks.

ASTA (*With tears in her eyes*): They're a last greeting to you from—from little Eyolf.

ALLMERS (*Looks at her*): From the little Eyolf who's out there? Or from you?

ASTA (*Softly*): From both of us. (*Picks up her umbrella*) Come along. We'll go to Rita, now.

ALLMERS (*Picks up his hat from the table, and says sadly—in a whisper*): Asta. Eyolf. Little Eyolf—! (*He follows her up the path.*)

CURTAIN

ACT THREE

SCENE: *A high place overgrown with bushes in* ALLMERS' *garden. At the back a sheer drop, with a railing along the edge, and steps on the left leading downwards. A view over the fjord below. A flagstaff with lines, but no flag, stands by the railing. Downstage right a summerhouse overgrown with vines and creepers. Outside it, a bench. It is a late summer evening with a clear sky. Dusk falls during the act.*

*   ASTA *sits on the bench with her hands in her lap. She has on a coat and hat, has her parasol beside her, and a small traveling bag is slung by a strap over her shoulder.*

*   BORGHEJM *comes up from left. He too has a traveling bag over his shoulder. He carries a rolled-up flag.*

BORGHEJM (*Catching sight of* ASTA): I didn't know you were up here!

ASTA: I was just taking a last look at the view.

BORGHEJM: Then I'm glad I happened to come up.

ASTA: Have you been looking for me?

BORGHEJM: Yes. I wanted to say good-bye to you. Though not for the last time, I hope!

ASTA (*With a faint smile*): You're very persevering.

BORGHEJM: In my job you have to be.

ASTA: Have you seen anything of Alfred? Or of Rita?

BORGHEJM: Yes, I saw them both.

ASTA: Together?

BORGHEJM: No. They weren't together.

ASTA: What are you doing with that flag?

BORGHEJM: Mrs. Allmers asked me to come up here and raise it.

ASTA: Raise a flag? Now?

BORGHEJM: Yes—at half-mast. She wants to see it flying day and night, she said.

ASTA (*With a sigh*): Poor Rita. And poor Alfred.

BORGHEJM (*Busy with the flag*): I see you're all ready for a journey. How can you bear to go away and leave them now?

ASTA (*In a low voice*): I *must* go.

BORGHEJM: Well—if you *must*—

ASTA: You're going away too, aren't you? Tonight?

BORGHEJM: Yes—I must go too. I'm taking the train. Are you?

ASTA: No. I'm going by the steamer.

BORGHEJM (*Glancing at her*): Each our separate way, then. (*She watches him as he raises the flag to half-mast. When he's finished he comes over to her.*)

BORGHEJM: Miss Asta—I can't tell you how sorry I am about little Eyolf.

ASTA (*Looks up at him*): I'm sure you are.

BORGHEJM: It's an awful feeling. I'm not used to grief.

ASTA (*Raises her eyes to the flag*): Time is a great cure for sorrow. It will pass.

BORGHEJM: Does *all* sorrow pass, do you think?

ASTA: Yes; like a sudden storm. You'll see—once you're far away from here—

BORGHEJM: It will have to be very far away indeed.

ASTA: Then—you have your new job to look forward to.

BORGHEJM: Yes—but I've no one to help me with it.

ASTA: Of course you have.

BORGHEJM (*Shakes his head*): No, no one. No one to share
the joy with—that's the hardest part. Joy needs to be
shared.

ASTA: More than suffering and hardship?

BORGHEJM: Much more! One can easily put up with them
alone.

ASTA: But joy—must be shared, you think.

BORGHEJM: Yes. It has no value otherwise.

ASTA: I see what you mean. Perhaps you're right.

BORGHEJM: Of course one can go along for a while being
happy all by oneself—but it's not much use in the long run.
It takes two to be *really* happy.

ASTA: Must it be limited to two? Can't several people be
happy together? *Many* people, perhaps?

BORGHEJM: Ah, but then it becomes quite a different thing,
Miss Asta!—Are you sure you could never make up your
mind to share joy and happiness—and suffering and hardship too—with someone? With just one person—all alone,
I mean?

ASTA: I tried it—once.

BORGHEJM: *You* did?

ASTA: Yes. When my brother—when Alfred and I lived together.

BORGHEJM: Oh, your brother. But that's quite different
too. I should think that would be more like peace than
happiness.

ASTA: It was lovely all the same.

BORGHEJM: Well, if *that* seemed lovely to you—just think
what it would have been if he hadn't been your brother!

ASTA: Yes—but then we shouldn't have lived together. I was
just a child at the time; and he wasn't much more than a
child himself.

BORGHEJM (*After a pause*): Was that *really* such a happy
time?

ASTA: Indeed it was.

BORGHEJM: You experienced true happiness?

ASTA: I did. I was unbelievably happy—now that I look back on it.

BORGHEJM: Tell me about it, Miss Asta—will you?

ASTA: There's not very much to tell. It consisted of a lot of little things.

BORGHEJM: Like what, for instance?

ASTA: Like the time Alfred passed his examination with such distinguished honors. Or, later, when he started getting better and better jobs at different schools. Or the time when he read me a particularly successful article he'd written—and actually had it accepted by one of the magazines.

BORGHEJM: It must have been a happy, peaceful time—I can see that. A brother and sister sharing all their joys and triumphs. (*Shakes his head*) I've never understood how your brother could bear to give you up.

ASTA (*With suppressed emotion*): He wanted to get married.

BORGHEJM: Was it very hard for you?

ASTA: It was at first. I thought I'd completely lost him.

BORGHEJM: Well, fortunately, it didn't come to that.

ASTA: No—it didn't.

BORGHEJM: Still, I don't see how he could bring himself to do it—get married, I mean. Not while he had the chance of being with you.

ASTA (*Gazing in front of her*): He was subject to the Law of Change, I suppose.

BORGHEJM: The Law of Change?

ASTA: Yes; that's what Alfred calls it.

BORGHEJM: It sounds like a very stupid law to me. I'd never be fool enough to believe in a law like that.

ASTA (*Rising*): You may, in time; who knows?

BORGHEJM: No—never! (*Insistently*) Listen to me, Miss Asta! Please be reasonable for once! It's a question of—

ASTA (*Interrupting*): Don't let's discuss that any more!

BORGHEJM (*Continuing as before*): But I *must*. It's quite impossible for me to give you up! After all—your brother has the sort of life he wanted; he's perfectly content without you; he doesn't really need you any more. And this dreadful thing that's happened, has changed your whole position here—

ASTA (*With a start*): What do you mean?

BORGHEJM: The loss of the child, of course. What else?

ASTA (*Recovering her self-control*): Little Eyolf's gone—it's true.

BORGHEJM: There's no longer any reason for your being here. There's no little crippled boy for you to look after any more. You're under no obligation here—there's no claim on you of any sort—

ASTA: Don't talk like that, dear Mr. Borghejm. You make things very hard for me.

BORGHEJM: I'd never forgive myself if I didn't use every effort to persuade you. Soon I'll be leaving town; heaven knows when I'll see you again—perhaps not for a long, long time. And, meanwhile, who knows—*anything* might happen!

ASTA (*With a grave smile*): You're afraid of the Law of Change after all, I see.

BORGHEJM: I'm not. Not in the least! (*With a bitter laugh*) And, as far as you're concerned, I don't suppose there's any change to hope for. It's quite obvious you don't care anything about me!

ASTA: You know that isn't true.

BORGHEJM: Not *enough*, then! Not as I want you to. (*More forcibly*) Asta—Miss Asta—can't you see how wrong you are in this? There could be so much happiness ahead for us! We've no right to let it go! We shall regret it all our lives—can't you see that?

ASTA (*Quietly*): I don't know. But we've got to let it go—I do know that.

BORGHEJM (*Controlling himself, looks at her*): Then—must I build my roads alone?

ASTA (*Warmly*): I wish I could help you build them! Help you through the hardships—share the joy—

BORGHEJM: Would you—if you could?

ASTA: Yes—indeed I would!

BORGHEJM: But you *can't!* Are you absolutely sure?

ASTA (*Looking down*): If I were only *half* yours—would you be satisfied with that?

BORGHEJM: No. I'd want you to be *all* mine.

ASTA (*Looks at him and says quietly*): Yes. Then I can't, you see.

BORGHEJM: Well—In that case I suppose I'd better say good-bye, Miss Asta.

(*He starts to go.* ALLMERS *comes up from the left.* BORGHEJM *stops.*)

ALLMERS (*As he comes up the last steps, points, and says in a low voice*): Is Rita in there—in the summerhouse?

BORGHEJM: No. There's no one here but Miss Asta.

ASTA (*Goes towards him*): Shall I go down and look for her? Ask her to come up here?

ALLMERS (*Prevents her from going*): No, no—don't do that. (*To* BORGHEJM) Was it you who raised the flag just now?

BORGHEJM: Yes. Mrs. Allmers asked me to. That's the reason I came up here.

ALLMERS: And—you're going away tonight?

BORGHEJM: Yes. Tonight I leave for good.

ALLMERS (*Glancing at* ASTA): In pleasant company, I hope?

BORGHEJM (*Shakes his head*): I'm going alone.

ALLMERS (*With surprise*) Alone!

BORGHEJM: Yes—quite alone.

ALLMERS (*Absent-mindedly*): Indeed?

BORGHEJM: And I expect to remain alone.

ALLMERS: There's something dreadful about being alone. It's such a *cold* feeling—

ASTA: But, Alfred dear, *you*'re not alone!

ALLMERS: That can be dreadful too.

ASTA (*Oppressed*): Don't say such things! Don't even think them!

ALLMERS (*Without listening to her*): Then—since you've decided not to go with him—? Since you're not bound in any way—? Why don't you stay on here with me—and Rita?

ASTA (*Uneasily*): I can't. I must get back to town.

ALLMERS: You won't go anywhere else, though—will you, Asta?

ASTA: No.

ALLMERS: And you promise to come out here again soon?

ASTA (*Quickly*): I dare not promise to do that—not for a while, at least.

ALLMERS: Very well. Just as you like. We'll meet in town then.

ASTA (*Imploringly*): Alfred—you mustn't leave Rita at a time like this!

ALLMERS (*Doesn't answer; turns to* BORGHEJM): In a way—perhaps it's best for you to be going by yourself.

BORGHEJM (*Grudgingly*): I don't see how you can say that!

ALLMERS: You never know; you might meet someone else—a little later on—

ASTA (*Involuntarily*): Alfred!

ALLMERS: Someone who'd prove to be your real companion —the only right one. Then it would be too late. Too late!

ASTA (*Softly, tremulously*): Alfred! Alfred!

BORGHEJM (*Looking from one to the other*): I don't understand. What do you mean by that—?

(RITA *comes up the steps on the left.*)

RITA (*Plaintively*): Please don't leave me—all of you!

ASTA (*Goes towards her*): You said you'd rather be alone—

RITA: Yes. But I'm afraid. It's getting darker—and I can't seem to escape from those wide-open eyes. I see them staring at me!

ASTA (*Tenderly and sympathetically*): What of it! There's nothing in those eyes for you to be afraid of, Rita.

RITA: You don't know what you're saying!

ALLMERS (*Insistently*): Asta! I beg you, I implore you, stay here with—with Rita!

RITA: Yes, and with Alfred too! Stay, Asta—I beg of you!

ASTA (*Struggling with herself*): I want to—more than I can say—

RITA: Then, do it! Alfred and I can't go through this suffering and agony alone!

ALLMERS (*Darkly*): This agony of remorse! Why not admit it?

RITA: I don't care what you call it—all I know is, we can't bear it alone! I implore you, Asta, stay and help us! Stay with us and take Eyolf's place—

ASTA (*Wincing*): Eyolf's—!

RITA: She may do that—mayn't she, Alfred?

ALLMERS: If she can—and if she cares to.

RITA: You used to call her your little Eyolf, didn't you? (*Seizes her hand*) Once again you shall be Eyolf, Asta: you shall be *our* Eyolf from now on.

ALLMERS (*With concealed emotion*): Asta—stay and share our life with us; with Rita, and with me. With me—your brother!

ASTA (*Decisively, snatching her hand away*): No, no. I can't! (*Turning*) What time does the boat leave, Borghejm?

BORGHEJM: Almost at once.

ASTA: Then I must get on board. Will you go with me?

BORGHEJM (*In a suppressed outburst of joy*): Go with you! Yes! Oh, yes!

ASTA: Come, then!

RITA (*Slowly*): I see. Then, of course—it's impossible for you to stay with us.

ASTA (*Throws her arms round her neck*): Thank you for everything, dear Rita. (*Goes up to* ALLMERS *and takes his hand*) Alfred—goodbye! A thousand times—goodbye!

ALLMERS (*Softly and intently*): It's as though you were running away, Asta. Why are you doing this?

ASTA (*With subdued anguish*): I *am* running away.

ALLMERS: Running away—from me!

ASTA (*In a whisper*): From you—and from myself.

ALLMERS (*Shrinks back*): Ah—!

(ASTA *rushes down the steps on the left.* BORGHEJM *waves his hat and follows her.* RITA *leans against the entrance of the summerhouse.* ALLMERS, *profoundly moved, goes to the railing and stands there looking down. A pause.*)

ALLMERS (*Turns and says with forced composure*): Here comes the steamer. Look, Rita—over there.

RITA: I dare not look at it.

ALLMERS: How do you mean—you *dare* not?

RITA: It has two great shining eyes. A red one, and a green one.

ALLMERS: They're only lights, you know.

RITA: To me—they're eyes. Staring out of the darkness. Staring in the dark.

ALLMERS: She's putting in to shore.

RITA: Where will she dock this evening?

ALLMERS (*Coming towards her*): At the pier—as usual.

RITA (*Straightening up*): She can't possibly dock *there!*

ALLMERS: There's no other place.

RITA: But that's where Eyolf—! Oh! How *can* they!

ALLMERS: Life's a pitiless business, Rita.

RITA: Men are so heartless. They have no pity, either for the living, or the dead.

ALLMERS: You're right. Life continues on its way—as though nothing had happened.

RITA (*Gazing straight before her*): Nothing *has* happened—to *them*. Only to us.

ALLMERS (*The pain reawakening*): It all seems so senseless, Rita. You bore him in such pain and anguish. And now he's gone—without even a trace.

RITA: Only the crutch was saved.

ALLMERS (*Angrily*): Stop it! Don't let me hear that word again!

RITA (*Plaintively*): I can't bear the thought of having lost him!

ALLMERS (*Coldly and bitterly*): While he was still with us you managed to get on very well without him. You'd let the whole day pass without ever laying eyes on him.

RITA: But I always knew I could see him any time I wanted to.

ALLMERS: And so we wasted the little time we had him with us.

RITA (*Listening, in terror*): Listen, Alfred! There's that bell again!

ALLMERS: It's just the steamer bell. She's on her way.

RITA: I didn't mean *that* bell. It's been ringing in my ears all day— There it is, again!

ALLMERS (*Goes to her*): You're mistaken, Rita.

RITA: I'm not—I hear it plainly. It rings very slowly—like a knell. And always the same words!

ALLMERS: Words? What words?

RITA (*Marking time with her head*): "The crutch—is—floating," "the crutch—is—floating." Surely you must hear it too?

ALLMERS (*Shakes his head*): I hear nothing. There *is* nothing to hear.

RITA: I don't care what you say—I hear it plainly.

ALLMERS (*Looks out over the railing*): They're on board now, Rita. The steamer's under way.

RITA: I don't see how you can fail to hear it! "The crutch—is —floating," "the crutch—"

ALLMERS (*Comes forward*): Don't stand there listening to sounds that don't exist! I was talking to you. I said that Asta and Borghejm were on board. The steamer's left. Asta is gone.

RITA (*Gives him a timid look*): Then, I suppose, you'll soon be going too.

ALLMERS (*Quickly*): What do you mean by that?

RITA: You'll go with your sister, won't you?

ALLMERS: Has Asta told you anything?

RITA: No. But you said yourself it was because of Asta that you married me.

ALLMERS: Yes. But you won me over. I'm bound to you by all the years we've lived together.

RITA: Only now you don't find me "devastatingly beautiful" any more.

ALLMERS: Who knows—the Law of Change may keep us together, after all.

RITA (*Nods slowly*): I've changed—it's true. It's an agonizing feeling.

ALLMERS: Agonizing?

RITA: Yes. It's a kind of birth, it seems to me.

ALLMERS: Or, perhaps, a rebirth. The beginning of a higher way of life. A regeneration, if you like.

RITA (*Gazing sadly before her*): But it means losing all one's happiness.

ALLMERS: Perhaps to lose it is to gain it, Rita.

RITA (*Vehemently*): Those are just words—just phrases! After all—we're creatures of the earth! You can't change that!

ALLMERS: But there's a lot of the sea—and a lot of the heavens in us, too.

RITA: Not in me. In you, perhaps.

ALLMERS: In you too, Rita. Much more than you suspect.

RITA (*Takes a step towards him*): Alfred— What would you think of taking up your work again?

ALLMERS: The work you always hated?

RITA: I'm no longer so difficult to please. I'd be willing to share you with the book.

ALLMERS: Why would you?

RITA: Just to keep you here—to have you near me.

ALLMERS: I'm afraid I can't be of much help to you.

RITA: But, perhaps, I could help you.

ALLMERS: With the book, you mean?

RITA: No. Just to live your life.

ALLMERS (*Shakes his head*): I don't know that I have a life to live.

RITA: To *bear* life, then.

ALLMERS (*Somberly, looking away from her*): I think it would be better if we parted. Best for both of us.

RITA (*Looks at him curiously*): Where would you go? To Asta?

ALLMERS: No—never again to Asta.

RITA: Where then?

ALLMERS: Into the great solitude.

RITA: You mean—up to the mountains?

ALLMERS: Yes.

RITA: That's just a dream, Alfred. You could never live up there.

ALLMERS: Still—that's where I want to go.

RITA: Why? Explain it to me.

ALLMERS: Sit down. There's something I'd like to tell you.

RITA: Something that happened to you while you were up there?

ALLMERS: Yes.

RITA: Something you never told us—neither Asta nor me?

ALLMERS: Yes.

RITA: You're always so silent about everything. You shouldn't be.

ALLMERS: Sit down. I'll tell you all about it.

RITA: Yes—tell me. (*She sits on the bench outside the summerhouse.*)

ALLMERS: I was all alone up there—up among the mountain peaks. I came to the edge of a lake—a large, desolate lake. I wanted to reach the other side, but I didn't know how to go about it. There was no sign of a boat; there was nobody in sight; the place was utterly deserted.

RITA: Well? What happened then?

ALLMERS: To one side of the lake was a small valley. I thought it might lead to a pass, through which I could reach the other side—beyond the stretch of water. So I followed it.

RITA: And you lost your way?

ALLMERS: I lost all sense of direction. There was no road, you see—not even a path. I walked on all day, and all the following night. I began to despair of ever getting back to civilization. I thought I was lost for good.

RITA: Did you think you'd never see any of us again? You *did* think of us—didn't you?

ALLMERS: No—strangely enough, I didn't. You and Eyolf

seemed remote and far away from me. And Asta, too.

RITA: What did you think of?

ALLMERS: I didn't think at all. As I clung to the bare edge of the precipice, I caught myself longing—with a sense of joy—for the peace and luxury of death.

RITA (*Jumping up*): How could you have a sense of joy about anything so ghastly!

ALLMERS: It didn't seem ghastly to me at all. I felt no fear. It was as though death were there beside me, like a good comrade. It all seemed right, and natural. In my family, people are used to dying young—

RITA: Stop talking about it, Alfred! It's over now—you got back safely, after all.

ALLMERS: Yes. Quite suddenly I found myself beyond the lake—just as I'd planned.

RITA: Now that it's passed, I suppose you won't admit it—but it must have been a terrifying night!

ALLMERS: That night was a turning point for me. I came to a definite decision. I knew what I must do. And I came straight home—to Eyolf.

RITA: And then—it was too late.

ALLMERS: Yes. It wasn't until death—my comrade—came and took him, that I felt the terror of it all. For, in spite of everything, the thought of leaving here fills us with dread. We're all of us earthbound, Rita.

RITA (*With a gleam of joy*): You see! You feel that too! (*Goes nearer to him*): Let's live our life together, Alfred— as long as we can!

ALLMERS: Our life? What life have we to live! It's all become so senseless—an empty void.

RITA (*In fear*): You're going to leave me, Alfred—I know it! Sooner or later you will leave me.

ALLMERS: You mean—to join my comrade?

RITA: No—worse than that. You'll leave me of your own free will. It's only with me that life seems empty to you. That's true, isn't it? Answer me!

ALLMERS (*Looks at her steadily*): What if it were—?

(*The sound of a violent disturbance—angry voices quarreling—is heard from below in the distance.* ALLMERS *goes to the railing.*)

RITA: What's happening? (*In an outburst*) They must have found him!

ALLMERS: No one will ever find him.

RITA: Then—what is it?

ALLMERS: The usual scenes—the usual violence.

RITA: Down at the shore?

ALLMERS: Yes. That whole community should be wiped out. The men are back from work—drunk, as they always are. They're beating up the children. The women are shouting for help. You can hear the children screaming.

RITA: Perhaps we should send someone to help them.

ALLMERS (*Harshly and angrily*): They didn't help Eyolf, did they? Let them suffer—as they let Eyolf suffer!

RITA: Don't say such things, Alfred! Don't even think them!

ALLMERS: I can't help it— All those shacks should be torn down!

RITA: Then where would those poor people go?

ALLMERS: Let them go somewhere else.

RITA: But, what about the children?

ALLMERS: Does it make any difference what becomes of them?

RITA (*Quietly and reproachfully*): You're forcing yourself to be harsh, Alfred.

ALLMERS (*Vehemently*): I've a right to be harsh! A *duty* to be harsh!

RITA: A duty?

ALLMERS: Yes—to Eyolf. His death must be avenged—I'm right in what I say, Rita! Think it over. That place should be razed to the ground—every stick and stone of it. See that you have it done—after I'm gone.

RITA (*Looks at him intently*): After you're gone?

ALLMERS: Yes. It'll give you something to do—something to occupy your time with. That's important for you.

RITA (*Firmly—with decision*): It is—you're right. Have you any idea what I plan to do—after you're gone?

ALLMERS: No—what?

RITA: As soon as you've left me, I plan to go down to the shore, make friends with all those poor neglected children —those ragged little urchins—and bring them home with me.

ALLMERS: What for? What would you do with them?

RITA: Take them to my heart.

ALLMERS: *You!*

RITA: Yes. That's what I plan to do, after you leave me. They shall all live up here with me—and be my children.

ALLMERS (*Shocked*): In our little Eyolf's place!

RITA: In our little Eyolf's place. They shall live in Eyolf's rooms. Read Eyolf's books. Play with his toys, and take turns sitting in his chair at table.

ALLMERS: This is fantastic! That you, of all people—! You're the last person in the world to undertake a thing like that!

RITA: Then I shall simply have to learn. I shall have to train myself; discipline myself.

ALLMERS: Are you really serious about all this? Do you really mean it? If so—you must be very changed.

RITA: I am, Alfred. You've seen to that. My heart is totally empty—thanks to you. I must try and fill it with something; something resembling love.

ALLMERS (*Stands for a moment lost in thought; then looks at her*): The truth is—we've never done very much for those poor people.

RITA: We've done nothing for them.

ALLMERS: We've scarcely thought of them, in fact.

RITA: Never with any sympathy.

ALLMERS: No. We never shared our "gold and our green forests."

RITA: We closed our hands to them. And our hearts too.

ALLMERS (*Nods*): Perhaps it was only natural, after all, that they didn't choose to risk their lives in trying to save Eyolf.

RITA (*Softly*): I wonder, Alfred—would we have risked ours, do you think?

ALLMERS (*With an uneasy gesture, pushing the thought away from him*): You must never doubt *that*, Rita.

RITA: We're both earthbound, remember.

ALLMERS: What will you try and do for these poor neglected children?

RITA: I'd like to help them to discover a happier, finer life—

ALLMERS: If you succeed in doing that—then Eyolf was not born in vain.

RITA: And he won't have died in vain, either.

ALLMERS (*Looks at her steadily*): I think you should face one thing clearly, Rita: It's not love that's making you do this.

RITA: I know. At least—not yet.

ALLMERS: What is it? Do you know?

RITA (*Half evasively*): I used to hear you talk to Asta about human responsibility, Alfred.

ALLMERS: That book you hated so—

RITA: Yes—and I hate it still. But I listened to what you told her. And now I'd like to try and go on with that book— in my own way.

ALLMERS (*Shakes his head*): It's not just because of an unfinished book—

RITA: No. There's still another reason.

ALLMERS: Well?

RITA: I want to make my peace with those wide-open eyes.

ALLMERS (*Moved, fixing his eyes on her*): I wish I could help you in that! May I try to, Rita?

RITA: Would you?

ALLMERS: Yes—if I thought I could.

RITA (*Hesitatingly*): But then—you'd have to stay here.

ALLMERS (*Softly*): Things might still work out between us; let us try, and see.

RITA (*Almost inaudibly*): Yes, Alfred—let us.

(*They are both silent. Then Alfred goes to the flagstaff and hoists the flag to the top. Rita stands by the summerhouse and watches him in silence.*)

ALLMERS (*Comes towards her again*): We have a lot of work before us, Rita.

RITA: Yes, we have. But there'll be peaceful moments too— you'll see. A kind of Sunday stillness.

ALLMERS (*Quietly, with emotion*): And, in that stillness— we shall feel their presence.

RITA (*Whispering*): Their presence?

ALLMERS (*As before*): Yes—those we've lost. We'll feel their spirits close to us.

RITA (*Nods slowly*): Our little Eyolf. And your big Eyolf, too.

ALLMERS (*Looks straight before him*): And then, who knows —if we look hard enough—every now and then, we may even catch a glimpse of them.

RITA: Where shall we look for them, Alfred?

ALLMERS (*Fixing his eyes upon her*): We must look upwards.

RITA (*Nods in agreement*): Upwards—yes.

ALLMERS: Up towards the mountain peaks. Towards the stars. Upwards—towards the great silence.

RITA (*Gives him her hand*): Thanks!

CURTAIN

John Gabriel Borkman

A PLAY IN FOUR ACTS

1896

CHARACTERS

JOHN GABRIEL BORKMAN, *formerly a bank president*

MRS. GUNHILD BORKMAN, *his wife*

ERHART BORKMAN, *their son, a student*

MISS ELLA RENTHEIM, *Mrs. Borkman's twin sister*

MRS. FANNY WILTON

VILHELM FOLDAL, *a subordinate clerk in a government office*

FRIDA, *his daughter*

MALENE, *Mrs. Borkman's maid*

> *A winter evening, at the old family residence of the Rentheims, in the neighborhood of Christiania.*

ACT
ONE

SCENE: MRS. BORKMAN's *drawing room. It is furnished with old-fashioned faded splendor. At the rear, an open sliding door leads into a conservatory, with windows and a glass door, through which a view of the garden can be seen. A driving snow in the twilight. On the right, a door leading from the hall. Farther forward, a large old-fashioned iron stove, the fire lighted. On the left, towards the back, a single smaller door. In front, on the same side, a window, covered with heavy curtains. A horsehair sofa stands between the window and the door. A table in front of the sofa is covered with a cloth. On the table, a shaded lamp. Beside the stove an armchair with a high back.*

MRS. GUNHILD BORKMAN *sits on the sofa, knitting. She is an elderly lady, of cold, distinguished appearance, with stiff carriage and immobile features. Her hair is very gray, her delicate hands transparent. She is dressed in a gown of heavy dark silk, which had at one time been attractive, but is now somewhat worn and shabby. A woolen shawl is thrown over her shoulders.*

She sits for a time erect and rigid at her knitting. The bells of a passing sledge are heard.

MRS. BORKMAN (*Listens; her eyes sparkle with enthusiasm and she whispers involuntarily*): Erhart! At last! (*Presently the maid,* MALENE, *enters from the hall with a visiting card on a small tray.*)

GUNHILD: Is that Mr. Erhart?

MARLENE: No Ma'am—it's a lady—

GUNHILD (*Putting aside her knitting*): Oh, Mrs. Wilton I suppose—

MALENE (*Coming nearer*): No Ma'am; it's a strange lady—

GUNHILD (*Taking the card*): Let me see— (*Reads it; rises quickly and looks intently at the girl*) Are you sure this is for me?

MALENE: I understood it was for you, Ma'am.

GUNHILD: Did she ask to speak with Mrs. Borkman?

MALENE: Yes, she did.

GUNHILD (*Abruptly, resolutely*): Very well! Say I am at home.

(THE MAID *opens the door for the strange lady and goes out.* MISS ELLA RENTHEIM *enters. She resembles her sister; but her face reveals suffering rather than hardness of expression. It still shows signs of great beauty and strong character. She has luxuriant snow-white hair, drawn back from the forehead in natural waves. She is dressed in black velvet, with a hat and a fur-lined cloak of the same material. The two sisters stand silent for a time, and look searchingly at each other. Each is evidently waiting for the other to speak first.*)

ELLA (*Still standing near the door*): You're surprised to see me, Gunhild.

GUNHILD (*Erect and immovable between the sofa and the table, resting her finger tips upon the cloth*): You must have made a mistake. The superintendent lives in the other wing, you know.

ELLA: I haven't come to see the superintendent.

GUNHILD: You've come to see me, then?

ELLA: Yes, I have a few words to say to you.

GUNHILD (*Advancing to the middle of the room*): Well—sit down, then.

ELLA: Thank you. I'd rather stand.

GUNHILD: Just as you please—but at least loosen your cloak—

ELLA (*Unbuttoning her cloak*): Yes—it's very warm here—

GUNHILD: I am always cold.

ELLA (*Looking at her for a time with her arms resting on the back of the armchair*): Well, Gunhild, it's nearly eight years since we saw each other last.

GUNHILD (*Coldly*): Since last we spoke, you mean—

ELLA: Quite right—since last we spoke. I expect you've seen me, now and then, on my yearly visit to the superintendent.

GUNHILD: Once or twice, I have—

ELLA: And I've occasionally caught a glimpse of you—there at the window.

GUNHILD: You must have seen me through the curtains then. You have good eyes. (*Harshly and cuttingly*) But the last time we spoke to each other was here in this room—

ELLA (*Trying to stop her*): Yes, yes—I know, Gunhild—

GUNHILD: The week before he was—set free—

ELLA (*Moving towards the back*): Don't speak of that!

GUNHILD (*Firmly but in a low voice*): It was the week before he was set at liberty.

ELLA (*Coming down*): Yes—I shall never forget that day! But it's too heartbreaking to think of; one can't bear to dwell on it—even for a moment—

GUNHILD (*Gloomily*): And yet one's thoughts can dwell on nothing else! (*Vehemently; clenching her hands together*) I can't understand it—I never shall! That such a thing— such an appalling thing—could happen in our family! Such an old, distinguished family—that we should have been made to suffer!

ELLA: We were not the only ones to suffer, Gunhild.

GUNHILD: I dare say not; but the others don't trouble me much. In their case it was only a matter of a little money —a few investments. But for us! For me! And then for Erhart; he was a mere child at the time! why should we two innocent people have been made to suffer all the shame—the hideous disgrace!

ELLA (*Cautiously*): How does he bear it, Gunhild? Tell me.

GUNHILD: Erhart, you mean?

ELLA: No, Borkman himself! How does he bear it?

GUNHILD (*Scornfully*): Do you think I ever ask about that?

ELLA: Ask? You surely don't need to ask!

GUNHILD (*Looks at her, surprised*): You don't suppose I ever have anything to do with him? That I ever see him—?

ELLA: Not even that!

GUNHILD: A man who was in jail for five years! (*Covers her face with her hands*) The bitter shame of it! (*With rising vehemence*) And then to think what the name of John Gabriel Borkman used to mean! No! I shall never see him again—never!

ELLA (*Looks at her for a moment*): You have a hard heart, Gunhild.

GUNHILD: Towards him—yes!

ELLA: After all, he is your husband.

GUNHILD: Didn't he say at the trial that it was I who caused his ruin? That I spent money so recklessly?

ELLA (*Tentatively*): Wasn't there perhaps some truth in that?

GUNHILD: It was he who insisted on it. He insisted on our living in such an absurdly lavish style—

ELLA: I know; but that's just where you should have used your influence—and that, you never did—

GUNHILD: How was I to know it wasn't his own money he gave me to squander, and that he used to squander too, ten times more than I did—?

ELLA (*Quietly*): Well, I suppose his position forced him to do that—to some extent—

GUNHILD (*Scornfully*): Yes, it was always the same thing! We had to live up to his position! He lived up to it right enough!— Drove about in a four-in-hand as if he were a king; let people bow and scrape to him, as if he were a king! (*Laughing*) They called him by his first name all over the country, as if he were the King himself! "John Gabriel"! "John Gabriel"! Everyone knew what a great man John Gabriel was!

ELLA (*Warmly and emphatically*): He *was* a great man then!

GUNHILD: Yes, so it seemed. But he never breathed a word to me as to his real position; never gave a hint as to where his money came from—

ELLA: No—other people didn't know that either—

GUNHILD: I don't care about the others! But it was his duty to tell me the truth. And he never did. He kept on lying to me—lying disgracefully!

ELLA (*Interrupting*): That's not true, Gunhild! He may have kept things from you, but I'm sure he didn't lie!

GUNHILD: Call it what you like—it comes to the same thing! Then it all went to pieces; and that was the end of his glory and his greatness!

ELLA (*To herself*): Yes, it all went to pieces—for him—and for others!

GUNHILD (*Drawing herself up menacingly*): But I tell you this, Ella—I haven't given up yet—! I shall still redeem myself—you'll see!

ELLA (*Eagerly*): Redeem yourself? What do you mean by that?

GUNHILD: Redeem my good name—my honor—my fortune. Redeem my ruined life—that's what I mean! Thank God I have someone near me who will atone for all the past—

ELLA: Gunhild! Gunhild!

GUNHILD (*Her excitement rising*): Someone who will atone for all his father's sins.

ELLA: Erhart, I suppose.

GUNHILD: Yes, my son, Erhart! He will redeem our home, the family name—all that can be redeemed and perhaps more besides.

ELLA: How do you expect him to do that, Gunhild?

GUNHILD: I don't know how—but somehow it must and shall be done! (*Looks searchingly at her*) Isn't that what you've had in mind too, Ella, ever since he was a child?

ELLA: I wouldn't quite say that.

GUNHILD: No? Then why did you take charge of him when the crash came?

ELLA: You couldn't very well look after him yourself at that time, Gunhild—

GUNHILD: No, I couldn't. And his father had a good enough excuse—he was safely under lock and key—

ELLA (*Indignant*): How can you say such things!

GUNHILD (*With a venomous expression*): And how could you bring yourself to take care of the child of a—John Gabriel! Just as if he were your own—take him from me—home to you, and keep him with you, year after year; until he was nearly grown up. (*Looks suspiciously at her*) What was your real reason, Ella? Why did you keep him with you?

ELLA: I grew to love him so dearly—

GUNHILD: More than I—his mother?

ELLA (*Evasively*): I don't know about that. And then, Erhart was rather a delicate child—

GUNHILD: Erhart—delicate!

ELLA: Yes, he seemed so at that time. And you know quite well the climate is milder on the West Coast than it is here.

GUNHILD (*Smiling bitterly*): Is it indeed? (*Breaking off*) It's true—you've done a great deal for Erhart. (*Changing her tone*) But, of course, you could afford it. (*Smiling*) You were so lucky, Ella. You managed to save all your money.

ELLA (*Hurt*): I didn't manage anything about it, I assure you: I had no idea until long, long afterwards, that my securities had been left untouched.

GUNHILD: I understand nothing about such things—I only say you were lucky. (*Looking inquiringly at her*) But when you insisted on educating Erhart for me—what was your motive in that?

ELLA (*Staring at her*): My motive—!

GUNHILD: Yes, you must have had some motive. What did you want to do with him? To make of him, I mean?

ELLA (*Deliberately*): I wanted Erhart to become a happy human being.

GUNHILD (*Contemptuously*): People in our position have something besides happiness to think of!

ELLA: Indeed? What, for instance?

GUNHILD (*Steadily and earnestly*): Erhart's first duty is to win such a brilliant position for himself that no one will dare remember the shadow his father has cast over our lives.

ELLA (*Searchingly*): Is this what Erhart himself demands of his life?

GUNHILD (*Slightly taken aback*): Yes—I should hope so—!

ELLA: Isn't it rather what you demand of it?

GUNHILD (*Curtly*): Erhart naturally feels as I do.

ELLA (*Sadly and slowly*): Are you so sure of your son, Gunhild?

GUNHILD (*With veiled triumph*): Yes, I am! Thank heaven!

ELLA: Then I should think you must be very happy—in spite of all the rest.

GUNHILD: So I am—as far as that goes. Yet—I can't help it—each moment all the rest comes rushing over me—like a storm.

ELLA (*Changing her tone*): Tell me something, Gunhild; you'd best be honest with me—for that's really why I've come—

GUNHILD: Tell you what?

ELLA: Something I felt I must talk to you about. It seems Erhart doesn't live out here with you—?

GUNHILD (*Harshly*): Erhart can't possibly live out here. He has to live in town—

ELLA: So he wrote me—

GUNHILD: He must, on account of his studies. But he comes to visit me—every single evening.

ELLA: Then—may I see him? I'd like to talk to him at once.

GUNHILD: He's not here yet. But I expect him any minute.

ELLA: He must be here, Gunhild; I hear his footsteps overhead—

GUNHILD: Up in the gallery, you mean?

ELLA: Yes—I've heard him pacing about up there ever since I came.

GUNHILD (*Looking away from her*): That is not Erhart, Ella.

ELLA (*Surprised*): Not Erhart? Who is it then?

GUNHILD: It's he.

ELLA (*With restrained anguish*): Borkman. John Gabriel Borkman!

GUNHILD: He walks up and down like that, back and forth, from morning to night, day in and day out.

ELLA: I've heard rumors of this—

GUNHILD: I dare say. No doubt people find plenty to say about us.

ELLA: It was Erhart who told me about it in his letters. His father usually keeps to his room upstairs, he said; while you stay down here and keep to yours.

GUNHILD: That's how we've lived, Ella, all these eight long years. Ever since they set him free and sent him home to me!

ELLA: I didn't believe for a moment it could be true—it seemed so utterly impossible!

GUNHILD (*Nods*): It is true—and it can never be otherwise.

ELLA (*Looking at her*): This must be a terrible life, Gunhild.

GUNHILD: Worse than terrible—almost unendurable.

ELLA: It must be.

GUNHILD: Always to hear his footsteps up there; from early morning till far into the night. One can hear them so clearly. There's no escaping them.

ELLA: No—there's no escaping them.

GUNHILD: I often feel as though I had a sick wolf pacing his cage up there. Right over my head. (*Listens and speaks in a whisper*) Listen! Listen! Back and forth—back and forth, goes the wolf!

ELLA (*Tentatively*): Can nothing be done about this, Gunhild?

GUNHILD (*With a gesture of repulsion*): He's never tried to change it—

ELLA: What about you?

GUNHILD (*Indignantly*): I! After all the wrong he's done me! No thank you! Let the wolf go on pacing up there!

ELLA: It's too warm for me here—I think I'll take my things off after all.

GUNHILD: I asked you to—

(ELLA *takes off her hat and cloak and lays them on a chair beside the door leading to the hall.*)

ELLA: But—when he goes out— Don't you ever meet him then?

GUNHILD (*With a bitter laugh*): In society, you mean?

ELLA: When he goes out for a walk—through the woods, or—

GUNHILD: The great Mr. Borkman never ventures out.

ELLA: Not even after dark?

GUNHILD: Never.

ELLA (*With emotion*): I suppose he can't bring himself to—

GUNHILD: I suppose not. His hat and cloak are still hanging in the closet—the closet in the hall you know—

ELLA (*To herself*): The closet we used to hide in when we were little—

GUNHILD (*Nods*): Sometimes, late at night, I hear him come down, as though intending to go out. But he always stops —halfway down the stairs—and turns back—back to his own room again.

ELLA (*Quietly*): Do none of his old friends ever come to see him?

GUNHILD: He has no old friends—

ELLA: He had so many—once.

GUNHILD: He chose a good way to get rid of them. He was a costly friend to his friends, was John Gabriel.

ELLA: Yes—I dare say you're right, Gunhild.

GUNHILD (*Vehemently*): I must say I think it's petty, mean, contemptible—to make so much of the insignificant losses they may have suffered. They were only money losses after all!

ELLA (*Not answering her*): So he lives up there all by himself: utterly alone!

GUNHILD: Yes, I suppose so. I have heard there's an old clerk, some old accountant, who comes to see him now and then.

ELLA: That must be Vilhelm Foldal. They were boyhood friends, I believe.

GUNHILD: I believe they were. I know nothing about him. He didn't move in our circle—when we had a—

ELLA: But he comes to see Borkman now?

GUNHILD: Yes, he deigns to. But of course, only after dark.

ELLA: This Foldal—didn't he lose money when the bank failed?

GUNHILD (*Carelessly*): I believe he lost something—some trifling sum—

ELLA (*With slight emphasis*): It was all he possessed, Gunhild.

GUNHILD (*Smiling*): What he possessed couldn't have been much. Nothing to speak of.

ELLA: No; and he made no mention of it—at the trial.

GUNHILD: In any case, I can assure you, Erhart has made up for any little loss he may have suffered.

ELLA (*With surprise*): Erhart? How could Erhart have done that?

GUNHILD: He's taken an interest in Foldal's youngest daughter—helped her with her studies—given her a chance to make something of herself and someday earn her living. That's a great deal more than her father could have done.

ELLA: Yes—I dare say he couldn't afford to do much.

GUNHILD: Erhart has also arranged for her to have music lessons. She's already made such progress that she sometimes goes up to—up to his room—and plays for him.

ELLA: He's still fond of music then?

GUNHILD: I suppose he is. He has that piano you sent here—when he was expected back—

ELLA: And she plays to him on it—?

GUNHILD: Yes, now and then. In the evenings. That was Erhart's idea, too.

ELLA: But how does the poor child manage to get home? It's a long way all by herself.

GUNHILD: Erhart has arranged for her to stay with a lady who lives near here—a Mrs. Wilton—

ELLA (*With interest*): Mrs. Wilton!

GUNHILD: A very rich woman. You don't know her.

ELLA: I've heard her name. Mrs. Fanny Wilton, isn't it?

GUNHILD: Yes, quite right.

ELLA: Erhart has mentioned her several times in his letters. Does she live out here now?

GUNHILD: She's taken a house here. She moved out from town some time ago.

ELLA (*With slight hesitation*): They say she's divorced from her husband.

GUNHILD: Her husband's been dead for several years.

ELLA: Yes, but they were divorced; he divorced her—

GUNHILD: He deserted her—that's what he did! She was in no way to blame!

ELLA: Do you know her at all intimately, Gunhild?

GUNHILD: I know her pretty well. She lives close by. She often drops in to see me.

ELLA: Do you like her?

GUNHILD: She's very understanding—has unusually clear judgment—

ELLA: About people you mean?

GUNHILD: Yes—especially about people. She's made a deep study of Erhart, of his character, of his whole mind—and of course, she idolizes him, as might be expected.

ELLA (*With a touch of finesse*): Then perhaps she knows Erhart even better than she knows you.

GUNHILD: Erhart saw a good deal of her in town—before she moved out here.

ELLA (*Without thinking*): Yet she moved out of town in spite of that.

GUNHILD (*Taken aback, looking keenly at her*): In spite of that! What do you mean?

ELLA (*Evasively*): Nothing—nothing in particular—

GUNHILD: You said that so strangely. You did mean something by it, Ella—

ELLA (*Looking her straight in the eyes*): Yes, as a matter of fact, Gunhild, I did mean something by it.

GUNHILD: Then why not be frank about it!

ELLA: First I must tell you this; I, too, feel that I have a certain claim on Erhart. But perhaps you don't agree?

GUNHILD (*Glancing around the room*): I suppose you have
—after all the money you've spent on him—

ELLA: Not because of that, Gunhild; but because I love him.

GUNHILD (*Smiling scornfully*): Love my son? Is it possible—
in spite of everything?

ELLA: Yes, in spite of everything, I love Erhart—love him as
much as I can love anyone at my time of life.

GUNHILD: What if you do?

ELLA: That's why I'm troubled when I see anything threatening him.

GUNHILD: Threaten Erhart! What should threaten him, or
who?

ELLA: You, first of all—in your own way—

GUNHILD (*Vehemently*): I!

ELLA: —and I'm afraid of this—Mrs. Wilton, too.

GUNHILD (*Looks at her for a moment in speechless surprise*):
You can think such things of my son! Of Erhart—who has
his great mission to fulfill!

ELLA (*Lightly*): His mission—!

GUNHILD (*Indignantly*): How dare you say that so scornfully!

ELLA: Do you think a young man of Erhart's age, full of health
and spirits—is going to sacrifice his life for such a thing as
a "mission"?

GUNHILD (*Emphatically*): Erhart will—I know he will!

ELLA (*Shaking her head*): You neither know it nor believe
it, Gunhild.

GUNHILD: Not believe it!

ELLA: No! It's only a dream you cling to! Without it you
might utterly despair.

GUNHILD: I should indeed despair. (*Vehemently*) I dare say
that's what you'd like to see, Ella.

ELLA (*With head erect*): I'd rather see that—than see you
triumph at Erhart's expense.

GUNHILD (*Threateningly*): You want to come between
mother and son—you want to come between us!

ELLA: I want to free him from your power—your will, your influence.

GUNHILD (*Triumphantly*): You're too late! You had him in your clutches all those years—until he was fifteen—but I've won him back again, you see!

ELLA: Then I shall win him back again from you. (*Hoarsely, half whispering*) This is not the first time we two have fought over a human being.

GUNHILD (*Looking at her in triumph*): And it was I who won the victory!

ELLA (*With a smile of scorn*): You still think that victory was worth the winning?

GUNHILD (*Darkly*): No— God knows you're right in that!

ELLA: This victory will not be worth the winning either.

GUNHILD: Not worth it! When I'm fighting to keep my power over my son!

ELLA: No! Because it's only power you want!

GUNHILD: And you?

ELLA (*Warmly*): I want his heart—I want his love—

GUNHILD (*With an outburst*): You'll never have that again! I can assure you!

ELLA (*Staring at her*): I suppose you've taken care of that!

GUNHILD (*Smiling*): Indeed I have! Couldn't you see that in his letters?

ELLA (*Nods slowly*): Yes, I could see nothing but you—in his letters of late.

GUNHILD (*Provokingly*): I haven't wasted these eight years!

ELLA (*Controlling herself*): What have you said to Erhart about me? Is it the sort of thing you can tell me?

GUNHILD: I can tell you well enough! I've only told him the truth—

ELLA: Well?

GUNHILD: I've constantly impressed upon him, that he must never forget, that we have you to thank for being able to live as we do—for being able to live at all!

ELLA: Is that all?

GUNHILD: That's the sort of thing that rankles—I feel that in my own heart.

ELLA: But Erhart's always been aware of that—

GUNHILD: When he came home to me, he imagined that you did it all out of the goodness of your heart. He doesn't believe that any longer, Ella.

ELLA: What does he believe, now?

GUNHILD: He believes what is the truth!—I asked him how he accounted for the fact that Aunt Ella never came to visit us—

ELLA (*Interrupting*): He knew my reasons already—

GUNHILD: He knows them better, now! You led him to believe that it was to spare me—and his father—

ELLA: And so it was—

GUNHILD: Erhart doesn't believe that for a moment now!

ELLA: What have you told him of me?

GUNHILD: That you're ashamed of us—that you despise us! Don't attempt to deny it! Didn't you once plan to take him away from me entirely? Think, Ella; you surely can't have forgotten that.

ELLA (*With a gesture of denial*): But that was at the height of the scandal—when the case was before the court. I have no such plans now!

GUNHILD: It wouldn't matter if you had! Erhart has his mission to fulfill; my son needs me—not you! He's as good as dead to you—and you to him!

ELLA (*Coldly and resolutely*): We shall see; for now, I've decided to remain here—

GUNHILD: Here—in this house?

ELLA: Yes, here!

GUNHILD: Here, with us? You mean—all night?

ELLA: All the rest of my life, if need be.

GUNHILD (*Collecting herself*): Well, Ella—the house is yours—

ELLA: Oh, come now—

GUNHILD: Everything is yours! This chair I'm sitting in—the

bed I lie and toss in at night—the very food we eat—all belong to you!

ELLA: It was the only way to arrange things. Borkman can hold no property of his own—his creditors would take it away from him at once!

GUNHILD: How well I know it! We're obliged to live on your pity—on your charity!

ELLA: I can't prevent you from looking at it in that light, Gunhild.

GUNHILD: No, you can't!— When do you want us to move out?

ELLA (*Looking at her*): Move out?

GUNHILD (*In great excitement*): You don't imagine I'd ever live under the same roof with you! I'd rather go to the poorhouse, or tramp the roads!

ELLA: Very well; then let Erhart come with me—

GUNHILD: Erhart! My son!

ELLA: Yes, then I shall go straight home again.

GUNHILD (*After reflecting a moment, firmly*): Erhart himself shall choose between us!

ELLA (*Looking doubtfully and hesitatingly at her*): Erhart choose?—You dare risk that, Gunhild?

GUNHILD (*With a hard laugh*): Dare you say! Let my son choose between his mother and you! Yes—indeed I dare!

ELLA (*Listening*): Is someone coming? I thought I heard—

GUNHILD: It must be Erhart— (*There is a sharp knock at the door leading in from the hall, which is immediately opened.* MRS. WILTON *enters in evening dress, and with outer wraps. She is followed by* THE MAID, *who has not had time to announce her, and looks bewildered. The door remains half open.* MRS. WILTON *is a strikingly handsome, well-developed woman in her thirties. Her lips are full, red, smiling, her eyes sparkling. She has luxuriant dark hair.*)

MRS. WILTON: Good evening, my dear Mrs. Borkman!

GUNHILD (*Rather dryly*): Good evening, Mrs. Wilton. (*To* THE MAID) Malene, light the lamp. (MAID *lights the lamp and exits.*)

MRS. WILTON (*Seeing* ELLA): Oh, I beg your pardon—you have a visitor—

GUNHILD: It's only my sister; she's just arrived from— (ER-HART BORKMAN *flings the half-open door wide open and rushes in. He is a young man with bright, cheerful eyes; his mustache is beginning to grow.*)

ERHART (*Radiant with joy; on the threshold*): What did I hear—? Aunt Ella—? (*Rushing up to her and seizing her hands*) Aunt Ella! I can't believe it! Is it really you?

ELLA (*Throws her arms around his neck*): Erhart, my dear, dear boy! How you've grown! How good it is to see you again!

GUNHILD (*Sharply*): What does this mean, Erhart? What were you doing—hiding in the hall?

MRS. WILTON (*Quickly*): Erhart—Mr. Borkman—came with me.

GUNHILD (*Looking hard at him*): So you didn't come to see your mother first?

ERHART: I had to stop in at Mrs. Wilton's for a moment—to call for little Frida.

GUNHILD: Is that Miss Foldal with you too?

MRS. WILTON: Yes; she's just taking off her things.

ERHART (*Addressing someone through the open door*): You can go right upstairs, Frida!

(*Pause.* ELLA *observes* ERHART. *He seems embarrassed and a little impatient; his face has assumed a nervous and colder expression.*)

GUNHILD (*With forced politeness*): Well, Mrs. Wilton—will you give us the pleasure of your company this evening?

MRS. WILTON: Many thanks, my dear Mrs. Borkman, but I'm afraid I can't. We have another engagement—we're going to the Hinkel's.

GUNHILD (*Staring at her*): We?—Who do you mean by "we"?

MRS. WILTON (*Laughing*): I really ought to have said "I." But the ladies of the house begged me to bring Mr. Bork-man with me—that is—if I should happen to see him.

GUNHILD: And you did happen to see him, it appears.

MRS. WILTON: Yes; it was lucky, wasn't it? You see, he was good enough to drop in at my house, to call for little Frida.

GUNHILD (*Dryly*): But Erhart—I didn't know you knew these people—these Hinkels.

ERHART (*Irritated*): Well, I don't exactly know them. (*Adds rather impatiently*) You know best, Mother, what people I know or don't know!

MRS. WILTON: Oh, what does it matter! They're such a charming, gay, hospitable family—they'll soon put you at your ease! The house is always full of young people.

GUNHILD (*With emphasis*): If I know my son, Mrs. Wilton, it would not be the right sort of company for him.

MRS. WILTON: Good heavens, Mrs. Borkman, he's young, too, you know!

GUNHILD: Yes, he is young—fortunately. He has much to accomplish.

ERHART (*Concealing his impatience*): Well, Mother, it's obvious I can't go to the Hinkels this evening! Naturally I'll stay here with you and Aunt Ella.

GUNHILD: I was sure you would, Erhart.

ELLA: No, Erhart, you mustn't stay home on my account—

ERHART: Of course I'll stay, Aunt Ella—I wouldn't think of going. (*Looking doubtfully at* MRS. WILTON) But what excuse can we make?— Can I get out of it? You've said "yes" for me, haven't you?

MRS. WILTON (*Gaily*): What nonsense!— Not get out of it! When I make my entrance, deserted and forlorn, into those festive halls—I shall simply say "no" for you!

ERHART: Well—if you really think I can get out of it—?

MRS. WILTON: I'm not afraid of saying either "yes" or "no"— I'm used to being on my own, you see. And you can't possibly leave your aunt the moment she's arrived. For shame, Monsieur Erhart! Would that be behaving like a good son?

GUNHILD: Son?

MRS. WILTON: Well, adopted son then, Mrs. Borkman.

GUNHILD: I'm glad you concede that!

MRS. WILTON: You know—I sometimes think we should be more grateful to a good foster mother than to our real mother.

GUNHILD: Has that been your own experience?

MRS. WILTON: I knew so little of my own mother, alas! But perhaps if I'd had a really good foster mother—I shouldn't have become so—so disreputable as people say I am! (*To* ERHART) So, you're going to stay quietly at home, like a good little boy, and drink tea with Mamma and Auntie! Good-bye, good-bye, dear Mrs. Borkman! Good-bye, Miss Rentheim.

ERHART: I'll go part of the way with you.

MRS. WILTON: You shan't go a step with me. I'm quite used to going about alone— But you'd better beware, Mr. Borkman, I warn you!

ERHART: What am I to beware of?

MRS. WILTON: As I go down the road—deserted and forlorn, as I said before—I shall try and cast a spell over you!

ERHART: Are you going to try that again?

MRS. WILTON: Yes, just you beware! As I go down the road, I shall say over and over—from the very center of my being—I shall say: Mr. Erhart Borkman, take up your hat at once!

GUNHILD: And I suppose you think he will?

MRS. WILTON: Of course he will! He'll snatch it up instantly! And then I shall say: Put on your overcoat like a good boy, Erhart Borkman—and your galoshes—for goodness' sake don't forget your galoshes— And then follow me—be a good obedient boy—and follow me!

ERHART: Of course—you know I will—

MRS. WILTON: Follow me! Follow me!— Good night! (*She laughs and nods to the ladies and exits.*)

GUNHILD: Well!— Does she really go in for tricks of that sort?

ERHART: Of course not, Mother—she's only joking—but don't let's talk about Mrs. Wilton. (*He makes* ELLA RENTHEIM *sit down in an armchair by the stove. He stands and gazes at her for a moment*) Well—Aunt Ella—I can't believe you're here. Ought you to have taken such a long journey —and in winter too?

ELLA: I found I had to, Erhart.

ERHART: Had to?— Why, Aunt Ella?

ELLA: I had to come here to consult a specialist.

ERHART: I think that's splendid!

ELLA (*With a smile*): Do you, Erhart?

ERHART: I mean—I'm glad you made up your mind to it at last.

GUNHILD (*In a cold voice*): Are you ill, Ella?

ELLA (*Looks at her sharply*): You know perfectly well that I'm ill, Gunhild.

GUNHILD: I knew you weren't strong—and hadn't been for years—

ERHART: I was always trying to persuade you to go to a doctor—don't you remember—?

ELLA: Yes—I know—but I had no faith in any of the doctors there; besides, at that time, I didn't feel it quite as much.

ERHART: You mean—you're worse, Aunt Ella?

ELLA: Yes, dear; I'm afraid I am.

ERHART: But—it's nothing dangerous, is it?

ELLA: That depends on how you look at it.

ERHART (*Eagerly*): In that case, Aunt Ella, you mustn't think of hurrying home—

ELLA: I don't intend to, Erhart.

ERHART: You must stay here in town—where you can have the choice of the best doctors—

ELLA: Yes—that's what I thought when I left home.

ERHART: And you must find some nice comfortable rooms; in a quiet hotel, perhaps—

ELLA: I went back this morning to the one I stayed in once before—

ERHART: Well—you were quite comfortable there—

ELLA: But I've decided not to stay there after all.

ERHART: Oh?—why not?

ELLA: After coming out here, I changed my mind.

ERHART (*Surprised*): Really? Changed your mind—?

GUNHILD (*Continues to crochet; without looking up*): Your aunt will live here, in her own house, Erhart.

ERHART: Here!— Here with us?— Is this true, Aunt Ella?

ELLA: Yes; that's what I've decided.

GUNHILD (*As before*): It all belongs to your aunt, you know.

ELLA: I plan to stay out here—for a while at any rate. I'll furnish some rooms of my own. I thought perhaps, in the superintendent's wing—

ERHART: Quite right, Aunt Ella; your rooms are always kept ready for you there— (*With sudden animation*) But, Aunt Ella—aren't you awfully tired after your long journey?

ELLA: Yes; I suppose I am a little tired.

ERHART: Then I should think you'd want to go to bed early; get a good rest—

ELLA (*Looks at him with a smile*): That's what I plan to do.

ERHART (*Eagerly*): And then we can have a really good talk tomorrow—or some other day, perhaps. We can really talk things over—you, and Mother, and I. Don't you think that's a good idea, Aunt Ella?

GUNHILD (*With an outburst, rising from the sofa*): Erhart— I can tell—you're going to leave me!

ERHART (*Starts*): What do you mean by that?

GUNHILD: You're going to that party—to the Hinkels!

ERHART (*Involuntarily*): Oh, that! (*Collects himself*) Well, you wouldn't have me sit here and keep Aunt Ella up half the night. Remember—she's ill, Mother!

GUNHILD: You're going to the Hinkels!

ERHART (*Impatiently*): Good heavens, Mother! I don't really see how I can get out of it!— What do you think, Aunt Ella?

ELLA: I want you to feel quite free, Erhart.

GUNHILD (*Goes up to her menacingly*): You want to take him from me!

ELLA (*Rising*): Yes, if I only could!
   (*Music is heard from above.*)

ERHART (*Writhing as if in pain*): Oh, I can't stand all this!

(*Looking round*) What have I done with my hat? (*To* ELLA) Do you know what that music is, Aunt Ella?

ELLA: No, Erhart.

ERHART: It's the *Danse Macabre*. The Dance of Death. Don't you know the Dance of Death, Aunt Ella?

ELLA (*Smiling sadly*): Not yet, Erhart.

ERHART: Mother!—I implore you—let me go!

GUNHILD: Away from your mother— Is that what you want?

ERHART: But I'll come back again—tomorrow perhaps—

GUNHILD (*With passionate emotion*): You want to leave me —to be with a lot of strangers—with—with— No, I'll not even think of it!

ERHART: There are bright lights down there—and young, happy faces—and there's music, Mother—

GUNHILD (*Pointing upwards*): There's music here too, Erhart—

ERHART: It's just that kind of music that drives me out of the house.

ELLA: Do you grudge your father a moment's self-forgetfulness?

ERHART: No—of course not! I'm only too glad that he should have it—if only I don't have to listen to it!

GUNHILD (*Looks solemnly at him*): Be strong, Erhart! Be strong, my son! Remember—you've devoted your life to a great mission!

ERHART: Oh, Mother— Do stop talking about that! —I wasn't cut out to be a missionary! Good night, dear Aunt Ella—good night, Mother! (*He goes hastily out through the hall.*)

GUNHILD (*After a short silence*): Well, Ella—it didn't take you long to win him back.

ELLA: I wish I could believe it.

GUNHILD: But you won't be allowed to keep him long, you'll see.

ELLA: By you, you mean?

GUNHILD: Or by the other one.

ELLA: Then rather she than you.

GUNHILD (*Nodding slowly*): That I understand. I say the same. Rather she than you.

ELLA: And whatever happens to him in the end—

GUNHILD: —wouldn't greatly matter, I should say.

ELLA (*Taking her outdoor things upon her arm*): This is the first time in our lives we twin sisters have agreed— Good night, Gunhild. (*She goes out by the hall. The music sounds louder from above.*)

GUNHILD (*Stands still for a moment, starts, shrinks together, and whispers involuntarily*): The wolf is whining again— the sick wolf! (*She stands still for a moment, then flings herself down on the floor, writhing in agony and whispering*) Erhart, come back to me! I can't bear this life—I can't bear it any longer!

CURTAIN

ACT TWO

SCENE: *The great gallery on the second floor of the Rentheim house. The walls are covered with old tapestries, representing hunting scenes, all in faded colors. A folding door to the left and farther forward a piano. In the left-hand corner, at the back, a door, cut in the tapestry, and covered with tapestry, without any frame. Against the middle of the right wall, a large writing table of carved oak. There are many books and papers. Farther forward on the same side, a sofa with a table and chairs in front of it. The furniture is all of a stiff Empire style. Lighted lamps on both tables.*

JOHN GABRIEL BORKMAN *stands, his hands behind his back, beside the piano listening to* FRIDA FOLDAL, *who is playing the last bars of the* Danse Macabre.

BORKMAN *is of medium height, a well-knit, powerfully built man, well on in the sixties. His appearance is distinguished, his profile finely cut, his eyes piercing, his hair and beard curly and grayish white. He is dressed in a slightly old-fashioned black coat, and wears a white necktie.* FRIDA *is a pretty, pale girl of fifteen, with a somewhat weary and overstrained expression. She wears a light-colored dress, attractive but obviously inexpensive.*

The music ceases. A pause.

BORKMAN: Can you guess where I first heard tones like these?

FRIDA (*Looking up at him*): No, Mr. Borkman.

BORKMAN: It was down in the mines.

FRIDA (*Not understanding*): Really! Down in the mines?

BORKMAN: I'm a miner's son, you know. Or perhaps you didn't know?

FRIDA: No, Mr. Borkman.

BORKMAN: A miner's son. And sometimes my father took me down with him into the mines. The metal sings down there.

FRIDA: Really—sings?

BORKMAN: Yes, when it's loosened. The hammer strokes that loosen it—they are the midnight bells striking to set it free. That's why the metal sings, in its own way, for gladness.

FRIDA: Why does it do that, Mr. Borkman?

BORKMAN: It wants to come into the light of day, and serve mankind. (*He paces up and down the gallery, always with his hands behind his back.*)

FRIDA (*Sits waiting a little, then looks at her watch and rises*): I beg your pardon, Mr. Borkman, but I'm afraid I'll have to go now.

BORKMAN (*Stopping before her*): Must you go so soon?

FRIDA (*Putting her music in its case*): I really must. You see I have an engagement this evening.

BORKMAN: An engagement—for a party?

FRIDA: Yes.

BORKMAN: Are you to entertain the guests? Are you going to play for them?

FRIDA (*Biting her lip*): No; at least, I'm only to play dance music.

BORKMAN: Only dance music?

FRIDA: Yes, there's to be a dance after supper.

BORKMAN (*Stands and looks at her*): Do you like playing dance music? At other people's parties?

FRIDA (*Putting on her outdoor clothes*): If I'm lucky enough to get an engagement—it means I can earn a little money.

BORKMAN (*Interested*): Is that what you think of, as you sit playing for the dancers?

FRIDA: No; I usually think how hard it is that I mayn't join in the dance myself.

BORKMAN (*Nodding*): That's just what I wanted to know. (*Pacing restlessly about the room*) Yes, yes—not to be able to join in the dance one's self, that is the hardest thing of all. (*Stopping*) But there's one thing that makes up for all that, Frida.

FRIDA (*Looking questioningly at him*): What could that be, Mr. Borkman?

BORKMAN: That you have ten times more music in you than all the dancers put together.

FRIDA (*Smiling shyly*): I'm not so sure of that.

BORKMAN (*Holding up his forefinger warningly*): You must never be mad enough to doubt yourself!

FRIDA: But, if no one knows about it—

BORKMAN: As long as you know about it yourself—that's all that matters. Where is it you're to play this evening?

FRIDA: At Mr. Hinkel's.

BORKMAN (*With a swift, keen glance at her*): Hinkel's, you say!

FRIDA: Yes.

BORKMAN (*With a cutting smile*): Do people go to that man's house? Can he actually get people to visit him?

FRIDA: Yes, he has lots of visitors—at least, that's what Mrs. Wilton says—

BORKMAN (*Vehemently*): What sort of people are they? Can you tell me that?

FRIDA (*A little nervously*): I really don't know. Oh, but I do know that young Mr. Borkman will be there this evening.

BORKMAN (*Taken aback*): Erhart! My son?

FRIDA: Yes, he's to be there.

BORKMAN: How do you know that?

FRIDA: He told me so himself. An hour ago.

BORKMAN: Is he out here today?

FRIDA: Yes, he was with Mrs. Wilton all afternoon.

BORKMAN (*Inquiringly*): Did he come here, too? Do you know whether he talked to anyone—downstairs?

FRIDA: He went in to see Mrs. Borkman.

BORKMAN (*Bitterly*): I might have known it.

FRIDA: She had a lady calling on her, I think.

BORKMAN: Did she indeed! Well, I suppose people still call on Mrs. Borkman now and then.

FRIDA: Later on—if I should happen to see young Mr. Borkman—shall I tell him to come and call on you too?

BORKMAN (*Harshly*): You'll do nothing of the sort! I forbid it —do you hear? The people who want to see me can come of their own accord. I ask no one.

FRIDA: Well then, I won't say anything. Good night, Mr. Borkman.

BORKMAN (*Pacing up and down and growling*): Good night, Frida.

FRIDA: Do you mind if I run down the back stairs? It's the shortest way.

BORKMAN: Go any way you like. Good night to you.

FRIDA: Good night, Mr. Borkman. (*She goes by the little tapestry door.* BORKMAN, *lost in thought, goes up to the piano, and is about to close it, but changes his mind. Looks around the great empty room, and sets to pacing it from the corner beside the piano to the corner at the back on the*

*right. Pacing backward and forward nervously and inces-
santly. At last he goes up to the writing table, listens in the
direction of the folding door, hastily snatches up a hand
mirror, looks at himself in it, and straightens his necktie. A
knock at the folding door,* BORKMAN *hears it, looks rapidly
towards the door, but remains silent. In a little while there
comes another knock, this time, louder.)*

BORKMAN (*Standing beside the writing table with his left
hand resting upon it, and his right thrust in the breast of
his coat*): Come in. (VILHELM FOLDAL *comes softly into the
room. He is a bent and worn man with mild blue eyes
and long, thin gray hair straggling down over his coat
collar. He has a portfolio under his arm, a soft felt hat, and
large horn spectacles, which he pushes up on his forehead.*
BORKMAN *changes his attitude and looks at* FOLDAL *with a
half-disappointed, half-pleased expression*) Oh, it's only
you.

FOLDAL: Good evening; yes—it's only me, John Gabriel.

BORKMAN (*With a stern glance*): It seems to me you're
rather late.

FOLDAL: It's quite a long way you know. Especially if you
have to walk.

BORKMAN: Why do you always walk, Vilhelm? The tramway
passes your door.

FOLDAL: It's good for you to walk—and then you always save
the carfare. Well—tell me, has Frida been playing for you
lately?

BORKMAN: She just this moment left. Didn't you see her as
you came in?

FOLDAL: No, I haven't seen her for a long time. Not since she
went to live with this Mrs. Wilton.

BORKMAN (*Seating himself at his desk, motioning toward a
chair*): You may sit down, Vilhelm.

FOLDAL (*Seating himself on the edge of a chair*): Many
thanks. (*Looks mournfully at him*) You can't imagine how
lonely I feel since Frida left home.

BORKMAN: Oh, come now—you have plenty left.

FOLDAL: Yes, heaven knows I have—five of them! But Frida was the only one who seemed to understand me a little. (*Shaking his head sadly*) The others don't understand me at all.

BORKMAN (*Gloomily, gazing straight before him drumming on the table with his fingers*): That's just the point! That is the curse that we rare—we exceptional men—are forced to bear. The average man—the mediocrities that make up the common herd—they don't understand us at all, Vilhelm.

FOLDAL (*With resignation*): It's not so much the lack of understanding. With a little patience one can wait for that awhile. (*His voice choked with tears*) No, there's something much more bitter—

BORKMAN (*Vehemently*): There is nothing more bitter than that!

FOLDAL: Oh, yes there is, John Gabriel. I had a dreadful scene at home—just before coming here—

BORKMAN: What about?

FOLDAL (*With an outburst*): I'm afraid my family despise me—

BORKMAN (*Indignantly*): Despise!

FOLDAL (*Wiping his eyes*): I've suspected it for quite some time. But today it was unmistakable.

BORKMAN (*After a short pause*): I'm afraid you made a bad choice when you married.

FOLDAL: I had practically no choice in the matter. And, after all, you feel like settling down when you get on in years. And, at that time, I was so crushed—so broken in spirit—

BORKMAN (*Jumping up in anger*): Are you accusing me? Is this a reproach?

FOLDAL (*Alarmed*): No, for God's sake, John Gabriel—!

BORKMAN: Yes, you're thinking of the failure of the bank! I can see you are!

FOLDAL (*Soothingly*): But I don't blame you for that! Heaven knows I don't—

BORKMAN (*Growling, resumes his seat*) Well, that's a good thing at any rate—

FOLDAL: Besides, you mustn't think it's my wife I'm complain-
ing of. She hasn't much polish, poor thing, that's true
enough—but she's a good sort, all the same. No, it's the
children—

BORKMAN: I might have known it.

FOLDAL: After all—they've had a much better education—
and so, of course, they demand more of life.

BORKMAN (*Looking at him sympathetically*): And for that
reason they despise you, Vilhelm?

FOLDAL (*Shrugging his shoulders*): Well, I haven't made
much of a career, you see, there's no denying that.

BORKMAN (*Moving nearer to him, laying his hand on his
arm*): But surely they must know that you are a poet—
that you've written a tragedy?

FOLDAL: Yes, of course they know that. But it doesn't seem
to make much impression on them.

BORKMAN: Then they have no understanding. Your tragedy
is good—I'm firmly convinced of that.

FOLDAL (*Brightening up*): Yes, don't you think there are
some good things in it, John Gabriel? Heavens! If I could
only get it produced—(*Opens his portfolio, and begins
eagerly turning over the contents*) Look here! I want to
show you a few changes I've just made—

BORKMAN: Oh, you've brought it with you, have you?

FOLDAL: Yes, I did bring it. It's so long since I've read it to
you. I thought it might amuse you to hear an act or two—

BORKMAN (*Rising, with a negative gesture*): No, no; we'll
save that for some other time.

FOLDAL: Just as you like.

(BORKMAN *paces up and down the room.* FOLDAL *puts the
manuscript away.*)

BORKMAN (*Stopping in front of him*): You're right in what
you just said—you haven't made a career for yourself. But
I promise you this, Vilhelm; when the time is ripe; when
my power is restored to me—

FOLDAL (*Making a movement to rise*): Thank you, thank
you—

BORKMAN (*Waving his hand*): No—you may remain seated. When the time is ripe, I say—when my power is restored to me—when they realize they can no longer do without me; when they come to me here and grovel at my feet, begging me to take charge of the bank again—the new bank which they have founded but are totally incapable of managing—I shall stand here and receive them, and the whole world shall know what conditions John Gabriel Borkman imposes before he—(*Has taken position beside the writing table in the same attitude as before. Stops suddenly and stares at* FOLDAL) You look as if you doubted me. Perhaps you don't believe that they'll come—that they *must* come to me one day? Don't you believe it?

FOLDAL: Yes, God knows I do, John Gabriel.

BORKMAN (*Seating himself again on the sofa*): I firmly believe it. I'm immovably convinced—I *know* that they'll come. If I didn't believe that, I should have put a bullet through my head long ago.

FOLDAL: No! Not that, John Gabriel—!

BORKMAN: But they'll come! They'll come, I tell you! I expect them any day now—any moment. And, as you see, I'm ready to receive them.

FOLDAL (*With a sigh*): If only they'd come quickly—

BORKMAN: Yes, time passes; the years go by; life—no, I dare not think of that! Do you know what I sometimes feel like?

FOLDAL: No, John Gabriel—?

BORKMAN: I feel like a Napoleon who was shot and maimed in his first battle.

FOLDAL (*With his hand on his portfolio*): I understand that feeling.

BORKMAN: Perhaps— But on a smaller scale, of course.

FOLDAL: My little world of poetry means a great deal to me, John Gabriel.

BORKMAN: But think of me! I—who could have controlled millions! Think of the vast mining operations I had in mind —the veins of metal I would have exploited. The waterfalls! The quarries! I would have controlled trade routes and steamship lines all the wide world over! I would have accomplished all this—I, alone!

FOLDAL: I know. Nothing was too vast for you to undertake, John Gabriel.

BORKMAN: And now I'm forced to sit here like a wounded eagle, and watch these other men outstrip me in the race.

FOLDAL: That's my fate too.

BORKMAN (*Not listening*): And I was so near the goal—only think of it! If I'd only had a week to take my bearings, all the deposits would have been covered; the securities I had used so daringly would have been replaced as before; just another day or two and all my vast schemes would have succeeded; not a soul would have lost a single penny—

FOLDAL: Yes; success was almost within your grasp—

BORKMAN: And then treachery defeated me—just at the crucial moment! (*Looks at* FOLDAL) Do you know what I consider the most infamous deed a man can commit?

FOLDAL: No—tell me.

BORKMAN: It's not murder. It's not robbery or theft. It's not perjury. Men commit such crimes against people they hate; or against strangers, to whom they are indifferent.

FOLDAL: Then, what is the most infamous deed, John Gabriel?

BORKMAN: The most infamous deed a man can commit is to betray his friend's confidence.

FOLDAL (*Thoughtfully*): Yes; but, after all—

BORKMAN (*Violently*): I know what you're about to say—but that's all nonsense! None of the securities would have been lost—how often do I have to tell you that! They would all have been returned to their respective owners. No, I say —the most infamous deed a man can commit is to misuse his friend's letters—to expose to all the world what had been confided to him in the closest secrecy—like a whisper in an empty, dark, securely locked room. The man who is

capable of such an act is an archscoundrel; a creature
thoroughly depraved in mind and spirit. I had such a
friend— And it was he who caused my ruin.

FOLDAL: I can guess who you mean, John Gabriel.

BORKMAN: I had confided all my plans to him, down to the
smallest detail. And, then—just at the crucial moment—
he turned against me the weapons I myself had placed in
his hands.

FOLDAL: I never could understand, why he—of course there
were many rumors at the time.

BORKMAN: What sort of rumors? Tell me. I know nothing. I
had to go straight into—isolation. What were the rumors,
Vilhelm?

FOLDAL: You were to have been minister of finance, they
said.

BORKMAN: They offered me the post, but I refused it.

FOLDAL: Then, you didn't stand in his way in that respect?

BORKMAN: No—that was not why he betrayed me.

FOLDAL: In that case, I can't imagine—

BORKMAN: I may as well tell you, Vilhelm.

FOLDAL: Well?

BORKMAN: It had to do with a woman.

FOLDAL: A woman? But John Gabriel, surely—?

BORKMAN (*Interrupting*): Don't let's discuss it any further.
As things turned out, neither of us became minister of
finance. Neither he nor I.

FOLDAL: But he rose to great power.

BORKMAN: And I was hurled to my destruction.

FOLDAL: What a terrible tragedy, John Gabriel!

BORKMAN (*Nodding to him*): Almost as terrible as yours,
now I come to think of it.

FOLDAL (*Simply*): Yes; at least as terrible.

BORKMAN (*Laughing quietly*): But, if you look at it from
another point of view, it's really quite a comedy as well.

FOLDAL: A comedy—?

BORKMAN: Yes, it has its comic aspects. Just listen to this—

FOLDAL: Well?

BORKMAN: You didn't meet Frida just now, when you came in?

FOLDAL: No.

BORKMAN: While we sit here talking, she is down there playing dance music for the man who betrayed and ruined me.

FOLDAL: I knew nothing about that—

BORKMAN: Yes; she took her music and went straight from here to the great man's house!

FOLDAL (*Apologetically*): Well—naturally the poor child doesn't—

BORKMAN: But you'll never guess who's listening to her music, down there with all the others.

FOLDAL: Who?

BORKMAN: My son.

FOLDAL: What!

BORKMAN: What do you think of that, Vilhelm! My son is dancing down there this evening. Wasn't I right in calling it a comedy?

FOLDAL: Then, of course, he knows nothing of the circumstances.

BORKMAN: What doesn't he know?

FOLDAL: He surely can't know how he—how that man—

BORKMAN: Don't be afraid of the name. I can quite well bear it now.

FOLDAL: I'm certain that your son knows nothing of the circumstances, John Gabriel.

BORKMAN (*Gloomily, sitting and striking the table*): He knows, as surely as I'm sitting here.

FOLDAL: Then how could he bring himself to set foot inside that house!

BORKMAN (*Shaking his head*): My son doesn't see things with my eyes. I'd take my oath he's on my enemies' side. He thinks, as they do, that Hinkel only did his confounded duty when he betrayed me.

FOLDAL: Who could have made him see things in that light?

BORKMAN: Who? Have you forgotten who brought him up?

First his aunt—from the time he was six or seven years
old—and in recent years—his mother!

FOLDAL: I believe you're doing them an injustice.

BORKMAN (*Flaring up*): I never do anyone an injustice! Both
of them have poisoned his mind against me!

FOLDAL (*Soothingly*): Well, well—perhaps they have.

BORKMAN (*Indignantly*): Oh, these women! They ruin and
corrupt our lives! Prevent us from fulfilling our triumphant destiny!

FOLDAL: Not all of them, John Gabriel.

BORKMAN: Indeed? Can you name one that's good for anything?

FOLDAL: That's the trouble—the few I know are good for
nothing.

BORKMAN (*With a snort of scorn*): Then what's the use of it?
What's the use of such women existing—if you never know
them?

FOLDAL (*Warmly*): It is of some use, John Gabriel. It's com-
forting and reassuring to think that somewhere in the
world, far away, the true woman exists after all.

BORKMAN (*Moving impatiently on the sofa*): Do spare me
that poetical nonsense!

FOLDAL (*Looks at him, deeply wounded*): You call my most
sacred belief poetical nonsense?

BORKMAN (*Harshly*): Yes, I do! That's the kind of thing that's
always prevented you from getting on in the world. Get
rid of all those silly notions and I might still be able to help
you—help put you on your feet again.

FOLDAL (*Boiling inwardly*): You'll never be able to do that—

BORKMAN: Why not? Once I regain my power—

FOLDAL: That's a remote prospect, I'm afraid.

BORKMAN (*Vehemently*): What do you mean? Perhaps you
think that time will never come? Answer me!

FOLDAL: I don't know what to answer.

BORKMAN (*Rising, cold and dignified, and waving his hand
toward the door*): Then I no longer have any use for you.

FOLDAL (*Starting up*): No use—!

BORKMAN: Since you don't believe that the tide will turn for me—

FOLDAL: How can I believe it in the face of all reason! You'd have to be cleared of guilt—

BORKMAN: Go on! Go on!

FOLDAL: I may not be a lawyer, but I've read enough to know—

BORKMAN (*Quickly*): That it's impossible, you mean?

FOLDAL: There's no precedent for such a thing.

BORKMAN: Exceptional men are above precedent.

FOLDAL: The law makes no such distinction.

BORKMAN (*Harshly and decisively*): You are no poet, Vilhelm.

FOLDAL (*Unconsciously folding his hands*): You really mean that—seriously?

BORKMAN (*Dismissing the subject, without answering*): We're only wasting each other's time. You'd better not come here again.

FOLDAL: You want me to leave you, then?

BORKMAN (*Without looking at him*): I no longer have any use for you.

FOLDAL (*Softly, taking his portfolio*): No; I dare say not.

BORKMAN: You've been lying to me all these years.

FOLDAL (*Shaking his head*): Never lying, John Gabriel.

BORKMAN: Yes, lying! Haven't you filled me with hope and trust and confidence?

FOLDAL: But it wasn't a lie so long as you believed in my poetry. So long as you believed in me, I believed in you.

BORKMAN: So we've just been deceiving each other; and perhaps deceiving ourselves, both of us.

FOLDAL: But isn't that the essence of friendship, John Gabriel?

BORKMAN (*Smiling bitterly*): Yes, you're right there! Friendship means—deception. I've learned that once before.

FOLDAL (*Looking at him*): I have no poetic talent. You could actually tell me that so brutally—

BORKMAN (*In a gentler tone*): I don't pretend to know much about these things—

FOLDAL: Perhaps you know more than you're aware of. For I have had doubts myself, you see. The terrible doubt that I may have wasted my life, pursuing a dream—

BORKMAN: If you doubt yourself, you can never succeed.

FOLDAL: That's why it was such a comfort to come here and talk to you, John Gabriel, because you believed. Now you have become a stranger to me.

BORKMAN: And you to me.

FOLDAL: Good night, John Gabriel.

BORKMAN: Good night, Vilhelm. (FOLDAL *goes out to the left;* BORKMAN *stands for a moment gazing at the closed door. He makes a movement as though to call* FOLDAL *back, but changes his mind, and begins to pace the floor with his hands behind his back. Then he stops at the console table, puts out the lamp. The room becomes half dark. After a short pause, there comes a knock at the tapestry door.*)

BORKMAN (*At the table, starts, turns, and asks in a loud voice*): Who is that knocking? (*No answer; another knock*) Who is it? Come in! (ELLA RENTHEIM, *with a lighted candle in her hand, appears in the doorway. She wears her black dress, as before, with her cloak thrown loosely over her shoulders.* BORKMAN *stares at her*) Who are you? What do you want of me?

ELLA (*Closes the door and advances*): It is I, Borkman. (*She puts down the candle on the piano and remains standing beside it.*)

BORKMAN (*Stands as though thunderstruck, stares fixedly at her and says in a half whisper*): Is it—is it Ella? Ella Rentheim?

ELLA: Yes. It's "your Ella," as you used to call me once; in the old days—many years ago.

BORKMAN (*As before*): Yes, it is you, Ella—I see that now.

ELLA: Can you recognize me?

BORKMAN: I'm beginning to—

ELLA: The years have been hard on me. Don't you think so, Borkman?

BORKMAN (*In a strained voice*): You are a good deal changed —just at first glance—

ELLA: I no longer have my dark curls, Borkman. Those curls you loved to twine around your fingers.

BORKMAN (*Rapidly*): That's true—you're wearing your hair differently.

ELLA (*With a sad smile*): Yes—it's the way I do my hair that makes the difference.

BORKMAN (*Changing the subject*): I knew nothing about your being here.

ELLA: I've only just arrived.

BORKMAN: What made you undertake this journey now—in midwinter?

ELLA: I'll tell you all about it.

BORKMAN: Did you come to see me?

ELLA: You—as well as others. But I shall have to go back over the years if I'm to tell you the real reason for my visit.

BORKMAN: You must be tired.

ELLA: Yes, I am tired.

BORKMAN: Won't you sit down? There—on the sofa—

ELLA: Thank you. It'll be good to sit down a bit. (*Pause. She crosses to the right and seats herself in the extreme forward corner of the sofa.* BORKMAN *stands beside the table with his hands behind his back looking at her. Short silence*) It seems like an eternity since we saw each other last, Borkman.

BORKMAN (*Gloomily*): It is a long, long time ago. Terrible things have come to pass since then.

ELLA: A whole lifetime has passed. A wasted lifetime.

BORKMAN (*Looking keenly at her*): Wasted!

ELLA: Yes, wasted. For both of us.

BORKMAN (*In a cold tone*): I don't consider my life wasted yet.

ELLA: What about mine?

BORKMAN: You've only yourself to blame, Ella.

ELLA (*With a start*): You dare say that!

BORKMAN: You could have been perfectly happy without me.

ELLA: You think so?

BORKMAN: If you'd only made up your mind to it.

ELLA (*Bitterly*): There was someone else only too anxious to marry me, that's true enough—

BORKMAN: But you refused him.

ELLA: Yes, I did.

BORKMAN: Time after time you refused him. Year after year—

ELLA (*Scornfully*): Year after year I refused happiness—I suppose you think?

BORKMAN: You could quite well have been happy with him. And then I would have been saved.

ELLA: You—?

BORKMAN: You could have saved me, Ella.

ELLA: How do you mean?

BORKMAN: He thought I was responsible for your obstinacy— your perpetual refusals. And he took his revenge. It was easy enough for him; he had all those letters of mine—in which I confided in him—trusted him; and he made good use of them. And that was the end of me—for the time being, at any rate. You're to blame for all that, Ella.

ELLA: I see, Borkman. So, according to you, it's I who am the guilty one.

BORKMAN: It depends on how you look at it. I know I have much to thank you for. You bought up this house and property at the auction, and placed it entirely at my disposal—and your sister's. You took charge of Erhart and cared for him in every way—

ELLA: As long as I was allowed to—

BORKMAN: By your sister, you mean. I've never concerned myself with these domestic details. As I was saying—I know all the sacrifices you have made for me and for your sister. But you were in a position to do so, Ella, and you mustn't forget that it was I who placed you in that position.

ELLA (*Indignantly*): It's very wrong of you to say that, Borkman! It was my devotion to Erhart—and to you—that made me do it!

BORKMAN (*Interrupting*): My dear Ella, I don't choose to discuss matters of sentiment. I only mean that if you acted generously, it was I who gave you the power to do so.

ELLA (*Smiling*): Power—power!

BORKMAN (*Vehemently*): Yes, the power! At the height of the battle, at the decisive moment, when I couldn't afford to spare either relative or friend—when I was forced to take—when I *did* take—the millions that were entrusted to me, I spared everything that was yours. I left your fortune intact—though I could have taken it and used it as I did all the rest.

ELLA (*Coldly and quietly*): That is quite true, Borkman.

BORKMAN: Yes, it is. And that's why, when they came and took me, they found all your securities untouched in the safe at the bank.

ELLA (*Looking at him*): I've often thought about it—what really made you spare all my property? That, and that alone? Why did you do it?

BORKMAN: Why?

ELLA: Yes, why? Tell me.

BORKMAN (*Harshly and scornfully*): Perhaps you think I wanted to have something to fall back on, if things went wrong?

ELLA: Oh, no—I'm sure you never would have thought of that!

BORKMAN: Never! I was so absolutely certain of victory.

ELLA: But then why—?

BORKMAN (*Shrugging his shoulders*): Good heavens, Ella, it's not so easy to remember one's motives of twenty years ago. I only remember pondering silently and alone on all the vast projects I had in mind. I used to feel like an explorer about to start out on a balloon voyage. Night after sleepless night I spent inflating my giant balloon, preparing to soar over the perilous uncharted oceans of the world.

ELLA (*Smiling*): You, who never had the slightest doubt of victory?

BORKMAN (*Impatiently*): Men are like that, Ella. They both doubt and believe at the same time. (*Gazing before him*) I suppose that was why I didn't want to take you and yours with me in the balloon.

ELLA (*Eagerly*): But why—I ask you? Tell me why?

BORKMAN (*Without looking at her*): You hesitate to take what you hold dearest in the world on such a risky voyage.

ELLA: But you *were* risking what you held dearest in the world—your whole future life—

BORKMAN: Life is not always what one holds dearest.

ELLA (*Breathlessly*): Was that how you felt at that time?

BORKMAN: Yes, I believe I did.

ELLA: You mean to say that I was the dearest thing in the world to you?

BORKMAN: Yes, I believe you were—now that I look back on it.

ELLA: And yet many years had passed, since you deserted me, and married—married another!

BORKMAN: I deserted you, you say? You must realize quite well that higher motives—well then, other motives—compelled me to do it. Without his support, I could have achieved nothing.

ELLA (*Controlling herself*): So you deserted me—for higher motives.

BORKMAN: I couldn't do without his help—and he made you the price.

ELLA: And you paid the price—paid it in full—without the slightest protest.

BORKMAN: I had no choice. I had to conquer or fall.

ELLA (*In a trembling voice, looking at him*): Can this be true? At that time I was the dearest thing in the world to you?

BORKMAN: Yes, both at that time and long afterwards—long, long afterwards—

ELLA: And yet you drove a bargain for me. You drove a bargain for my love. To gain control over the bank, you sold me to another man!

BORKMAN (*Gloomily and bowed down*): I was driven by inexorable necessity, Ella.

ELLA (*Rises from the sofa, quivering with passion*): Criminal!

BORKMAN (*Starts, but controls himself*): I've heard that word before.

ELLA: Don't think for a moment I'm referring to anything you may have done against the law! What did it matter to me what use you made of all those papers—those securities—or whatever you want to call them! If I'd only been allowed to be beside you—close to you—when the storm broke over you—

BORKMAN (*Eagerly*): What then, Ella?

ELLA: Believe me, I would have borne the ruin, the shame, the disgrace with you so gladly. I would have helped you to bear it, Borkman—

BORKMAN: Would you have had the strength—the courage?

ELLA: Indeed I would! For at that time, you see, I knew nothing of your great, your dreadful crime—

BORKMAN: What are you talking about? What crime?

ELLA: A crime for which there can be no forgiveness.

BORKMAN (*Staring at her*): You're out of your mind, Ella.

ELLA (*Approaching him*): You're a murderer! You are guilty of the one mortal sin!

BORKMAN (*Falling back toward the piano*): You're beside yourself!

ELLA: You've killed love in me. Robbed my whole life of tenderness. (*Still nearer him*) I don't suppose you realize what that means! In the Bible they speak of a mysterious sin for which there can be no forgiveness. I never understood what it could be. I know it now. The great unpardonable sin is to murder love in a human soul.

BORKMAN: And I've done that, you say?

ELLA: You have done that! I never knew until this moment what really happened to me. When you deserted me and turned to Gunhild instead—I took that for common fickleness on your part—and heartless scheming on hers. I think I even despised you a little—in spite of everything. But I see things clearly now: *I* was the woman you loved, and you deserted me! You were ready to sacrifice the one you held dearest in the world for money and for power. You have been twice guilty of murder. You've not only killed my soul—you've killed your own as well!

BORKMAN (*With cold self-control*): I see you're just as violent and passionate as ever, Ella. I suppose it's only natural you should see things in that light. After all you are a woman, and to you these are the only things that matter.

ELLA: Yes—indeed they are!

BORKMAN: Things that affect your feelings and emotions.

ELLA: Yes! To me these are the only things that count!

BORKMAN: But I am a man; I see things differently. It's true that as a woman I held you dearest in the world. But if the worst comes to the worst—one woman can always take the place of another.

ELLA (*With a smile*): Was that your experience when you married Gunhild?

BORKMAN: No, but my vast plans for the future helped me to bear that, too. I dreamt of exploiting all the sources of power throughout the country. I wanted to become master of all the wealth that lay hidden in the earth, in the mountains, the forests and the sea; so that, through me, it might benefit the lives of countless thousands.

ELLA (*Lost in recollection*): I know. We spent many an evening talking about your plans—

BORKMAN: Yes, Ella; I could talk to you.

ELLA: I sometimes used to tease you—do you remember? I asked if you wanted to awaken all the sleeping spirits of the earth.

BORKMAN (*Slowly*): All the sleeping spirits of the earth. (*Nodding*) I remember that expression.

ELLA: You always took me seriously. You used to answer: "Yes, Ella! That is precisely what I want to do."

BORKMAN: And so it was. But I had to get my foot into the stirrup—and only that one man could help me to do that. He was willing to give me control over the bank, on one condition—

ELLA: That you agree to give up the woman you loved, and who loved you so deeply in return.

BORKMAN: I knew of his consuming passion for you—I knew that on no other condition would he—

ELLA: And so you struck the bargain.

BORKMAN (*Vehemently*): Yes, Ella—I struck the bargain. I had to. My desire for power was uncontrollable, you see! He helped me halfway towards my goal. Each year I climbed higher; year after year—higher and higher—

ELLA: And I was as though wiped out of your life.

BORKMAN: Yet, in spite of that, he destroyed me, Ella. All on account of you.

ELLA (*After a short, thoughtful silence*): It's almost as though there had been some sort of curse on our relationship. Has that ever occurred to you, Borkman?

BORKMAN (*Looking at her*): A curse?

ELLA: Yes. Doesn't it seem so?

BORKMAN (*Uneasily*): Perhaps. But why? (*With an outburst*) Oh, Ella, I no longer know which of us is right—you or I!

ELLA: You were the guilty one. You killed all joy in me.

BORKMAN (*Anxiously*): Don't say that, Ella.

ELLA: All a woman's joy, at any rate. I've lived as though under an eclipse ever since you went out of my life. As time passed it became harder and harder for me—and at last utterly impossible—to love any living thing. Neither people, nor animals, nor plants. There was just one—

BORKMAN: Whom do you mean?

ELLA: Erhart, of course.

BORKMAN: Erhart—?

ELLA: Erhart—your son, Borkman.

BORKMAN: Was he really so close to your heart?

ELLA: Why else do you suppose I took him with me? And kept him near me all those years?

BORKMAN: I thought it was out of pity—like all the rest.

ELLA (*With strong inward emotion*): Pity, you say! Ha! I haven't known pity since you deserted me. I was incapable of feeling it. Whenever a poor starving child came to my door, begging for food and shelter—I turned it over to the servants. I had no desire to look after it myself, to warm it at my own fireside, to set food before it and watch it eat its fill. Yet I was not meant to be like that. You cast a blight over my life, Borkman. My heart grew cold and barren.

BORKMAN: Except towards Erhart.

ELLA: Yes, except towards your son. I could feel no tenderness for any other living thing. You cheated me of a mother's joy and happiness in life. And—what was worse, perhaps—of a mother's sorrow and tears as well.

BORKMAN: You mustn't say that, Ella—

ELLA: Who knows? Perhaps a mother's sorrow and tears were what I needed most. But at that time the loss of all this seemed to me unbearable. That's why I took Erhart with me. I had completely won his heart; and then—!

BORKMAN: What, Ella?

ELLA: And then his mother—his mother in the flesh, I mean —took him away from me again.

BORKMAN: But eventually he would have been obliged to leave you—

ELLA (*Wringing her hands*): I can't endure the loss of your son's heart, Borkman. The emptiness—the loneliness!

BORKMAN (*An evil expression in his eyes*): You're mistaken, Ella, I assure you! Hearts are not easily lost to a certain person in the room below.

ELLA: She's won him back again. I've lost him to her. Or, if not to her—to someone else. The letters he occasionally writes me have made that very clear to me.

BORKMAN: So you've come to take him home with you?

ELLA: If it were only possible——!

BORKMAN: It's possible enough, if you've set your heart on it. After all, you have the strongest claim on him.

ELLA: Claim! What's the good of having claims! If he doesn't belong to me of his own free will, he doesn't belong to me at all! But I must have him with me now——I need him! I need his undivided love!

BORKMAN: Remember Erhart is already in his twenties. You could hardly expect to keep his "undivided love" for very long.

ELLA (*With a melancholy smile*): It wouldn't have to be for very long.

BORKMAN: Indeed? I should have thought anything you wanted, you'd want for life.

ELLA: That's true. That's why I say it needn't be for very long.

BORKMAN (*Taken aback*): What do you mean by that?

ELLA: You know, of course, that I've been ill for many years?

BORKMAN: Have you been ill?

ELLA: Yes. Didn't you know that?

BORKMAN: No; not really——

ELLA (*Looking at him in surprise*): Hasn't Erhart told you?

BORKMAN: I really can't remember——at the moment——

ELLA: Perhaps he never even mentioned me.

BORKMAN: Oh, yes——I'm sure he must have mentioned you. The fact is, I very seldom see him——scarcely ever. There's someone downstairs who keeps him away from me. Keeps him away, you understand.

ELLA: You're sure of that?

BORKMAN: Quite sure. (*Changing his tone*) So you've been ill, Ella?

ELLA: Yes, I have. This autumn it grew so much worse——I decided to come here to consult a specialist.

BORKMAN: Has he given his opinion?

ELLA: Yes, this morning.

BORKMAN: What did he say?

ELLA: He told me what I've long suspected——

BORKMAN: Well—?

ELLA (*Calmly and quietly*): He says my illness is incurable.

BORKMAN: No—surely not!

ELLA: Yes—quite incurable. The doctors can do nothing for it—they must just let it take its course. They can ease the pain a little—that's always something.

BORKMAN: But it's sure to take a long time, Ella—

ELLA: I may, perhaps, live through the winter.

BORKMAN (*Without thinking*): The winter here is long.

ELLA: It will be long enough for me, at any rate.

BORKMAN (*Eagerly, changing the subject*): But what could have caused this illness? You, who have lived such a normal well-regulated life—? What could have caused it?

ELLA (*Looking at him*): The doctors thought that perhaps at some time in my life—I'd had to go through some great stress of emotion—

BORKMAN (*Firing up*): Emotion! You mean that I'm to blame!

ELLA (*With increasing inward agitation*): It's too late to go into that. But I've only a short time to live. I must have my boy close to me again before I go. It's hard to leave this life—and vanish into darkness—knowing that not a soul here will remember me. That no one will mourn for me, or think of me with tenderness—as a son thinks of the mother he has lost.

BORKMAN (*After a short pause*): Take him, Ella, if you can win him back.

ELLA (*With animation*): Do you give your consent? Can you?

BORKMAN (*Gloomily*): Yes. And it's no great sacrifice—since he's not mine to give.

ELLA: All the same—thank you for the sacrifice! Now, there's something else I want to ask of you, Borkman; it means a great deal to me.

BORKMAN: What is it? Tell me.

ELLA: I don't suppose you'll understand; you'll think it childish of me.

BORKMAN: What is it, Ella?

ELLA: I'll leave a good deal of money, as you know—

BORKMAN: Yes, I dare say.

ELLA: I intend to leave it all to Erhart.

BORKMAN: Well—you've no one closer to you.

ELLA: No. There's no one closer to me.

BORKMAN: No one of your own family, I mean. You are the last.

ELLA (*Nodding slowly*): Yes, that's just the point. When I die, the name of Rentheim will die with me. That's such a bitter thought. To be wiped out of existence, even to one's very name—

BORKMAN (*Firing up*): Ah—I see now what you're driving at!

ELLA: Don't let that happen to me, Borkman! Let Erhart bear my name after me!

BORKMAN (*Looking harshly at her*): I understand. You want to spare my son from bearing his father's name. Is that it?

ELLA: No—never that! I myself would have borne it with such pride, such happiness! But—when a mother is at the point of death— You may not think it or believe it, Borkman—but a name can be a powerful bond—

BORKMAN (*Coldly and proudly*): Very well, Ella. I am man enough to bear my own name alone.

ELLA (*Seizing and pressing his hand*): Thank you—thank you, Borkman! You've made up to me for all the past! For when I die Erhart Rentheim will live on after me!

(*The tapestry door is thrown open.* MRS. BORKMAN, *with the large shawl over her head, stands in the doorway.*)

GUNHILD (*Violently agitated*): Erhart shall never bear that name!

ELLA (*Shrinking back*): Gunhild!

BORKMAN (*Harshly and threateningly*): I allow no one to come up here!

GUNHILD (*Advancing a step*): I ask no one's permission—

BORKMAN (*Going toward her*): What do you want of me?

GUNHILD: I shall fight for you—protect you from the powers of evil.

ELLA: The worst powers of evil are in yourself, Gunhild.

GUNHILD (*Harshly*): That may be. (*Menacingly*) But let me tell you this—he shall bear his father's name—and restore it to its former honor. And I will be his mother—I alone! My son's heart shall be mine. Mine and no other's. (*She goes out by the tapestry door and shuts it behind her.*)

ELLA (*Shaken*): Borkman, Erhart's whole life will be wrecked by this. You must come to an understanding with Gunhild. We must go down to her at once.

BORKMAN (*Looks at her*): We? I too, you mean?

ELLA: Yes—both of us.

BORKMAN (*Shaking his head*): She is hard, Ella. Hard as the metal I once dreamed of hewing out of the rocks.

ELLA: Try it, Borkman! Try it now!

CURTAIN

ACT THREE

SCENE: MRS. BORKMAN'S *drawing room. The lamp is still burning on the table beside the sofa. The conservatory at the back is quite dark.* MRS. BORKMAN, *with the shawl still over her head, enters, in violent agitation, by the hall door, goes up to the window, draws the curtain a little aside, and looks out; then she seats herself beside the stove, but immediately springs up again, goes to the bell cord and rings. Stands beside the sofa and waits a moment. No one comes. Then she rings again, this time more violently.* THE MAID *presently en-*

*ters from the hall. She looks sleepy and out of temper, and
appears to have dressed in great haste.*

GUNHILD (*Impatiently*): Where have you been, Malene? I
rang twice!

MALENE: Yes, Ma'am, I heard you.

GUNHILD: Then why didn't you come?

MALENE (*Sulkily*): I had to put some clothes on first I suppose!

GUNHILD: Yes, dress yourself properly. And go and fetch my
son at once.

MALENE (*Looking at her in astonishment*): Fetch Mr. Erhart?

GUNHILD: Yes, tell him to come home at once, I want to speak
to him.

MALENE (*Grumbling*): Then I'll have to go over to the superintendent, and wake the coachman.

GUNHILD: Why should you do that?

MALENE: He'll have to harness the sleigh—there's a lot of
snow tonight.

GUNHILD: Good heavens—it's only just around the corner.

MALENE: Why, Ma'am, you can't call that just around the
corner.

GUNHILD: Of course it is. You know where Mr. Hinkel lives.

MALENE (*Maliciously*): Oh, so young Mr. Borkman's there
this evening is he?

GUNHILD (*Taken aback*): Where else should he be, may I
ask?

MALENE (*With a slight smile*): I only thought he might be
where he usually is.

GUNHILD: Where do you mean?

MALENE: At that Mrs. Wilton's—as she calls herself.

GUNHILD: Mrs. Wilton? My son's not often there—

MALENE (*Half muttering*): Every day of his life—I've heard
it said.

GUNHILD: Nonsense, Malene! Go to Mr. Hinkel's and get
hold of him at once.

MALENE (*With a toss of her head*): Very well, Ma'am, I'm going.

(*She is on the point of going out by the hall, but just at that moment the hall door is opened, and* ELLA *and* BORK-MAN *appear on the threshold.*)

GUNHILD (*Draws back a step*): What does this mean?

MALENE (*Terrified, instinctively folding her hands*): Lord save us!

GUNHILD (*Whispers to* THE MAID): Tell him he must come at once!

MALENE (*Softly*): Yes, Ma'am.

(ELLA *and, after her,* BORKMAN *enter the room.* THE MAID *sidles past them to the door, goes out, and closes it after her. A short silence.* MRS. BORKMAN, *having recovered her self-control, turns to* ELLA.)

GUNHILD: What does he want, here in my room?

ELLA: He wants to come to an understanding with you, Gunhild.

GUNHILD: He's never attempted that before.

ELLA: He wants to now.

GUNHILD: The last time we saw each other, was in court, when I was summoned to give an account—

BORKMAN (*Coming nearer*): I intend to give my own account tonight.

GUNHILD (*Staring at him*): You!

BORKMAN: Not of my actions; they were proclaimed before the world—

GUNHILD (*Sighing bitterly*): That's true enough!

BORKMAN: But no one understood my motives. No one saw that I acted as I did because I was obliged to; because I was myself—I was John Gabriel Borkman—myself, and not another. That's what I shall attempt to explain to you tonight.

GUNHILD (*Shaking her head*): It's of no use. Explanations and excuses acquit no one.

BORKMAN: They may acquit one in one's own eyes.

GUNHILD (*With a gesture of repulsion*): Spare me all this!

I've had plenty of time to think over your criminal behavior.

BORKMAN: During those five endless years in prison—I had time to think about it too. And during those eight years up there in my study I had still more time to think. I've retried the whole case by myself—time after time I've retried it. I've been my own accuser, my own defender and my own judge. I venture to say I've been more impartial than anyone else could be. For hours on end I've paced the floor up there, turning over in my mind every one of my actions. I've analyzed them from every angle, as impartially, as pitilessly as any lawyer could. And each time I arrived at the same verdict. The only crime I committed was against myself.

GUNHILD: What of me? What of your son?

BORKMAN: I include you both, when I speak about myself.

GUNHILD: What of the hundreds of others you're said to have ruined?

BORKMAN (*More vehemently*): I felt the power within me. I was driven by an inexorable force. The potential riches imprisoned in the earth cried out to me. They called on me to free them! No one else paid any heed to them. I alone heard their cry.

GUNHILD: And you disgraced the name of Borkman!

BORKMAN: If the others had had the power, don't you suppose they would have behaved exactly as I did?

GUNHILD: No! No one but you would have done it!

BORKMAN: Perhaps not. But only because they didn't have my vision. And, had they tried to do it, they wouldn't have had my aims in mind. Their motives would have been quite different. In short—I've acquitted myself.

ELLA (*Gently and appealingly*): You dare say that so positively, Borkman?

BORKMAN (*Nodding*): Acquitted myself—at least on that score. But there's something else for which I accuse myself most bitterly.

GUNHILD: And what is that?

BORKMAN: I wasted eight long invaluable years up there. The very day I was set free I should have made up my mind to face reality—to face the cold hard facts. I should have started over again, in spite of everything—and worked my way up to even greater heights.

GUNHILD: You would have done the same thing all over again—believe me.

BORKMAN (*Shakes his head and looks at her with a sententious air*): Nothing new ever happens, that's true enough. But what has happened is never exactly repeated either. It's all in the point of view. An old action may be transformed when seen from a new angle. But you don't understand that, of course.

GUNHILD (*Curtly*): I don't understand it—no.

BORKMAN: That's the curse I've had to bear—I've never found a single soul to understand me.

ELLA (*Looking at him*): Never, Borkman?

BORKMAN: Just one, perhaps. Long, long ago, when I didn't think I needed understanding. Since then no one has understood me. There's been no one aware enough, alert enough to spur me on—inspire me to renew my efforts— convince me that I'd done nothing irreparable.

GUNHILD (*With a scornful laugh*): So, after all, you need to be convinced of that?

BORKMAN (*With increasing indignation*): When the whole world proclaims that I'm a beaten man—there are moments when I come close to believing it. (*Raising his head*) But, sooner or later, my unconquerable faith rises up in me. And that acquits me!

GUNHILD (*Looking harshly at him*): Why have you never come and asked me for what you call understanding?

BORKMAN: What good would it have been to come to you?

GUNHILD (*With a gesture of repulsion*): You've never loved anything but yourself—that's the crux of the whole matter.

BORKMAN (*Proudly*): I have loved power—

GUNHILD: Power, yes!

BORKMAN: The power to create happiness; to enrich the lives of thousands.

GUNHILD: You once had the power to make me happy. Have you never thought of that?

BORKMAN (*Without looking at her*): Someone usually goes down in a shipwreck—

GUNHILD: What about your son? Have you used your power, have you lived and worked, to make him happy?

BORKMAN: I don't know him.

GUNHILD: That's true. You don't even know him!

BORKMAN (*Harshly*): You, his mother, have taken care of that!

GUNHILD (*Looking at him with a lofty air*): There are other things I've taken care of.

BORKMAN: You?

GUNHILD: Yes; I alone!

BORKMAN: What, for instance?

GUNHILD: Your memory.

BORKMAN (*With a short, dry laugh*): My memory! That sounds as if I were already dead and buried.

GUNHILD (*Emphatically*): And so you are.

BORKMAN (*Slowly*): Perhaps you're right! But no! No! Not yet! I've been close to death—but now I have awakened. I am myself again. I still have many years before me. A new and radiant life awaits me. I can see it—and you shall see it too.

GUNHILD (*Raising her hand*): Never dream of life again. Stay buried in your grave!

ELLA (*Shocked*): Gunhild! Gunhild! How can you!

GUNHILD (*Not listening to her*): I shall raise a monument over your tomb.

BORKMAN: A monument to my shame, I suppose you mean—?

GUNHILD: It will be no monument of metal or stone; and it will bear no scornful epitaph. I shall see that your grave is hidden away behind a thick hedge of trees and bushes.

All memory of John Gabriel Borkman will be wiped out forever.

BORKMAN (*Hoarsely and cuttingly*): And you will perform this labor of love?

GUNHILD: I could never hope to accomplish it alone. But I have someone near me who has dedicated his life to this. His own life shall be so pure and bright, that all your burrowing in the dark will be as though it had never been.

BORKMAN (*Darkly and threateningly*): If you mean Erhart, why not say so!

GUNHILD (*Looking him straight in the eyes*): Yes, I do mean Erhart—my son! He whom you're so willing to renounce— in atonement for your own acts.

BORKMAN (*With a look toward* ELLA): In atonement for my greatest sin.

GUNHILD (*Repelling the idea*): A sin towards a stranger— What about your sin towards me? (*Looking triumphantly at both*) But he won't listen to you! When I call out to him for help he'll come to me! For he wants to be with me! I'm the one he needs! (*Suddenly listens and cries*) There he is! I hear him!— Erhart!

(ERHART *hastily opens the hall door and enters the room. He is wearing an overcoat and has his hat on. Pale and anxious.*)

ERHART: Mother! What in heaven's name—! (*Seeing* BORKMAN, *who is standing beside the door leading into the conservatory, he starts and takes off his hat. After a moment's silence he asks*) What is it, Mother? What's the matter?

GUNHILD (*Stretching out her arms toward him*): I had to see you, Erhart; I want you near me—always!

ERHART (*Stammering*): Near you—always? What do you mean by that?

GUNHILD: I want you—need you, Erhart. There's someone who wants to take you from me.

ERHART (*Recoiling a step*): Ah—so you know about it!

GUNHILD: You know about it too?

ERHART (*Surprised, looking at her*): Of course I know—
but—

GUNHILD: So it was all planned—behind my back! Oh, Erhart! Erhart!

ERHART (*Quickly*): Mother—tell me what it is you know!

GUNHILD: I know that your aunt has come here to take you
from me.

ELLA: First listen to me, Erhart!

GUNHILD (*Continuing*): She wants me to give you up to her.
She wants to take your mother's place; she wants you to
be her son, not mine. She wants to leave everything to
you—but you're to give up your own name and take hers
instead!

ERHART: Aunt Ella, is this true?

ELLA: Yes, Erhart.

ERHART: I knew nothing of all this. Why do you want me
back with you again?

ELLA: Because I feel I've lost you here.

GUNHILD (*Harshly*): Lost him to me—yes! That's only natural.

ELLA (*Looks beseechingly at him*): I can't afford to lose you,
Erhart. I'm a lonely, dying woman.

ERHART: Dying—?

ELLA: Yes—dying. Be like a son to me! Stay with me to the
end!

GUNHILD (*Interrupting*): And betray your mother? And your
purpose in life as well? Do you want to do that, Erhart?

ELLA: Answer me, Erhart. I haven't long to live.

ERHART (*Warmly, with emotion*): Aunt Ella—you've always
been so good to me, I owe so much to you. You gave me
the happiest childhood any boy could wish for—

GUNHILD: Erhart—Erhart!

ELLA: Thank you for saying that!

ERHART: —but it's impossible. I can't stay with you now.

GUNHILD (*Triumphantly*): I knew it! You shan't have him,
Ella!

ELLA: I see—so, after all, you've won him back.

GUNHILD: Yes, he's mine. And mine he will remain! We still have a long way to go together, Erhart—you and I!

ERHART (*Struggling with himself*): Mother—you'd better know the truth—

GUNHILD (*Eagerly*): Well?

ERHART: I can't stay with you, either.

GUNHILD (*As though thunderstruck*): What do you mean?

ERHART (*Summoning up spirit*): I'm young, Mother! I feel stifled in this airless room!

GUNHILD: Here—with me?

ERHART: Yes, Mother; here with you.

ELLA: Then come with me, Erhart.

ERHART: It wouldn't be any better for me there, Aunt Ella. It would be different, but no better. There'd be the same scent of dried lavender and rose leaves. The air would be just as stifling there!

GUNHILD (*Shaken, but having recovered her composure with effort*): You can say such things about your mother's house?

ERHART (*With growing impatience*): I don't know how else to put it! All this morbid watchfulness—this constant adulation—I can't endure it any longer!

GUNHILD (*With deep solemnity*): Remember what you've dedicated your life to, Erhart!

ERHART (*In an outburst*): Say rather what you've dedicated my life to, Mother! You've been my will; I've never been allowed to have one of my own. But I won't endure it any longer! I'm young; I've my own life to live! (*With a polite, considerate glance at* BORKMAN) I can't give it up in atonement for another; no matter who that other may be.

GUNHILD (*With growing anxiety*): I don't recognize you. Who has changed you, Erhart?

ERHART: Who? I suppose you can't conceive that I myself have—?

GUNHILD: No, no! You've come under some strange power. You don't belong to your mother any more—nor to your foster mother, either.

ERHART (*With labored defiance*): I've discovered my own power, Mother. And my own will, as well!

BORKMAN (*Advancing towards* ERHART): Then perhaps it's time for me to speak, at last.

ERHART (*Distantly and with calculated politeness*): What do you mean——? What does Father mean by that?

GUNHILD (*Scornfully*): I'd like to know that too.

BORKMAN (*Proceeding undisturbed*): Why not join forces with me, Erhart? No one can atone for another person's actions. These are mere illusions they've tried to foster in you here in this airless room. Even if you were to live your life like all the saints together——what good would it do me?

ERHART (*With measured respectfulness*): That's very true indeed, Sir.

BORKMAN: Yes, it is. And what good would it do me to spend the rest of my life in abject penitence? For years I've tried to feed myself on hopes and dreams; but I could never be satisfied with that. And now I've done with dreaming.

ERHART (*With a slight bow*): Then——what will you do now, Sir?

BORKMAN: I shall make a fresh start; work out my own redemption. A man can only atone for his past through his present and his future; through work——incessant work. I shall fulfill the youthful ambitions that meant the world to me. And now my vision has grown clearer; I see things on an even greater scale. Help me in this new life, Erhart! Join forces with me!

GUNHILD (*Raising her hand warningly*): Don't do it, Erhart!

ELLA (*Warmly*): Do it——do it! Help him, Erhart!

GUNHILD: You advise him to do that? You——the lonely, dying woman?

ELLA: I'm not thinking of myself.

GUNHILD: No; as long as I'm not the one to take him from you!

ELLA: Exactly——Gunhild.

BORKMAN: Well——Erhart?

ERHART (*Torn with pain*): Father, I can't. It's utterly impossible!

BORKMAN: Then—what do you plan to do?

ERHART (*With a sudden glow*): I'm young! I've a life of my own, and I intend to live it!

ELLA: Couldn't you give me just a little time? Two short months, Erhart?

ERHART: If I only could, Aunt Ella! But—it's impossible!

ELLA: You know how much I love you—!

ERHART: It's impossible, Aunt Ella. I can't—I tell you!

GUNHILD (*Looks at him sharply*): Does your mother mean nothing to you, either?

ERHART: Mother—you know I'll always care for you. But I can't sacrifice my life to you. There's no life here for me!

BORKMAN: Then join me, Erhart. For life is work. We two will live and work together!

ERHART (*Passionately*): Father—I can't think of work just now. I'm young! It's as though I'd just discovered that! I've suddenly discovered all the warmth and joy of life. I don't want to work. I only want to live—!

GUNHILD (*With a cry of divination*): What will you live for, Erhart?

ERHART (*With sparkling eyes*): For happiness, Mother.

GUNHILD: And where do you expect to find it?

ERHART: I have found it already.

GUNHILD: Erhart!

(ERHART *goes quickly to the hall door and throws it open.*)

ERHART: Fanny! You can come in now.

(MRS. WILTON *in outdoor wraps, appears on the threshold.*)

GUNHILD (*With hand aloft*): Mrs. Wilton!

MRS. WILTON; May I—?

ERHART: Yes—come in! I've told them everything.

(MRS. WILTON *comes forward into the room.* ERHART *closes the door behind her. She bows formally to* BORKMAN, *who returns her bow in silence. A short pause.*)

MRS. WILTON (*In a subdued firm voice*): You've told them?— Then I suppose I'm not any too welcome in this house.

GUNHILD (*Slowly, looking hard at her*): You have robbed me of my last hope in life—(*With an outburst*)—but all this is impossible!

MRS. WILTON: I dare say it seems impossible to you, Mrs. Borkman.

GUNHILD: Surely you must see that yourself.

MRS. WILTON: It's improbable, I grant you. But it's true all the same.

GUNHILD (*Turning*): You're really serious about this, Erhart?

ERHART: It means happiness to me, Mother—the greatest happiness in life. I can't say more than that!

GUNHILD (*Clenching her hands together*): Oh, my poor son! You've bewitched him—you've tricked him into this—!

MRS. WILTON (*Raising her head proudly*): I've done nothing of the sort.

GUNHILD: You have—I say!

MRS. WILTON: Erhart came to me of his own free will. And of my own free will I went halfway to meet him.

GUNHILD (*Measuring her scornfully with her eye*): That I can well believe!

MRS. WILTON (*With self-control*): There are certain forces in life that you seem to know very little about, Mrs. Borkman.

GUNHILD: What forces, may I ask?

MRS. WILTON: Forces that compel two people to join their lives irrevocably—regardless of the consequences.

GUNHILD (*With a smile*): I thought you were already irrevocably bound to another—

MRS. WILTON (*Abruptly*): He deserted me.

GUNHILD: He's still alive, they say—

MRS. WILTON: He's dead to me.

ERHART (*Insistently*): That's true, Mother. Besides, this other man makes no difference to me.

GUNHILD (*Looking sternly at him*): So you know about the other—!

ERHART: Of course I do. Fanny has told me everything.

GUNHILD: And yet you say it makes no difference!

ERHART (*With a defiant petulance*): This means happiness to me, Mother. I'm young! I insist on living my own life!

GUNHILD: Yes, you are young, Erhart—too young for this.

MRS. WILTON (*Firmly and earnestly*): Believe me, Mrs. Borkman, I've said the same thing to him. I've told him all
about my life. Over and over again I've pointed out to him
that I'm seven years older than he is—

ERHART (*Interrupting*): What difference does that make!
Besides—I've known that all along.

MRS. WILTON: But, I assure you—nothing was of any use.

GUNHILD: Indeed? Why didn't you refuse to see him? Close
your door to him? You should have done that from the
start.

MRS. WILTON (*Looks at her, and says in a low voice*): I simply couldn't do that, Mrs. Borkman.

GUNHILD: Why couldn't you?

MRS. WILTON: This meant happiness for me too, you see.

GUNHILD (*Scornfully*): Happiness, happiness—!

MRS. WILTON: I'd never known happiness before; I couldn't
drive it away from me simply because it came so late.

GUNHILD: How long do you think this happiness will last?

ERHART (*Interrupting*): Whether it lasts or not, Mother—
that's of no importance now!

GUNHILD (*Angrily*): How can you be so blind? Can't you see
where this is leading you?

ERHART: I don't care about the future— I only know this
means all of life to me!

GUNHILD (*In anguish*): You call this life, Erhart?

ERHART: Can't you see how lovely she is!

GUNHILD (*Wringing her hands*): So I must learn to bear this
shame as well!

BORKMAN (*At the back of the room, harshly and cuttingly*):
You're used to bearing things of that sort, Gunhild—

ELLA (*Imploringly*): Borkman!

ERHART: Father!

GUNHILD: Day after day I shall be forced to see my son linked
to a—to a—

ERHART (*Interrupting her harshly*): You'll be forced to see nothing of the sort, Mother! You can be sure of that! I don't intend to stay here.

MRS. WILTON (*Quickly and decisively*): We're going away, Mrs. Borkman.

GUNHILD (*Turning pale*): Going away! Together, no doubt?

MRS. WILTON (*Nodding*): I'm leaving for abroad—I'm going South. I'm taking a young girl with me; and Erhart is coming with us.

GUNHILD: With you—and a young girl?

MRS. WILTON: Yes. The young girl who's been living with me, —little Frida Foldal. I want her to go abroad—where she can perfect her music.

GUNHILD (*Suppressing a smile*): What do you say to all this, Erhart?

ERHART (*Embarrassed, shrugging his shoulders*): Well, Mother—it's what Mrs. Wilton wants—so—

GUNHILD (*Coldly*): And when does this distinguished company leave—if I may ask?

MRS. WILTON: We leave at once. Tonight. My sleigh is waiting outside the Hinkels' house.

GUNHILD (*Appraising her*): So that is the explanation of the party!

MRS. WILTON (*Smiling*): There was no party; just Erhart and me. And Frida, too, of course.

GUNHILD: Where is she now?

MRS. WILTON: She's waiting in the sleigh.

ERHART (*In painful embarrassment*): Mother—surely you can understand. I wanted to spare you this. Spare all of you—

GUNHILD (*Looks at him, deeply pained*): You'd have gone away without saying goodbye!

ERHART: I thought that would be best. Best for all of us. Everything had been arranged—our things were packed. But, of course, when you sent for me— (*Holding out his hands to her*) Goodbye, Mother.

GUNHILD (*With a gesture of repulsion*): Don't come near me!

ERHART (*Gently*): Is that your last word?

GUNHILD (*Sternly*): Yes.

ERHART (*Turning*): Then, goodbye to you, Aunt Ella.

ELLA (*Clasping his hands*): Goodbye, Erhart—live your life —and be happy! As happy as ever you can!

ERHART: Thank you, Aunt Ella. (*Bowing to* BORKMAN) Goodbye, Father. (*To* MRS. WILTON) Come! Let's be off!

MRS. WILTON (*In a whisper*): Yes, let's.

GUNHILD (*With a malignant smile*): Mrs. Wilton—do you think you're wise to take that young girl with you?

MRS. WILTON (*Returning the smile, half ironically, half seriously*): Men are so fickle, Mrs. Borkman—and women, too. When Erhart tires of me, and I of him, it might be as well for both of us if he, poor fellow, has someone to fall back on.

GUNHILD: But what about you?

MRS. WILTON: Oh, I shall manage—I assure you! Goodbye to you all!

(*She bows and goes out by the hall door.* ERHART *stands for a moment as though wavering; then he turns and follows her.*)

GUNHILD (*Dropping her folded hands*): Childless!

BORKMAN (*As though awakening to a resolution*): Then I must brave the storm alone. My hat and coat—! (*He goes hastily toward the door.*)

ELLA (*In terror, stopping him*): Where are you going, John Gabriel?

BORKMAN: Out into the storm of life, I tell you—let me go!

ELLA (*Restraining him*): No! You're ill, John Gabriel! I can see it in your face!

BORKMAN: Let me go, I say! (*He tears himself away from her, and goes out by the hall.*)

ELLA (*In the doorway*): Help me to hold him, Gunhild!

GUNHILD (*Coldly and sharply, in the middle of the room*): I shall never try to hold on to anyone again! Let them go away from me! Let them go where they like—both of them! (*Suddenly, with a cry of anguish*) Erhart! Don't leave me!

(*She rushes with outstretched arms toward the door.* ELLA *stops her.*)

CURTAIN

ACT
FOUR

SCENE: *An open space outside the main building, which lies to the right. A projecting corner of it is visible, with a door approached by a flight of low stone steps. The background consists of steep fir-clad slopes, quite near. On the left, a fringe of trees, forming the margin of a wood. The snowstorm has ceased; but the newly fallen snow has drifted deep around. The night is dark with drifting clouds. Now and then the moon gleams out faintly. Only a dim light is reflected from the snow.*

BORKMAN, GUNHILD *and* ELLA *are standing upon the steps,* BORKMAN *leaning wearily against the wall of the house. He has an old-fashioned cape over his shoulders, holds a soft gray felt hat in one hand and a thick knotted stick in the other.* ELLA *carries her cloak over her arm.* GUNHILD'S *great shawl has slipped down over her shoulders, so that her hair is uncovered.*

ELLA (*Barring the way*): Don't try to follow him, Gunhild!

GUNHILD (*In fear and agitation*): Let me get by, I say—he mustn't leave me!

ELLA: It's useless, I tell you! You'll never overtake him.

GUNHILD: Still—let me pass! I'll go down the road and keep on calling to him. He's bound to hear his mother's cry!

ELLA: How can he! He's probably already in the sleigh—

GUNHILD: They can't have started yet.

ELLA: He's in the sleigh—he must be!

GUNHILD: Then he's with her—with her!

BORKMAN (*With a sardonic laugh*): And he won't choose to hear his mother's cry.

GUNHILD: No—he won't hear it. (*Listening*) Sh! What is that?

ELLA (*Also listening*): It sounds like sleigh bells—

GUNHILD: It's her sleigh—hers!

ELLA: Perhaps it's someone else's—

GUNHILD (*With a stifled cry*): No! It's Mrs. Wilton's covered sleigh; I know those silver bells! Listen! They're coming! They've started down the hill!

ELLA (*Rapidly*): If you must call out to him, Gunhild—call out now! Perhaps, after all, he— (*The sound of the bells is heard close by*) Hurry, Gunhild! They're passing just below us!

GUNHILD (*Stands for a moment undecided; then she stiffens and says in a stern, cold voice*): No. I won't call out to him. Let Erhart Borkman go away from me. Far, far away —to what he calls life and happiness.

(*The sound of the bells dies away in the distance.*)

ELLA: One can no longer hear the bells—

GUNHILD (*After a pause*): They sounded like funeral bells to me.

BORKMAN (*With a dry laugh*): They're not tolling for me— not yet.

GUNHILD: No, but for me—and for him who has gone from me.

ELLA (*Nodding thoughtfully*): Who knows, Gunhild: in spite of everything, they may be ringing in new life and happiness for him.

GUNHILD (*Suddenly animated, looking hard at her*): Life and happiness, you say!

ELLA: For a little while, at any rate.

GUNHILD: Can you bear the thought of his finding life and happiness—with her?

ELLA (*With warmth and feeling*): Indeed I can!— With all my heart!

GUNHILD (*Coldly*): Then you're richer than I am, in the power of love.

ELLA (*Looking far away*): Perhaps it's the lack of love that keeps that power alive.

GUNHILD (*Fixing her eyes on her*): If that is true, Ella, I shall soon be as rich as you are.

(*She turns and goes into the house.* ELLA *stands for a time looking with a troubled expression at* BORKMAN; *then lays her hand cautiously upon his shoulder.*)

ELLA: John, you must come in, too.

BORKMAN (*As if awakening*): I?

ELLA: This cold is too much for you—I can see that. Come in with me; come inside, where it's warm.

BORKMAN (*Angrily*): Upstairs again, I suppose you mean?

ELLA: Why not downstairs with her—?

BORKMAN (*His anger flaming*): I shall never set foot inside that house again!

ELLA: But it's so late, John. Where could you go now?

BORKMAN (*Putting on his hat*): First I must go and see to all my hidden treasures.

ELLA (*Looking anxiously at him*): I don't understand you, John—

BORKMAN (*With laughter, interrupted by coughing*): I'm not talking about stolen goods, Ella! Don't be afraid of that! (*Stopping and pointing*) Do you see that man there? Who is it?

(VILHELM FOLDAL, *in an old cape, covered with snow, with his hat brim turned down, and a large umbrella in his hand, advances toward the corner of the house, laboriously stumbling through the snow. He is noticeably lame in his left foot.*)

BORKMAN: Vilhelm! What are you doing here again?

FOLDAL (*Looking up*): You! Out on the steps, John Gabriel!

Good heavens! (*Bowing*)—and Mrs. Borkman too, I see!

BORKMAN (*Abruptly*): This is not Mrs. Borkman.

FOLDAL: Oh, I beg your pardon—I lost my glasses in the snow. But to think of your being outdoors, John Gabriel—!

BORKMAN (*Carelessly and gaily*): It's about time, isn't it? After three years in detention; five years in prison; eight years in that room upstairs, alone—

ELLA (*Distressed*): Borkman, I implore you!

FOLDAL: Yes, yes—

BORKMAN: What is it you want of me?

FOLDAL (*Still standing at foot of steps*): I had to come and see you, John Gabriel; I simply had to.

BORKMAN: Even after I'd shown you the door?

FOLDAL: I couldn't let that stand in the way—

BORKMAN: What's the matter with your foot? You're limping.

FOLDAL: Yes. You see—I was run over.

BORKMAN: Run over?

FOLDAL: Yes, by a covered sleigh—

BORKMAN: Aha—!

FOLDAL: With two horses. They came down the hill at a gallop; I couldn't get out of their way fast enough, and so they—

ELLA: They ran over you?

FOLDAL: They came right down upon me, Madam—or perhaps I should say Miss. They came right down upon me— and I rolled over and over in the snow. I lost my glasses— broke my umbrella; and I twisted (*Rubbing his leg*) my foot too.

BORKMAN (*Laughing inwardly*): Do you know who was in that sleigh, Vilhelm?

FOLDAL: No, how should I? It was a closed sleigh, and they had the curtains drawn. And the coachman didn't stop a moment to see if— But what difference does it make? (*With an outburst*) I'm so happy! So very happy!

BORKMAN: Happy?

FOLDAL: I don't know how to put it—but I think happy is the only word for it. Something so wonderful has happened!

That's why—I couldn't help it—I had to come and share
my happiness with you, John Gabriel.

BORKMAN (*Harshly*): Well—share away then!

ELLA: First ask your friend to come in, Borkman—

BORKMAN (*Sternly*): I told you—I'll never set foot inside that
house again!

ELLA: But didn't you hear him say he'd been run over?

BORKMAN: We are all of us run over sometime or other in life.
The thing to do is to pick oneself up again—as though
nothing had happened.

FOLDAL: That's a profound saying, John Gabriel. But I can tell
you about it here. It'll only take a second—

BORKMAN (*More mildly*): Yes—do that, Vilhelm.

FOLDAL: When I got home tonight, just after leaving you—
you'll never believe this!—there was a letter waiting for
me. Can you guess who it was from?

BORKMAN: From your little Frida, I expect.

FOLDAL: Exactly! Think of your guessing that! Yes, it was a
long—a fairly long letter from little Frida. A servant
brought it. And what do you suppose the letter was about?

BORKMAN: Was it, perhaps, a farewell letter to her parents?

FOLDAL: Right again, John Gabriel! How good you are at
guessing! She wrote to say that Mrs. Wilton has invited
her to go abroad with her! She's taken such an interest in
the child's gift for music that she wants her to have further
training. And she's actually arranged for a tutor to accom-
pany them, to help Frida with her other studies too. Her
education has been rather neglected, in some respects, you
see.

BORKMAN (*Shaken with inward laughter*): Yes; I see the
whole thing very clearly, Vilhelm—

FOLDAL (*Continuing eagerly*): And, just imagine—she only
found it out this evening! At that party. Hm—you know
the one I mean. And yet she took time to write me all
about it. And it's such a warm affectionate letter too.
There's not a trace of contempt for her father in it, I assure you! And wasn't it tactful of her to say goodbye in

writing, before going away? (*Laughing*) But I shan't allow it, all the same.

BORKMAN (*Looks inquiringly at him*): What do you mean?

FOLDAL: She says they plan to leave tomorrow, very early in
the morning—

BORKMAN: Tomorrow, eh? She wrote you that?

FOLDAL (*Laughing and rubbing his hands*): But she doesn't
know her father—! I'll surprise her! I'm on my way to Mrs.
Wilton's now—

BORKMAN: Tonight?

FOLDAL: Good heavens, it's not so very late. And if they've
locked up for the night, I'll ring the doorbell; for I simply
must see my Frida before she goes. Good night, good night!
(*Makes a movement to go.*)

BORKMAN: You may as well spare yourself that long walk,
Vilhelm.

FOLDAL: Oh, you're thinking of my foot—

BORKMAN: In any case, you won't be able to get in.

FOLDAL: Oh, yes I will! I'll stand at the door and ring and ring
—I don't care what they think! I'm determined to see my
Frida and say good-bye to her.

ELLA: Your daughter has already left, dear Mr. Foldal.

FOLDAL: Left? Already? Are you sure? Who told you that?

BORKMAN: The young man who is to be her tutor.

FOLDAL: Indeed? Who is he?

BORKMAN: He happens to be Erhart Borkman.

FOLDAL (*Beaming with joy*): Your son, John Gabriel! Is he
the one who's going with them?

BORKMAN: Yes! He is to help Mrs. Wilton with little Frida's
education.

FOLDAL: But this is splendid! Then the child is in the very
best of hands. So they've really left. You're absolutely
positive?

BORKMAN: They were in that sleigh that ran over you on the
road, just now.

FOLDAL (*Clasping his hands*): Think of my little Frida—
traveling in such luxury!

BORKMAN: Yes, Vilhelm! Your daughter is traveling in great style— And young Mr. Borkman, too! Did you notice the silver bells?

FOLDAL: Silver bells, you say? Real silver? Genuine silver bells?

BORKMAN: Quite genuine, Vilhelm, I assure you! Everything about that sleigh was genuine throughout.

FOLDAL (*With quiet intensity*): How wonderful life is! My little gift for poetry hasn't been wasted after all; it has taken the form of music in my Frida. And now she's setting forth into that great wide world that I so often longed to see. She sets forth in a splendid sleigh, to the tune of silver bells—

BORKMAN: —and runs over her father.

FOLDAL (*Happily*): What does it matter about me! As long as the child is— So I'm too late after all. I'd better go home and comfort her poor mother. I left her crying in the kitchen.

BORKMAN: Crying, you say?

FOLDAL: Yes—just imagine! She was sobbing her heart out when I left.

BORKMAN: And you are laughing, Vilhelm?

FOLDAL: That's different! She understands nothing about such things, you see. Well—goodbye. It's a good thing the tramway passes my door. Goodbye, goodbye, John Gabriel. Goodbye, Miss. (*He bows, and limps laboriously out the way he came.*)

BORKMAN (*Stands silent a moment, gazing before him*): Goodbye, Vilhelm! It's not the first time you've been run over in life, old friend!

ELLA (*Looking at him with suppressed anxiety*): You look so pale, John; so very pale!

BORKMAN: That's the result of being in prison up there, all these years.

ELLA: I've never seen you look like this.

BORKMAN: You've never seen an escaped convict before, I expect.

ELLA: John—please come inside with me!

BORKMAN: It's no use trying to persuade me! I've already told you—

ELLA: John, I implore you! For your own sake—

(THE MAID *opens the door and stands in the doorway*.)

MALENE: I beg your pardon; but Mrs. Borkman told me I was to lock the front door now.

BORKMAN (*In a low voice, to* ELLA): You see! They want to lock me up again!

ELLA (*To* THE MAID): Mr. Borkman isn't feeling well. He wants to stay out in the fresh air a little while.

MALENE: But Mrs. Borkman told me—

ELLA: Just leave the key in the door! I'll lock it presently.

MALENE: Very well, Miss. Lord save us—! (*She goes into the house*.)

BORKMAN (*Stands silent for a moment and listens; then goes hastily down the steps and out into the open space*): Now I'm outside the walls, Ella. Now they'll never get hold of me, again!

ELLA (*Who has gone down to him*): You're a free man, John! You can come and go just as you please!

BORKMAN (*Softly, as though in terror*): I never want to live under a roof again! It's so good to be out here in the night! If I were to go back into that room of mine, ceiling and walls would shrink together and crush me—crush me flat as a fly!

ELLA: But where will you go?

BORKMAN: I'll go on, and on, and on. Try and win my way back to freedom, and life, and human beings again. Will you come with me, Ella?

ELLA: I? Go with you? Now?

BORKMAN: Yes, now—at once!

ELLA: How far are you going, John?

BORKMAN: I shall go on until my strength gives out.

ELLA: It's such a raw, cold night. Hadn't you better—?

BORKMAN (*In a very hoarse voice*): I see! The lady is worried about her health—!

ELLA: No! I'm worried about yours!

BORKMAN: A dead man's ͙͗ͣlth? I can't help laughing at you, Ella! (*He moves onward.*)

ELLA (*Following him, holding him back*): What did you call yourself?

BORKMAN: A dead man, I said. Don't you remember, Gunhild told me to stay quietly in my grave?

ELLA (*With resolution, throwing her cloak around her*): I'm going with you, John.

BORKMAN: Yes, we two belong to each other, Ella. (*Advancing*) Come with me!

(*They have gradually passed into the low wood on the left. It conceals them little by little, until they are quite lost to sight. The house and the open space disappear. The landscape, consisting of wooded slopes and ridges, slowly changes and grows wilder and wilder.*)

ELLA'S VOICE (*In the wood to the right*): Where are we going, John? I don't recognize this place.

BORKMAN'S VOICE (*Higher up*): Just follow my footsteps in the snow.

ELLA'S VOICE: Why do we have to climb so high?

BORKMAN'S VOICE (*Coming closer*): We must go up this winding path.

ELLA (*Still hidden from sight*): I don't think I can go much farther.

BORKMAN: (*Nearer, on edge of wood to right*): Come! We're not far from the view now. There used to be a bench up there—

ELLA (*Appearing among the trees*): Ah! You remember it—

BORKMAN: There you can rest.

(*They have emerged upon a small high-lying open plateau in the wood. The mountain rises abruptly behind them. To the left, far below, an extensive fjord landscape, with high ranges in the distance, towering one above the other. On the plateau to the left, a dead fir tree with a bench under it. The snow lies deep upon the plateau.* BORKMAN, *and*

after him, ELLA *enter from the right and wade with difficulty through the snow.*)

BORKMAN (*Stopping at the verge of the steep declivity on the
left*): Now, Ella! Come and see!

ELLA (*Coming up to him*): What is it you want to show me,
John?

BORKMAN (*Pointing outwards*): See—how free and open the
country lies before us!

ELLA: We've often sat on this bench before and looked out
over a much farther distance—

BORKMAN: It was a dreamland we looked out at then.

ELLA (*Nodding sadly*): The dreamland of our life, yes! And
now that land is covered with snow— And the old tree is
dead.

BORKMAN (*Not listening to her*): Can you see the smoke of
the great steamships out there on the fjord?

ELLA: No, John.

BORKMAN: I can see it! All over the world they go—spreading friendship and understanding— Bringing light and
warmth to thousands of homes. That's what I dreamed of
doing!

ELLA (*Softly*): And it remained a dream.

BORKMAN: Yes, it remained a dream. (*Listening*) And down
there by the river—the factories are humming! Can you
hear them? My factories! All those I would have created! The night shift's on; so, you see, they're working night
and day! Listen! The engines are throbbing; the wheels are
turning—round and round they go! Can't you hear them,
Ella?

ELLA: No, John.

BORKMAN: I can hear them!

ELLA (*Anxiously*): I think you're mistaken, John.

BORKMAN (*More and more inspired*): But these are only
the outworks of the kingdom!

ELLA: The kingdom? What kingdom?

BORKMAN: *My* kingdom of course! The kingdom I was on
the point of conquering, when I—when I died.

ELLA (*Shaken in a low voice*): Oh, John, John!

BORKMAN: And there it lies, defenseless—masterless; a prey to thieves and robbers!—Ella! Do you see that mountain range in the far distance? Do you see the great peaks soaring—towering one behind the other? That is my vast, my infinite, my inexhaustible kingdom!

ELLA: An icy wind blows from that kingdom, John!

BORKMAN: It is the breath of life to me! It comes to me like a greeting from subject spirits. I can see all those imprisoned millions! I can feel the veins of metal stretching out their arms to me; their wide-spread, branching, luring arms! In the vaults of the bank that night, as I stood there with a lantern in my hand, they came to me as in a vision. You begged to be liberated and I tried to free you. But my strength failed me, and the treasure sank back into the earth again. (*With outstretched hands*) But I must whisper it to you now—here in the stillness of the night: I love you, as you lie there, dormant, buried in the darkness! I love you, unborn forces yearning for the light! I love you with all your dazzling train of power and glory! I love you, love you, love you!

ELLA (*In suppressed but rising agitation*): Yes; now—as always, John—your love lies buried there. But here—in the light of day—there was a warm human heart that yearned for you. And you took that heart and crushed it. You did worse than that—far worse! You sold it! Sold it for—

BORKMAN (*Trembles; a cold shudder seems to go through him*): The Kingdom, the Power and the Glory, you mean?

ELLA: The Kingdom, the Power and the Glory—yes! I accused you earlier tonight of murdering love in the heart of the woman who loved you; and whom you loved in return—as much as you were capable of loving anyone. (*With uplifted arm*) And because of this I prophesy, John Gabriel Borkman: you will never receive the price you demanded for that murder. You will never enter in triumph into your cold, dark, kingdom!

BORKMAN (*Staggers to the bench and seats himself heavily*):
I fear your prophecy will come true, Ella.

ELLA (*Going up to him*): Never fear it, John. It would be the
best thing that could happen to you.

BORKMAN (*Cries out, clutching at his breast*): Ah— Now it
let me go again.

ELLA (*Shaking him*): What was it, John!

BORKMAN (*Sinking down again against the back of the seat*):
A hand of ice clutched at my heart.

ELLA: John! You still feel it, John?

BORKMAN (*Murmurs*): No— No ice hand— It was a metal
hand.

(*He sinks down upon the bench.* ELLA *tears off her cloak
and throws it over him.*)

ELLA: Stay where you are. I'll go for help—(*She goes a step
or two toward the right; then stops, returns, and carefully
feels his pulse and touches his face. She spreads the cloak
tighter around him, and sinks down in the snow in front of
the bench. A short silence. Then* GUNHILD, *wrapped in a
mantle, comes through the wood on the right.* THE MAID
goes before her carrying a lantern) It's best so, John Gabriel; best—for you.

MALENE(*Throwing the light upon the snow*): Look, Ma'am;
here are their footsteps in the snow—

GUNHILD (*Peering around*): Yes; they're here. They're sitting
over on the bench. (*Calls*) Ella!

ELLA (*Rising*): Are you looking for us?

GUNHILD (*Sternly*): What else could I do?

ELLA (*Pointing*): There he is, Gunhild.

GUNHILD: Asleep?

ELLA: A long, deep sleep, I think.

GUNHILD (*With an outburst*): Ella! (*Controls herself and asks
in a low voice*) Did he do it of his own accord?

ELLA: No.

GUNHILD (*Relieved*): Not by his own hand then?

ELLA: No, an icy metal hand clutched at his heart.

GUNHILD (*To* THE MAID): Go for help. Get the men up from the farm.

MALENE: Yes, Ma'am. (*To herself*) Lord save us! (*She goes out through the wood to the right.*)

GUNHILD (*Standing behind the bench*): The night air must have killed him—

ELLA: Yes—

GUNHILD: Strong man that he was.

ELLA (*Coming in front of the bench*): Won't you look at him, Gunhild?

GUNHILD (*With a gesture of repulsion*): No, no! (*Lowering her voice*) He was a miner's son, John Gabriel Borkman, he couldn't live in the fresh air.

ELLA: I think it was the cold that killed him.

GUNHILD (*Shakes her head*): The cold, you say? The cold— that had killed him long ago!

ELLA (*Nodding to her*): And changed us into shadows.

GUNHILD: You're right in that.

ELLA (*With a painful smile*): A dead man, and two shadows —that is what the cold has made of us.

GUNHILD: Yes, coldness of heart— Perhaps now, we can hold out our hands to each other, Ella.

ELLA: I think we can, now.

GUNHILD: We twin sisters over him we have both loved.

ELLA: We two shadows, over the dead man.

(GUNHILD *behind the bench and* ELLA *in front of it take each other's hand.*)

CURTAIN

When We Dead Awaken

A DRAMATIC EPILOGUE
IN THREE ACTS

1899

CHARACTERS

PROFESSOR ARNOLD RUBEK, *a sculptor*

MAJA RUBEK, *his wife*

INSPECTOR AT THE WATERING PLACE

ULFHEJM, *a landed proprietor*

LARS, *his servant*

A FOREIGN LADY

A DEACONESS, *her companion*

Waiters, guests at the resort, and children

ACT
ONE

SCENE: *Outside the hotel at a watering place; part of the building is seen on the right. It is an open clearing in a park. There is a fountain, fine old trees and shrubbery. On the left is a small pavilion almost entirely overgrown with ivy and Virginia creeper. A table and a chair stand outside it. In the background a view of the fjord, clear out to the sea, with cliffs and small islets in the distance. A calm, warm, sunny summer morning.*

PROFESSOR RUBEK *and* MAJA RUBEK *are seated in wicker chairs at a table set for two, on the lawn outside the hotel. They have just had breakfast. They are drinking champagne and seltzer water, and each has a newspaper.* THE PROFESSOR *is an elderly man of distinguished appearance, wearing a black velvet jacket over light summer clothes.* MAJA *is quite young, full of animation, with merry mischievous eyes; she seems a little tired. She wears fashionable traveling clothes.*

MAJA (*Seems to be waiting for* THE PROFESSOR *to say something; then she lets her paper drop and heaves a deep sigh*): Oh dear, oh dear—!
RUBEK (*Looks up from his paper*): Well? What's the matter, Maja?
MAJA: Listen to that silence!
RUBEK (*With a tolerant smile*): So— You're able to hear that, are you?
MAJA: What?
RUBEK: The silence.
MAJA: Of course I am!

RUBEK: I know what you mean, *mein Kind*. It really does seem audible.

MAJA: It *is* audible! It's positively overwhelming!

RUBEK: Here in particular, you mean?

MAJA: No; everywhere here at home. The town was noisy enough, it's true—but even the noise had something dead about it.

RUBEK (*Gives her a searching look*): You don't seem very happy at being home again.

MAJA (*Looks at him*): Are *you* happy?

RUBEK (*Evasively*): I—?

MAJA: Yes, you. You've been away ever so much longer than I have—but can you honestly say you're happy to be home again?

RUBEK: No, as a matter of fact, I'm not, particularly.

MAJA (*With animation*): There, you see! I knew it!

RUBEK: Perhaps I've been away too long. It doesn't seem like home to me any more.

MAJA (*Eagerly, moving her chair closer to him*): Then why don't we go away again? Let's leave as soon as possible!

RUBEK (*Somewhat impatiently*): Isn't that what we plan to do, Maja dear?

MAJA: Why can't we leave at once? We have our nice new house to go to; we'd be ever so much more comfortable there.

RUBEK (*Smiles indulgently*): Our nice new *home*, I suppose you mean.

MAJA (*Sharply*): I prefer *house*. Let's stick to that.

RUBEK (*His eyes dwelling on her*): You're a strange little creature, aren't you?

MAJA: Do you think so?

RUBEK: Yes, I do.

MAJA: Why? Simply because I'm bored with hanging about up here?

RUBEK: Who was it who insisted on coming North this summer?

MAJA: I suppose I did.

RUBEK: Well—*I* certainly didn't.

MAJA: How was I to know things would be so different? It's only about four years since I left here—and everything's completely changed.

RUBEK: Yes—it's four years since you left here and got married.

MAJA: *Married?* What's that got to do with it?

RUBEK: Four years since you became the Frau Professor, and the mistress of a delightful home—I beg your pardon, *house,* I mean—as well as a villa on Lake Taunitz, which is now the height of fashion. All very elegant and distinguished, Maja, you must admit. And roomy, too. We needn't always be getting in each other's way—

MAJA: Oh, there's room enough; I grant you that.

RUBEK: You'd never known that sort of luxury before; your life at home was very different.

MAJA (*Looks at him*): So you think it's *I* who've changed?

RUBEK: Yes, Maja—I do.

MAJA: Don't you think the people here have changed at all?

RUBEK: I suppose they have, to some extent. And not for the better, I must admit.

MAJA: I'm glad you admit that, at least!

RUBEK (*Changing the subject*): Do you know what I think of, when I see the lives these people lead?

MAJA: No—tell me.

RUBEK: I keep thinking of that night on the train—on the journey up here—

MAJA: You were sound asleep.

RUBEK: No—not really. I noticed how quiet it was at all the little stations— I felt like you, Maja: I could actually *hear* the silence—

MAJA: Hm. Like me; yes, I dare say.

RUBEK: —and then I realized we must have crossed the border; that we were really home again. The train stopped at every little station, for no apparent reason—

MAJA: Why did it have to stop, then?

RUBEK: I don't know. Nobody got off, and nobody got on, and yet there were these endless waits. And at each station two guards—one of them with a lantern in his hand— paced up and down the platform, carrying on a totally unnecessary conversation, in low hushed voices—

MAJA: It's true, there always seem to be two men carrying on an unnecessary conversation—

RUBEK: —about absolutely nothing. (*In a livelier tone*) Never mind! Tomorrow things will be different! We'll get aboard that splendid ship that's waiting for us in the harbor, and sail North along the coast, way up to the Arctic sea.

MAJA: But I thought you wanted to see something of the country—and the people?

RUBEK (*Shortly and snappishly*): I've seen more than enough.

MAJA: Perhaps a sea voyage might be better for you—

RUBEK: At least it'll be a change.

MAJA: Well—as long as it does you good—

RUBEK: What do you mean, "does me good"? There's nothing wrong with me.

MAJA (*Rises and goes to him*): Yes there is, Rubek. Aren't you aware of it yourself?

RUBEK: My dear Maja—what could possibly be the matter with me?

MAJA (*Stands behind him, leaning on his chair*): That's what I wish you'd tell me. You've grown so restless lately; you can't settle down anywhere. Whether we stay home, or whether we go abroad—it's the same thing. And you've begun to shy away from people; it's as though you were avoiding them.

RUBEK (*With a touch of sarcasm*): Well, well! You've noticed that, have you?

MAJA: No one who knows you could fail to notice it. And then I think it's such a pity that you seem to have lost all interest in your work.

RUBEK: So you've noticed that too, have you?

MAJA: Yes. You used to work incessantly—from morning until night. You used to be absolutely tireless!

RUBEK (*Gloomily*): Used to be—yes.

MAJA: But ever since you finished that great masterpiece of yours—

RUBEK (*Nodding thoughtfully*): "The Resurrection Day"—

MAJA: Yes. It's been shown all over the world. It's made you famous—

RUBEK: Perhaps that's the trouble, Maja.

MAJA: What do you mean?

RUBEK: After I'd finished this masterpiece of mine— (*With a violent gesture*) for "The Resurrection Day" *is* a masterpiece! At least, it was at first. No—it *is!* It *must*—it *must* be a masterpiece!

MAJA (*Looks at him in amazement*): Of course it is! All the world knows that!

RUBEK (*With a gesture of dismissal*): All the world! What does the world know! It knows and understands nothing!

MAJA: Well—at least it recognizes—

RUBEK: What? Something that isn't even there! Something I never intended to convey! It hasn't the faintest understanding of my meaning, but it goes into ecstasies all the same! (*Growling to himself*) What's the good of it all. What's the use of spending one's life slaving for the Masses—for "All the world"!

MAJA: Do you think it's better to do what you're doing now? Turning out an occasional portrait-bust? Do you think that's worthy of you?

RUBEK (*With a sly smile*): I wouldn't dismiss them as "portrait-busts," if I were you.

MAJA: What else are they, I'd like to know! For the past two or three years that's all you've done. As soon as "The Resurrection Day" was finished, as soon as it was out of the house, you—

RUBEK: But they're not just "portrait-busts," I tell you!

MAJA: What are they, then?

RUBEK: They're not what they seem to be; they're not just

simple, straightforward portraits. They're charged with
irony, with satire, with a hidden comment. People don't
see this, of course, but—

MAJA: Well?

RUBEK: I see it; and it amuses me immensely. They all exclaim: "What a speaking likeness! How marvelous! How
remarkable!" But they don't see what's hidden behind that
"speaking likeness," as they call it. They don't suspect
that it conceals the portraits of fatuous, self-satisfied asses,
pompous, self-righteous horses, cringing curs, greedy swine,
and ruthless, brutal bulls—

MAJA (*Indifferently*): All the dear domestic animals, in fact.

RUBEK: Exactly—the dear domestic animals. All the animals
Man has depraved into his own image, and that have depraved him in turn. (*Empties his glass of champagne and
laughs*) And, in their innocence, countless worthy, prosperous plutocrats order these insidious works of art, and
actually pay me for them; pay me most handsomely.

MAJA (*Fills up his glass*): Come! Drink and be happy,
Rubek!

RUBEK (*Passes his hand several times over his forehead and
leans back in his chair*): I am happy, Maja. Really happy.
That is—in a way. (*Short silence*) After all, there's a certain happiness in being free and independent; in being able
to satisfy one's every wish—in a material sense, that is.
Don't you agree?

MAJA: Yes, I suppose so. It's all right, in its way. (*Looking
at him*) But do you remember what you promised me
that day when we agreed to—when we made the difficult
decision?

RUBEK: When we agreed to get married, you mean. It was a
difficult decision for you, I realize that.

MAJA (*Continues, unruffled*): We agreed I was to leave here
and go abroad with you, and have a happy, carefree life.
Do you remember what you promised me that day?

RUBEK (*Shakes his head*): I can't say I do. What did I
promise you?

MAJA: You said you'd take me up to a high mountain and show me all the glory of the world.

RUBEK (*With a start*): Did I promise *you* that, too?

MAJA (*Looks at him*): What do you mean? Who else did you—?

RUBEK (*Indifferent*): No, no—I simply meant, did I really promise to show you—?

MAJA: —all the glory of the world. That's what you said. And you said all that glory would be ours.

RUBEK: That's an old saying—a kind of metaphor. I often used to use it.

MAJA: A metaphor—I see.

RUBEK: Even as a boy I used to use it; when I wanted to persuade the other children to come and play with me—to run off to the woods or to the mountains.

MAJA (*Looks at him intently*): Then perhaps you only wanted to persuade *me* to come out and play with you? Is that so, Rubek?

RUBEK (*Passing it off as a joke*): Don't you think it's been a fairly pleasant game?

MAJA: I didn't go with you to play games.

RUBEK: I dare say not.

MAJA: And you never did take me up to a high mountain, and show me—

RUBEK (*With irritation*): —all the glory of the world? That's true—I didn't. Somehow I don't think you were made for mountain climbing, little Maja.

MAJA (*Trying to control herself*): You seemed to think so then.

RUBEK: That was four or five years ago. (*Stretches himself in his chair*) Four or five years is a long, long time.

MAJA (*Looks at him bitterly*): Has it seemed so very long to you, Rubek?

RUBEK: It begins to seem a bit long. (*Yawns*) Just now and then.

MAJA (*Goes back to her chair*): I shan't bore you any longer.

(*She sits down, picks up her newspaper, and begins glancing through it. They are both silent.*)

RUBEK (*Leans his elbows on the table and stares at her; then says in a teasing tone*): The Frau Professor is offended!

MAJA (*Coldly; without looking up*): Not in the least.

(*Visitors to the Baths, mostly ladies, begin to pass, singly and in groups, through the park from the right and out to the left. Waiters bring refreshments from the hotel and go off behind the pavilion.* THE INSPECTOR, *wearing gloves and carrying a cane, comes from his rounds in the park, meets visitors, bows politely, and exchanges a few words with some of them.*)

INSPECTOR (*Advances to* PROFESSOR RUBEK'S *table and politely takes off his hat*): Allow me to wish you good morning, Mrs. Rubek. Good morning, Professor.

RUBEK: Good morning, Inspector.

INSPECTOR (*To* MAJA): I trust you had a restful night, Mrs. Rubek?

MAJA: Yes, thank you, indeed I did; but then I always sleep like a top!

INSPECTOR: I'm delighted to hear it. Sometimes the first night in a strange place can be a little trying. How about you, Professor?

RUBEK: I'm not so lucky, I'm afraid. I can't seem to get much sleep—especially lately.

INSPECTOR (*Sympathetically*): Oh, that's too bad. But a few weeks here at the Baths will soon remedy that.

RUBEK (*Looks up at him*): Tell me, Inspector—do any of your patients take the baths at night?

INSPECTOR (*Astonished*): At night? No—not to my knowledge.

RUBEK: Is that so?

INSPECTOR: I know of no one here seriously ill enough to require such treatment.

RUBEK: Then—do any of your guests take midnight walks, here in the park?

INSPECTOR (*Smiles and shakes his head*): No—that would be against the rules, Professor.

MAJA (*Impatiently*): I told you, Rubek—you must have dreamt it!

RUBEK: Must I, indeed! (*Turns to* THE INSPECTOR) I happened to get up last night—I couldn't sleep; I went to the window to see what sort of a night it was—

INSPECTOR: Yes?

RUBEK: And I caught sight of a white figure, out there, among the trees.

MAJA (*Smiling; to* THE INSPECTOR): The Professor claims it was wearing a white robe—

RUBEK: Something of that sort, I said. I couldn't see it very clearly; it was white, at any rate.

INSPECTOR: How very strange. Was it a lady or a gentleman?

RUBEK: I'm almost sure it was a lady. It was followed by another figure; a dark figure—like a shadow.

INSPECTOR (*With a start*): Dark? All in black, perhaps?

RUBEK: Yes, I think so.

INSPECTOR (*Light dawns on him*): And was this black figure following the white one? Close behind her?

RUBEK: Yes—at a little distance—

INSPECTOR: Aha! Then I think I can explain it, Professor.

RUBEK: Tell me—what was it?

MAJA (*Simultaneously*): Do you mean to say the Professor *wasn't* dreaming?

INSPECTOR (*Lowers his voice to a whisper as he directs their attention towards the background to the right*): Hush! Look over there— Don't say anything now.

(A THIN LADY, *wearing a robe of fine white cashmere, and followed by* A DEACONESS *in black, with a silver cross on her breast, come round the corner of the hotel and cross the park towards the pavilion downstage left. Her face is pale, almost masklike. Her eyelids droop over her eyes, which seem almost sightless. Her long robe falls in sculptured folds to the ground. She wears a large white crepe*

*shawl which covers her head, neck, breast, shoulders and
arms. Her arms are crossed over her breast. She walks
stiffly with measured steps.* THE DEACONESS *also walks with
a measured tread and has the appearance of a servant.
She never takes her dark, prominent eyes from the lady.
Some waiters with serviettes over their arms come to the
door of the hotel and watch the two strange women with
curiosity. The women pay no attention and go into the
pavilion, looking neither to right nor left.*)

RUBEK (*Has risen slowly and involuntarily and stands staring at the closed door of the pavilion*): Who was that lady?

INSPECTOR: She's a foreign lady; she's rented the pavilion.

RUBEK: A foreigner, you say?

INSPECTOR: Yes, presumably. At least, they arrived here from
abroad—about a week ago. We've never seen them here
before.

RUBEK (*Decisively; looking at him*): It was she I saw in the
park last night.

INSPECTOR: Yes; I thought it must have been.

RUBEK: What is the lady's name?

INSPECTOR: She's registered as Madame de Satow, and companion. That's all we know about her.

RUBEK (*Reflecting*): Satow? Satow—?

MAJA (*With a mocking laugh*): Do you know anyone of that
name, Rubek?

RUBEK (*Shakes his head*): No—no one. Satow. It sounds
Russian. Slavic, certainly. (*To* THE INSPECTOR) What language does she speak?

INSPECTOR: When she talks to her companion, it's in a language I don't recognize. But she speaks Norwegian like a
native.

RUBEK (*Exclaims, with a start*): Norwegian? You're sure
you're not mistaken?

INSPECTOR: How could I be?

RUBEK (*Looks at him intently*): You've heard her yourself?

INSPECTOR: Yes; I've spoken to her several times. Only a few
words, however—she's very reticent— But—

RUBEK: It was Norwegian?

INSPECTOR: Thoroughly good Norwegian. Perhaps with a slight North-country accent.

RUBEK (*Gazes straight before him in amazement; in a whisper*): Strange!

MAJA (*Hurt, and a little shaken*): Could this lady have been one of your models, Rubek? Try and remember.

RUBEK (*Gives her a scathing look*): One of my models!

MAJA (*With a provoking smile*): Yes; you're supposed to have had innumerable models, aren't you? In your younger days!

RUBEK (*In the same tone*): You're mistaken, little Maja. I've actually had only one model. One single model—for all the work I've ever done.

INSPECTOR (*Who has turned away and is looking off toward the left*): If you'll excuse me, I think I'll leave you now. Here comes someone I don't particularly care to meet; especially in the presence of ladies.

RUBEK (*Looks in the same direction*): He looks as if he were going hunting. Who is he?

INSPECTOR: He's a certain Mr. Ulfhejm, who comes from—

RUBEK: Ulfhejm! Of course!

INSPECTOR: The bear killer, they call him.

RUBEK: I used to know him.

INSPECTOR: Who doesn't?

RUBEK: Very slightly, however. Has he become a patient of yours, at last?

INSPECTOR: No; strangely enough he hasn't. At least—not yet! He stops off here once a year—on his way to the hunting grounds. If you'll excuse me— (*He starts towards the hotel.*)

ULFHEJM'S VOICE (*From off stage*): Wait a minute! Wait—damn you! Do you hear? Who are you running away from?

INSPECTOR (*Stops*): I'm not running away, Mr. Ulfhejm.

(ULFHEJM *comes in from the left followed by a servant with a pair of hunting dogs on a leash.* ULFHEJM *is dressed*

*in hunting clothes, with high boots and a felt hat with a
feather in it. He's a thin, tall, sinewy man, with thick
hair and beard. He is loud-voiced; of indefinite age, though
no longer young.*)

ULFHEJM (*Pouncing on* THE INSPECTOR): A nice way to
greet a stranger, I must say! Dashing off with your tail between your legs—as if the devil himself were after you!

INSPECTOR (*Calmly, without answering him*): Did you just
get in by the steamer, Mr. Ulfhejm?

ULFHEJM (*Growls*): What the hell would I want with a
steamer! (*Arms akimbo*) You know damn well I sail my
own ship! (*To his* SERVANT) Take good care of your fellow creatures, Lars. But keep them ravenous all the same.
Fresh meat bones—but not too much meat on 'em, do you
hear? And they must be raw and bloody. And get something in your own belly while you're at it. (*Aims a kick at
him*) Get the hell out of here, and be quick about it!
(THE SERVANT *takes the dogs round the corner of the
hotel.*)

INSPECTOR: Would you care to go into the dining room, Mr.
Ulfhejm?

ULFHEJM: That flytrap filled with corpses? Thanks—not for
me!

INSPECTOR: Just as you please.

ULFHEJM: But tell the housekeeper to have my hamper prepared as usual. Plenty of food, and lots of brandy—! You
can tell her either Lars or I will raise hell with her if it
isn't—

INSPECTOR (*Interrupting*): We know what to expect from
you. (*Turning*) Is there anything you'd like, Professor?
Shall I send the waiter? How about you, Mrs. Rubek?

RUBEK: Thank you—nothing for me.

MAJA: Nothing for me, either.
(THE INSPECTOR *goes into the hotel.*)

ULFHEJM (*Stares at them a moment, then raises his hat*):
Well—by God! I seem to have strayed into highly distinguished company!

RUBEK (*Looks up*): What do you mean by that, Mr. Ulf-hejm?

ULFHEJM: The great sculptor Rubek, if I'm not mistaken?

RUBEK (*Nods*): We've met a couple of times, I believe. It must have been that last autumn I spent here at home.

ULFHEJM: That was many years ago—you weren't so famous then! In those days even a lousy bear hunter like me might venture to approach you.

RUBEK (*Smiles*): I don't bite even now.

MAJA (*Looks at* ULFHEJM *with interest*): Do you really hunt bears, Mr. Ulfhejm?

ULFHEJM: Preferably bears, Madame. But I hunt almost anything that comes my way: eagles, wolves, women, elk or reindeer; anything that's fresh and juicy and full-blooded—

MAJA (*Gives him a bold look*): But preferably bears?

ULFHEJM: Preferably, yes. One gets a chance to use a knife on them. (*With a slight smile*) Your husband and I both work in hard material, Madame. He struggles with great blocks of marble, I presume; and I struggle with the quivering sinews of the bear. And in the end we conquer—both of us. In spite of its resistance, we master our material and vanquish it.

RUBEK (*Thoughtfully, gazing before him*): There's a lot of truth in what you say.

ULFHEJM: Yes. I'm sure marble puts up a good fight too. It's dead, and it resents being hammered into life. And when you try to prod a bear out of his lair—he resents it too!

MAJA: Do you go hunting in the forests?

ULFHEJM: No—in the mountains. I don't suppose you've ever been up to the high mountains?

MAJA: No, never.

ULFHEJM: Then you should come there now! I'll take you with me—both of you.

MAJA: Thanks; but Rubek's decided on a sea voyage.

RUBEK: Yes; we're going to cruise along the coast to the far North.

ULFHEJM: In all those stinking fjords, I suppose! Why should
you want to flounder about in all those foul gutters full of
stagnant water. Sewer water, I call it!

MAJA: Do you hear that, Rubek?

ULFHEJM: You'd much better come with me up to the mountains. Up there you can get away from men—and all their
filth. I can't tell you what that means to me! But, I suppose, to a delicate young lady— (*He breaks off abruptly.*
THE DEACONESS *comes out of the pavilion and goes into the
hotel.*)

ULFHEJM (*Follows her with his eyes*): What's that black
crow doing here? Did you see her? Is someone getting
buried?

RUBEK: I haven't heard of—

ULFHEJM: There must be someone getting ready to kick the
bucket, then. The sooner they get it over with the better.
The only thing to do with sick people is to bury them.

MAJA: Have you never been sick, Mr. Ulfhejm?

ULFHEJM: Never. If I had been I shouldn't be here now.
My comrades have been sick though—poor creatures.

MAJA: And what did you do for your comrades?

ULFHEJM: Shot them, of course.

RUBEK (*Looks at him*): Shot them?

MAJA (*Pushes back her chair*): You mean—you killed them?

ULFHEJM (*Nods*): I never miss.

MAJA: You've actually shot people?

ULFHEJM: I wasn't speaking about people.

MAJA: But, you said—your comrades.

ULFHEJM: My comrades are my dogs, of course.

MAJA: Your dogs?

ULFHEJM: Certainly. I have no other comrades. My dogs are
honorable, loyal and faithful. But when one of them gets
sick or feeble—bang!—I send him packing—into the unknown.

(THE DEACONESS *comes out of the hotel carrying a tray of
bread and milk. She places it on the table outside the
pavilion and goes inside.*)

ULFHEJMK (*With a scornful laugh*): And they call that food for human beings! Milk! Pap!—Ha! You should see my comrades eat! Would you like to?

MAJA (*Smiles at* RUBEK *and gets up*): Very much.

ULFHEJM: You're a game one! Come along, then. They devour great meatbones dripping with blood. They gulp them down—vomit them up—and gulp them down again. It's a great sight! Come along—I'll show you. And we can arrange about your coming to the mountains, too—

(*He goes round the corner of the hotel followed by* MAJA. *Almost simultaneously* THE FOREIGN LADY *comes out of the pavilion and sits down at her table. She raises the glass of milk to her lips, and is about to drink, when she catches sight of* RUBEK *and stares at him with vacant, expressionless eyes. He remains seated, but stares at her intently and persistently. At last he gets up and takes a few steps towards her, stops, then speaks in a low tone.*)

RUBEK: I knew you at once, Irene.

IRENE (*In a toneless voice, putting down her glass*): So you recognized me, Arnold.

RUBEK (*Without answering*): I see you know me too.

IRENE: Yes; but that's different.

RUBEK: Why?

IRENE: *You're* still alive.

RUBEK (*Not understanding*): Alive?

IRENE (*After a pause*): Who's the other one? The woman who was sitting with you—at the table?

RUBEK (*With some reluctance*): That was—that is my wife.

IRENE (*Nods slowly*): I see. That's good. She doesn't concern me, then.

RUBEK (*Uncertainly*): No—I suppose not—

IRENE: You found her later; after—after I'd ceased to be.

RUBEK (*Gives her a sudden penetrating look*): Ceased to be? What do you mean by that, Irene?

IRENE (*Without answering*): And the child? The child has fared well, Arnold. It has won its way to honor and glory. Yes. Our child lives on after me.

RUBEK (*Smiles as at a far-off memory*): Our child—yes; we used to call it that.

IRENE: When I was alive—yes.

RUBEK (*Attempting to take a lighter tone*): Yes, Irene; our child has become famous all over the world. You may have read about it.

IRENE (*Nods*): And has made its father famous too. That's what you always used to dream of.

RUBEK (*Softly, with emotion*): I owe it all to you, Irene. Thank you for that.

IRENE (*Lost in thought*): If I'd done what I had a right to do at that time, Arnold—

RUBEK: Well?

IRENE: I should have killed that child.

RUBEK: Killed it!

IRENE (*In a whisper*): Yes—killed it; before I left you. Crushed it. Ground it into dust.

RUBEK (*Shakes his head reproachfully*): You could never have done that, Irene. You would never have had the heart to do it.

IRENE: That's true: at that time my heart was different.

RUBEK: But, later? Afterwards?

IRENE: Later—I killed it innumerable times. Day and night I killed it in my thoughts. Killed it—in hatred, in revenge, in anguish.

RUBEK (*Goes right up to her table and asks softly*): Irene—why did you leave me? Surely you can tell me after all these years. Why did you run away like that and leave no trace? Why did you disappear completely?

IRENE (*Slowly shakes her head*): Oh, Arnold—why should I tell you now; now that I'm in another world.

RUBEK: Was there someone else you cared for?

IRENE: There was someone who no longer cared for me; to whom my life was of no further use.

RUBEK (*Changing the subject*): Don't let's dwell on the past, Irene—

IRENE: No; I'm on the other side now; lost in another world. Why dwell on things I can no longer touch.

RUBEK: Where have you been, Irene? I tried desperately to find you. Where did you go?

IRENE: I vanished into darkness—as the child stood there transfigured in the light.

RUBEK: Have you traveled, Irene? Have you been to many foreign lands?

IRENE: Innumerable foreign lands; all over the world.

RUBEK (*Looks at her with compassion*): What did you do with yourself?

IRENE (*Turns her eyes on him*): Wait a minute; let me see —Oh, yes—of course! I became a music-hall performer. I stood on a turntable, stark naked—and posed as a living statue. I made a lot of money out of it. That's more than I did with you—you never had a penny. I went with many men; they were mad about me—I used to drive them crazy. I could never do that to you, Arnold: you were invulnerable.

RUBEK (*Shying away from the subject*): And did you marry?

IRENE: Yes; I married one of them.

RUBEK: Who is your husband?

IRENE: He was a South American. A famous diplomat. (*Gazes before her with a stony smile*) I drove him insane; utterly insane; incurably insane! It was a fascinating game. I should have found it hilariously funny—if there'd been anything left alive in me.

RUBEK: Where is he now?

IRENE: Rotting in some churchyard, with an imposing monument over his grave, and a bullet rattling in his skull.

RUBEK: Did he kill himself?

IRENE: Yes. He was obliging enough to save me the trouble.

RUBEK: And do you never mourn his loss, Irene?

IRENE (*Not understanding*): What loss?

RUBEK: Von Satow's, of course.

IRENE: His name was not Von Satow.

RUBEK: Indeed?

IRENE: Von Satow is my second husband. He's a Russian.

RUBEK: What's happened to him?

IRENE: He's far away in the Ural Mountains—among his gold mines.

RUBEK: Does he live there all the time?

IRENE (*Shrugs her shoulders*): Live? Live, did you say? Actually—I've killed him.

RUBEK (*Starts*): Killed him!

IRENE: Yes, killed him. With a sharp, exquisite little dagger that I always keep under my pillow.

RUBEK (*Vehemently*): I don't believe a word of this, Irene!

IRENE (*With a gentle smile*): It's true, Arnold—I assure you.

RUBEK (*Looks at her compassionately*): Have you never had any children?

IRENE: Yes—I've had many children.

RUBEK: Where are they now?

IRENE: I've killed them.

RUBEK (*Severely*): Stop telling all these lies, Irene!

IRENE: I *did* kill them, I tell you. I murdered them, one after the other, with joy in my heart—long before they were even born.

RUBEK (*Sadly, earnestly*): You're speaking in riddles, Irene.

IRENE: How can I help that? I only tell you things that are whispered in my ear.

RUBEK: I suppose I'm the only one who knows the answer.

IRENE: You *should* be the only one.

RUBEK (*Leans across the table and looks at her intently*): Something in you has snapped, Irene.

IRENE (*Gently*): Doesn't that always happen, when a young, vital woman dies?

RUBEK: Irene! You must free yourself from these insane illusions. You're alive! You're alive! You must know that!

IRENE (*Rises slowly from her chair and says in a trembling voice*): I was dead for many years. They came and bound me—tied my arms behind my back. Then they lowered

me into a tomb. There were bars at the window and
padded walls; so that the shrieks from the tomb might not
disturb those in the world above. But now—I'm just beginning to rise again from the dead. (*She sits down again.*)

RUBEK (*After a short pause*): And you blame me for all this?

IRENE: Yes.

RUBEK: You blame me for what you call your death?

IRENE: I blame you for the fact that I *had* to die. (*Switches
to a more casual tone*) Why don't you sit down, Arnold?

RUBEK: Dare I?

IRENE: Yes— You needn't be afraid of being frozen. I
haven't quite turned to ice yet.

RUBEK (*Moves a chair over to her table and sits down*):
Strange, isn't it, Irene? We used to sit like this, together,
long ago.

IRENE: And always slightly apart from one another.

RUBEK (*Drawing nearer*): It had to be so, then.

IRENE: Did it, Arnold?

RUBEK (*Decisively*): We *had* to stay apart.

IRENE: Did we—really?

RUBEK (*Continuing*): Do you remember what you answered
when I asked you to leave everything and go away with
me?

IRENE: I raised my hand and swore that I would follow you
to the end of the world and to the end of life; and that I
would serve you in all things—

RUBEK: In my art—

IRENE: Yes—with my naked body—

RUBEK (*Deeply moved*): And you did serve me, Irene;
bravely, gladly, generously—

IRENE: I served you with every drop of blood in my young
body, Arnold.

RUBEK (*Nods, with a look of gratitude*): You have every right
to say that.

IRENE: I fell down at your feet and served you, Arnold.
(*Clenching her fists*) But, then—you—*you*—!

RUBEK (*Defensively*): I never harmed you in any way, Irene
—never!

IRENE: You did! You destroyed something deep within me—

RUBEK (*Drawing back*): I did—!

IRENE: Yes, you! I revealed myself to you unreservedly—
stood before you freely, without shame; you gazed at me
but you never really saw me. (*Softly*) You never once came
near me, Arnold.

RUBEK: Yet, time and again, I was as though intoxicated by
your beauty!

IRENE (*Continues, as though she hasn't heard*): Yet if you
had come near me—if you had ever touched me—I think
I should have killed you. I always used to carry a small,
silver bodkin hidden in my hair. (*Thoughtfully; stroking
her forehead*) But—all the same—that you could—

RUBEK (*With an eloquent look*): I was an artist, Irene.

IRENE (*Darkly*): Yes; that's just it.

RUBEK: An artist—above all. I was in a fever—struggling to
create my masterpiece. (*Loses himself in memories*) It was
to be called "The Resurrection Day." I saw it in the shape
of a young woman waking from the sleep of death—

IRENE: Our child, yes—

RUBEK: She was to be the Ideal Woman; the noblest, purest
woman the world had ever known. Then, I found you—
and I knew you were the one I needed. And you agreed
to help me—joyfully, willingly. You left your people and
your home, and followed me.

IRENE: That was *my* resurrection. I awoke from the deep
slumber of childhood—and followed you.

RUBEK: Yes! That's why you alone could serve my purpose;
you became to me a hallowed creature—to be worshiped
in my most sacred thoughts. I was young then, Irene; it
would have seemed to me profanity to touch you—to desire you with my senses. I was afraid my vision would escape me—that I would be left powerless to accomplish the
work I was struggling to achieve— And I still think there
was some truth in that.

IRENE (*Nods with a touch of scorn*): First the work of art—
then the human being.

RUBEK: Condemn me if you must; but, at that time, I was
totally absorbed in my task, Irene. I was happy—utterly
enthralled by it.

IRENE: And you accomplished your task; you were victorious.

RUBEK: Yes, thanks to you—I was victorious. I wanted to
create the image of a pure young woman, awakening on
Resurrection Day. Nothing in that higher, freer, happier
region would seem strange to her—or new, or different.
While on earth she had known only joy, and purity, and
innocence; and, on awakening from the long sleep of
death, she finds herself unchanged. (*More softly*) The
Ideal Woman: that was my vision. I created her in your
image, Irene.

IRENE (*Spreads her hands out on the table and leans back
in her chair*): Then, you were finished with me—

RUBEK (*Reproachfully*): Irene!

IRENE: You had no further use for me—

RUBEK: How can you say that!

IRENE: —and you began to look about you for other "ideal
women"—

RUBEK: I found none. No one, after you.

IRENE: No other models, Arnold?

RUBEK: You were no model to me; you were the source of
all my inspiration.

IRENE (*Is silent for a moment*): And what poems have you
created, since the day I left you? What other poems have
you created out of marble?

RUBEK: No poems, Irene. I've merely done a little modeling.

IRENE: This woman you're living with—?

RUBEK (*Interrupts her vehemently*): Don't speak of her! Not
now!

IRENE: Where do you plan to go with her?

RUBEK (*Tired and spent*): On a long, dull trip—up North,
along the coast.

IRENE (*Looks at him with an almost imperceptible smile,*

and whispers): It would be better for you to go up into
the mountains. As high as you can go, Arnold. Higher,
higher—always higher!

RUBEK (*Expectantly, eagerly*): Will *you* be going there?

IRENE: Have you the courage to meet me once again?

RUBEK (*Uncertainly, with an inner struggle*): If we could—
oh, if we only could, Irene—!

IRENE: Why can't we do what we wish to do? (*Looks at him
imploringly with folded hands, and whispers*) Come to
me, Arnold! Come up there—to me!

(MAJA *comes round the corner of the hotel; she is radiant;
she goes quickly to the table where she and* ARNOLD *had
been sitting.*)

MAJA (*Speaks as she turns the corner, without looking up*):
I don't care *what* you say, Rubek, it's—(*Breaks off when
she sees* IRENE) Oh—excuse me! You've made an acquaintance, I see.

RUBEK (*Curtly*): Renewed an acquaintance. (*Rises*) What is
it? Do you want me?

MAJA: I only wanted to tell you— You can do as you like,
of course—but, I shan't go with you on that revolting
steamer!

RUBEK: Indeed? Why not?

MAJA: I'm going up into the forests—up into the mountains!
(*Coaxingly*) You *will* let me go, won't you, Rubek dear?
Then, afterwards, I'll be as good as gold—I promise you!

RUBEK: Who put that idea into your head?

MAJA: *He* did, of course! That dreadful bear killer. He's told
me such marvelous things about the mountains—and
about the life up there! He's told me such hideous, terrifying, *ghastly* stories—half of them lies, I expect—but thrilling all the same! You *will* let me go with him, won't you,
Rubek? Just to see if what he says is true! May I? May I,
Rubek?

RUBEK: As far as I'm concerned, you may. Just you go to the
mountains, little Maja! Go as far, and for as long, as you
like! I may be going in the same direction.

MAJA (*Quickly*): You needn't bother to go on my account!

RUBEK: I'm going to the mountains. I've made up my mind to go.

MAJA: Oh, thank you, Rubek! May I run and tell the bear killer at once?

RUBEK: You may tell the bear killer anything you like.

MAJA: Thank you, thank you! (*Is about to take his hand, but he withdraws it*) You're so kind and sweet today! (*She runs into the hotel. At that moment the door of the pavilion is seen to open noiselessly—and remains ajar.* THE DEACONESS *stands in the opening, watching intently. The others do not notice her.*)

RUBEK (*Decisively, turning to* IRENE): We'll meet up there, then?

IRENE (*Rises slowly*): Yes, we must. I've been searching for you for years.

RUBEK: When did you first begin to search for me, Irene?

IRENE (*With a touch of bitter humor*): From the moment I realized I'd given you something one can't live without, Arnold. Something one should never part with.

RUBEK (*Bows his head*): You gave me some of the best years of your youth—that's true enough. It fills me with remorse.

IRENE: I gave you far more than that—lavish fool that I was!

RUBEK: Yes—you were generous. You gave me all your naked loveliness—

IRENE: —to gaze at—

RUBEK: —and to glorify.

IRENE: For your own glory, Arnold— And the child's.

RUBEK: And for yours.

IRENE: But you've forgotten the most precious thing I gave you.

RUBEK: The most precious? What was that?

IRENE: My soul, Arnold. My young, vibrant soul. I had nothing left within me: I was soulless. (*Stares at him fixedly*) That's why I died.

(THE DEACONESS *opens the door wide, and makes room for her, as she passes into the pavilion.*)

RUBEK (*Stands looking after her and whispers*): Irene!

CURTAIN

ACT TWO

SCENE: *Near a health resort in the high mountains. The landscape is a vast, treeless plain by a mountain lake. Beyond the lake is seen a high range of mountains with snow in the crevasses. Downstage left, a mountain stream tumbles over a ledge of rock, and flows smoothly off right into the plain. Plants and bushes grow along the bed of the stream. On raised ground to the right, a stone bench. It is a summer afternoon, towards sunset. In the distance, on the plain beyond the brook, a flock of children are singing and dancing. Some wear ordinary clothes, others are in peasant costumes. Under the following dialogue is heard the distant sound of happy laughter.*

PROFESSOR RUBEK *sits up on the bench with a shawl over his shoulders, and watches the children at play.*

In a few moments MAJA *appears among the bushes in the middle distance, on the left. She peers about her, shading her eyes with her hand. She wears a flat sports hat, and a short skirt hiked up to just below the knees; she has on thick, high boots. She carries an alpenstock.*

MAJA (*From across the brook, catches sight of* RUBEK *and calls out*): Halloo-oo! (*She comes across the plain and with the help of her staff jumps over the brook and scrambles up the bank. Out of breath)* I've been looking for you for ages, Rubek!

RUBEK (*Nods indifferently and asks*): Have you just come from the hotel?

MAJA: That flytrap! Yes—I just escaped from it.

RUBEK (*Looks at her a moment*): I notice you didn't come in for lunch.

MAJA: No; we had our lunch out in the open.

RUBEK: Who do you mean by "we"?

MAJA: The bear killer and I, of course.

RUBEK: I see.

MAJA: And tomorrow morning early we'll be going off again.

RUBEK: After bears?

MAJA: Yes; we hope to bag a big one.

RUBEK: Have you seen any tracks?

MAJA (*In a superior tone*): You don't find bears out in the open!

RUBEK: Indeed—where then?

MAJA: Hidden away in the thickest part of the forest. In remote places where ordinary city folk would never dare to venture.

RUBEK: And the two of you are going there tomorrow?

MAJA (*Flings herself down on the heather*): We plan to; we may even start this evening—that is, if you've no obejction.

RUBEK: I? Far be it from me—

MAJA (*Hurriedly*): Lars and the dogs will be with us, of course.

RUBEK: Lars and the dogs are no concern of mine. (*Changing the subject*) Hadn't you better come and sit here on the bench?

MAJA (*Drowsily*): No, thanks; this heather is so soft and comfortable.

RUBEK: You look tired.

MAJA (*Yawning*): I'm beginning to feel a little tired, I think.

RUBEK: It creeps up on one. In the first excitement one doesn't feel it—

MAJA (*Sleepily*): I think I'll close my eyes for a few moments.

(*A short pause.*)

MAJA (*Suddenly impatient*): How can you bear to hear those children screaming! Why you should want to watch their silly antics—!

RUBEK: In spite of their "silly antics," as you call them—there's a wonderful grace, a sort of harmony, in their movements now and then. It's like music. Those moments are worth waiting for.

MAJA (*With a slightly scornful laugh*): Always the artist—aren't you, Rubek?

RUBEK: Yes—I hope so.

MAJA (*Turns over on her side with her back to him*): He's not a bit of an artist.

RUBEK (*Attentively*): Who isn't?

MAJA (*In a sleepy tone*): The other one, of course.

RUBEK: The bear killer, you mean?

MAJA: Yes. He's not a bit of an artist. Not a bit!

RUBEK (*Smiles*): I'm sure you're right in that.

MAJA (*Vehemently, but without moving*): And then he's so ugly! (*Picks a tuft of heather and throws it away*) So incredibly ugly! Ugh!

RUBEK: Do you find that reassuring? Is that why you're willing to go off into the wilds with him?

MAJA (*Curtly*): I don't know. (*Turns towards him*) You're ugly too, Rubek.

RUBEK: Have you only just discovered that?

MAJA: No—I've been aware of it for quite some time.

RUBEK (*Shrugs his shoulders*): One grows older, little Maja; one grows older.

MAJA: That's not the kind of ugliness I mean. But there's a weariness in your eyes—an expression of defeat. You look at me with a resigned expression—that is, when you deign to look at me at all.

RUBEK: I see. That's what you think.

MAJA: Yes—I've watched it grow on you. Your eyes have become almost evil; I sometimes feel you're hatching some awful plot against me.

RUBEK: Really? (*In a friendly but serious tone*) Come here and sit beside me, Maja. It's time we had a little talk.

MAJA (*Half rising*): Will you let me sit on your knee, then? You used to like me to—remember?

RUBEK: No, not here—in full view of the hotel. (*He makes room for her*) But you may sit on the bench next to me.

MAJA: No thanks; in that case I'd rather stay where I am. I can hear you well enough from here. (*Looks at him inquiringly*) What is it you want to say to me?

RUBEK (*Begins slowly*): Why do you suppose I agreed to come up here this summer?

MAJA: Well among other things—you said it was because you thought it would do me so much good. But—

RUBEK: But—?

MAJA: I don't believe a word of all that now. I believe you had another reason—

RUBEK: Indeed?

MAJA: Yes. I think you came on account of that pale lady.

RUBEK: Madame von Satow—!

MAJA: Well—we can't seem to get rid of her. Yesterday she even turned up here.

RUBEK: What on earth—!

MAJA: You obviously knew her intimately, Rubek—long before you knew *me*.

RUBEK: Yes, and I'd forgotten her long before I knew you, too.

MAJA (*Sitting upright*): Do you forget so easily?

RUBEK (*Curtly*): Very easily. (*Adds harshly*) When I choose to.

MAJA: Even a woman who's been your model?

RUBEK (*Dismissing this*): When I no longer had any use for her, then—

MAJA: A woman who has posed before you naked?

RUBEK: That means nothing—to an artist. (*With a change of tone*) And how, may I ask, was I to know that she was in this country?

MAJA: You might have seen her name on a Visitor's List, in one of the local newspapers.

RUBEK: Her present name would have meant nothing to me. I never heard of Herr von Satow.

MAJA (*With pretended weariness*): Oh, well—! Then I suppose you had some other reason for deciding to come here.

RUBEK (*Seriously*): Yes, Maja, I had. A very different reason. I think it's about time we discussed it.

MAJA (*In a fit of suppressed laughter*): You look so solemn, Rubek!

RUBEK (*Looks at her suspiciously*): Unnecessarily solemn, perhaps.

MAJA: How do you mean?

RUBEK: And that might be as well for both of us.

MAJA: Now I'm beginning to get curious!

RUBEK: Only curious? Not the slightest bit uneasy?

MAJA (*Shakes her head*): Not in the least.

RUBEK: Good. Then, listen. The other day, down at the Baths, you said you'd noticed how restless I've become of late—

MAJA: And so you have.

RUBEK: What do you think is the reason for this restlessness?

MAJA: How should I know? (*Briskly*) Perhaps you're bored with my companionship; we've been together constantly—

RUBEK: Constantly? Why not say, perpetually?

MAJA: Day in and day out, yes. In the past four or five years we've scarcely been apart a single moment. We've been alone together—just the two of us.

RUBEK (*With interest*): Well? What then?

MAJA (*Slightly oppressed*): You're not a particularly sociable man, Rubek. You prefer to be alone—you actually need solitude. And I don't know how to talk about the things that interest you; about art—and things like that. I know nothing about art and (*With an impatient gesture*) God knows, I don't care anything about it! .

RUBEK: I know. That's why we usually end up sitting by the fire, talking about the things that interest *you*.

MAJA: And there's nothing very stimulating about that!

RUBEK: Not stimulating, perhaps—but it helps to pass the time.

MAJA: That's just it—pass the time! And time is passing; it's slipping away from you, Rubek. I think *that's* what makes you so uneasy—

RUBEK (*Nods vehemently*): And so restless! (*Shifts about on the bench*) It's such a meager kind of life. I don't think I can put up with it much longer.

MAJA (*Rises and stands looking at him for a moment*): If you want to get rid of me—just say so.

RUBEK: Get rid of you! What an expression!

MAJA: I mean it! If you've had enough of me, just tell me—and I'll go.

RUBEK (*With an almost imperceptible smile*): Is that supposed to be a threat?

MAJA: How could that possibly be a threat to you?

RUBEK (*Rising*): It's true; you're right. (*Adds after a pause*) We can't go on like this.

MAJA: And, so—?

RUBEK: There's no "and, so" about it. (*Emphasizing his words*) Simply because we can't go on living alone together—that doesn't necessarily mean we have to part. .

MAJA (*With a scornful smile*): What have you in mind? A temporary separation?

RUBEK (*Shakes his head*): That's not necessary, either.

MAJA: Then, what? Out with it! What do you want to do with me?

RUBEK (*With some hesitation*): What I need—and I feel this strongly, almost desperately—is the companionship of someone who could be really close to me—

MAJA (*Interrupts him tensely*): And I'm—not that?

RUBEK: Not in the way I mean. I mean closeness in the sense of sharing an understanding of my work—of all the things I strive for. I need someone to supply the things I lack—someone to complete me, if you like.

MAJA (*Slowly*): I'm of no use to you in things like that, it's true. They're much too hard for me.

RUBEK: I'm afraid they're not much in your line.

MAJA (*In an outburst*): No! And I wouldn't want them to be, either!

RUBEK: I'm well aware of that. I had no such illusions when I married you.

MAJA (*Observing him closely*): You have someone definite in mind, haven't you? I can tell.

RUBEK: Indeed? Since when have you become a mind reader?

MAJA: I know you, Rubek. I know you very well.

RUBEK: Who do you think I have in mind? Do you know that too?

MAJA: Of course I do!

RUBEK: Who? Tell me!

MAJA: That former model of yours. The one you used for— (*With a sudden change of thought*) People down at the hotel think she's mad; did you know that?

RUBEK: Really? And what do people down at the hotel think of you and the bear killer?

MAJA: What's that got to do with it? (*Continues her former train of thought*) But you were thinking of the pale lady, weren't you?

RUBEK (*Calmly*): Yes, I was. When I'd finished my work, and I had no further use for her— In any case, she left me—disappeared—without a word—

MAJA: —then you took me as a sort of makeshift, I suppose.

RUBEK (*More unfeelingly*): Frankly yes, little Maja—something of the sort. For a year, or a year and a half, I'd been alone, you see, struggling to put the last, the final touches to my work. "The Resurrection Day" went all over the world and brought me fame, and all the good things that went with it. (*With greater warmth*) But I no longer cared about my work. I became disgusted with all the praise and all the laurels that were heaped upon me. I was filled with despair and loathing; I wanted to run away—bury myself—hide myself in some remote corner of the woods. (*Looks at her*) Since you're a mind reader, I suppose you can guess what I decided to do then?

MAJA (*Lightly*): You decided to make portrait-busts of ladies and gentlemen—that's simple!

RUBEK: To order—yes. And behind each portrait lurked the face of an appropriate animal. I gave them that for nothing; threw it in for good measure, so to speak. (*With a smile*) But I wasn't thinking so much of that—

MAJA: What, then?

RUBEK (*Again seriously*): It suddenly struck me that this whole business about art—this cant about an artist's vocation, an artist's sacred mission—was a lot of hollow nonsense; basically unsound and meaningless.

MAJA: What would you have instead?

RUBEK: Life, Maja.

MAJA: Life?

RUBEK: Yes; beauty, sunshine, life itself. Isn't that the all-important thing? Far more important, certainly, than burying oneself in a dark dismal hole, exhausting one's strength in a constant battle with lumps of clay and blocks of marble.

MAJA (*With a little sigh*): I've always thought so, certainly.

RUBEK: And I'd grown rich enough to live in luxury; to enjoy basking in the sunshine. I could afford to build myself the villa at Lake Taunitz, the palatial house in town, and all the rest of it.

MAJA (*Taking his tone*): And last but not least, you could afford to buy me as well, and to give me a share in all your treasures.

RUBEK (*Jokingly; changing the tone of the conversation*): Didn't I promise to take you with me up to a high mountain and show you all the glory of the world?

MAJA (*With a gentle expression*): You've perhaps taken me

up to a high enough mountain, Rubek—but you haven't shown me all the glory of the world.

RUBEK (*With a laugh of irritation*): How insatiable you are, Maja! How utterly insatiable! (*Bursts out violently*) But the most hopeless thing of all—! Can you guess what that is, I wonder?

MAJA (*With quiet defiance*): The fact that you're bound to me for life; isn't that it?

RUBEK: I shouldn't have had the heart to express myself so crudely.

MAJA: But you have the heart to think it, all the same.

RUBEK: You can't begin to understand the feelings of an artist, Maja.

MAJA: Good heavens! I can't even understand my *own* feelings, if it comes to that!

RUBEK (*Continues undisturbed*): I live at such high speed —all artists do. I've lived through a whole lifetime in the few years since we met. I realize there can be no happiness for me in idleness. It's useless for men like me to attempt that kind of life. I must go on working and creating —working and creating, to my dying day. (*Forcing himself to continue*) That's why I can't go on with you any longer, Maja; not with you alone.

MAJA (*Quietly*): You're tired of me, in other words.

RUBEK (*In an outburst*): Yes, I'm tired! Unspeakably tired, and bored, and enervated by our life together. Now you know the truth. (*Controlling himself*) These are cruel, harsh words I know, and you've done nothing to deserve them; I admit that freely. It's solely and entirely due to me. I've started a new cycle; I've awakened; I've come to myself again.

MAJA (*Involuntarily folding her hands*): Then why, in heaven's name, shouldn't we part?

RUBEK (*Looks at her in astonishment*): Would you be willing to?

MAJA (*Shrugs her shoulders*): Of course—if there's no other way—

RUBEK (*Eagerly*): But there is another way; there's an alternative—

MAJA (*Holding up her forefinger*): You're thinking of the pale lady again, aren't you?

RUBEK: Why hide it? Since seeing her again I've thought about her constantly. (*Takes a step towards her*) I'll tell you a secret, Maja.

MAJA: Well?

RUBEK (*Points at his breast*): All my dreams—the visions that inspire my work and feed it—are hidden away in a little box here in my breast; this box has a special safety-lock, and only one key can open it. When she left me and disappeared, she took that key away with her. The box snapped shut, and it was impossible for me to open it. You had no key, little Maja; all these years the treasure has lain there useless. And time is passing!

MAJA (*Trying to hide a sly smile*): You should get her to unlock it for you, Rubek.

RUBEK (*Not understanding*): Maja—?

MAJA: She's here, isn't she? I expect that's why she came.

RUBEK: I've never said a word to her about it.

MAJA (*With an innocent expression*): But it's all so simple, Rubek dear. What is there to make a fuss about?

RUBEK: Simple—you think?

MAJA: Of course! If she's the one you need, by all means keep her near you. (*Nods to him*) Don't worry! I shall find a place to go.

RUBEK: Where do you mean?

MAJA: There's always the villa; if need be I can move out there. But why should that be necessary? God knows, the house in town is big enough! With a little good will, there'd certainly be room for three.

RUBEK (*Uncertainly*): You really think that would work out?

MAJA (*Lightly*): Why not? And if it doesn't, it doesn't— that's all! There's no point in discussing it.

RUBEK: But if it doesn't work out, Maja—then, what shall we do?

MAJA: Then we shall simply have to part—part for good. I'll manage to find a new life for myself somewhere; a free life! Free! Free!—No need to worry about that, Professor Rubek! (*Suddenly points off to the right*) Look! There she is!

RUBEK (*Turns*): Where?

MAJA: Striding across the plain—like a marble statue. She seems to be coming here.

RUBEK (*Gazing off, shading his eyes with his hand*): She looks like "The Resurrection" come to life. (*To himself*) How could I have been fool enough to change it; to overshadow her with—!

MAJA: What are you talking about?

RUBEK: Nothing. Nothing you would understand.

(IRENE *comes from the right over the plain. The children at their play have caught sight of her and run to meet her. She is surrounded by them; some appear confident and at ease, others shy and timid. She talks to them in a low voice, and indicates they are to go down to the hotel; she herself will rest awhile beside the brook. The children run down the slope on the left, stage center.* IRENE *goes to where the water pours over the wall of rock and lets it flow over her hands to cool them.*)

MAJA (*In a low voice*): Go down and have a talk with her, Rubek. Talk to her alone.

RUBEK: Meanwhile—where will you go?

MAJA (*Gives him a significant look*): I'll go my own way, from now on. (*She jumps down from the hillock, leaps the brook by the aid of her alpenstock, and stops beside* IRENE.) Madame von Satow—Professor Rubek's up there waiting for you.

IRENE: What does he want?

MAJA: He wants you to help him open a little box that has snapped shut.

IRENE: Can I help him in that?

MAJA: He says you're the only one who can.

IRENE: Then I shall have to try.

MAJA: Yes, do, Madame von Satow. You really must! (*She goes down the path towards the hotel. In a few moments* RUBEK *comes down to* IRENE, *but stops with the brook between them.*)

IRENE (*After a short pause*): She—the other one—said you were waiting for me.

RUBEK: I realize now, I've been waiting for you for years.

IRENE: I couldn't come to you, Arnold. I was down there in the tomb; in a deep sleep filled with dreams.

RUBEK: But now you have awakened.

IRENE (*Shakes her head*): My eyes are still weighed down with sleep.

RUBEK: A new dawn awaits us, Irene—you shall see!

IRENE: You mustn't believe that.

RUBEK: But I do believe it! I'm convinced of it! Now that I've found you again—

IRENE: Risen from the dead.

RUBEK: Transfigured!

IRENE: Risen from the dead—but not transfigured, Arnold.

RUBEK (*He crosses over to her on the stepping stones below the cascade*): Where have you been all day, Irene?

IRENE (*Pointing*): Far out on the dead stretches of the moor—

RUBEK (*Changing the conversation*): Your—your friend is not with you today, I see.

IRENE (*Smiling*): All the same, my friend—is keeping a sharp eye on me.

RUBEK: Does she always do that?

IRENE (*Glances furtively around*): Always. I'm never out of her sight—no matter where I go. (*Whispers*) One of these fine days, I'll have to kill her.

RUBEK: Would you do that?

IRENE: With the utmost joy—if I could only manage it.

RUBEK: Why should you want to?

IRENE: Because she's a witch—a black magician. (*Mysteriously*) Think of it, Arnold! **She's** actually changed herself into my shadow.

RUBEK (*Trying to calm her*): There, there, Irene! We must all have a shadow, after all.

IRENE: I'm my own shadow. (*In an outburst*) Don't you understand that!

RUBEK (*Sadly*): Yes—of course I do, Irene.

(*He sits down on a stone beside the brook. She stands behind him leaning against the wall of rock.*)

IRENE (*After a pause*): Why do you turn your eyes away from me?

RUBEK (*Softly, shaking his head*): I dare not look at you.

IRENE: Why shouldn't you dare to look at me any more?

RUBEK: You are tormented by a shadow; I'm tormented by my conscience.

IRENE (*With a glad cry of liberation*): At last!

RUBEK (*Springs to his feet*): What is it, Irene?

IRENE (*Motions him away*): Quiet! Quiet! (*Takes a deep breath and speaks as though relieved of some heavy burden*) They've let go of me—for a while, at least— Now we can sit down and talk as we used to—when I was alive.

RUBEK: If we only could, Irene.

IRENE: Sit down where you were sitting; I'll come and sit beside you. (*He sits down again; she sits on another stone close to him.*)

IRENE (*After a short silence*): I've come back to you now, Arnold. From an immense distance—I've come back to you.

RUBEK: Back from an endless journey.

IRENE: Home to my lord and master—

RUBEK: To our home—to our own home, Irene.

IRENE: You knew I'd come, didn't you, Arnold? Did you look for me every single day?

RUBEK: I didn't dare look for you.

IRENE (*With a sidelong glance*): Didn't dare? No, I suppose not. For you understood nothing.

RUBEK: Is it true, Irene, that there was no one else? Didn't you leave me for someone else's sake?

IRENE: Mightn't it have been for your sake, Arnold?

RUBEK (*Looks at her doubtfully*): I don't understand—

IRENE: Don't you see, Arnold? After I'd given myself body and soul to serve you, and the statue was finished—our child, as you called it—I laid at your feet the most precious offering of all; I withdrew—disappeared from your life forever.

RUBEK (*Bows his head*): And left me desolate.

IRENE (*Flaring up suddenly*): That was exactly what I wanted. Never again were you to create anything—never again! I wanted our child to stand alone.

RUBEK: Then—was it jealousy?

IRENE (*Coldly*): It came closer to being hatred.

RUBEK: Hatred? Hatred for me?

IRENE (*Vehemently*): Yes. It was the artist I hated in you. The artist, who made use of a young vibrant human being —unscrupulously, almost carelessly—and destroyed its soul to create a work of art.

RUBEK: How can you say that, Irene! You looked upon my art as something sacred; you shared in it—rejoiced in it! Each day we met as though before an altar!

IRENE (*Coldly, as before*): I'll tell you one thing, Arnold.

RUBEK: Well?

IRENE: I didn't love your art before I met you—I loved it still less afterwards.

RUBEK: But the artist, Irene?

IRENE: I hate the artist.

RUBEK: The artist in me too?

IRENE: In you most of all. Each time I took off my clothes and stood before you naked—I hated you.

RUBEK (*Violently*): You're lying, Irene! That's not true!

IRENE: I hated you because you were so unmoved—

RUBEK (*Laughs*): Unmoved! You couldn't have thought that!

IRENE: —so maddeningly objective—so self-controlled; because you were an artist, not a man! (*Her tone changes to one of tenderness and warmth*) But I loved the statue;

I loved that moist clay that came to life under your touch. Out of that formless mass our child was born—your child and mine, Arnold.

RUBEK (*Sadly*): In spirit and in truth.

IRENE: It's for the sake of our child that I've undertaken this long pilgrimage.

RUBEK (*Suddenly alert*): For the statue's—?

IRENE: Call it what you like. I call it our child.

RUBEK (*Uneasily*): You mean—you want to see it? You want to see it finished? In the marble you always thought so cold? (*Eagerly*) It's far away in one of the great museums, Irene; don't you know that?

IRENE: I've heard a rumor to that effect.

RUBEK: And you always hated museums, don't you remember? You used to call them graveyards—

IRENE: Then I shall make a pilgrimage to where my soul, and my soul's child, lie buried.

RUBEK (*Uneasy and alarmed*): You must never see that statue—do you hear? Never try to see it, I implore you!

IRENE: Why not? Do you think if I saw it again I should die a second time?

RUBEK (*Clenches his hands*): I don't know what to think— I never dreamed this statue would haunt you in this way, Irene. After all—you left me before it was completed—

IRENE: It *was* completed. I should never have left you otherwise. I should never have left you to finish it alone.

RUBEK (*Sits with his elbows on his knees, rocking his head from side to side, with his hands over his eyes*): It's no longer quite the same as when you saw it last.

IRENE (*Quietly, but quick as lightning, she half draws a narrow-bladed knife concealed in her breast, and says in a hoarse whisper*): Arnold—you haven't harmed our child?

RUBEK (*Evasively*): Harmed it?—How can I be sure what you would call it?

IRENE (*Breathless*): What have you done to the child? Tell me!

RUBEK: I'll tell you, if you promise to listen quietly to what I have to say.

IRENE (*Hides the knife*): I'll listen as quietly as a mother can, when she—

RUBEK (*Interrupting*): And you mustn't look at me while I'm telling you.

IRENE (*Moves to another stone behind his back*): I'll sit here behind you. Now—tell me.

RUBEK (*Takes his hands from before his eyes and gazes straight before him*): When I first discovered you, I knew I had to use you to create my masterwork.

IRENE: "The Resurrection Day" you called it; I call it "our child."

RUBEK: I was young in those days; and I had very little knowledge of life. I chose the figure of a beautiful, virginal young woman as the symbol of the Resurrection Day. Her life on this earth had left her pure and untouched as a child; and when she awoke in the glorious light, she had no evil to atone for.

IRENE (*Rapidly*): Yes— And I still stand there like that in our work—?

RUBEK (*Hesitating*): Perhaps not quite in the same way, Irene.

IRENE (*In rising excitement*): Not quite—? Not as I always used to stand for you?

RUBEK (*Without answering*): In the years that followed I learned worldly wisdom. I saw the Resurrection Day in a more complex form. The base on which your figure stood —erect and solitary—seemed too small to carry all the wealth of images I now wanted to add—

IRENE (*Gropes for the knife but stops short*): What did you add then? Tell me!

RUBEK: The images of things I'd seen around me in the world. I was compelled to do it, Irene. I *had* to. I enlarged the base to make room for this new conception. I added a curved segment of the earth, and out of various crevasses swarmed human beings with dimly-suggested animal faces. They were men and women as I'd come to know them in real life.

IRENE (*In breathless suspense*): But my figure as the radiant young woman still stands in the center? It does, doesn't it, Arnold?

RUBEK (*Evasively*): Perhaps not directly in the center. For the sake of the over-all effect I had to move the figure back a little way, you see. It would have dominated the whole composition otherwise.

IRENE: But the glorious light? Is it still reflected in my face?

RUBEK: Of course, Irene. That is—in a way. Subdued, perhaps, a little—to suit my new conception.

IRENE (*Rising noiselessly*): This new conception—does it express life as you now see it, Arnold?

RUBEK: Yes—I suppose it does.

IRENE: And, in this new conception, I've been subdued and moved into the background; I'm no more than a figure in a group. (*She draws the knife.*)

RUBEK: Certainly not into the background, Irene. A figure in the middle distance, perhaps.

IRENE (*Whispers hoarsely*): You've just pronounced your own death sentence, Arnold.

RUBEK (*Turns and looks up at her*): My death sentence?

IRENE (*Quickly hides the knife and says as though choked with anguish*): My whole soul—you and me—we two, we and our child—were in that solitary figure.

RUBEK (*Intensely, taking off his hat and mopping his brow*): I'm part of the group, too—I want you to know, Irene, how I've portrayed *myself*. There's a man weighed down by guilt, sitting in the foreground by a stream—like this one here. He finds it almost impossible to break loose from the earth. I call him "remorse for a wasted, perjured life." He tries to wash his hands clean in the spring water, and he's in despair because he knows he can't succeed. Never, in all eternity, will he know resurrection. He must remain forever in his hell.

IRENE (*Harshly and coldly*): Poet!

RUBEK: Why poet?

IRENE: Because you're weak and superficial. You condone and make excuses for all your sins—even those you have committed in your thoughts. You killed my soul—(*Smiles*) but you think your account is clear because you portray yourself, in a statue, as an abject contrite penitent.

RUBEK (*Defiantly*): I'm an artist; I'm not ashamed of any weakness that may cling to me. You see, Irene, I was *born* to be an artist—I can never be anything else.

IRENE (*Looks at him with a subtle, evil smile, and says gently and softly*): You are a poet, Arnold. (*Gently strokes his hair*) Can't you see that? You great, beloved, aging child?

RUBEK (*Annoyed*): Why do you keep calling me a poet?

IRENE (*With a malign look in her eyes*): Because there's something apologetic in that word, my friend; it implies forgiveness of sins; it spreads a cloak over all human frailty. (*With a sudden change of tone*) But *I* was a human being —then! I, too, had a life to live—a destiny to fulfill. I gave up all that in order to become your slave. It was suicide; a deadly sin against myself. (*Half whispering*) I shall never be able to atone for it.

(*She sits down near him beside the brook and keeps close watch on him, though he is unaware of it; as though absent-mindedly she picks some flowers from the shrubs around them.*)

IRENE (*With apparent self-control*): My destiny was to bring children into the world. Many children. Real children. Not the kind that are hidden away in graveyards. I should never have served you—poet.

RUBEK: Those were wonderful days, Irene. Wonderful, marvelous days—now that I look back on them—

IRENE (*Looks at him with a gentle expression*): Do you remember a word you used when you had finished—finished with me and with our child? (*Nods at him*) Do you remember it, Arnold?

RUBEK (*Looks at her inquiringly*): A word I used then—
that you still remember?

IRENE: Yes. Don't *you* remember it?

RUBEK (*Shakes his head*): I can't say I do—at least, not for
the moment.

IRENE: You took both my hands in yours, and pressed them
warmly. I held my breath in expectation. Then, you said:
"Thank you from my heart, Irene. This has been a blessed,
glorious episode."

RUBEK (*Looks at her doubtfully*): Did I say "episode"? It's
not a word I'm apt to use.

IRENE: You said "episode."

RUBEK (*With assumed cheerfulness*): Well—after all, I suppose in a way it *was* an episode.

IRENE (*Curtly*): At that word I left you.

RUBEK: You take things so painfully to heart.

IRENE (*Passes her hand over her forehead*): Yes—perhaps
you're right. Let's try and shake off everything sorrowful
and painful. (*Plucks off the petals of a wild rose and
strews them on the brook*) There go our birds, Arnold!
Just look at them swimming!

RUBEK: What sort of birds are they?

IRENE: Can't you see? They must be flamingos—because
they're pink.

RUBEK: Flamingos don't swim; they only wade.

IRENE: They're not flamingos, then—they're sea gulls.

RUBEK: Sea gulls with red beaks, perhaps. (*He picks some
broad green leaves and throws them into the brook*) I'll
send my ships out after them.

IRENE: But the birds must not be harmed.

RUBEK: They shall not be harmed. (*Smiles at her*) Do you
remember the summer we used to sit like this beside Lake
Taunitz—outside the little peasant hut?

IRENE (*Nods*): On Saturday evenings, yes—when we'd finished our week's work—

RUBEK: We took the train out, and stayed there over Sunday.

IRENE (*With an evil gleam of hatred in her eyes*): Only an episode, Arnold.

RUBEK (*As though not hearing*): You used to send birds swimming on the water then; water lilies mostly—

IRENE: White swans, they were.

RUBEK: White swans, of course! I tied a leaf to one of them —remember? A large dock leaf, I think it was—

IRENE: And it became Lohengrin's boat—drawn by a swan.

RUBEK: You loved that game, Irene!

IRENE: Yes—we often used to play it.

RUBEK: All through that summer. Every single Saturday.

IRENE: You said I was the swan that drew your boat; do you remember?

RUBEK: Did I? Yes—I expect I did. (*Absorbed in the game*) Just look at the sea gulls swimming down the stream!

IRENE (*Laughing*): And all your boats have run ashore!

RUBEK (*Throws more leaves into the brook*): I have plenty in reserve. (*He throws in more leaves and follows them with his eyes; then says after a pause*) Irene—I've bought that little peasant house beside Lake Taunitz.

IRENE: You've bought it, have you? You always said you would as soon as you could afford it.

RUBEK: The time came when I could afford it; and I bought it.

IRENE (*With a sidelong look at him*): And so you live there now; in our old house?

RUBEK: No; I had it torn down long ago. I've built a beautiful villa on the site, surrounded by a park. That's where we usually—(*Stops and corrects himself*)—that's where I usually spend the summer.

IRENE (*Controlling herself*): So you, and the other woman— live there now.

RUBEK (*With a touch of defiance*): Yes; unless my wife and I are traveling—as we are this year.

IRENE (*Gazing off into the distance*): How beautiful life was on Lake Taunitz—how very beautiful.

RUBEK (*As though gazing into himself*): And yet, Irene—

IRENE (*Completing his thought*): And yet we let all that beauty go.

RUBEK (*Softly and urgently*): Is it too late for repentance?

IRENE (*Doesn't answer; sits silent for a moment, then points towards the mountains*): Look over there, Arnold. Look at the sun setting behind those peaks. How red it is! You'd think the heather was on fire.

RUBEK (*Looks to where she is pointing*): It's a long time since I've watched a sunset in the mountains.

IRENE: And, what about a sunrise?

RUBEK: I don't think I've ever seen a sunrise.

IRENE (*Smiles as though lost in memories*): I once saw a marvelous sunrise.

RUBEK: Did you? Where was that?

IRENE: High, high up on a mountain top—at a dizzy height— It was you who lured me up there. You promised to show me all the glory of the world, if I would only—

RUBEK: If you would only—? Well?

IRENE: I obeyed you, and went with you up to the heights. And there I fell on my knees—and worshiped you. And served you. (*Is silent for a moment, then says softly*) Then —I saw the sunrise.

RUBEK (*Turning the conversation*): Irene—would you like to come and live with us, down at the villa?

IRENE (*Looks at him with a scornful smile*): With you— and the other woman?

RUBEK (*Urgently*): With *me*—as in the days when we were working and creating. You can free the treasure locked up within me; won't you help me to do that?

IRENE (*Shakes her head*): I no longer have the key to you, Arnold.

RUBEK: You have! You're the only one who has it! (*Imploringly*) Help me, Irene! Help me to start my life again.

IRENE (*Immovable as before*): Empty dreams, Arnold! Dead, idle dreams! There can be no resurrection for the life we had together.

RUBEK (*Curtly, breaking off*): Then we'd better go on playing.

IRENE: Yes; just playing, Arnold.

(*They sit and strew leaves and petals over the brooks, and watch them float away. In the background* ULFHEJM *and* MAJA, *dressed for hunting, are seen coming up the slope from the left.* THE SERVANT *with the leash of dogs follows them and goes out to the right.*)

RUBEK (*Catches sight of them*): There goes little Maja, with the bear killer.

IRENE: Your lady, yes.

RUBEK: Or his, perhaps.

MAJA (*Looks round as she crosses the moor, sees them sitting by the brook and calls out*): Good night, Professor! I'm off in search of adventure! Be sure and dream of me!

RUBEK (*Calls back*): What kind of an adventure will it be?

MAJA (*Coming nearer*): I'm going to try *life* for a change—instead of all that other stuff.

RUBEK (*Mockingly*): Well, fancy, little Maja! Are you going to try that, too?

MAJA: Indeed I am! I've made up a song about it—listen! (*Sings triumphantly*)

> I am free! I am free! I am free!
> No more life in the prison for me!
> I am free as a bird! I am free!

Do you know something? I believe I'm awake at last!

RUBEK: So it would seem.

MAJA (*Takes a deep breath*): Waking up is such a marvelous feeling!

RUBEK: Good night, Frau Maja—and good luck to the—

ULFHEJM (*Interrupting, calls out*): Stop that, blast you! Don't give us any of your damned good wishes! Can't you see we're going out to shoot—!

RUBEK: What will you bring me home from the hunt, little Maja?

MAJA: I'll bring back a bird of prey for you to use as a

model. You'll see! I'll put a bullet through its wing and
bring it down—

RUBEK (*Laughs mockingly and bitterly*): A bullet through
its wing—of course! In your ignorance, you've always had
a way of winging things!

MAJA (*Tosses her head*): Don't worry! I'll look after myself
from now on! (*Nods and laughs roguishly*) Goodbye—
have a nice peaceful summer night out on the moors.

RUBEK (*Jokingly*): Thanks! And bad cess to you and to
your hunting!

ULFHEJM (*Roaring with laughter*): Ah! That's more like it!

MAJA (*Laughing*): Thanks, thanks, thanks, Professor!
(*They have both crossed the visible part of the moor, and
go out through the bushes on the right.*)

RUBEK (*After a short pause*): A summer night out on the
moors. Yes—that would have been life!

IRENE (*Suddenly, with a wild expression in her eyes*): Will
you spend a summer night out on the moors—with me?

RUBEK (*Opens his arms wide*): Yes; yes, come!

IRENE: My beloved lord and master.

RUBEK: Oh, Irene!

IRENE (*Hoarsely, smiling and groping in her breast*): It will
only be an episode— (*Quickly, whispering*) Hush! Don't
look round!

RUBEK (*Also in a low voice*): What is it?

IRENE: A face—staring at me.

RUBEK (*Turns involuntarily*): Where? (*With a start*) Ah—!
(THE DEACONESS'S *head is partly visible among the
bushes beside the path to the left. Her eyes are immovably
fixed on* IRENE.)

IRENE (*Rises and says softly*): We must part now. No—don't
get up! And don't come with me. (*Bends over him and
whispers*) Till we meet again. Tonight. Out on the moors.

RUBEK: You will come, Irene?

IRENE: I shall come. Wait for me here.

RUBEK (*Repeats dreamily*): A summer night out on the

moors. With you. With you. (*His eyes meet hers*) That might have been our life, Irene. And we let it go.

IRENE: We only recognize the things we've lost, when— (*Breaks off.*)

RUBEK (*Looks at her inquiringly*) When?

IRENE: When we dead awaken.

RUBEK (*Shakes his head sadly*): And, then—what do we really see?

IRENE: We see that we have never lived. (*She goes towards the path to the left.* THE DEACONESS *makes way for her to pass and follows her down the path.* RUBEK *remains sitting motionless beside the brook.*)

MAJA (*Is heard singing triumphantly, off in the hills*):

> I am free! I am free! I am free!
> No more life in the prison for me!
> I am free as a bird! I am free!

CURTAIN

ACT THREE

SCENE: *A wild craggy mountainside with sheer precipices at the back. Snow-clad peaks rise on the right and lose themselves in drifting mist. To the left, on a mound of stones, stands an old half-ruined hut. It is early morning. Dawn is breaking. The sun has not yet risen.*

MAJA, *flushed and angry, comes down over the stones on the left.* ULFHEJM *follows her, half amused, half angry, holding on to her firmly by the sleeve.*

MAJA (*Trying to wrench herself free*): Let me go! Let me go, I say!

ULFHEJM: What's the matter? You're not going to bite me, are you? You're as ferocious as a wolf!

MAJA (*Strikes his hand*): Let me go, I tell you! And keep quiet!

ULFHEJM: Damned if I will!

MAJA: Then I won't go another step with you, do you hear? Not a single step!

ULFHEJM: How do you think you can get away from me up here?

MAJA: If necessary, I can always jump over the precipice—

ULFHEJM: And smash yourself into dogs' meat? Nice, juicy dogs' meat? (*Lets her go*) There you are! Go on! Jump over the precipice if you like. It's a sheer drop. There's nothing but a goat path—almost impassable.

MAJA (*Brushes off her skirt with her hand, and looks at him with furious eyes*): You're a nice one to go out hunting with!

ULFHEJM: Don't you care for this kind of sport?

MAJA: You call it sport, do you?

ULFHEJM: Certainly! The best sport in the world!

MAJA (*Tosses her head*): Well—I must say! (*After a pause, looks at him intently*) Why did you let the dogs loose up there?

ULFHEJM (*Blinking his eyes and smiling*): I thought they'd like the chance to do a bit of hunting on their own.

MAJA: That's not true—and you know it! You didn't do it for their sake.

ULFHEJM (*Still smiling*): What *did* I do it for, then? Tell me!

MAJA: You wanted to get rid of Lars, that's all. You told him to go after them and find them. And, meanwhile— It was disgusting of you!

ULFHEJM: Meanwhile—what?

MAJA (*Curtly breaking off*): It doesn't matter.

ULFHEJM (*In a confidential tone*): Lars won't find them,

you know; you can take an oath on that. It'll be quite some time before he comes back—you'll see.

MAJA (*Looks at him angrily*): Yes, I suppose so.

ULFHEJM (*Catching at her arm*): Lars understands my methods.

MAJA (*Eludes him and measures him with a glance*): Do you know what you look like, Mr. Ulfhejm?

ULFHEJM: Like myself, I'd say.

MAJA: Precisely; because you look exactly like a satyr.

ULFHEJM: A satyr?

MAJA: A satyr—yes.

ULFHEJM: That's some sort of a monster, isn't it? A wood-demon—or something of that sort?

MAJA: It's a creature just like you. With goats' legs, and a beard like a goat. And a satyr has horns, too.

ULFHEJM: Well, well! He has horns too, has he?

MAJA: Yes, a pair of ugly horns—like yours.

ULFHEJM: So you can see my poor little horns, can you?

MAJA: Yes, I believe I can; quite plainly.

ULFHEJM (*Takes the dogs' leash out of his pocket*): In that case, I'd better tie you up.

MAJA: Tie me up! Have you gone mad?

ULFHEJM: If I'm a demon, then I must behave like one! So —you can see my horns, can you?

MAJA (*Soothingly*): Now—do try and be nice, Mr. Ulfhejm! (*Breaking off*) By the way, where's that splendid hunting lodge you bragged so much about? I thought it was supposed to be somewhere around here.

ULFHEJM (*Points to the hut with a flourish*): There it is—in front of you.

MAJA (*Looks at him*): That old pigsty!

ULFHEJM (*Laughing in his beard*): It's sheltered more than *one* fair princess, I can tell you.

MAJA: Was that where that horrible man came to the princess in the form of a bear?

ULFHEJM: The very place, most charming fellow-hunter!

(*With a gesture of invitation*) Won't you step inside——?

MAJA: I'd rather die than set foot in there! Ugh!

ULFHEJM: It's a splendid place for a couple to drowse away a summer night! Or even a whole summer, if it comes to that.

MAJA: Thanks! The idea doesn't appeal to me! (*Impatiently*) I'm thoroughly sick of you and of your hunting. I'm going back to the hotel before they wake up down here.

ULFHEJM: And how will you get there, pray?

MAJA: That's up to you. There must be *some* way down, I'm sure of that.

ULFHEJM (*Points toward the back*): Yes, there's a way of sorts; right down the face of the precipice——

MAJA: Oh, well; I'll manage somehow——

ULFHEJM: Just try it! You'd never dare!

MAJA (*Doubtfully*): You really don't think I can do it?

ULFHEJM: Not in a million years—unless I help you.

MAJA: Come and help me, then! What else are you here for, may I ask?

ULFHEJM: Shall I carry you on my back?

MAJA: Don't be absurd!

ULFHEJM: Or in my arms, perhaps?

MAJA: Now don't start all that again!

ULFHEJM (*With suppressed anger*): I picked up a young girl, once—picked her up out of the gutter and carried her in my arms; carried her close to my heart. All through life I would have carried her like that—lest haply she should dash her foot against a stone. Her shoes were worn pretty thin when I found her, you see——

MAJA: Yet you carried her close to your heart?

ULFHEJM: Yes; I lifted her high up out of the mud and bore her in my arms with tender care. (*With a growl of laughter*) And what did I get for my pains? Can you guess that?

MAJA: No. What?

ULFHEJM (*Looks at her, smiles and nods*): Horns. The

horns you see so plainly. How's that for a funny story, Madame Bear Killer?

MAJA: It's funny enough. But I know one that's even funnier.

ULFHEJM: How does *that* story go?

MAJA: Like this: There was once a stupid girl, who had both a father and a mother—but they were poor, and their home was very humble. One day a high-and-mighty gentleman came by, and saw the girl. He picked her up in his arms—just as you did—and took her far away with him—

ULFHEJM: Did she go with him because she wanted to?

MAJA: Yes; for she was very stupid.

ULFHEJM: And, no doubt, he was a brilliant handsome man?

MAJA: No—he wasn't particularly handsome. But he pretended that he was going to take her with him up to the very highest mountain; a mountain bathed in light and radiant with sunshine.

ULFHEJM: So he was a mountain climber, was he?

MAJA: Yes—in a way.

ULFHEJM: And he took the girl up with him—?

MAJA: Far from it! Instead—he lured her into a cold damp cage, where there was neither sunshine nor fresh air—or so it seemed to her. There was only a lot of gilding, and huge stone images of phantoms were ranged along the walls.

ULFHEJM: Damned if I don't think it served her right!

MAJA: But don't you think it's a funny story, all the same?

ULFHEJM (*Looks at her a moment*): Listen to me, my dear, good fellow-hunter—

MAJA: What is it now?

ULFHEJM: Couldn't we two patch the rags of our lives together, somehow?

MAJA: Does the thought of patching up old rags appeal to you?

ULFHEJM: Why not? We might tack them together here and there and use them to make one fairly decent life.

MAJA: What if the rags are too rotten to stand patching?

ULFHEJM (*With an expansive gesture*): Then we'll do without them, and stand free and unashamed—as the man and woman we really are!

MAJA (*Laughs*): You with your goats' legs—yes!

ULFHEJM: And you with your— Well—let that go.

MAJA: Let *us* go, you mean. Come on!

ULFHEJM: Stop! Where to, comrade?

MAJA: Down to the hotel, of course.

ULFHEJM: And then?

MAJA: Then we'll simply say good-bye, and thanks for pleasant company.

ULFHEJM: But *we* can't part. Do you really think we *can*?

MAJA: You didn't manage to tie me up, you know.

ULFHEJM: I can offer you a castle—

MAJA (*Pointing to the hut*): Like that one there?

ULFHEJM: It's not in ruins yet.

MAJA: And all the glory of the world, perhaps?

ULFHEJM: I said, a castle.

MAJA: Thanks! I've had enough of castles.

ULFHEJM: It's surrounded by miles of splendid hunting grounds.

MAJA: Are there works of art in this castle of yours?

ULFHEJM (*Slowly*): No; there are no works of art; but—

MAJA (*Relieved*): Thank God for that!

ULFHEJM: Will you go with me, then? As far as I want you to go—and for as long as I want you?

MAJA: There's a tame bird of prey that keeps watch over me.

ULFHEJM (*Wildly*): Maja! We'll put a bullet through his wing!

MAJA (*Looks at him a moment and says resolutely*): Then —carry me down into the depths!

ULFHEJM (*Puts his arm round her waist*): We're just in time; the mist is rising.

MAJA: Is the way down very dangerous?

ULFHEJM: The mountain mist is more dangerous still.

(*She shakes him off, goes to the edge of the precipice and looks over, but starts back quickly.*)

ULFHEJM (*Goes towards her laughing*): What is it? Does it make you dizzy?

MAJA (*Faintly*): Yes—that, too. But, look over the edge. Do you see them coming up?

ULFHEJM (*Goes and bends over the edge of the precipice*): It's only your bird of prey—and his strange lady.

MAJA: Can't we get past without their seeing us?

ULFHEJM: Impossible! The path's too narrow. And there's no other way.

MAJA (*Nerving herself*): Very well—we'll face them here!

ULFHEJM: Spoken like a true bear killer, comrade!

(RUBEK *and* IRENE *appear over the edge of the precipice at the back. He wears a shawl over his shoulders; she has a fur cloak thrown loosely over her white dress, and a swans-down hood over her head.*)

RUBEK (*Still only half visible above the edge*): Well, Maja! So, after all, we meet again!

MAJA (*With assumed assurance*): Your servant, Professor! Won't you come up?

(RUBEK *climbs up and holds out his hand to* IRENE, *who also climbs right to the top.*)

RUBEK (*To* MAJA, *coldly*): I see you've been on the mountains all night too—just as we have.

MAJA: I've been out hunting, yes. You gave me permission, you know.

ULFHEJM (*Pointing downward*): Did you come up that path?

RUBEK: Yes—as you saw.

ULFHEJM: And the strange lady, too?

RUBEK: Of course. (*With a glance at* MAJA) The strange lady and I have decided to travel the same path in future.

ULFHEJM: Don't you realize how dangerous that path is?

RUBEK: We thought we'd try it all the same. It didn't seem too difficult at first.

ULFHEJM: Nothing seems too difficult at first. But you're apt to reach a tough spot, where you can neither advance nor yet go back; you're trapped. Mountain-bound, we hunters call it.

RUBEK (*Looks at him and smiles*): You actually talk like an oracle, Mr. Ulfhejm!

ULFHEJM: God forbid! (*Urgently, pointing up toward the peaks*) But there's a storm coming—can't you see? Listen to those blasts of wind!

RUBEK (*Listening*): They sound like a prelude to the Resurrection Day.

ULFHEJM: They're a prelude to a raging storm, man! Look at those great clouds gathering up there! Very soon they'll descend on us, like a shroud.

IRENE (*With a shudder*): I know how a shroud feels!

MAJA (*Tugging at* ULFHEJM's *sleeve*): Let's get away.

ULFHEJM (*To* RUBEK): I can only help one at a time. Take shelter in the hut while the storm lasts. When it's over I'll send some people up to fetch you.

IRENE (*Terrified*): To fetch us! No! No—!

ULFHEJM (*Harshly*): To take you down by force, if need be. It's a matter of life and death, I tell you. You've been warned. (*To* MAJA) Come—you can trust your comrade.

MAJA (*Clinging to him*): If I get down alive—I shall sing and shout with joy!

ULFHEJM (*Starts to descend and calls back to the others*): Wait in the hut, mind—till the men come up with ropes to fetch you. (ULFHEJM, *with* MAJA *in his arms, clambers rapidly but warily down the precipice.*)

IRENE (*Looks for a while at* RUBEK *with terror-stricken eyes*): Did you hear, Arnold? They're going to send men up to fetch me! A lot of men will come up here, and—!

RUBEK: Don't be afraid, Irene!

IRENE (*In growing terror*): And that woman in black—she will come too. She must have missed me long ago. She'll seize me, Arnold; and put me in the strait jacket. She has it with her in her trunk. I've seen it—

RUBEK: No one will be allowed to touch you.

IRENE (*With a wild smile*): No—I have means to prevent it.

RUBEK: What means, Irene?

IRENE (*Drawing out the knife*): This!

RUBEK (*Trying to seize it*): You have a knife—!

IRENE: I always carry it. Day and night—even in bed.

RUBEK: Give me that knife, Irene!

IRENE (*Hiding it*): You shan't have it. I may have use for it myself.

RUBEK: What use could you have for it up here?

IRENE (*Looks at him fixedly*): It was meant for *you*, Arnold.

RUBEK: For me!

IRENE: Yes. Last evening, when we were sitting by Lake Taunitz—

RUBEK: By Lake Taunitz—?

IRENE: Outside the peasant hut; we played with swans and water lilies—

RUBEK: Yes? And then?

IRENE: —and when I heard you say in that icy tone of voice, that I was only an episode in your life—

RUBEK: I never said that! It was *you* who said it—*you*, Irene!

IRENE (*Continuing*): —I had this knife in my hand. I was going to stab you in the back.

RUBEK (*Somberly*): Why didn't you do it, Irene? What stopped you?

IRENE: The dreadful thought suddenly came to me that you were dead already—had been dead for a long time.

RUBEK: Dead?

IRENE: Dead. Dead—just as I am. We sat there by Lake Taunitz, we two corpses—and played together.

RUBEK: I don't call it being dead. But you don't understand me.

IRENE: What has become of the burning desire you had for me—the desire you struggled so against—when I stood before you naked, as the young woman in "The Resurrection Day"?

RUBEK: Our love is not dead, Irene.

IRENE: The love that we knew on earth—this glorious, marvelous earth—this mysterious earth—that love is dead in both of us.

RUBEK (*Passionately*): It's that very love that I feel burning in me now—as strongly and as ardently as ever! Don't you know that, Irene?

IRENE: Have you forgotten what I am?

RUBEK: It makes no difference what you say you are. To me you are the woman I've made you in my dreams.

IRENE: I stood naked on a turntable in a music hall and showed myself to countless men—after I left you.

RUBEK: It was I who drove you to it—blind fool that I was! I set a work of art—a thing of clay—above human happiness and love!

IRENE (*Looking down*): Too late—too late!

RUBEK: Nothing you've done in the years between has lowered you in my eyes, Irene.

IRENE (*With head erect*): Nor in my own.

RUBEK: Then, don't you see?—We're free! There's still enough time left for us to live.

IRENE (*Looks at him sadly*): But all desire for life is dead in me. Now I have arisen; I searched for you and found you. And I see that both you and life itself are dead—just as I was.

RUBEK: You're mistaken, Irene; utterly mistaken! Life still surges all around us—and within us too.

IRENE (*Smiles and shakes her head*): The young woman of your "Resurrection Day" can see all of life stretched out on its bier.

RUBEK (*Throws his arms round her passionately*): Then, if we two are dead, let us live life just once more to the full, before we go back to our graves.

IRENE (*With a cry*): Arnold!

RUBEK: But not here in the darkness; not here, enveloped by a hideous shroud of mist—

IRENE (*Passionately*): No, no—high up in the glorious light; on the very summit of life's promise!

RUBEK: There we shall celebrate our marriage, Irene—my beloved!

IRENE (*Proudly*): The sun shall witness it, Arnold.

RUBEK: All the powers of light shall witness it; and all the powers of darkness too. (*Seizes her hand*) Bride of my spirit—will you follow me?

IRENE (*As though transfigured*): I will follow my lord and master, with joy in my heart.

RUBEK (*Draws her after him*): We must first go through the mist, Irene—

IRENE: Through the mist—yes. And then we shall stand at the very top of the tower that glitters in the sunrise.

(*The clouds of mist close in over the scene.* RUBEK *and* IRENE *hand in hand climb up over the snow-clad slope on the right and are lost to sight among the lowering clouds. Blasts of wind whistle through the air.* THE DEACONESS *appears near the mound of stones to the left. She stops and peers round silently, searchingly.*)

MAJA (*Can be heard singing triumphantly from the depths below*):

> I am free! I am free! I am free!
> No more life in the prison for me!
> I am free as a bird! I am free!

(*A sound like thunder is heard from the snow field above. The avalanche glides and whirls downwards with dizzy speed.* RUBEK *and* IRENE *are dimly seen as they are whirled along with the masses of snow and are buried under them.*)

THE DEACONESS (*Gives a loud cry and stretches out her arms towards them*): Irene! (*She stands silent for a moment, then makes the sign of the cross before her in the air, and says*) Pax vobiscum!

(MAJA'S *triumphant song is heard from still farther away, down below.*)

CURTAIN